Committees and Commissions in India
1977

Concepts in Communication
Informatics & Librarianship-51

General Editor : **S.P. Agrawal**

Committees and Commissions in India 1977

Volume 15

PART A

A Concept's Project

Compiled by a team of professionals
guided by
VIRENDRA KUMAR

CONCEPT PUBLISHING COMPANY, NEW DELHI 110059

ISBN 81-7022-484-5 (Vol. 15, Part A)

First Published 1993

Published and Printed by
Ashok Kumar Mittal
Concept Publishing Company
A/15-16, Commercial Block, Mohan Garden
NEW DELHI 110059 (India)

Lasertypeset by
Printing Express
H-13, Bali Nagar
NEW DELHI 110015

GENERAL EDITOR'S INTRODUCTION

In the context of the changing world, the role of the government – be it at central, state or local level – is becoming more prevasive in the modern society. Everyday, it has to encounter new problems and face new issues which demand quite a new thinking and novel strategies to overcome them. Thus, the increasing role of the government in every sphere of people's life has broadened its functions and responsibilities tremendously and enlarged its activities to such an extent that the government machinery of its own can hardly manage its affairs. Moreover, its functions are becoming more complicated and complex requiring the assistance of outside specialists, technocrats and specialized agencies.

In view of this, the modern government has to set-up committees and commissions and working or study groups on various problems and issue from time to time. In the light of the recommendations of these committees and commissions, the government takes decisions on key issues and problems. Often the government is obliged to seek the assistance of a committee to evaluate some of its schemes in operation so that on the basis of the evaluation reports of the committee, it may either continue, modify or scrap the on-going schemes. In other words, the committees or commissions, etc., exercise a great deal of pivotal force in shaping the policies and programmes of the government and for this purpose submit a large number of reports.

In these volumes of *Committees and Commissions in India*, now being published under the *Concepts in Communication Informatics and Librarianship (CICIL)* series, an attempt has been made to cover the period from 1974 onwards. The volumes include the vital data about only those reports of the committees and commissions which have been constituted by the Central Government. We have made every endeavour to include the digest of all the important reports on various vital issues of great importance and on major areas of national development.

We have also an ambitious plan to publish the digests of the important reports of the committees and commissions appointed by different state governments, the semi-government organisations and the learned bodies as also the reports published during the period of the British Government.

The publication has been brought out under the guidance of Shri Virendra Kumar, specialist in his own right with vast experience of working in Government Documents Section in the Central Secretariat Library and having the privilege of the blessings of Dr. S.R. Ranganathan – the father of Indian Library Science. I also put on record the collaborative help provided by Shri M.W.K. Sherwani.

We are sure that this compilation will prove a very useful reference tool for researchers, serious students and scholars of the public administration and political science, administrators, policy-makers, educationists and historians.

S.P. AGRAWAL

PREFACE

This volume of *Committees and Commissions in India* attempts to understand the activities of the various Committees and Commissions during the period 1974.

A 'Commission' is a governmental agency created to perform a particular function such as special investigations or on governmental regulations of business. It is appointed mainly when it is thought that a matter involves some financial questions. There are other reasons for which a Commission is appointed, e.g., in matters pertaining to welfare of the State and its citizens and or improving the efficiency in an administration. The status of a 'Committee' is also the same as that of a 'Commission', but it does not possess as wide powers as are enjoyed by a Commission and has to limit itself to specific work assigned to it under its terms of reference. While arriving at decisions in the form of recommendations, a Commission or Committee ensures that such decisions are representative of interests of various types of people and also a safeguard against abuse of power.

A Committee or a Commission comprises a Chairman, the Members and Member Secretary (sometimes there is also an Assistant Secretary). In some cases, there are even One-man Commissions and the enquiry in such Commissions is entrusted to an Officer-on-Special Duty.

The Chairman of a Commission is a person well-versed mostly in legal matters and is often a retired judge of a High Court or the Supreme Court of India. Occasionally, a Member of Parliament is also appointed as the Chairman of a Commission. On the other hand, the Chairman of the Committee is mostly a specialist in the subject of the Committee. He can be a Leader or a Convenor also, if he heads a Panel, a Study Group or a Delegation, etc.

The Members of a Commission, Committee, Panel, Study Group etc., are specialists in their respective fields and provide valuable guidance to the Commission or the Committee in making recommendations.

The Member-Secretary or Secretary is generally nominated from among the experienced officials who have the requisite competent knowledge of the subject on which the Commission or the Committee is appointed.

Committees and Commissions in India provides in chronological order vital information about Committees and Commissions appointed by the Government from time to time. Information for each Committee or Commission is presented in a compact form in four parts, namely; Constitution; Appointment; Terms of Reference and Recommendations.

CONTENTS

PART B

PART C

RAILWAY ACCIDENT INVESTIGATION REPORT ON COLLISION BETWEEN 9UP BARAUNI-KANPUR (M.G.) EXPRESS AND DOWN GARHARA (B.G.) GOODS SPECIAL AT BACHWARA STATION OF NORTH-EASTERN RAILWAY AT ABOUT 20.38 HOURS ON FEBRUARY 2, 1977[1]

One Man Commission Shri A.G. Jacob, Additional Commissionr of Railway Safety, North Eastern Circle

Appointment

The Commission was constituted under the Ministry of Tourism and Civil Aviation (Commission of Railway Safety) in accordance with Rule 4 of the Statutory Investigation into Railway Accident Rules, 1973 vide Notification No. RS.13-T(8)/71 dated April 19, 1973 on February 2, 1977.

Terms of Reference

To enquire into the collision between 9Up Barauni-Kanpur (M.G.) Express and Down Garhara (B.G.) Goods Special at Bachwara Station of North-Eastern Railway at about 20.38 hours on February 2, 1977.

Contents

Summary; Inspection and Inquiry; Relief Measures; Composition of

---

1. Delhi, Controller of Publications, 1983, 24 p.

Trains and Damage; Local Features; Summary of Evidence; Tests and Observations; Discussion; Conclusions; Remarks and Recommendations; Annexure; Railway Board's Comments on Various Paras of the Report.

Conclusions

55. On full consideration of the factual, material and circumstantial evidence, I have come to the conclusion that the collision between 9Up Barauni-Kanpur (MG) Express and Down Garhara (BG) Goods Special at 20.38 hours on 24-2-77 at Bachwara Jn. Station on the Samastipur Division of North-Eastern Railway was caused by the Driver, Sri Anoop Lal of Down Garhara (BG) Goods Special failing to control his train in time and thus passing the Down Home Signal at danger.

56. *Responsibility*

1. Responsibility for causing the accident must rest with Sri Anoop Lal,* Driver of the Goods Train, who failed to obey the Down Home Signal thus Contravening G.R. 76 (Extract at Annexure I).

2. Responsibility for working the goods train with Brake Power below specified standards should rest normally with Train Examiner, Sri Motiur Rahman of Narayanpur Anant and Guard Ram Ekbal Prasad, Guard of the Goods Train who worked the train without a vacuum gauge and signed the vacuum certificate without the pressure in the brake van being entered therein. However, it is seen from the Railway's files that the practice of working trains with less than required pressure in the brake van is known to the Railway Administration and has their tacit approval. This is clear from the fact that a quarterly statement of such trains is being prepared and submitted to Railway Board. Responsibility for working the Goods Trains with vacuum pressure below 20 cm. in the brake van should rest, therefore, with the Railway Administration.

Driver Binda Singh of Sonpur, Driver of 9 Up is guilty of negotiating the Diamond Crossing at 15 KMPH when there is a speed restriction of 10 KMPH on the same.

---

* Since breathed his last on 24-4-78 while functioning as resting crew of SC 9 Up Goods train.

[*Bio-data of Driver Sri Anoop Lal*:

Driver Sri Anoop Lal who is now 52 was first appointed as Cleaner in 1946. He has been successfully promoted as Fireman 'C'. Fireman 'B', Shunter 'B', Shunter 'A', and finally as Driver 'C' on 14-1-1970. While working as Shunter 'B' he had been reverted as Fireman 'B' for one year for 'fusion of lead plug'. Though he has had no punishment, for charges arising out of accidents in the last 5 years, he has a number of them for charges arising out of indiscipline. His accident index neglecting all punishments other than that for accident cases is 400 against desirable limit of 300. He has not attended any refresher courses.]

57. *Relief Measures*: Reference details of ordering and running of Medical Van given in Para 52 and Para 54, it is considered as stated in para 54 that the working of Medical Vans was not entirely satisfactory. However, local doctors, Civil authorities and local railway staff carried out rescue and relief operations promptly, to the extent possible within resources available.

Recommendations

58.1 It is of importance to ascertain why a Driver passed Signals at Danger. An attempt within the capacity of this inquiry has been made in Para 51. It is, however, felt that in all such cases of human failure resulting in serious accidents a properly trained Psychologist must be available to examine those involved and try to understand why the individual failed as he did at the particular time and place in spite of years of training and experience.

58.2 An attempt to study the accident pronounces of individual Drivers was made by the Board as a result of which instruction about classifying Drivers, their counselling and training was issued vide Railway Board's letter No. 69/Psych/14 of 15-10-1969. This was a step in the right direction but there does not appear to have been much follow up on these, as was revealed in this inquiry. The Railway Board may like to take steps to see that the orders contained in this letter are implemented. It may perhaps be desirable to make this the responsibility of the Safety rather than that of the Mechanical Department.

58.3 Incidentally, the list of irregularities to be taken into consideration as listed in Para 2 of the above letter do not include acts of indiscipline such as "not turning on duty", "careless working",

"Obstructive working", etc. It is considered that these also should be included in this list as these offences are those of one who is not duty conscious and, therefore, likely to cause accidents.

58.4 Again the present formulae is:

$$\text{Accident Index} = \frac{\text{No. of Accidents} \times \text{Seventy}}{\text{Total length of service as Fireman onwards}} \times 100$$

This allows for calculation of the Index at one particular point of time but does not convey any information about change for better or worse in the Driver's accident proneness over the years. It is, therefore, suggested that both numerator and denominator in the above formulae be limited to a specified period say 5 or 10 years as considered by the RDSO to be suitable. The exercise of checking on Loco running staff's accident proneness at these intervals must then be made a regular work of the Safety Departments on the Railway who should also be responsible to see that the Mechanical Department follow up with counselling and refresher in case of individuals whose accident index exceeds the desirable maximum. The Railway Board may like to consult the Psycho-Technical Wing of RDSO on the suggested changes in the procedure and issue orders.

59.1 There can be no two opinions that a Diamond Crossing of two Main Lines represent a particularly vulnerable spot insofar as danger of collision is concerned. In a number of previous cases of collision at Diamond Crossings the concerned A.C.R.S. had recommended the imposition of a speed restriction of 50 KMPH at such crossing on the basis of GR 90(C). Reference may be made to the ACRS's recommendation in the case of collision of Hijli, on S.E. Railway on 22-2-68 and collision at Saktigarh on Eastern Railway on 14-11-75. However, Railway Board have not agreed to the assumption that Para GR 90(C) is applicable in such cases and have based their decision on Para 147(C) of Indian Railway Signal Engineering Manual. Whatever the merits of the arguments regarding the applicability or otherwise of GR 90(C) to cases of Diamond Crossing, it is considered that there is a case for speed restriction on Diamond Crossing to mitigate the consequences of human failure as in this case and that as layouts involving Diamond Crossings are not so numerous, the effect of such speed restriction on operating speeds would not be significant.

59.2 A permanent speed restriction of 15 KMPH on such crossing is desirable except perhaps in Sub-urban Areas where it would be impractical as switching from slow to fast lines and vice versa over Diamonds would be frequently necessary. It is true that in spite of the existence of 15 KMPH (on BG) and 10 KMPH (on MG) speed restriction in this case the accident did occur involving considerable casualties but the casualties would have been incomparably larger had 9 Up been at full speed. It is therefore, recommended that a permanent speed restriction of 15 KMPH be imposed on all Diamond Crossings of Main Lines.

60.1 In the Chapter on 'Discussion' I have dealt with in detail the various aspects of the brake power of the B.G. Down Goods. The conclusion I could reach based on the conditions obtaining on this train and other instances which have come to notice in respect of brake power such as absence of gauge in the brake, deficiency of vacuum pressure at the brake, large number of cylinders with less or more than the limits of travel laid down for piston travel, etc., is that there is in the Railway Administration, no real earnestness in enforcing Safety parameters if it is likely to affect the daily operation. It can be only because of this that the Railway Board, after laying down parameters to be observed in respect of brake power, has called for statistics on and continue to tolerate running of trains not satisfying these parameters over the years.

60.2 It is, therefore, recommended that parameters laid down for Brake Power of Goods trains be made mandatory in respect of following provisions and it be made the rule that no trains not satisfying these parameters should be allowed to leave an originating station:

(1) Percentage of operative cylinders. An operative cylinder with piston travel not lying within the limits prescribed should be treated as in-operative.
(2) Minimum vacuum pressure in rear Brake Van and average vacuum pressure in engine and brake van together.
(3) Existence of a vacuum gauge in the brake of the train.

If the parameters so laid down is contravened *en route* due to attachment of additional wagons or otherwise maximum train speed should be halved till the parameters are restored at the first opportunity.

61. It has already been stated in Para 49.2 that speed of 9 Up over the Diamond was above 15 KMPH as against 10 KMPH

prescribed. Similarly, from the final speed of collision of B.G. Down Goods, it is clear that in site of existence of a 15 KMPH Speed restriction, the Driver had not earlier tried to control his train sufficiently. It is a matter of common observance that Drivers do not normally observe such speed restrictions strictly. Thus many passenger trains negotiate turn-outs at speeds much higher than 15 KMPH and in fact many Officers turn a blind eye to this as they feel that otherwise punctuality will suffer. It is, therefore, suggested that periodical drives be organised on all Railways when speeds over permanent speed restrictions are monitored by Officers without the knowledge of Drivers and strict action taken for non-observance of speed restrictions.

62. In the chapter on 'Discussion' and heading 'Relief Arrangements', I have referred to the fact that in this case the nearest medical van at Barauni was not only ordered late but also appears to have left after the maximum time prescribed. It appears that Railways are not carrying out enough Mock Drills in respect of turning out of Medical Vans to assess the actual time that will be taken in an emergency to do so and to remove any snags, that may become apparent as a result of such trials. I would suggest that a periodicity of once in a quarter be laid down for such trials; that these be ordered by the D.S. personally without notice; results maintained in a special register and action taken to bring the time taken within the limits laid down.

63. Referring to para 50.4, it is recommended that at Junction Stations where block instruments are provided in Cabins, but the nomination of line is done by a platform Assistant Station Master as distinct from Cabin Asstt. Station Master, the two operations of granting permission to approach and lowering of signals for reception be dealt with as two separate operations and private numbers be exchanged between those concerned separately for each operation. The proforma of train registers used at these stations may perhaps then require to be modified which should also be done.

64.1 According to Para 711(7) of the Indian Railway Medical Manual, passengers other than Railway staff injured in a railway accident are to be shifted to the nearest Civil Hospital as soon after the accident as possible if their condition permit such transfer. My visit to Civil Hospitals where such patients are undergoing treatment has shown that such Hospitals are unbearably over-crowded, nursing is poor and surroundings un-hygienic. It is considered that the payment of an *ex gratia* amount to the injured do not absolve the Railway of the moral responsibility to ensure that these injured in a Railway accident receive the best medical aid available and this in the present circumstances is available in the Railway Hospitals.

64.2 It is considered that a large organisation like the Railway has the resources to make available the additional accommodation, equipment, medicines and personnel required for this purpose at short notice and that, therefore, except in cases where exceptionally good Civil Hospitals such as those attached to Medical Colleges or in large Cities like Bombay where better specialist attention can be given, are available, the effort should be to treat the injured in Railway Hospitals until they are fit to be discharged. It is recommended that the Medical Manual be amended accordingly.

Railway Board's Comments on Various Paras of the Report

Para 58.1: From time to time the Psycho-technical Cell of the RDSO has been making case studies of the staff involved in accidents, since 1968. Instructions have been issued that normally on receipt of a reference from the A.C.R.S. the Psycho-technical Cell should undertake the case study of the staff involved in the accident. However, in case of any difficulty arising out of lack of resources, the ACRS may be advised and the matter decided mutually between the RDSO and ACRS.

Para 58.2: In terms of Board's circular letter No. 69/Psych/14/1 dated 15-10-1969, special steps are required to be taken to correct and counsel the staff are accident prone (i.e., whose accident index is above 300). It is the responsibility of the Safety Counseller/Loco Inspector to watch and counsel such staff. The Divisional Officers (DME/DSO) are also required to informally interview some cases as a part of remedial measures. Also highest priority is to be given for sending such staff to Refresher Courses and Safety Camps. The extent instructions on the subject have been reiterated by the railway administration to all Divisions for strict compliance. The railway is also taking up the staff responsible for not following the instructions and for not sending the driver for refresher courses.

It is seen that CRS has noted the action taken by the railway administration.

Paras 58.3 and 58.4: The formula for calculating the accident index, as envisaged in Board's circular letter No. 69/Psych/14 dated

15-10-1969, has been subjected to review in respect of steam drivers by the RDSO, and the same is under trial on the Western Railway. In the revised formula, it has been decided to take into account only those irregularities which are related to accidents directly or indirectly so that it is easier to identify hard core potential safety risks and expose them to corrective measures. Bringing all the irregularities within the scope of computation of the accident index, irrespective of their nature, is likely to make the index less effective. In calculating the accident index in terms of revised procedure, the irregularities committed during the entire service period, in a given capacity, are not taken into account. Instead the range is restricted to cover only a period of 5 years with provision for periodical reviews. A further advantage offered the revised procedure is that it helps to distinguish repeated offenders or accident prone from casual offenders.

The RDSO is also working on a revised formula for calculating accident index in respect of Diesel/Electric Drivers and Motormen.

Para 59: The matter has been given a careful consideration by this Ministry and it has been decided that para 3 of Section III of Chapter VII of Rules for opening of a Railway pertains to isolation between different reception lines at a station and does not refer to the isolation between block section lines forming a running junction. Isolation of such lines is not required, as long as they are provided with complement of signals indicated in para 147 of the Signal Engineering Manual.

Necessary instructions on the subject have been issued to all the Railways, vide Board's circular letter No. 76/W3/SG/G/10 dated 27-8-1977, a copy of which was endorsed to CRS also.

Para 60: The Railway Ministry are extremely concerned about the safety of Travelling Public, and is earnest about the implementation of means of ensuring such safety. It is to this effect that a number of instructions have been issued specifying various parameters of Brake Powers. The very fact that statements of cases where requisite Brake Power has not been maintained are called for, indicates the close monitoring done at the highest level.

Para 61: The railway administration has noted the recommendation for compliance. It may be mentioned that instructions already exist that speed of trains should be checked by the Officers and Inspectors and that deterrent action should be taken against those found violating the speed restrictions. Instructions have also been issued to the Railways that during the observance of the Annual

Safety Week surprise checking of the speed of the trains should be one of the important activities.

Para 62: Detailed instructions are being issued to the Railways that mock drills in regard to turning out of medical vans and break down trains should be conducted once in a quarter, unless these trains have actually been turned out in a particular quarter in connection with an accident.

Para 63: The matter was given a careful consideration by the Board as early as in 1967 and after taking into account the views expressed by the Railways, it was decided that to avoid multiplicity of private numbers. It would be sufficient if only one private number is exchanged for the entire transaction consisting of nomination of line and releasing of S.M.'s control on the Home Signal and that the exchange should take place only prior to the release of S.M.'s control over the Signal, i.e., at the end of the transaction. As explained by the railway administration, it is not necessary to exchange private numbers at the time the Cabin ASM grants line clear for a train, since he can grant permission to approach for a train when the conditions for the same are fulfilled. Nomination of reception line not essential at the time of granting permission to approach and there is, therefore, no need for exchange of private number between the ASM and the Cabin ASM at that time.

It is seen that the CRS has noted the position explained by the railway administration.

Para 64: The practice followed on the railways with regard to treatment of the persons injured in railway accidents is set out in para 711(7) of the Indian Railway Medical Manual, which reads as under:

(7) The injured persons other than Railway beneficiaries should be shifted, as far as possible, to the nearest non-railway hospitals except in the following circumstances:

- (i) Non-availability of non-railway hospital.
- (ii) Want of accommodation in the non-railway hospital.
- (iii) Unsuitability of the non-railway hospital to render efficient aid.
- (iv) Difficulty of transport.
- (v) Serious condition of the patient.
- (vi) In other circumstances considered justifiable by the attending medical officer.

It would be seen from the above that the interests of the injured have been well guarded even in the provisions of the existing rules.

The background in which these provisions that the injured persons, other than railway employees, should preferably be taken to a non-railway hospital, have been followed over years is that in train accidents, there is a general feeling that the railways are guilty party. In the past, there were also allegations that railways deliberately destroyed evidence of the correct number of injured or dead. Even now, once in a while, such allegations are made. If the treatment is undertaken in a railway hospital as a rule and in preference to a non-railway hospital, it will expose the railways to avoidable criticism that the best possible treatment was not made available. In this background, this Ministry consider that the provisions contained in the Indian Railways Medical Manual need not be changed.

2

RAILWAY ACCIDENT INVESTIGATION REPORT ON THE COLLISION OF NO. 16 UP NEW DELHI-MADRAS GRAND TRUNK EXPRESS TRAIN WITH THE REAR OF VIJAYAWADA-MADRAS DIESEL-11 UP GOODS TRAIN BETWEEN THE UP DISTANT AND HOME SIGNALS OF ONGOLE STATION OF THE VIJAYAWADA-GUDUR SECTION OF SOUTH-CENTRAL RAILWAY AT ABOUT 04-10 HOURS ON FEBRUARY 8, 1977[1]

8th February 1977 – 27th April, 1977

One Man Commission Shri K.N. Kamath, Additional Commissioner of Railway Safety

Appointment

The Commission was constituted under the Ministry of Tourism and Civil Aviation (Commission of Railway Safety) in accordance with Rule 4 of the Statutory Investigation into Railway Accident Rules, 1973 vide Notification No. RS.13-T(8)/71 dated April 19, 1973 on February 8, 1977.

Terms of Reference

To enquire into the collision of No. 16 Up New Delhi-Madras Grand Trunk Express Train with the rear of Vijayawada-Madras Diesel-11 Up Goods Train between the Up Distant and Home Signals of Ongole Station of the Vijayawada-Gudur Section of South-Central Railway at about 04-10 hours on February 8, 1977.

---

1. Delhi, Controller of Publications, 1980, 19 p.

Contents

Summary; Inspection and Inquiry; Relief Measures; The Trains; Local Features; Summary of Evidence; Observations and Tests; Discussion; Conclusions; Remarks and Recommendations; Annexures; Railway Board's Comments in Various Parts of the Report.

Conclusions

30. (a) *Cause*: On full consideration of the factual, material and circumstantial evidence, I have reached the conclusion that the accident involving the collision of No. 16 Up G.T. Express with the rear of BMD-11 Up Goods train which occurred at about 04-10 hours on 8th February, 1977 at km. 291/13-14 between the Up Distant and Home Signals of Ongole station was caused as a result of the G.T. Express having been admitted the Block Section which was already occupied by BMD-11.

(b) *Responsibility*: The primary responsibility for this accident lies on Shri N. Ch. Venkata Reddy,* Switchman, North Cabin, Ongole, who granted Line Clear for No. 16 Up without personally having seen the BMD-11 arrive and pass the Cabin. He contravened provisions of General Rule 248A and para 51(*a*)(1) of the Block Working Manual and para 10-B(*g*) Note (iv) of the Station Working Institutions.

[*Bio-data of Switchman*:

Shri N.Ch. Venkatareddy, was first appointed as a Railway Porter in December 1962. After attending the training for the post of Switchman in the Zonal Training School at Tiruchirappalli for four months and having passed the same he was promoted to officiate as Switchman and posted to hold independent charge in November 1965. He had last attended the Refresher Course from 3-8-1974 to 2-9-1974 and the Safety Camp from 23-8-1973 to 28-8-1973. He has been censured once for Block failure and has had no other punishment.]

*Assistant Station Master, Shri I. Peddi Raju of Ongole, contributed to the accident in giving the 'Out' report for BMD-11

---

* The accused were convicted and released.

without himself seeing the train pass and also misleading the North Cabin Switchman. He contravened Subsidiary Rule 124(5)*(a)* and *(c)*.

[*Bio-data of ASM:*

Shri I. Peddi Raju, was first appointed as Probationary Junior Clerk in December 1946 and promoted as Assistant Station Master in May 1951. He has been working as an Assistant Station Master at Ongole from June 1971. He last attended the Refresher Course from 27-1-1976 to 25-2-1976 and the Safety Camp from 22-8-1975 to 28-8-1975. He has been cautioned on several occasions mostly in connection with Commercial Work. He has also been censured several times for causing detention to trains. His annual increment has been withheld on three occasions—once for failing to issue Caution Order to the Driver of a train regarding working of a dip lorry which resulted in an accident and twice for detention to trains at the signals. Consequent on a criminal charge during the May 1974 strike in the Court he was ordered to be dismissed from service by the Divisional Superintendent from 21-5-1974 but on review this was modified* as reduction in time scale by two stages for 24 months.]

*Switchman, Shri A. Samson, of South Cabin, Ongole, also contributed to the accident by failing to personally observed BMD 11 pass before he had give the slot to the North Cabin Switchman for reception of No. 16 Up G.T. Express.

[*Bio-data of Switchman*:

Shri A. Sampson, Switchman, was first appointed as a Relieving Porter in December 1962, after attending the training course for the post of Switchman between December 1965 and April 1966 and having passed the same he was promoted to officiate as Switchman in independent charge in May 1967 at Ongolc.

He has been censured once for causing detention to a train. His annual increment was withheld for three months (non-recurring) for causing detention to No. 4 Mail in May 1970].

[NOTE — Extracts of rules contravened are at Annexure III.]

---

* The accused was convicted and released.

(c) *Relief Measures:* With reference to Section II of the Report, I am satisfied that the medical aid was as prompt as could be expected under the circumstances. The injured passengers in the Railway Hospital at Vijayawada were being well looked after and they were satisfied with the attention given to them in the hospital.

Recommendations

31. According to para 3(*f*) of the Block Working Manual of the Southern Railway, applicable to Vijayawada Division of South Central Railway also, the emergency release button (with counter) provided on the Block instrument is used if the operating handled gets locked in the 'Train On Line' position under any of the following conditions and it is necessary to turn the handled to the 'Line Closed' position: (i) Blocking Back, (ii) Blocking Forward, (iii) When a train is received without clearing the Home or (iv) when the operating handled has been turned to 'Train On Line' by error.

It is, however, seen from the emergency release register of the North Cabin that this was used 67 times in November 1976 (excluding several operations for testing), 44 times in December 1976, 53 times in January 1977 and 28 times in February 1977. On most occasions the use has been attributed to the Last Vehicle Track having not operated. It was also understood that the Signal and Telecommunication maintenance staff (stationed at Ongole) were not even verbally informed regarding these failures. It is, therefore, clear that this release which is provided as an operational facility is being used indiscriminately. This misuse has nullified the several mechanical and electrical safety measures provided at the station, viz., track circuiting of the running lines, interlocking of the Block instrument with the Home Signal, the Last Vehicle Track circuit and the lock bar provided between the Home Signal and the first facing points. On the Secunderabad Division of the South Central Railway the emergency release button has not been provided and it is understood that this practice obtaining on the Central Railway before this Division was merged with the South Central Railway. On the Block Instruments provided in the Secunderabad Division facility exists for Blocking back and Blocking forward and the instrument handle is free to be turned to the 'Line Closed' position thereafter. I consider that this is a very much safer condition and recommend that the facility of emergency release button provided not only on the

Vijayawada Division but also elsewhere on the South Central Railway and other Railways should be withdrawn in the interest of safety. If it is not possible to give effect to this immediately in view of the alterations that might be required to the signalling and interlocking mechanism, it is suggested that the key of the padlock which is provided on the emergency release button should be kept in the personal custody of the Station Master on duty and every time the emergency release button is required to be used, Private Numbers should be exchanged by the Switchmen and the Assistant Station Master and the reason for the use recorded clearly in the Emergency Release Register.

32. Several shortcomings were noticed in regard to the use of the emergency release button. At Surareddipalem, on separate Register was maintained for recording the use of button. In the Train Registers of Ongole Cabins the use of the button was not recorded when it had to be used after Blocking back or Blocking forward, etc. Moreover, at the time of taking over and handling over charge, the Switchmen had not indicated the counter number on some occasions. Suitable action may be taken to ensure that the various instructions regarding the use of the emergency release button are scrupulously followed by all train passing staff.

33. According to para 9*(f)* of the Block Working Manual — Double (and Quadruple) Lines with Modified S.G.E. Lock and Block Instruments — 1962 of the Southern Railway 'No erasures or overwriting must be made in the Train Register Book. If any entry is found to be incorrect, a line must be drawn lightly through it, so that it can be read at any time and the correct entry made above it and initialed. In respect of the entries against BMD-11 the Switchmen of both South Cabin, Ongole and North Cabin, Surareddipalem did not follow these instructions. Suitable action may be taken in this regard.

34. According to para 10*(a)* of the Block Working Manual, *ibid.* the Train Register must be examined and signed by the Station Master in-charge daily and his signature given in the remarks column. It was seen that this was not being done at Ongole—probably this may be the case at other stations also. If these instructions are followed any irregularities are likely to be brought to light before any harm is done. Action may be taken for strict compliance of these instructions.

35. According to para 10*(b)*, the Train Register should also be examined and signed by the Traffic Inspector and the Inspector,

Telegraphs and Phones of the section whenever they visit the stations in the course of their duties. It appears that the Register of North Cabin, Ongole was not inspected by any Supervisory staff as otherwise the large number of failures attributed to the Last Vehicle Track circuit necessitating frequent use of the emergency release button would have come to light much earlier and corrective action could have been taken in time. The matter needs to be looked into and suitable action taken for compliance of these instructions.

36. When I carried out test in the North Cabin at Ongole the Block instrument was in the 'Train On Line' position. When I attempted to turn it to 'Line Closed' position before the train had arrived the handle did not turn. But the Block instrument could not be normalised even after the train had arrived probably as the contact had broken. The emergency release had, therefore, to be used to normalise the instrument. This is something undesirable as the instrument should not get locked like this if an attempt is made by mistake to turn it to the 'Line Closed position. The reason of this needs to be looked into and suitable action taken to make the instrument more hardy and dependable.

37. The Last Vehicle Track circuit (L.V.T) is provided on a short length of two rails ahead of the Home Signal and similar to the First Vehicle Track which is provided ahead of the Advanced Starter Signal. A scrutiny of the Emergency Release Register showed that whereas the Last Vehicle Track in the North Cabin had been reported to have failed frequently there was not a single case where First Vehicle Track had failed. If he First Vehicle Track fails it would not be possible to take off the Last Stop Signal. This leads to conclude that either something was wrong in the circuitry in the Block instrument or more probably the staff have been misusing the emergency release and attributing it wrongly to failure of the L.V.T. This needs to be investigated and action taken to improve either the circuitry if any defects are discovered or to ensure that the staff do not attribute the use of the button to failure of the L.V.T. everytime.

38. In the Caution Order issued to the Driver of No. 16 Up by the Station Master, Vijayawada, the kilometrage where a speed restriction of 15 km/h. was to be observed (on Bridge No. 589) had been wrongly given as 290/13-15 (instead of 295/13-15). The Driver, therefore, was taken unawares when he saw somebody waving a green hand signal near km. 291. Though he claims to have slowed down to 20/25 km./h. It is doubtful if this is true particularly as the

Guard of the train has said he does not remember an speed restriction having been observed after leaving Karavadi. In fact, had the restriction been on account of some temporary arrangement for rebuilding a bridge or for some similar work, an accident would have probably been caused at that site. Suitable action may be taken against the staff at fault and also to ensure that staff take great care in the preparation of Caution Orders.

39. The Switchman of the North Cabin, Ongole, had been working during the previous week or so on 12-hour shifts against the normal 8-hour shifts due to shortage of Switchmen. The shorter duty hours would no doubt have been fixed on the basis of the increased rail traffic and consequent increase in the work load of the Switchmen. It was, therefore, not at all desirable to make them work for longer hours of duty for days together. Suitable steps may be taken to ensure that this does not recur.

40. On the Vijayawada-Gudur section as also or several other trunk routes there has been considerable increase of traffic in recent years. A number of fast trains have been introduced and several of the existing Express and Mail trains have been speeded up by reducing the number of stoppages. All these have led to a greater burden on the train passing staff. On top of this, very great importance is being attached to the punctuality of some of the more important trains and any detentions to these trains are viewed with severity. In fact it appears to me that there is a certain amount of 'fearpsychosis' among the train passing staff which leads them to take short cut methods in order to prevent any detention to these important trains. While punctuality is not doubt important it should not be attempted to be achieved by reducing the emphasis on safety. I would, therefore, recommend that an in-depth study be made of this aspect by the Railway Board in order to devise suitable means to reconcile these two somewhat conflicting objectives. It is necessary that the staff should feel assured that in cases of detentions due to genuine causes they would not be taken up. In the present case the fear that No. 16 Up might suffer detention was probably responsible to some extent in making the station staff ignore the safety rules.

41. The provisions of para 51*(a)* (2) and (3) of the Block Working Manual were not being followed in the North Cabin, Ongole. Necessary steps may be taken to ensure compliance with these instructions.

42. The speed chart on locomotive No. WDM_2 18469 of No. 16

Up was not recording the speed. It is regrettable that despite repeated instructions on this subject the chart was not functioning even on an important train like No. 16 Up. The matter needs to be looked into and necessary action taken to ensure that speed charts do not fail to record the speed at any time.

Railway Board's Comments on Various Paras of the Report

Paras 31 & 32: Action has already been taken by the railway administrations to modify the Block Instruments by removing the Emergency Release facility wherever existing and also making the locking of the Block Instrument free in 'train on line' position when the handle is turned from 'line closed' to 'train online' in order to facilitate blocking and blocking forward. These modifications have since been completed.

Pending the completion of the modifications, the Railway had issued instructions that the of the padlock, provided on the Emergency Release Button, should be kept in the personal custody of the Station Master on duty instead of Switchman in the cabin and handed over to the Switchman only when absolutely necessary, after exchanging private numbers and recording the reasons for its use in the Emergency Release Register.

Paras 33 & 34: Attention of the staff has already been drawn to the instructions in force and a drive instituted by the railway to ensure strict compliance thereof. The railway administration would also take suitable action against the staff concerned for failure on their part.

Para 35: Instructions have been issued to the inspecting officials by the railway administration to ensure strict compliance of the instructions laid down in the Blocking Manual.

Para 36: The observation made by ACRS was a result of equipment failure which could take place at any time. It is seen that the incidence of such failures is not high. The railway administration has, however, completed the job of modifying the instruments so that the handled does not get locked if it is turned directly from "Line Closed" to "Train on line" position and has also taken care of the defects observed by ACRS.

Para 37: It has been explained by the railway administration that the circuitory of the Block Instrument for the last vehicle track is exactly the same as the first vehicle track circuit. The question of defects in the circuitory of the block instrument would, therefore, not arise. However, since the usage of the emergency release has been attributed to failures of the last vehicle circuit, the reasons for frequent use of the emergency key are under investigation by the railway administration. In any case, as mentioned earlier the emergency release facility has been removed.

Para 38: The defaulting staff would be taken up by the railway administration.

Para 39: Steps are being taken to ensure implementation of Hours of Employment Regulations as accepted by the Government after the Railway Labour Tribunal, 1969 award. In the mean time, on South Central Railway, the Divisional Superintendent, Vijayawada has already issued instructions to the staff to avoid over hours of work as far as possible. The implementation of the Railway Labour Tribunal, 1969 award is connected with the creation of a large number of Rest Giver and Leave Reserve posts on railways and only after the proposals are accepted by the Board, can these posts be created. This will take some more time. The matter is being pursued with the railways for submission of vetted figures and with the Finance Directorate for issue of authorisation where proposals have been received.

Para 40: There is no evidence which could be indicative of a 'fear-psychosis' among the train passing staff. In the day-to-day administration of the railways, there is emphasis on movement, but there is even greater emphasis on 'safety', which cannot be sacrificed for the sake of punctuality. Necessary instructions have already been issued to the Railways to educate the staff to develop a balanced outlook regarding observance of safety *vis-a-vis* detention to trains.

Para 41: Necessary action has been taken by the railway administration to draw the attention of the staff to the rules in the Block Working Manual. Meanwhile, the work removal of Emergency Release button was taken up by the railway administration, which has since been completed.

Para 42: Instructions already exist to ensure that speed recorders are provided on the locomotives working Mail/Express trains. The railways have to ensure that they are in proper working condition. Instructions are being reiterated to the railways to ensure that speed recorders/speedometers titted on locomotives are maintained in proper working condition.

RAILWAY ACCIDENT INVESTIGATION REPORT ON DERAILMENT OF 104 DOWN KATHGODAM-BAREILLY PASSENGER IN THE CATCH SIDING AT HALDWANI STATION OF IZATNAGAR DIVISION OF NORTH EASTERN RAILWAY AT ABOUT 05.12 HOURS ON 7th FEBRUARY, 1977

February 9, 1977 – July 22, 1977[1]

One Man Commission Shri Suresh Chandra, Additional Commissioner of Railway Safety, North- Eastern Circle, Gorakhpur

Officers Present Shri G.P. Srivastava; Shri S.T. Awatramani; Shri A.K. Johri; Shri G.S. Kang

Appointment

The Commission was constituted under the Ministry of Tourism and Civil Aviation (Commission of Railway Safety) in accordance with Rule 4 of the Statutory Investigation into Railway Accident Rules, 1973 Vide Notification. No. RS. 13-T(8)/71 dated April 19, 1973 on February 2, 1977.

Terms of Reference

To enquire into the derailment of 104 Down Kathgodam-Bareilly Passenger in the Catch Siding at Haldwani Station of Izatnagar Division of North-Eastern Railway at about 05.12 Hours on 7-2-1977.

---

1. Ministry of Tourism and Civil Aviation (Commission of Railway Safety), Government of India, New Delhi, 1984, ii + 15 p.

Contents

Summary; Relief Measures; Composition of Train and Damage; Local Features; Summary of Evidence; Observations and Tests; Discussion; Conclusions; Remarks and Recommendations; Annexures from A to D; Railway Board's Comments on Various Paras of the Report.

Conclusions

47. *Cause*: On full consideration of the factual, material and circumstantial evidence, I have come to the conclusion that the derailment of 104 Down Kathgodam-Bareilly Passenger in the catch siding of Haldwani Station on Kathgodam-Bareilly section of North-Eastern Railway at about 05.12 hours on 7-2-1977 was due to inadequate brake power on the train.

48. *Responsibility*: The responsibility for the accident rests equally on:

(a) Shri Mohd. Saddiq,* the train engine Driver, who, according to his own deposition and threading recorded by him in the Brake-Power Certificate Book, has admitted that the vacuum in the train engine was only 30 cms. against 46 cms. minimum specified. He thus contravened instructions under para 793(c) of the N.E. Railways Operating Circular No. 12 and N.E. Railway's letter No. M/32/0 of 29/30 May 1968 (copy at Annexure 'A').

(b) Shri R.C. Masand,* Guard of the train who did not ensure that the train had the required minimum vacuum of 38 cms. in the gauge of the brakevan before he started the train. He did not also record the brakevan vacuum gauge reading in the Brake-Power Certificate Book of the TXR. He thus contravened the instructions under para 79(3)(c) and (c) of the North Eastern Railway Operating Circular No. 12 and N.E. Railway's letter of May 1968 (copy at Annexure 'A').

(c) Shri T.R. Sharma*, Train Examiner, Kathgodam, who did not ensure that the minimum specified level of vacuum was available on the engine and the brakevan of the train. As per para

* Since acquitted in the Sessions Court, Haldwani.

3.10.1 of the I.R.C.A. Rules, Part IV (extract placed at Annexure 'B', he is required to record these vacuum gauge readings on the Brake Power Certificate and obtain the signatures of the Driver and the Guard which he failed to comply with and the train left Kathgodam with inadequate brake power. The minimum vacuum required should have been as indicated in Annexure 'A'.

Bio-data of Driver:

Shri Mohd. Saddiq, Driver of train engine No. 30085/YB joined service as a Cleaner on the N.E. Railway on 1-12-1946 and was promoted as a Driver from 12-9-1959. During his service, he has been punished on 51 occasions including one reversion and withholding of increment on 20 occasions. He had passed the refresher course in December 1975.

Bio-data of Guard:

Shri R.C. Masand, Guard, joined railway service as Guard Grade 'C' on 25-4-1953 and was promoted to Grade 'B' on 19-12-1965. He passed the refresher course in August 1975. During his service, he has been 'censured on 8 occasions and his increment has been withheld on four occasions.

Bio-data of Train Examiner:

Shri Tirath Ram Sharma, Train Examiner, Kathgodam, joined railway service as Carriage Cleaner on 23-9-1951 and was promoted as S.S. Painter on 19-5-1954 and as Painter from 22-5-1957. He was promoted as Train Examiner on 6-2-1973. He has not received any punishments during his service career.]

49. *Relief Measures*: I am satisfied that medical aid was arranged promptly and the relief measures were satisfactory. The Railway Administration may, in a suitable manner, convey their appreciation to Dr. U.S. Khurana, a private Medical Practitioner of Haldwani, for his prompt response on being advised of the accident.

Recommendations

50. Strict instructions should be issued to the staff directly responsible, viz., Drivers, Guards and Train Examiners that under no

circumstances should a train leave unless it has the minimum prescribed brake-power. There should be special vacuum examination in ghat sections with gradients steeper than 1 in 100. The inspecting officials of the Mechanical and Operating Departments should make periodical checks in this respect and strictly deal with cases of default.

51. Vide para 17(5) of North Eastern Railway's Operating Circular No. 12 (extract placed at Annexure 'C') certain targets for punctuality have been prescribed and it has been stated that these should be "maintained at all costs". Such an undue emphasis on punctuality *regardless of costs* is likely to give rise to a tendency amongst the staff to compromise with safety and run trains with inadequate brake-power which can lead to disastrous consequences. The relevant instructions in the circular referred to should be suitably modified.

52. The catch siding at Haldwani is sanded and has a depth of sand of about 3" above top of the rail. The plan of the catch siding requires sanding to be started from the heel of the crossing with the depth of sand being gradually increased within a distance of 30′ so as to attain a depth of 3" of sand above the rail top. This depth of sand is then required to be maintained for the remaining length of the catch siding. The depth of sand in catch sidings needs to be carefully fixed as neither too much nor too little sand over the rails is desirable. If the depth of sand is excessive, it is likely to head up against the leading vehicle and is most likely to derail a train. On the other hand, too little sand is useless. A catch siding should function in such a manner as to bring a train entering the siding to a stop without derailing. For this purpose it is necessary that the leading wheels should be able to keep their flanges in contact with the rail right through. If this contact is lost at any instant due to the wheels not being able to sink deep enough into the sand, either due to excessive depth of sand or on account of its poor quality, a derailment is almost a certainty. The Railway Administration should, therefore, fix the depth of sand to be provided on different stretches of the catch siding in consultation with the R.D.S.O. so that trains entering the catch siding come to a stop without derailing.

53. The grades in catch sidings should be parabolic so that the kinetic energy of a moving train which enters the catch siding gets destroyed. Similarly a sharp curve in the catch siding is also not desirable from the point of view of stability of vehicles on the rails.

Curves in the alignment of the catch siding should, therefore, be avoided or made as flat as possible. Catch sidings taking off from a curve should also be tangential to the curve on the main line so that there is no violent change in the direction of any vehicle entering the catch siding which may lead to instability. The Railway Administration, may, therefore, examine the existing grades and lay out of the catch siding at Haldwani and make necessary changes as required. In this connection it may also be mentioned that some members of the public appeared at the Inquiry and represented against the present location of the catch siding which they desired to be shifted across to the other side of the yard. The Railway Administration may consider the suggestion when examining the existing lay out of the siding.

54. The sand provided in the catch siding should be dry, coarse and gritty and no caking should be allowed. Instructions to this effect as also regarding the periodicity of inspection have been laid down in the Chief Engineer's Permanent Way Circular No. 1 of 1960 issued by the N.E. Railway. These instructions should be reiterated for strict compliance by the maintenance staff.

55. The Railway Administration has licensed some land adjacent to the catch siding for construction of shops. In view of the risk posed by a train derailing and capsizing in the catch siding, the land adjacent of the catch siding should be kept free from any structures.

56. The speedometer of the train engine No. 30085/YB was not in working order as testified by the Driver. The Railway Administration should ensure that speedometers on the engines of passenger trains are maintained in working order.

57. The Station Working Rules for Haldwani provide for the reception of a Down train from Kathgodam side on line No. 1 without stopping at the Outer signal after obtaining specific and personal permission by the Assistant Station Master on duty from the D.O.S. or D.S.O./Izatnagar on control phone. This provision in the working rules can lead to serious consequences if the train goes out of control or the brakes fail to apply as in this case. It is, therefore, recommended that the provision for direct reception of a Down train without stopping at the Outer signal should be deleted from the Station Working Rules.

58. The brake adjusting rod of the train engine No. 30085/YB broke as a result of the accident and the broken surface indicated the presence of an old flaw. The metallurgical examination (copy of report at (Annexure 'D') revealed the presence of slag and porosity

in the weld metal. There was superficial welding all round the circumference with practically no fusion between the weld metal and the parent metal. Brake adjusting rod is an important component, the breakage of which can render the locomotive brakes ineffective. It is, therefore, recommended that ultrasonic testing to detect flaws in important components of rolling stock should be carried out in the sheds and workshops to avoid chances of a failure and a serious mishap on the run.

59. Only one coach was overdue P.O.H. by one month and the return date for another coach was February 1977. The Railway Administration should ensure that the coaches are booked for P.O.H. by the due return date.

60. The overhauling of the Station Master' lock-up box and of the relays at Haldwani which are overdue should be completed without further delay. Similar action should be taken at other stations on the section where overhauling is due.

61. Since the arm and light of the Down Outer and Home signals and the Up Outer signal are not visible from the Cabin from where they are operated, repeaters for these signals should be provided in the Cabin as required vide G.R. 26.

62. As indicated in para 43, the extraction of key 'Q' from the lever frame locks the point lever but the lock lever still remains free which can be operated by anyone thus unlocking the catch siding points at site. This is in violation of G.R. 37 and paras 151(ii) and 171(d) of the Signal Engineering Manual. This shortcoming should be set right so that after extraction of key 'Q', it should not be possible for the lock lever to be operated.

Railway Board's Comments on Various Paras of the Report

Para 50: Instructions with regard to availability of minimum brake power before a train starts, already exist. These have been reiterated by the railway administration to all concerned for strict compliance, emphasising, *inter alia*, that the inspecting officials should carry out periodical checks and take up cases of default severely.

Paras 52 & 53: The Railway has already undertaken the work of examining the existing design of the catch siding in all its aspects with a view to effecting improvements. The Railway would be asked to expedite this.

Para 54: Instructions regarding provision of proper quality sand in the catch siding, its maintenance and periodicity of inspections of the sidings as laid down in the Engineers Permanent Way Circular No.1 of 1960 have been re-iterated by the Railway to the concerned officials.

Para 55: The Railway has initiated action for removal of the shops, etc., from the railway land adjoining the catch siding. The Railway would be asked to expedite action.

Para 56: The Railway is keeping a close watch on the proper maintenance of the speedometers. With the provision of spares, there would normally be no case of engine running without or with defective speedometers. A drive was also launched by the Railway to ensure that the train engines are provided with speedometers in working order.

Para 57: The Station Working Rules of Haldwani have since been amended to prohibit direct reception of Down trains without stopping short of the Outer signal.

Para 58: The brake adjusting rod is normally not required to be welded. The Railway has issued instructions to the shops that whenever welding of the brake adjusting rod is resorted to, there should be proper fusion between the weld metal and the parent metal. As for ultrasonic testing of the rolling stock, it may be mentioned that while the axles are being tested ultrasonically, the brake adjusting rods are not suited for such tests.

It is seen that CRS has noted the position explained by the railway administration.

Para 59: As explained by the Railway, the POH of the coaches were regulated during December 1976 and January 1977. The extension of the return dates of the coaches due POH was, however, permitted only after ensuring that the coaches were free from defects and fit to run.

Para 60: Action has been taken by the Railway Administration accordingly. This has been noted by CRS.

Para 61: This recommendation has been implemented by the Railway.

Para 62: Necessary action has been taken by the railway administration to ensure that it is not possible for the lock lever to be operated after extraction of key 'Q'.

4

COMMITTEE TO CONDUCT STUDY AND MAKE RECOMMENDATIONS FOR THE DEVELOPMENT OF INDUSTRIES BASED ON ETHYL ALCOHOL, 1977 – REPORT[1]

Chairman Shri A. Swaminathan, Managing Director, HOC Ltd., Bombay

Members Shri S.S. Sachdeva; Smt. Lata Singh; Shri S.P. Bhattacharya; A representative of CSIR; One representative each from the States of U.P., Maharashtra, Tamil Nadu and Gujarat; Representative of AIDA, New Delhi; Representative of All-India Alcohol Based Industries Development Association

M. Secy. Dr. K.S. Tiwari

Appointment

The Government of India decided to set up a Committee to make a study and prepare a report regarding planning of alcohol-based industry. The Committee was constituted vide office order No. L-15021(i) 77-ch-II dated 17th February 1977 issued by the Ministry of Chemicals and Fertilizers, Government of India.

Terms of Reference

(i) To prepare the present status of the industries based upon alcohol, i.e., total approved capacities, actual installed capacities and the production achieved.

(ii) To work out estimates of capacity likely to materialise by the end of the 5th Plan, i.e., 1978-79.

---

1. Ministry of Chemicals and Fertilisers, Government of India, New Delhi, 1977, iii + 205 p.

(iii) To assess long range demand estimates for a period say 15 years.

(iv) To recommend specific areas of alcohol-based industries in which future growth needs to be planned.

(v) To examine the constraints on the development and growth of the alcohol-based industries and recommend suitable remedial measures.

(vi) To make any other recommendation which may help in increasing the availability and utilization of alcohol for industrial purpose.

Contents

Summary; Introduction and Scope of Committee's Work; Present Status of Alcohol Industry and Chemicals based on Alcohol; Present Trends; Recommended Trends; Conclusions and Recommendations; Note of Dissent; Appendices; Office Order Constituting the Committee; Shri A.B. Roy Chowdhury's report on visit to Brazil; Memorandum submitted by All India Alcohol-based Industries Association; Report of Dr. Bhalerao; A note by Shri Y.V.S.S. Murthy; View of Experts; Visits to Distilleries; Questionnaires; AABIDA note on problems of alcohol-based industries; AIDA Note; Jalan Committee Report; Dr. Tiwari's Report on Working of Distilleries; Summary of Replies Received to Questionnaires; Minutes of Meeting with AABIDA on 18-8-1977; Statistical Information compiled by Somaiya Organics (India) Ltd.

Recommendations

A. Alcohol Industry

(1) Our survey of the alcohol industry revealed that adequately technically qualified staff is not employed in the distilleries. Sufficient attention is not paid to the reaction parameters. There is an urgent need to employ qualified people in the distilleries to a minimum of atleast one person in each shift as a supervisor. Our survey of technical educational institutes indicates that the three year degree course in Biochemicals Engineering available with H.B.T. Institute at Kanpur is suitable for such personnel.

(2) In order to follow up the implementation of modern tech-

nology in the industry, A.I.D.A. should form a technical cell and hold periodic discussions and visits to the industries. Appropriate consultants such as EIL/FEDO should be engaged by them on a periodic basis for advice on modernisation of existing plant.

(3) It is necessary to follow a standard method of calculation of efficiency. Such standard methods have been arrived at but all units are not following them. Some of the units cultivate their own culture which requires molasses as feedstock while others use ready made yeast and save the material required to produce the yeast. In addition to this there is no uniform pattern regarding taking total sugar or fermentable sugar as the basis of calculations. In some factories the quantity of molasses is not weighed.

(4) The industry requires to modernise and remove bottlenecks in the process. Provision of instruments to measure and control temperatures, rates of flow, quantities of materials put in and taken out, steam consumption, etc., is required. Necessary laboratory facilities are essential. It is recommended that a cess of 3 paise per litre of alcohol be levied and the amount utilised to promote Research and Development activity for alcohol industry and alcohol-based industry.

(5) It is recommended that molasses-based alcohol be totally reserved for industrial purpose. If this is not possible, then the most desirable course for the growth of alcohol-based chemical industry would be to freeze the alcohol allocation to the potable liquor industry to its present level. The next best course would be to restrict the alcohol allocation to country liquor as it affects the State's revenue. For the planning of alcohol based industry on a national level, alcohol should get the same consideration as other basic feedstock like naphtha — that is to say there should be a central control.

(6) A controlling body should be formed and entrusted with the work to provide guidelines to the industry, monitor the progress of the industry, administer funds for Research and Development. The existing Central Molasses Board could be strengthened to perform these functions. The central body should draw up a five year plan on the requirements of the industry, of raw materials and finished products and an yearly plan for distribution of molasses to distilleries as well as alcohol to the industry. Once an annual plan has been made it should ordinarily not be disturbed. The sugar factories from which the distilleries will take the molasses for the year should be ear-marked before the commencement of the season and similarly

the distilleries that will supply alcohol to the industries should be earmarked. The average distance over which a distillery is required to transport molasses should preferably be within 50 kilometre, such that there is equitable distribution of molasses distance-wise.

(7) There is enough scope to improve the yield of alcohol per tonne of molasses by implementing a few improvements which would not cost much investment. A few such suggestions are:

(a) Selection of a suitable strain of yeast to generate higher concentration of alcohol, which can stand high temperature in summer months. A mixed strain to convert the unfermentable portion of sugar can also be utilised.
(b) Laboratory checks during the fermentation process at every stage should be carried out.
(c) Instruments for measuring, controlling and recording temperature and flow at essential stages of the process must be provided.
(d) Fermentors should be thoroughly cleaned and steamed after completion of every batch to prevent contamination, i.e., thorough sterility should be maintained.
(e) Fermentors should be covered and alcohol escaping through carbon dioxide should be recovered.
(f) The quantity of Sulphuric Acid and inorganic nutrients required for the batch should be determined by actual analysis.
(g) Heat economy at various stages should be exercised by proper design of heat exchangers and lagging of distillation columns and pipelines.
(h) Independent check on sugar percentage of molasses is absolutely essential to calculate the yield.
(i) Proper conditions of storage of molasses must be maintained.

(8) In order to encourage distilleries to improve their efficiency and utilisation of raw materials, a policy of liberal and timely allocation of molasses to units which show better actual efficiency should be followed. This can be done by ascertaining the physical quantities of molasses consumed and alcohol produced.

(9) While planning a new distillery the availability of molasses in the region should be ascertained. The cost of transport of molasses should be kept to the minimum.

(10) It is preferable to attach a distillery to the sugar factory to

take the advantage of the utilities available and the other off-site facilities. The cost of production of alcohol of distilleries attached to sugar factory will be lower.

(11) The multiplicity of taxes and levies and administrative control by Government agencies has been criticised right from the 1955 report. It would be advisable to have separate units for manufacture of potable liquor and industrial alcohol. This should be gradually done over a period of years. There is no justification for having different rates of taxes in different States. Alcohol should be considered as a basic feedstock material like Naphtha and should be available at a uniform price all over the country. This matter requires serious and immediate attention. This is an artificial barrier causing hindrance to the progress of industry.

(12) It is desirable to utilise sugar-cane and its by-products economically. At present 60 per cent of the sugar-cane is utilised for *Gur* and *Khandsari.* The sugar extraction is poor and sugar is lost in bagasse and control on by-product utilisation is not easily possible. More and more sugarcane should be diverted to sugar factories and *Khandsari* molasses should be used for distillation so that finally it will enhance the production of alcohol.

(13) Small size distilleries below 10-12 million litres per year should not be encouraged except when they are attached to sugar factories.

(14) The raw-material for potable liquor, at least for Indian made foreign liquor must be obtained from alternative sources such as grains, starches, etc.

(15) The price of molasses should be brought down to keep the price of alcohol at the lowest level. The amount of Rs. 20 per tonne of molasses provided at present for the construction of storage tanks for molasses should be discontinued from the price of molasses. Instead a cess of Rs. 0.03 (3 paise) per litre, should be levied on the price of alcohol to provide funds for research and development work both in the distillery industry as well as alcohol-based chemicals industry. The bare price of molasses could still further be reduced. This is imperative for the growth of alcohol-based industry.

(16) Alcohol should preferably be used as a chemical feedstock and not as a fuel, for motive power or as a source of energy because its calorific value per unit weight is very low.

(17) At present, the Central Molasses Board meets once in a year at the beginning of the sugar season. There should be another meet-

ing in the middle of the season to review the situation so that any surplus molasses could be transported to the required ditilleries before the start of the rainy season.

(18) The distribution of alcohol is controlled by the State Government although the Central Government intervenes in allocation of alcohol from surplus to deficit States. The procedure followed causes lot of difficulties to the users. For release of alcohol, licence holder has to submit an application for a particular month's quota to Excise Commissioner who issues release order. On the basis of release order, the Excise Superintendent of the District gives a transport permit. After utilising the quota released in a permit, the licence holder has to submit another application for the release of the next month's quota. The same distillery may not be allotted from month to month. This situation needs rationalisation.

(19) While licensing new units, the availability of molasses within the region should be taken into consideration. Also preference should be given to existing units to expand as there is already adequate infrastructure available within the existing units.

(20) As an incentive to the distillers to produce alcohol more efficiently it may be worthwhile to allow the efficient distilleries who produce during the season at 240 litres per tonne of molasses to export about five per cent of alcohol produced.

(21) Established units in alcohol deficit States are finding great difficulty to maintain supply of alcohol because the surplus States are setting up alcohol based units to utilise their surplus alcohol. The well established units in deficit States must be assured of supply of alcohol without any interruption. This should be carefully kept in view while approving the further capacities.

B. Alcohol-based Chemical Industries

(1) The alcohol-based industries must be assured or their full requirements of alcohol before new units are licensed. In the case of alcohol deficit States, the surplus States that are required to release alcohol should be clearly marked and excessive distance for transport of alcohol be eliminated.

(2) The supply of alcohol to the industries should be regular and the procedure of submitting returns month by month and getting fresh quota should be done away with. Annual quota should be released. It should be appreciated that all alcohol-based industries

are continuous industries and if shut down for any reason result into loss of efficiency and loss of alcohol in start-up and shut down. This is a national waste.

(3) It is better to allocate the total production of individual distilleries to individual alcohol-based industries for a minimum period of one year from time to time so that other formalities like denaturants, transport permit and release order are planned.

(4) Industries which require relatively more alcohol per tonne of product should be given lower priority. However, the present units may be allowed to have a 3 to 4 per cent annual growth rate. In remote places where petrobased ethylene is not available alcohol-based ethylene units may be permitted.

(5) Apart from extensive Research and Development work for finding out alternate sources of alcohol and maximising production of alcohol from existing conventional sources, research and development work must be undertaken in the new avenues of fermentation technology in selective fermentation processes using the revolutionary new technique of immobilised enzymes. Alcohol can be directly converted into chemicals like Butanol and Acetone. The low energy technology is much more appropriate to India than the utilisation of conventional technologies.

Note of Dissent by the Representative of All-India Distillers' Association, New Delhi

1. The terms of reference for this Committee clearly stipulate that this Committee should prepare the present status of the *industries based on alcohol*, i.e., the total approved capacities, actual installed capacities and the production achieved. The Committee has to work out the estimates of the capacities likely to materialise by the end of 5th Plan, i.e., 1978-79 and to assess long-range estimates for a period of say 15 years and to recommend specific areas of alcohol-based industries, in which future growth needs to be planned. The Committee is to further examine the constraints on the development and growth of the alcohol-based industries and recommend suitable remedial measures. Besides, the Committee has been asked to make any other recommendation which may help in increasing the availability and utilisation of alcohol for industrial purposes.

2. Unfortunately the report, which has been finalised, does not deal with the subjects as envisaged in the terms of reference. The

Committee has not collected any reliable and adequate data from the alcohol-based industrial units regarding consumptions of raw materials for the past few years, theoretical production possible from the quantities of raw materials consumed, actual production achieved, efficiencies possible and actual efficiencies achieved, etc. Data regarding the technical working of these units has also been collected. In the absence of these figures, it is not possible for the Committee to give their comments on the *present status of the alcohol-based industries*. The reports primarily deals with the condition of Alcohol Industry and not Alcohol-based Industries. Even here, the Committee has not collected basic data regarding the actual number of distilleries existing in this country, their present licensed/installed capacities, the actual production of each distillery for the past five years, their efficiencies and the problems being faced by them with regard to the availability of adequate quantity of proper quality of raw materials, etc. They have commented upon the working of the Alcohol Industry not based on data collected; but have given their comments based on—somewhat prejudiced view of the working of this industry.

3. Even though our Association, had intimated to them that there are 101 distilleries in *production* with a licensed capacity of about 604 million litres, they have mentioned that there are only 71 distilleries in production *as per D.G.T.D. records* which also is contradictory as per data given in Appendix 8 where the number of distilleries is mentioned as 83 with a licensed capacity of 508 million litres. It is well within their knowledge that there are number of units which have been licensed by the State Excise Commissioners and have not so far been registered with D.G.T.D. The Committee should have assessed the installed capacities of the various units as well. The Committee secretariat should have taken the trouble of collecting all the latest data regarding the number of distilleries and their present capacities by contacting the various Excise Commissioners of the States concerned. This, according to me, has been a lapse in this report. Without this important data, it is very difficult to prepare a report indicating the present status of this industry and the possible production which can be achieved in the next few years.

4. It has been mentioned that during the last 30 years the distilleries have been working at a very low standard of efficiency and there has not been any improvement in their working. This statement is not based on any data collected for the past 30 years but is based

on prejudiced opinion. In fact, from the data available with the All India Distilleries' Association, the recovery of rectified spirit has gone up from 222 to 229 litres per tonne of molasses from 1972 to 1976. In fact, the recovery of alcohol per tonne of molasses is dependent on a number of factors such as quality of molasses, total fermentable sugar in molasses, continuous operation of distillery, etc. etc. This also depends on continuous supply of power, quality of coal to maintain steam pressure, etc.

5. It has also been mentioned that alcohol industry is letting out effluent without any treatment which can cause enough pollution. I submit that this subject is outside the purview of the terms of reference. The factual position is that the All India Distillers' Association has collected from its members large amounts and have given the same to various Research Institutions like N.S.I., Kanpur for working out a proper and economic solution of the problem. Some distilleries have already adopted lagooning method for treatment of effluent. Others have requested their State Governments to allot them land for this purpose. It may be further pointed out that nothing has been mentioned regarding the effluent being let out by the *alcohol based industry*. The report could deal with the problem of Effluents being let out by the Alcohol Based Industry as per terms of reference but unfortunately the report is silent on this.

6. The report does not deal with the problem of inadequate lifting of alcohol from distilleries which resulted in frequent stoppages of distilleries due to warehouse jamming. This has been one of the reasons for poor utilisation of installed capacities of the distilleries. The report does not deal with the requirement of adequate storage capacities for Alcohol with the Alcohol consuming units, the present position and the steps to be taken to augment the same, if necessary.

7. In the report it has been mentioned that there is no adequate technical control in the distillery. It is not fair to make such a sweeping remark against the distilleries without collecting any data from the distilleries in this regard and studying them carefully. There has been gradual improvement in production, efficiencies and other working data of the distilleries. The recovery and other efficiency figures would greatly depend upon the fermentable sugar in molasses. Without collecting and studying these data, it is not fair to come to any conclusion.

8. It has also been mentioned in the report that it is possible to

convert non-fermentable sugar by enzymatic action. It would have been desirable if the details of the process of fermentation of non-fermentable sugar or the reference from literature giving the details of the process could have been given in the report to enable the distilleries to benefit by this information.

9. The efficiency of conversion of alcohol into various alcohol-based chemicals is very important in the present context and unfortunately the Committee has not collected any data regarding the present conversion efficiency of alcohol into various alcohol based chemicals, what is the theoretical efficiency possible and where the industry stands at present. It is quite possible that the alcohol consuming industry could improve their conversion efficiencies by better process control and technology.

10. It is common knowledge that alcohol prices have been very uneconomic to the alcohol units during the past few years and due to which the industry has not been in a position to undertake any modernisation programme or technological improvements. Any proposal for any increase in alcohol prices has always been strongly opposed by the alcohol consuming industry. It would have been a very good exercise if this Committee had collected data pertaining to the percentage incidence of the existing ex-factory price of rectified spirit excluding taxes namely Rs. 589.1 per K.L. to the final sale price of their end products to the actual consumers. Unfortunately, the Committee has not thought it fit to collect such useful data which would be handy to the Government whenever this question comes up again in future.

11. It has been mentioned in the report that the yield of alcohol produced in Brazil from sugar factory molasses is 300 litres per tonne. It has been conveniently omitted to mention that the sugar content of molasses in Brazil is over 66 per cent whereas the sugar content of molasses in India is around 45 per cent to 47 per cent. Actually, the purity of final molasses in India is around 35 per cent whereas the same in Brazil goes up to 60 per cent. In Brazil, they are deliberately throwing out molasses rich in sugar since their policy has been to produce more alcohol and less sugar whenever the international price of sugar goes down. This is the position today and in Brazil they sacrifice efficiency of recovery of sugar in the sugar factory and pass on molasses of higher sugar content to the distillery to recover more alcohol, with a view to save foreign exchange in importing crude oil. In Brazil, the official policy has been to replace petrol

by power alcohol and as such the Government is giving a lot of encouragement for producing alcohol directly even from cane juice. If these facts are not mentioned, it is likely that inadequate data will mislead the authorities concerned. Our Association has recently sent a delegation to Brazil to study the working of distilleries and shortly a report in this regard will be submitted to the Government comparing their efficiencies and our efficiencies.

12. According to the Committee the delivered cost of alcohol on the present day basis has been suggested to be in the region of Re. 1 per litre to the user. This suggestion has been made without any study or supporting data. I am of the view that it is not possible because molasses and alcohol transport charges vary from distillery to distillery and consumer to consumer. With the allotment of molasses entirely in the hands of the State excise authorities, a uniform delivered price is not practicable. As at present, the molasses transport charges should be computed on actual basis, and reckoned as an incidence on the production of alcohol without any ceiling.

13. It has been recommended that a "Cess" of 3 paise per litre of alcohol may be realised and the amount be utilised to promote research and development activities. It is strange that the alcohol-based industry want to utilise the "Cess" to be collected by Alcohol Industry. As far as alcohol industry is concerned, it fully supports the idea of collecting a separate "Cess" and apportioning the same for R&D activity for the alcohol industry after payment of taxes, if leviable. Similarly the alcohol-based industry should have come forward to collect "Cess" out of the sale of their products rather than depending on alcohol industry for their R&D activities to be controlled by the Government and the alcohol industry only. Out Association is strongly opposed to any suggestion wherein the money collected by the alcohol industry is proposed to be utilised by the alcohol consuming industry.

14. The Committee has made a reference to the yield of alcohol from molasses in Brazil but has not discussed the reason as to why Brazil is going in a big way for promoting the use of power alcohol for motive purposes. In this regard, our country is also more or less similarly situated and we are already spending considerable foreign exchange in import of crude. We have to seriously study the reasons which led Brazil to encourage the use of alcohol as motor fuel and find out whether the same policy will suit our country also.

15. It has been recommended by the Committee that efficient distilleries who produce during the season 240 litres per tonne of molasses may be permitted to export 5 per cent of alcohol produced by them, without mentioning the sugar content of molasses which will be made available to the distillery concerned. This suggestion is vague. I agree with the spirit of the suggestion but the recovery of alcohol should have some relation to the sugar content of molasses. The base recovery should be 220 litres per tonne of molasses, based on the present performance.

16. The report has been made unnecessarily bulky by incorporating copies of all the representations received from various individuals/organisations. It is not a normal practice to include such papers in the final report of the Committee. These background papers and representations are meant for study by the members Committee and only the recommendations of the Committee alongwith supporting data should find a place in the report.

17. One of the graphs included in the report give a wrong impression. I would like to make a reference to the trend curves given for the price of alcohol and molasses. The alcohol prices have been increased only a few times and the recent steep increase was entirely due to increase in molasses price. These trends should have been indicated by a straightline joining the adjacent who points and not by a curve which is likely to mislead the authorities concerned. Besides, in the same graph both the graphs for alcohol and molasses have been given. The range of increase in prices of molasses is Rs. 10 to Rs. 60 (500%) and the range of increase in prices of alcohol from Rs. 200 to about Rs. 600 (200%). Even though the percentage increase in molasses is far higher than the percentage increase of alcohol price, the graph does not reflect this position correctly to a layman. The reason being that they have adopted the same scale even though the range of prices has been from Rs. 10 to Rs. 60 for molasses and from Rs. 200 to about Rs. 600 for alcohol. They should have used two different scales to represent the real picture regarding the extent of the percentage increase in the prices of these two commodities.

18. Our Association strongly supports the suggestion that a part of molasses price be funded as a sort of a "Cess" for Research and Development in Alcohol Industry. This fund should be jointly operated by the Alcohol Industry and a body which may be appointed by the Government of India.

Statement showing Comparative Position of Estimated Consumption of Industrial Alcohol

	By 1981 in million litres
(A) For Industrial uses	296.7
(B) Pesticides	6.0
(C) Pharmaceuticals	—
(D) Misc. Items (Potables)	180.0
(E) Other small scale users	90.0
(F) Paint & Varnishes	40.0
(G) Hospitals	40.0
Total	652.7

Note:

(1) Item No. A is compiled on basis of licences and 10 per cent growth by 1981 on basis of installed capacities of 1976 and new licencses (assumed to be implemented by 1980).

(2) Item No. B, C, D, E, F, and G as per figures of Fermentation Council's Figure (Please refer Annexure No. 12).

5

RAILWAY ACCIDENT INVESTIGATION REPORT ON DERAILMENT OF 387 DOWN BHUSAWAL-ALLAHABAD PASSENGER TRAIN AT MAJHGAWAN STATION ON SATNA-MANIKPUR SECTION OF CENTRAL RAILWAY AT 11.58 HOURS ON FEBRUARY 17, 1977[1]

One Man Commissioner Shri J.Y. Marathey, Additional Commissioners of Railway Safety, Bombay

Appointment

The Commission was constituted under Ministry of Tourism and Civil Aviation (Commission of Railway Safety) in accordance with Rule 4 of the Statutory Investigation into Railway Accidents Rules, 1973 vide Notification No. Rs. 13-T(8)/71 dated April 19, 1973 on February 17, 1977.

Terms of Reference

To enquire into the Derailment of 387 Down Bhusawal-Allahabad Passenger Train at Majhgawan Station on Satna-Manikpur Section of Central Railway on 11.58 hours on February 17, 1977.

Contents

Summary; Inspection and Inquiry; Relief Measures; Composition of Train and Damage; Local Features; Summary of Evidence; Observations and Tests; Discussion; Conclusions; Summary of Recommendations; Annexures.

---

1. Delhi, Controller of Publications, 1979, i + 21 p.

Conclusions

44. *Cause*: On full consideration of the factual, material and circumstantial evidence I have come to the conclusion that derailment of 387 Down Bhusawal-Allahabad passenger train at Majhgawan station on Satna-Manikpur section of the Central Railway at 11.58 hours on February 17, 1977 was due to:

(i) the left hand chipped and worn out tongue rail of 1 in 12 facing turn-out leading to the 1st Loop line at Bombay end of Majhgawan station not being replaced in time; and

(ii) the flange of the leading left wheel of wagon No. CR 65190 C having worn out at its root and tip beyond condemning limits over certain portions and the same not being detected in time.

45. *Responsibility*

(a) *Track*

(i) Shri V.B. Mehta, acting P.W.I., Manikpur is primarily responsible for the accident. The extendnuating circumstances may however be taken into account [para 43(a)(i)].

Shri V.B. Mehta aged 39 years joined Railway Service as an Apprentice P.W.I. on 26-5-1956. He was promoted as P.W.I. Grade III in Rs. 425-700 (R.S.) Scale on 15-10-65 but was officiating as P.W.I. Grade II in Rs. 550-750 (R.S.) Scale in a leave vacancy at the time of the accident. He has no previous punishments.

(ii) Shri S.L. Raikwar, P.W.I.-III, Markundi and Shri S.C. Gupta, Assistant Engineer, Satna must also share some responsibility for the accident [paras 43(a)(ii) and (iii)].

(b) *Rolling Stock*

(i) Shri P.A. Narkhede, TXR, Bhusawal is primarily responsible for the accident [para 43(b)(i)].

Shri P.A. Narkhede aged 48 years appointed as an Apprentice C & W (Carriage and Wagon) Khalasi on 1-7-52. He was promoted as Assistant TXR grade Rs. 55-130 (P.S.) from 9-1-56 and later promoted as TXR, grade Rs. 100-180 (A.S.)

from 5-3-58 in which capacity he was working at the time of the accident. He was warned three times, fined one time, censured two times and his increment withheld for three times for various minor offences.

(ii) Each of the TXRs at Khandwa, Itarsi, Jabalpur, Katni and Satna must also share some responsibility for the accident [para 43(b)(ii)].

46. *Relief Measures*: I am satisfied that the medical aid and relief measures were arranged promptly, satisfactorily and adequately.

Recommendations

47. The Points and Crossings Register showed that the left hand tongue rail of Point No. 8A at Majhgawan, which was on the outside of a curve, used to wear very fast and had to be replaced every now and then (para 28). The tongue rail was replaced on 11-9-76 but during the inspection on 11-10-76, i.e., within one month, it was found to be worn out and required to be kept under observations. The C & M (Chemical and Metallurgical) examination carried out showed that the tongue rail was a of normal rail steel and was not defective (Annexure III). As chipped and broken tongue rail is a safety hazard, it is suggested that in such locations, i.e., on outside of a curve, tongue rails made of special wear resisting steel such as manganese steel may be used.

As a trial measure it is also suggested that a check rail of adequate length (length greater than the maximum wheel base of rolling stock) may be provided on the inside of the curve on the approach to the facing turnout so that the leading outer wheel of a vehicle will not have a tendency to hug the outer rail and the tongue rail fixed to it. This might help in reducing the wear and tear of such tongue rail also. If the trial succeeds, it could be extended in other locations.

48. According to para 3.10 of the Conference Rules, Part IV, all trains have to be examined by the Train Examining staff and a certificate of fitness has to be issued to the Station Master who is not to despatch the train unless such a certificate is received. Form T 431 B has also been introduced for this purpose. It was, however, seen that this Form is not used in practice and the work is done on verbal messages. This is not satisfactory and the correct procedure should be

enforced.

49. Although according to Conference Rules, the TXR at the starting station as well as those enroute have to detect a faulty wheel profile, it was surprising that none of the Train Examining staff at Bhusawal, Khandwa, Itarsi, Jabalpur, Katni and Satna could detect the worn out flange of the wagon that had reached condemning limits. This leads one to think that a general laxity in working has crept in and this is indeed disturbing. Necessary corrective steps may be taken by the Administration.

50. Proper marshalling of the train and not been done according to extent rules. Had the train been properly marshalled, the casualties that occurred may not have occurred. Wrong marshalling of SLRs and trains having been repeatedly observed by the Commission, the same was pointedly brought to the notice of the Railway Board vide Commissioner of Railway Safety's letter No. 22-T (4)/73 of 15-10-74 but this case indicates that cases of wrong marshalling of trains continue to occur. The lapse in this case needs to be viewed seriously and necessary steps require to be taken to avoid such cases in future.

51. Arising out of Metre Gauge Mixed Train derailment, the Commission had made recommendations in the past that where mixed trains are a required to be run, the goods stock may be attached in the rear in order to reduce the consequence of their derailment on the coaching stock. The Railway Board vide their letter No. 72/Safety/(A&R)1/2 dated 16-12-72 had issued instructions that this should be done except where it would be difficult to attach and detach goods wagons in the rear of the train due to difficulties in the layout of the yards, reversal of engines, etc. During the Inquiry it was stated that the goods wagons of 387 Down are often booked to Naini where there are no shunting facilities available and therefore the wagons are attached in the front. A review of the marshalling of 387 Down done for the 3 months October to December 1976 showed that the goods stock was booked to Naini only on 15 days or so while on rest of the days it was booked to Allahabad, Jabalpur, Katni and/or Satna where shunting facilities are available. It was also seen that the goods stock is generally booked from Bhusawal Itarsi and Jabalpur and while at Jabalpur it is generally attached in the rear, at Bhusawal and Itarsi, it is attached in the front. The marshalling of goods stock on the train may be reviewed and instructions to attach the goods stock in the rear of the train except where it is unavoidable (in the

circumstances given in Board's letter) may be issued.

52. According to Working Time Table, 387 Down runs as a Mixed Train between Jabalpur and Manikpur. The implication of this apparently is that the goods stock put on this train between Jabalpur and Manikpur and detached at or before reaching Manikpur is fit for running at goods train speed only and is not made fit to run at passenger train speed. In that case, the booked speed of 387 Down between Jabalpur and Manikpur will have to be 58 km.p.h. and not 65 km.p.h. as shown in the Time Table, as the maximum permissible speed of goods train is 65 km.p.h. Necessary corrections may be made in the Working Time Table.

53. According to para 1407(C)—W.W., if the cause of a derailment is not indisputably known, measurements should be taken over a distance or 100 metres in rear of the place of derailment and 50 metres ahead of it. Contrary to these instructions, measurements were taken in this particular case for 50 metres only on either side of the point of derailment. This did not give a correct idea of the condition of the track in rear or in front of the place of derailment. It is surprising that the technical staff should make such mistakes in this important matter. Strict instructions may be issued to the staff to avoid such mistakes in future.

54. For assessment of the speed of the train, a lot of evidence had to be collected and some trials carried out and even then, the assessment cannot be said to be cent per cent correct. The only reliable way to find out the correct speed of the train is to fit the engine with a speed recorder. In the past, the fitment of speed recorders to passenger trains had been recommended but the Board vide their letter No. 74/Safety (A&R)/1/22 of 7-1-76 had stated that as passenger trains have to stop frequently, the chances of their overspeeding are remote and the indigenous supply of speed recorders is not adequate and hence it was not proposed to extend provision of speed recorders to passenger trains. In day-to-day working however, there are several instances of passenger trains taking the turn-outs at excessive speed and the only effective way to prevent this could be provide speed recorders on these trains and to take up with the Drivers wherever they are found to exceed the authorised speed. The supply of speed recorders could also be encouraged. The recommendation to provide speed recorders to passenger trains may therefore be reconsidered.

6

RAILWAY ACCIDENT INVESTIGATION REPORT ON COLLISION OF BPQD GOODS TRAIN WITH THE REAR OF NO. 76 UP WALTAIR-KAZIPET PASSENGER TRAIN ON THE UP MAIN LINE OF KESAMUDRAM STATION ON VIJAYAWADA-KAZIPET BG DOUBLE LINE SECTION OF SOUTH CENTRAL RAILWAY AT ABOUT 22.10 HOURS ON 25TH MARCH 1977[1]

March 28, 1977 – June 15, 1977

One Man Commission Shri K.N. Kamath, Additional Commissioner of Railway Safety, South Circle, Bangalore

Officers Present

Railway Shri S. Balasubramanian; Shri I.K. Puri; Shri P.K. Srinivasan; Shri Gulshan Rai

Civil Shri Mahbub Ali; Shri Kamal Kumar; Maj. Viswanatham

Appointment

The Commission was constituted under Ministry of Tourism and Civil Aviation (Commission of Railway Safety) in accordance with Rule 4 the Statutory Investigation into Railway Accident Rules, 1973 vide Notification No. RS.13-T(8)/71 dated April 19, 1973 on 25th March, 1977.

---

1. Ministry of Tourism and Civil Aviation (Commission of Railway Safety), Government of India, New Delhi, 1985; ii + 14 p.

Terms of Reference

To enquire into the collision of BPQD Goods Train with the rear of No. 76 Up Waltair-Kazipet Passenger train on the Up Main Line of Kesamudram Station on Vijayawada-Kazipet BG double line — section of South Central Railway at about 22.10 hours on March 25, 1977.

Contents

Summary; Inspection and Inquiry; Relief Measures; The Train; Local Features; Summary of Evidence; Observations and Tests; Discussion; Conclusions; Remarks and Recommendation; Annexures.

Conclusions

28. (a) *Cause of Accident*: On full consideration of the factual and circumstantial evidence and the results of tests I have reached the conclusion that the collision of the Up BPQD Goods train with the rear of No. 76 Up 'Waltair-Kazipet Passenger' train that occurred at about 22-10 hours on 25th March, 1977 at Km. 421/14 on the Up Main line of Kesamudram station on the Vijayawada-Kazipet Double line Broad Gauge section of South Central Railway was *caused as a result of the Up BPQD Goods* having been *driven past the Up Main Home Signal which was at Danger on to the Main line at the station which was* already occupied by No. 76 Passenger.

(b) *Responsibility*: Shri Doss Anthony, Driver of Up BPQD Goods is responsible for having passed the Up Main Home Signal of Kesamudram at Danger. He violated General Rules 76(a) and S.R. 76(1). He also violated General Rule 182 (b).

[*Bio-data of Shri Doss Anthony*:

Shri Doss Anthony was first appointed as an Engine Cleaner in February 1945 and promoted as Driver 'C' in October 1963. He has been working as a Diesel Driver since 1972. He has been censured on four occasions and fined on six occasions for various minor offences. His increment was withheld for one year in November 1966 for 'stalling a train'.]

Shri Sankaraiah, the Diesel Assistant, contributed to the accident in having failed to note the aspect of the Up Main home Signal and call out the same to the Driver. He contravened provisions of General Rules 122 and probably 182(b) also.

[Bio-data of Shri Sankaraiah:

Shri R. Sankaraiah was first appointed as a Yard Khalasi in August 1958 and promoted as Fireman 'C' in May 1966. He was promoted as Fireman 'B', in June 1973 and has been working as Diesel Assistant since 11-3-1976. He has been censured on one occasion and has had no other punishments.]

[NOTE: Extracts of Rules violated are at Annexure II.]

(c) *Relief Measures*: With reference to Section II of the Report, the relief arrangements were satisfactory. Dr. R. Reddy, a local Medial Practitioner of Kesamudram proceeded to the station immediately on being informed about the accident and rendered first-aid to the injured. Subsequently he gave them further medical aid in his dispensary situated nearby. The Railway administration may like to convey their appreciation to Dr. Reddy for his timely help.

Recommendations

29. The Assistant Station Master as well as the Switchman on duty in both the Cabins at Kesamudram had exchanged Private Numbers for the reception of BPQD Goods. They contravened the provisions of Para VII of the Station Working Order applicable to Kesamudram station according to which it is only when the nominated line is clear for the reception of the train and the facing and trailing points are correctly set and the facing point locked that Private Numbers should be exchanged by the Assistant Station Master with the Switchman. Exchange of Private Numbers in advance is hazardous and is a very undesirable practice. Suitable steps may be taken to ensure that the train passing staff do not take recourse to such measures.

30. A wooden bodied coach GS 3097, was attached next to the rear SLR of 76 Up contrary to the extant instructions of the Railway Board regarding marshalling of coaches on passenger trains. A steel bodied/anti-telescopic coach should have been marshalled here and such coaches were available in the train formation. There is, therefore, no reason why the wooden bodied coach should have been marshalled next to the SLR. This coach suffered the maximum damage

with complete demolition of the body and also caused several injuries. Had a steel bodied/anti-telescopic coach been attached it is probable that the casualties would have been less. The importance of correct marshalling of all passenger trains may be impressed on the railways.

31. According to Para 902(g) of the Indian Railways Signal Engineering Manual (Annexure II) track relays have to be periodically overhauled at intervals not exceeding 10 years but no such periodicity is laid down for 'line' relays. It is understood that the Signal Standards Committee is examining this issue. The matter may be expedited so that these relays are renewed in time.

32. Shri Anjaneyulu, Driver of 76 Up, whose Periodical Medical Examination was due on 26-2-1977 had not been sent for the same till the date of accident. It is necessary that staff are invariably sent for medical examination by the due date.

33. According to S.R. 36.6 (extract at Annexure II) of the Central and South Central Railways the Station Masters of all interlocked stations are to test the working of reception signals daily and record the results of the tests in the station/cabin diary. It was seen that in the station diary of Kesamudram only vague remarks that 'signals were tested' were made. It is necessary that the remark should give details of the signal tested and also whether the signals went back to danger when the Station Master's slide and the cabin slot were put back separately. It is suggested that the Station Masters should also test the track circuiting of the tracks by attempting to clear the concerned Home Signal when a track is occupied by a train. Very often when Drivers pass signals at danger they claim that the signals were cleared though the track circuiting would not have permitted this. The Drivers claim that the track circuit might have failed. If daily tests are carried out by the Station Master would be easier to decide the issue. It is, therefore, recommended that the subsidiary rules might be amplified to include testing of the track circuit also.

34. A scrutiny of the duties performed by Driver Shri Doss Anthony during the two days prior to the accident showed that after availing 8-1/2 hours rest at Balharshah he had signed on at 22-35 hours on 23-3-1977 and had signed off at Bellampalli at 18-05 hours on 24-4-1977. He was, therefore, on duty for *19 hours and 30 minutes*. Again he availed rest at Bellampalli for 8-1/2 hours before signing on at 02-35 hours on 25-3-1977 and signed off at Dornakal at 15-00 hours the same day having been on duty for *12 hours 25 minutes*. He

then availed only *4 hours 45 minutes* rest at Dornakal before signing on at 19-45 hours for working BPQD Goods. It will thus be seen that he had been made to work for periods very *much in excess of* 10 hours. He did not *have adequate rest also particularly on the 25th*. It is most undesirable to make Drivers work for *such long periods* as this would induce fatigue which in turn is liable to impair his capacity and cause accidents. The importance of not exceeding the 10-00 hours rule and giving adequate rest to engine crew may be impressed upon the Railways.

Railway Boards Views on Recommendations

Para 29: Necessary instructions have been issued by the Railway to all concerned. The defaulting staff is also being taken up.

It is seen that CRS has noted the action taken by the Railway.

Para 30: Instructions have been issued by the railway administration to all concerned for strict compliance of the extent orders. Disciplinary action is being taken against the defaulting staff.

Para 31: "*Requirements and Schedule for periodical overhauling of Signalling Relays*"

1. Track relays of all types should be overhauled periodically. Line relays of only shelf type should also be overhauled periodically. No. Periodical overhauling is required for other types of relays.

2.1 Periodicity of overhauling of track relays of all types should be every 10 years subject to the maximum of 12 years.

2.2 (i) Periodicity of overhauling of shelf-type line relays should be every 15 years,

(ii) The overhauling period is to be counted from the date of last overhaul/manufacture,

(iii) These limits may be reduced for track relays of all types and shelf type line relays depending upon the intensity of traffic and other local conditions obtaining on the sections such as heavy sub-urban and major Route Relay interlocking installations as decided by the Railway.

3. All vital relays should be visually inspected periodically as detailed in sub-committee's recommendations. The periodicity of inspection of track and line relays should be once in every 2 and 3 years respectively.

4. All non-proved miniature plug-in type relays other than

track relays should be overhauled only when removed from service due to a failure. All proved type relays should be checked and its contacts cleaned at site, if required when a failure take place. If the failure persists the relay should be removed and sent for overhauling.

5. RDSO should examine and submit necessary draft for amendment too para 902 and other connected paras of Signal Engineering Manual to incorporate all the suggestions of standards Committee.
6. RDSO should conduct studies on type of test that can reveal defective relays at site using simple portable instruments.
7. RDSO should collect data on all known cases of relays failing on the unsafe side both in the past and future. They should also collect data on all failures of relays on the safe side occurring in future. For this, they should issue a suitable proforma to be filled in by the Railways for each failure. After sufficient data have been collected, RDSO should report back to the signal standards committee so that the effect of the resolution passed by the Committee can be studied.
8. RDSO should also study the economics of overhauling. They should also study the test to be carried out after overhauling and recommend the type of instrument set-up other facilities required for the purpose accordingly.

Para 32: Instructions have been issued to the Supervisory Officials by the Railway to ensure that staff are sent for medical examination by due dates.

Para 33: Necessary instructions on the subject have been issued to all the Railways vide Board's circular letter No. 77/Safety (A&R) 1/6 dated 1-10-77.

Para 34: Instructions have been issued to the Railways, emphasising the importance of not exceeding 10-hours duty at a stretch for the engine crew and giving them adequate rest. A copy thereof is enclosed for CRS's information.

It may be mentioned here that all Mail/Express and Passenger trains and 85 per cent of goods trains are working to the schedule of 10-hour duty at a stretch. It has been decided to provide additional running staff to the extent of 2700 and it is hoped that the 10-hour duty rule will be implemented completely in a short time.

7

RAILWAY ACCIDENT INVESTIGATION REPORT ON COLLISION OF MOTOR CAR NO. USR 9063 AND PASSENGER TRAIN NO. 131 UPA 'B' CLASS LEVEL CROSSING ON THE LALKUA JN.-KASHIPUR JN. SECTION OF THE IZZATNAGAR DIVISION OF NORTH-EASTERN RAILWAY AT 18.45 HOURS ON MARCH 28, 1977[1]

One Man Commission Shri A.V. Jacob, Additional Commissioner of Railway Safety, North Eastern Circle, Gorakhpur

Appointment

The Commission was constituted under Ministry of Tourism and Civil Aviation (Commission of Railway Safety) in accordance with Rule 4 of the Statutory Invcstigation into Railway Accidents Rules 1973 Vide Notification No. RS. 13-T(8)/71 dated April 19, 1973 on March 28, 1977.

Terms of Reference

To enquire into the collision of Motor Car No. USR 9063 and the Passenger Train No. 131 Up A 'B' Class Level Crossing on the Lalkua Jn-Kashipur Jn. Section of the Izzatnagar Division of North-Eastern Railway at 18.45 hours on March 28, 1977.

Contents

Summary; The Accident; Inspection and Inquiry; Relief Measures;

---

1. Delhi, Controller of Publications, 1981, 9 p.

The Train and the Car; Local Features; Summary of Evidence; Test and Observations; Discussion; Conclusions; Remarks and Recommendations; Railway Board's Comments on Various Paras of the Report.

Conclusions

37. *Cause*: On full consideration of the factual, material and circumstantial evidence, I have come to the conclusion that collision of Ambassador Car No. USR 9063 with coach No. 7771 of 131 Up Lalkua-Kashipur Passenger at 18.45 hours on 28-3-77 was caused by the failure of the Driver of the Car to stop before the closed level crossing gate.

38. *Responsibility*: Responsibility for the accident lies with the Driver of the Car No. USR 9063.

39. *Relief Arrangements*: Reference Paras 6 and 7 of the report, I am satisfied that relief arrangements were satisfactory.

Recommendations

40.1 In the extant case the accident was caused either by the negligence of the Driver of the Car or failure of the Car brakes. However, casualties to train passengers would have been avoided had the locked gate not given away before the Car so easily.

40.2 The reasons for the failure of the padlocked gate to stop the Car has been dealt with in Para 35. Some of the reasons are due to wrong practice being followed by N.E. Rly. and the methods adopted for padlocking the gate. Non-provision of vertical bolts is a failure to follow standard drawing of N.E. Railway for such gates. But since even this appears to be widespread, I do not hold any individual employee responsible for this. North-Eastern Railway Administration may take urgent steps to re-site the Level Crossing gates, make them opening away from track with pegs or brackets preventing from swinging towards the track. Also either horizontal or vertical bolts be provided and locking arrangements modified to prevent direct force being applied on the padlock.

41. Incidentally, a large number of cases have been reported on N.E. Railway (though they have not been subject of ACRS Inquiry) where speeding trucks have crashed through lifting barriers and ended up on the track. The potentialities of these incidents for caus-

ing high casualty accidents is evident. It is, therefore, suggested that either lifting barriers be re-designed to prevent vehicles coming on to track or one or two bumps be provided before the barrier to slow down trucks.

42. In the extant case reasons for failure of the Car Driver, to stop in time, could only be presumed since no occupant of Car came forward as a witness, the Car could not be examined, nor could even details of investigation by the Police including their examination of Car be obtained. In every level crossing accident, a train and a road vehicle would be involved. As matters stand now, the A.C.R.S is fortunate if he can get details of the road vehicle and witnesses from that side. This greatly handicaps the inquiry. It is, therefore, suggested that the Railway Board take up the matter with State Government to arrange for presence of the Investigating Police Officer at the inquiry, who should be also made responsible for making the road vehicle available for inspection by A.C.R.S., as also witnesses who were occupants of the road vehicle.

43. In the present case engine of 131 Up did not have a Speedometer. According to the Izzatnagar Division, 2 YB Engines of passenger link at Kashipur are working without Speedometers because gear boxes have been sent to workshop on 22-2-77. Even though the question of speed of 131 Up is not a relevant issue in this case as far as the cause of accident is concerned, it is a matter of concern that passenger train engines continue to be run without Speedometers. Every time this failure is pointed out after an accident by the A.C.R.S., the Railway Board issue another Circular but there is no earnestness in seeing that trains are not run without this safety equipment. The reason obviously is that none on the Division worries about this unless it affects operating statistics. In order to impart a sense of urgency in this matter, I suggest that the maximum sanctioned speed for the engine or section which ever is lower be further restricted by 15 KMPH when a passenger train engine is not provided with a Speedometer or an Express/Mail engine with a Speed Recorder. This will also reduce the chances of the Driver exceeding the maximum speed which is the purpose of providing these instruments.

Railways Board's Comments on various Paras of the Report

Para 40: As per Indian Railways Way and Works Manual (Item 4 of

Annexure, Chapter 16) swing type gates may be provided for 'B' class level crossings opening either away from or towards the track, but not across the track. It is not, therefore, considered necessary for the Railway to re-site such level crossing gates as to make them open away from the track. Level crossing gates cannot be designed strong enough to prevent gate crashing by irresponsible drives of vehicles. There is nothing intrinsically wrong with gates opening towards the track and this has not in any way caused the accident. The Railway would, however, be asked to provide bolts and modify the design of swing gates so that application of direct force on the locks is avoided.

Para 41: Lifting barriers are of uniform design on all the Railways and it is not possible to redesign them as to prevent gate crashing vehicles from coming on to track.

Insofar as provision of bumps to the approaches of level crossing is concerned, the Ministry of Shipping and Transport are not in favour of the proposal as they feel that this results in impeding the flow of traffic. The matter has, however, been taken up with that Ministry who have been asked to reconsider their stand in view of the proven effectiveness of bumps. This is being pursued with them.

Para 42: The Indian Railways Act is under revision. It has been proposed to give powers of the civil court to the Commissioner of Railway Safety, which include Addl. Commissioners of Railway Safety also. If the proposed amendment is enacted, the Addl. Commissioners of Railway Safety will be able to ensure the attendance of witnesses production of documents, which will facilitate the conduct of enquiries into accidents.

Para 43: A drive has been launched by the railway administration to ensure availability of speedometers in working condition in every passenger train engine. Workshops have been specifically asked to repair the speedometers received from the sheds expeditiously and return the same to the concerned sheds. Action has also been taken to obtain adequate number of speedometers as spares which would go a long way in eliminating the incidence of train engines running without speedometers.

As for suggestion that the maximum sanctioned speed should be reduced by 15 km/h in the event of the engine of a passenger train running without speedometer and the engine of a Mail/Express train without a speed-recorder, it may be mentioned that this is not feasible as such a course would seriously affect train operation. It is notes that the CRS has also not insisted on this recommendation.

8

RAILWAY ACCIDENT INVESTIGATION REPORT ON THE DERAILMENT OF NO. 28 UP MANGALORE-MADRAS WEST COAST EXPRESS TRAIN AT SEVUR STATION ON THE JOLARPETTAI-MADRAS BROAD GAUGE DOUBLE LINE SECTION OF SOUTHERN RAILWAY AT ABOUT 12.50 HOURS ON MARCH 30, 1977[1]

One Man Commission Shri K.N. Kamath

Appointment

The Commission was constituted under Ministry of Tourism and Civil Aviation (Commission of Railway Safety) in accordance with Rule 4 of the Statutory Investigation into Railway Accidents Rules, 1973 vide Notification No. RS. 13-T (8)/71 dated April 19, 1973 on March 30, 1977.

Terms of Reference

To enquire into the Derailment of No. 28 Up Mangalore-Madras West Coast Express Train Sevur Station on the Jolarpettai-Madras Board Gauge Double line section of Southern Railway at about 12.50 hours on March 30, 1977.

Contents

Summary; Introduction; Relief Measures; The Train; Local Features; Summary of Evidence; Observations and Tests; Conclusions;

---

1. Delhi, Controller of Publications, 1982, 18 p.

Remarks and Recommendations; Railway Board's Comments on Various Paras of the Report.

Conclusions

42. (a) *Cause of Accident:* On full consideration of the factual, circumstantial and material evidence, the cause of the derailment of No. 28 Up 'Mangalore-Madras West Coast Express' train which occurred at about 12.50 hrs. on the 30th March, 1977 at Sevur station on the Jolarpettai-Madras Broad Gauge Double line section of Southern Railway could not be definitely established.

(b) *Responsibility:* In the circumstances explained in para 41, no responsibility can be fixed.

(c) *Relief Measures:* With reference to Section II of the Report, the relief arrangements were satisfactory. The Medical Officers of the Karigiri Hospital, who were the first to reach the site of accident, rendered great assistance to the injured. The Railway Administration may convey their appreciation in a suitable manner to the Hospital Authorities.

Recommendations

43. As discussed in para 41(h) it is possible that the deficiency of guide rollers in the 6th and 7th coaches of the train might have caused excessive flange forces that led to the derailment. The location of the turnout on the transitioned portion of a curve might have also contributed to the excess flange force. It has however been pointed out by the Railway Administration that according to Rules 4.7.4 of the IRCA Rules Part IV for Coaching Stock, guide roller is not marked as a safety item. Similarly according to para 812 of the Indian Railways' *Way and Works Manual* (reproduced below), turnouts can, in exceptional cases, be taken off from the transitioned portion of a main line curve:

> "812. *No change of superelevation over turn-outs*—There should be no change of cant between points 20 metres (60 ft.) outside the toe of the switch and nose of the crossing respectively, except in cases where points and crossings have to be taken off from the transitioned portion of a curve. Normally turnouts should not be taken off the transitioned portion of a Main Line curve. However,

in exceptional cases, when such a course is unavoidable, a specific relaxation may be given by the Chief Engineer of the Railway after personally examining each case. In such cases changes of cant and/or curvature may be permitted at the rates specified in para 807 or such lesser rates as may be prescribed."

The actual cant gradient in the case of W.7 was flatter than 1 in 720 as fixed in para 807. As regards the curvature, however, this could not be verified as the turnout was completely damaged as a result of the accident. In these circumstances, it is recommended that the Research Designs and Standards Organisation (RDSO) should examine as to what would be the effect of deficiency of guide rollers on the riding of the coach and whether combined with minor track irregularities, it could cause a derailment. Based on the results of this study, it could be decided whether the guide roller should be shown as a safety item in the I.R.C.A. Rules so that MAN/BEML coaches are not allowed to run without the full compliment of guide rollers.

44. It was noticed that the inside guide rollers were missing from several of the coaches of 28 Up, whereas none of the outside guide rollers were missing. It is understood that this is due to the frequent theft of these rollers which are made of brass. The outside guide rollers are so situated that it is very difficult to remove them. The possibility of manufacturing the rollers with some other metal which is not as much in demand as brass or devising some better means of securing the rollers to make their removal more difficult may be examined by the RDSO for further suitable action.

45. According to para 812 of the *Way and Works Manual*, turnouts should not be taken off the transitioned portion of a main line curve normally. The turnout W.7 at Sevur was laid on the transition portion of a 1° curve. It is recommended that when the new loop line is relaid, the location of the turnout should be wholly on the circular portion of the curve or on the straight. At other stations on the main line and trunk routes where turnouts are laid on the transitioned portion of a curve, it is recommended that action should be taken to have them relocated on a programmed basis. Until this is done, it is considered that a suitable speed restriction of say 75 km/h on the B.G. and 50 km/h on the M.G. should be imposed at these locations. The Railway Board may consider this question and issue suitable instructions.

46. A complaint was received after the inquiry that relatives of

the deceased passengers were not promptly advised and some of the dead bodies were not even identified. To expedite identification of the dead bodies, it is suggested that photographs of the unidentified bodies should be exhibited at the nearest railway station as well as the train starting station. Prompt action should also be taken to convey information to the relatives of deceased and seriously injured persons wherever their addresses are available.

47. It is well known that short stretches of wooden sleepers are vulnerable to buckling. The Railway Board in their letter No. 71/W.6/TK/19, dated 18th January, 1972 addressed to all GMs, had indicated where such vulnerable stretches usually exist and also enumerated the special precautions to be taken in order to ensure that conditions which are conducive to buckling are not created at these locations. A short stretch of wooden sleepers in close proximity to a turnout is one such vulnerable location. One of the measures recommended by the Board for strengthening these stretches is increase of sleeper density to N+6 (M+7). At Sevur on the short wooden sleeper stretch forming the LVT portion which was just butting against the turnout the sleeper density was only M+4. Though in the present case there has been no evidence of buckling of the track, nevertheless, the Railway Administration should have provided a higher sleeper density of M+7 at this location in addition to the other precautions indicated in the Railway Board's letter. Urgent action needs now to be taken to carry out a survey of all such short stretches of wooden sleepers and ensure that the instructions contained in the Rly. Board's letter are fully implemented at all the stretches. The Railway Board may reiterate their instructions to all Railways for immediate compliance where this has not already been fully implemented.

Railway Board's Comments on Various Paras of the Report

Para 43: The effect of deficiency of guide rollers in causing excessive flange forces and affecting the riding of the BEML coaches has been carefully studied and it has been found that even if all the inside guide rollers in the coaches are deficient, with outside guide rollers being in position, there is little possibility of the riding of the coach getting effected or excessive flange forces coming into play. The rollers are meant for providing lateral guidance only. It is considered that location of the 1 in 12 turnout on the transition portion of a 1°

curve should not cause flange forces very much in excess of those developed on a turnout taking off from straight track. Therefore, the conclusion that location of the turn-out on the transition portion of the 1° curve would have contributed to the excessive flange forces, supposed to be the cause of the accident, is not acceptable.

Para 44: The fixing arrangement for the inside guide rollers have been modified to make pilferage more difficult. With the provision of this arrangement, there will be no possibility of inside guide rollers being removed by the miscreants unless the bogie frame is lifted off the wheels. Instructions to the Railways are being issued by RDSO to carry out necessary modifications on the coaches at the time of POH.

Para 45: It is already laid down in para 812 of the IRWWM that turnouts should not normally be taken off the transition portion of a main line curve. These provisions do not altogether prohibit laying of turn-outs on the transition portion of a main line curve. Turn-outs are laid on the transition portion of a curve only where due to constraints of room or layout, etc. It is not considered feasible to lay these on the straight track or on the main curve.

The relocation of turn-outs existing on the transition portion of the main line curves to either straight track or to the main curve would involve large scale changes in the track layouts and huge expenditure. Such a course of action is therefore not considered necessary.

The maximum permissible speed on the main line curved track from which a turn-out takes off can be determined on the basis of the instructions laid down in paras 811, 813 and 814 of the IRWWM. It is, therefore, not considered necessary to impose a general special restriction of 75 Kmph on the BG and 50 Kmph on the MG to all such locations where turn-outs take off from the transition portion of a main line curve. The maximum permissible speeds while negotiating various types of turnouts are already laid down which are much less than the general speed restrictions suggested by the ACRS. These speed limits to be observed while negotiating the turn-outs are further subject to the maximum permissible speed as calculated on the basis of the instructions contained in paras 813 and 814 of the IRWWM, in case of turnouts located on curved track. No action is, therefore, considered necessary at this stage on suggestions of the ACRS contained in para 45 of his report. However, as suggested by the CRS, the Railways will be asked to keep the position under watch.

Para 46: The Railway would make necessary arrangement to exhibit photographs of the deceased persons at the nearest station as well as the starting station to facilitate identification of the dead.

As for promptly conveying the information about the accident to the relatives of the deceased and the seriously injured persons, this is always done whenever the addresses of the relatives are available.

Para 47: As suggested, the instructions contained in Railway Board's letter No. 71/W6/TK/19, dated 18th January, 1972 will be reiterated to the Railways for early compliance and submission of a report.

9

COMMITTEE ON NEWS AGENCIES, 1977 – REPORT[1]

Chairman Shri Kuldip Nayar

Members Shri D.R. Mankekar; Shri C.R. Irani; Shri A.K. Sarkar; Shri K.R. Malkani; Shri Rahul Barpute; Shri Ishrat Ali Siddiqui; Shri K. Chathunni Master; Shri Nikhil Chakravartty; Shri S.G. Munagekar; Dr. R. Rajagopalan

M. Secy. Shri L. Dayal

Appointment

In pursuance of Government's declared policy on the functioning of press and news agencies, it has been decided to appoint a Committee through Resolution No. 30/14/77 Press dated 19th April, 1977 to examine the functioning of Samachar and to make recommendations regarding its future set-up.

Terms of Reference

The terms of reference of the Committee will be:

(i) To review the situation arising from collection and dissemination of news by a single news agency within the country and abroad and make recommendations consistent with the freedom of press, independence of news agencies, and possibilities of competitive services freely to all users.

(ii) To report on the financial viability of 'Samachar' taking into account the grants-in-aid given by the Government to tide over its unsatisfactory financial situation.

(iii) To consider and make recommendations in regard to the

---

1. Ministry of Information and Broadcasting, Government of India, New Delhi, 1977, 165 p.

personnel of 'Samachar', their emoluments, their integration and absorption, fitments and replacements vis-a-vis the erstwhile news agencies.

(iv) To make suitable recommendations about the future set-up of 'Samachar' and other forms of news agencies if suggested keeping in view the need for providing complete, impartial, objective, accurate, and countrywide news service.

(v) To take a view on the functioning of 'Samachar' as a member of the News Agencies Pool of the Non-aligned Countries and its commitments with regard to bilateral arrangements with a number of news agencies of the Non-aligned countries for mutual exchange of news and the manner in which its obligation will be discharged.

(vi) To report on any other aspect of the problem relating to proper functioning of a news agency or news.

Contents

Introduction; The Role and Functions of News Agencies; News Agencies of India : Origin and Growth; The Formation and Functioning of Samachar; International Services; The Structure Recommended; Financial Resources; Summary of Recommendations; Note of Dissent by Shri C.R. Irani and Shri A.K. Sarkar; Observations by Shri Ishrat Ali Siddiqui; Note of Dissent by Shri K. Chathunni Master; Note of Chairman; Appendices I—XII.

Recommendations

The Role and Functions of News Agencies (Chapter II)

1. We regard objectivity, adequacy and independency as the three main attributes needed for the news agency system of the country. (Para 15)

2. The news agency system should adequately cover all aspects of the country's life and not merely political events and the news from urban areas. The rich milieu of contemporary Indian life should be fully reflected. (Paras 19-20)

3. Consequently the dissemination of news by the agencies has to take place increasingly through the different Indian languages. (Para 22)

4. Government must follow a self-denying policy of not inter-

fering in any way with the work of news agencies. (Para 23)

5. It is necessary that the news agency system also covers news which is not only outside the orbit of Government functioning but which may imply criticism of authority. It is essential in a democracy that dissent should get adequate coverage. (Para 24)

6. The news agency system should not get identified with any vested interests, economic, social, communal or, political. (Para 25)

7. The news agencies should maintain a high standard of performance which would itself be a protection against interference from outside sources, including Government. (Paras 26-27)

8. News agencies, even during such situations as hostilities or international tensions and disputes, should strive to keep the people informed of the realities of the situation and not confine themselves only to the so-called popular view of events. (Para 31)

9. Different techniques of internal checks and supervision as well as evaluation of the news supplied to the subscribers should be developed by news agencies in order to maintain a high standard of performance. (Para 32)

10. Specialisation should be developed in the reporting system in terms of subject-matter and styles of reporting. Expertise should also be promoted to achieve higher ranges of reporting where new and modern techniques of writings should be used. (Para 35)

11. Programmes for professional training of the staff should be organised on an adequate scale. These should include training in managerial functions. (Para 36)

12. Since news reporting is a creative activity, selection of personnel should always be made strictly on merits and there should be opportunities for promotion of talent. (Para 37)

The Formation and Functioning of Samachar (Chapter IV)

13. An investigation may be made and responsibility fixed for the distortions in the release of news and the loss of credibility of the news-despatches of Samachar which occurred during the period of the Emergency. (Para 78)

International Services (Chapter V)

14. There is full potential for India to develop international news services and a beginning must be made. (Para 82)

15. The receipt and utilisation of news from any part of the world must depend entirely on the discretion of India's own news agencies and newspapers. (Para 88)

16. India's continued participation in the news agencies Pool of Non-aligned countries, according to a sound and business-like plan of action, is recommended, but a detailed examination of the way it is being implemented should be made. The results are at present not commensurate with the expenditure being incurred. The scheme as a whole should also be assessed after one year, and its further prospects judged. (Paras 93, 104)

17. An attitude of confrontation or isolation is clearly disfavoured in all documents concerning the Pool. We do not, therefore, approve of the decisions taken by Samachar to cancel its agreements with UPI and DPA as a result of its participation in the Pool. (Para 94)

18. The two domestic agencies should jointly set up an organisation for international services to be named NEWS INDIA. (Para 105)

19. The programme of organising international services would have several components. First, bilateral agreements as well as arrangements with world agencies should be strengthened and activised. Consultations should take place regarding the use of the wordage, with an eye on promoting increased use of Indian wordage for outside press. Secondly, in the light of the advice of foreign affairs experts, Bureaux should be organised according to a phased scheme in different regions of the world. Thirdly, the Ministry of External Affairs, should come forward as a subscriber to the international services. (Para 106)

20. International news would be drawn by the two domestic Agencies from this special organisation on subscription rates which would take into account the financial commitments of the system as well as the subscription, which in the light of the considerations set out by us, should be made by Government in the Ministry of External Affairs. In addition, it would be open for newspapers to subscribe directly to NEWS INDIA if they wish to draw the full supply of world news on payment of certain charges, provided they are already subscribing to at least one domestic Agency. (Para 107)

21. It is visualised that a total of about 25 Correspondents and stringers may be established over a period of two years. For this, priority may be given to countries and regions of political, economic

and cultural importance to India, neighbouring countries and countries with sizeable India origin population. (Para 109)

22. The Ministry of External Affairs (XP Division) should confine its transmission to official news and information only and should subscribe to NEWS INDIA for a special Indian news round-up for the Indian Missions abroad. (Para 110)

The Structure Recommended (Chapter VI)

23. We recommend that the Samachar should be dissolved and in its place there should be two news agencies: VARTA and SANDESH. They in turn should set up jointly an organisation for international services which may be called NEWS INDIA. The whole set-up should be created under an Act of Parliament which should be reviewed after 10 years. (Para 113)

24. VARTA would be charged with the responsibility for organising and developing Indian language services but would include services in English. For regional news, originating in different areas, the local bureau should send an English version on its trunk services to the bureaux in different regions for being supplied to the papers in those regions in their own language or in Hindi (after translation) or in English itself, if they so desire. For the Indian language papers in its own region the bureau would supply news in the regional language using Roman script on the teleprinter till teleprinter in that language is available. It would provide news to Akashvani and Doordarshan in regional languages. This Agency should have a concrete programme of developing its services in all major languages adequately, over a period of time, and in selected major languages including English over a short period. The languages may be selected on the basis of circulation of daily papers. To begin with, such languages may be taken up as are having a total circulation of more than 5 lakhs in respect of dailies. Being independent, and combining English services, this Agency would also provide a source of 'competition' for the other Agency. (Para 124)

25. Government (P&T Department) should promote the production of teleprinter machines in Indian languages without insisting on a minimum requirement of 100 machines. (Para 125)

26. In addition to serving the Indian language press, VARTA should also develop the supply of regional news. (Para 126)

27. The news agency work in the English language should be or-

ganised under one independent body. The infrastructure should be so designed as to make for expansion of the coverage in terms of areas and subjects and to achieve high standards of efficiency. The agency may be named SANDESH. (Para 133)

28. The General Bodies of VARTA and SANDESH would consist of:

(i) newspaper subscribers;
(ii) other newspapers with a circulation of 5,000 or above, on payment of an admission fee of Rs. 2,500 and an annual membership fee of Rs. 500; and
(iii) Akashvani and Doordarshan, after they are converted into autonomous corporations.

The General Bodies of the Agencies would meet every year within six months of the close of its own financial year to transact mainly the following business:

(i) elect representatives out of subscriber-members in the Managing Board:
(ii) receive and adopt Annual Reports and Accounts; and
(iii) elect Auditors who will hold office till the next Annual General Meeting. (Para 134).

29. The highest editorial, and managerial functions should be combined in the Chief Editor in each of the two agencies. The Chief Editor would be appointed by the Government Board concerned. He should be appointed on 5-year contract, with provision of 6 months' notice on either side. The same pattern should be adopted for NEWS INDIA. (Para 135).

30. The VARTA should be managed by a Governing Board consisting of 13 Members. There should be, at the present stage, 9 elected subscriber-representatives, representing languages as explained in para 124 of this Chapter, provided that there are at least 3 subscribers from the language. There should be one representative elected by the employees; he must himself be an employee. The Chief Editor, who would also be combining the ultimate managerial functions, would be an ex-officio Member. In addition, the rest of the Members should co-opt two persons known for their expertise and distinction in journalism, education, culture, science or economics.

The Members should select, from amongst themselves a Chairman for the Board who would function not as a whole-timer, but as an honorary Chairman. When the Akashvani and Doordarshan are converted into autonomous corporations, they should also jointly send one representative, in the Board. Until then, the head of their News Division should attend Board meetings as an Invitee. The Manager should also attend the meetings as an Invitee. The composition would thus be as follows:

Subscriber-representatives	—9
Employees' representative	—1
Co-opted Members	—2
Chief Editor	—1
	13

(Para 138)

31. The Governing Board of SANDESH may also consist of 13 Members. These should include 9 representatives of subscribers, provided that at least one representative is taken from big, medium and small newspapers each. Employees should elect one representative to represent them in the Board. In addition, two persons should be coopted on the same principles as in the case of VARTA. The Chief Editor, who would also combine the highest managerial functions, should be an *ex-officio* Member. The Members should elect one of them as part time Chairman, as in the case of VARTA. After Akashvani and Doordarshan are converted into autonomous corporations, they should jointly send one representative. Until, then the head of their News Division should attend meetings as an Invitee. The Manager should also attend the meetings as an Invitee. The composition would thus be as follows:

Subscriber-representatives	—9
Employees' representative	—1
Co-opted Members	—2
Chief Editor	—1
	13

(Para 139)

32. We have recommended that VARTA and SANDESH should jointly create an organisation for international services which may be named NEWS INDIA. We suggest this organisation should be managed by a Managing Committee of 11 persons which should include three representatives from each of the two Boards and their Chief Editors. In addition, it should include the two experts whose association may be useful for organising and running international news services; these persons should be nominated jointly by the two Boards. The Board should select from among themselves a person who may function as Chairman of the Managing Committee of NEWS INDIA in an honorary capacity. The Managing Committee will appoint a Chief Editor who would also be in charge of the managerial functions at the highest level. Representation to Akashvani and Doordarshan should be allowed in the same way as in the case of VARTA and SANDESH. The composition of the Managing Committee would thus be as follows:

Representatives of the two Boards	—6
Chief Editors of VARTA and SANDESH	—2
Co-opted Members	—2
Chief Editor	—1
	13

(Para 140)

33. All elected and co-opted Members in the three organisations would have a 2-year tenure. (Para 141)

34. In order to maintain close association with the subscribers which is so necessary for keeping up the standard of reporting; Regional Committees of leading editors and news editors may be formed to review the performance of the Agencies continually. The senior office bearers and executives of the Agencies should participate in these discussions and take follow up action. (Para 142)

35. There would be an advantage both in investment and in technical supervision if communication services are created and maintained jointly by both the Agencies. This may be explored. (Para 143)

36. In the Act of Parliament provisions should be made to the effect that the collections and dissemination of news would be free

from any slant, pressure or interference exerted either by Government authorities or by any other source and that the news coverage would be fully impartial, objective and independent. (Para 145)

37. An interim body would have to be created with the responsibility of bringing about the transition from the present set up to what is proposed. The main tasks which must be completed before the new structure emerges would be:

(i) Incorporation of the Agencies;
(ii) Creation of a reasonable membership-base;
(iii) Division of assets and liabilities;
(iv) Fitment of personnel; and
(v) Review of subscription rates.

(Para 146)

38. One of the functions of the interim body will be to select the Chief Editors, keeping in view the complexity and the importance of the task of organising and developing these Agencies on the lines indicated in the Report. (Para 148)

39. Government may appoint a small body to effect the transition, as explained above. During this transitional period, steps would also have to be taken to introduce a Bill in the Parliament. We feel these tasks can be completed within a period of 3 months. (Para 149)

Financial Resources (Chapter VII)

40. The expenditure over NEWS INDIA should be shared in equal proportion by VARTA and SANDESH. (Para 167)

41. We envisage that SANDESH will have operations roughly corresponding to those of the English Wing of the existing Samachar. Under the new set-up, the SANDESH may require additional revenue of the order of Rs. 30 to 35 lakhs per annum at current subscription rates of Samachar, in addition to its share in the expenditure over NEWS INDIA. The combined additional annual revenue of the news agencies we have recommended for the future may have to be of the order of Rs. 170 lakhs at the current rates of subscription. It is necessary to make adequate provisions for it. (Paras 169-170).

42. Akashvani/Doordarshan should pay an annual subscription at the rate of Re. 1 per licensed radio set and Rs. 5 per licensed TV set. (Para 173)

43. The subscription of Akashvani and Doordarshan should be allocated to VARTA and SANDESH in the ratio of 60 per cent for VARTA and 40 per cent for SANDESH. (Para 173)

44. The above subscription rates should be made applicable from the commencement of the current financial year 1977-78, in order to meet the deficit. (Para 174).

45. The subscription payable by Akashvani and Doordarshan should be in terms of an automatic formula and not at Government's discretion. (Para 175)

46. It should be ensured that the proposed agencies have a sound capital structure. For this purpose, all the moneys received as admission fee from the members should be credited to a capital fund of the respective news agencies. In addition, VARTA and SANDESH should be required to transfer a sum of Rs. 10 lakhs from the current revenues to the capital fund till such time that the total capital fund accumulates to Rs. 1 crore in each case. Save as otherwise provided above, they should be required to conduct their operations on a non-profit and no-loss basis. (Para 176)

47. The remaining shares of all the four erstwhile news agencies should be acquired so that their ultimate dissolution may take place at the earliest possible time. On the dissolution of the SAMACHAR their assets and liabilities should be shared by VARTA and SANDESH in equal proportions. (Para 177).

10

RAILWAY ACCIDENT INVESTIGATION REPORT ON DERAILMENT OF 367 UP SEALDAH-LALGOLA PASSENGER TRAIN AT KM. 52/27-53/11, IN MADANPUR STATION YARD, ON SEALDAH-RANAGHAT SECTION, IN SEALDAH DIVISION OF EASTERN RAILWAY AT ABOUT 13.26 HOURS ON APRIL 20, 1977[1]

One Man Commission Shri B. Jayajaya Rao

Appointment

The Commission was constituted under the Ministry of Tourism and Civil Aviation (Commission of Railway Safety) in accordance with Rule 4 of the Statutory Investigation into Railway Accidents Rules, 1973 vide Notification No. RS. 13-T(8)/71 dated April 19, 1973, on April 20, 1977.

Terms of Reference

To enquire into the derailment of 367 Up Sealdah-Lalgola Passenger Train at Km. 52/27-53/11, in Madanpur station yard on Sealdah-Ranaghat section in Sealdah Division of Eastern Railway at about 13.26 hours on April 20, 1977.

Contents

Summary; Introduction; Relief Measures; The Train; Local Conditions; Summary of Evidence; Observation and Tests; Discussion; Conclusions; Remarks and Recommendations; Annexures; Railway

---

1. Delhi, Controller of Publications, 1982, 22 p.

Board's View.

Conclusions

51. (a) On careful consideration of the factual, material and circumstantial evidence, I have come to the conclusion that the Derailment of 367 Up Sealdah-Lalgola Passenger Train at Km. 52/27-53/11, in Madanpur station yard, on Sealdah-Ranaghat Broad Gauge electrified double line section of Eastern Railway, at about 13.26 hours on 20-4-77 was as a result of the breakage of the helical springs in the left outer nest of the front bogie of the 5th coach (No. ER 2455 GS) from the engine.

(b) Inadequacy in maintenance of track and coaches of '367 Up' to suit the maximum speed of 100 Km/h permitted on Kalyani-Madanpur section contributed to the accident.

Responsibility

52. (a) Apropos para 50, no individual Railway employee is held responsible.

(b) Apropos para 46, the Railway Administration is however to blame for going ahead with the increase of maximum permissible speed to 100 km/h from a virtual maximum of 80 km/h on Naihati-Ranaghat section without adequately preparing the track and coaches to suit the increased speed and without obtaining the sanction of the Additional Commissioner of Railway Safety as required in General Rule 89(a) (Extracted in Annexure III).

Relief Measures

53. I am satisfied that the medical relief was prompt and efficient.

Recommendations

54. (a) On Eastern Railway the push-pull type WAM-2 locomotives were switched over from EMUs to main line service from 24-9-73. But the original speedometers which were removed when the locomotives were on EMUs were not refitted with the result that the passenger trains were being hauled by these locomotives without

speedometers/speed-recorders. As a result of the Commission of Railway Safety pointing out from time to time the Railway Board stated on several occasions in the past that instructions had been issued to Zonal Railways to ensure fitment and proper working of speedometers/speed-recorders on Mail/Express passenger and high speed Goods trains. It is, therefore, disquieting to note that WAM-2 locomotives have been working Passenger Express trains on Eastern Railway without speedometers/speed-recorders for some years.

(b) In view of the prevailing unsatisfactory position of speedo-meters/speed-recorders on Indian Railways, the ACRS/ North Eastern Circle suggested, in connection with side collision of a car with 131 Up Passenger train at level crossing at km. 51/9-10 between Sarkara and Kashipur stations of North-Eastern Railway on 28-3-77 that the maximum sanctioned speed may be reduced by 15 Km/h when passenger/Express/mail engines are not fitted with Speedo-meters/Speed-recorders. Loss of punctuality in such cases will make the Railway Administrations more alive to this vital item. It is recommended that some such effective step is called for to set the matters right.

55. Apropos para 43, there is no proper definition of Super-fast Mail/Express, fast passenger, passenger and mixed trains on Eastern Railway and probably on other Railways also Several safety aspects, such as the standard of maintenance P.O.H. of coaches, marshalling of coaches, provision of speedo-meters/speed-recorders, blanking off alarm chain, etc., much depend upon proper classification of trains. Maximum speed should, no doubt, figure prominently in such a definition. For instance, ordinary passenger trains may not be permitted to run at more than 80 km/h on Broad Gauge in view of the fact that aged coaches are allotted to such trains, in fact passenger trains are booked at 65-72 Km/h speed, on Indian Railways. It is recommended that the Railway Board may evolve suitable definitions for various classes of trains, with speed as a dominant factor for uniform use on Indian Railways.

56. Eastern Railway blanked off the Alarm chain apparatus on all passenger trains without exception and on selected Express/Mail trains. This step is considered too drastic. Trains like '367 Up' which have the characteristics of Express trains should have alarm chain apparatus in working order like other Express trains in view of their high speed and non-stop runs at way side stations. Apropos para 49, the blanket blanking off alarm chains on all passenger trains, without

discrimination, on Eastern Railway also calls for review.

57. (a) The Railway Board in their letter No. 76-Chg-II/14/1 dated 4-6-77 have stated that the behaviour of rivetted design of steel coaches is similar to anti-telescopic all welded integral coaches for the purpose of marshalling of passenger trains. In the case of collision between 66 Down Dehra Dun-Varanasi Janata Express with stationary M-5 Up Goods train at Katghar station on Northern Railway on 21-2-74, the ACRS, who inquired into the matter, felt that casualties would have been less had an anti-telescopic coach been marshalled next to engine instead of a steel coach. As a result of correspondence between the Commission of Railway Safety and the Board, the latter accepted the superiority of anti-telescopic coaches over steel coaches and issued instructions in their letter No. 75-Chg-II/14/1 dated 19-4-75 that only anti-telescopic coaches should be utilised wherever anti-telescopic/steel bodied coaches were permitted previously. It is not known, whether the present instructions (dated 4-6-77) are based on any tests/calculations. This matter needs a review.

(b) It is also suggested that in matters concerning the safety of passengers, the Railway Board may consult the Commission of Railway Safety while issuing instructions, unless they are of an urgent nature to ensure safety immediately and particularly while revising any instructions issued at the instance of the Commission earlier.

58. Coach No. ER 6107-VP (8th from the engine), a wooden bodied coach with steel panelling, was marshalled immediately inside the Guard's brakevan on the ground that it was only a parcel van. But it was understood at the time of this inquiry that this Parcel Van was actually meant for vendors with season tickets to travel with their goods. This coach was badly damaged and the boy who died was from this coach. It is obvious that this coach ought to have been treated as a passenger coach based on its actual use and not based on its General Nomenclature, particularly when the Railway meant it as a passenger coach. Steps should be taken by Eastern Railway and other Railways also, where necessary, to avoid such obvious errors in classification of coaches and marshalling of passenger trains.

59. As per Railway Board's letter No. 72/MIW7/814/60 dated 29-4-72, the passenger coaching vehicles (PCVs) and other coaching vehicles (OCVs) on Express/Mail trains should receive P.O.H. once in 12 months and PCVs on other than Mail/Express trains once in 18 months and OCVs on other than Mail/Express trains once in 24th

months. As discussed in para 43, 367 UP ought to have been classified as an Express train in view of its maximum permissible speed being 100 km/h and its non-stopping nature at wayside stations on Sealdah-Ranaghat section. But ordinary passenger coaches, P.O.H. period of which is fixed at an interval of 18 months for PCVs were allowed on this train. Moreover, VPU and VP coaches (2nd and 8th from the engine) which were meant to carry vendors (passengers) were treated as OCVs with a P.O.H. interval of 24 months. In fact, the P.O.H. interval for coach No. ER 6106 VP was fixed at an interval of 36 months on the ground that it was a spare coach while actually it was on regular formation and in the absence of any positive instructions from the Board that P.O.H. interval for spare coaches of passenger trains can be increased. Further, there is no guarantee that the so-called spare coaches continue to remain as spare. It is necessary that the instructions for the maintenance of coaches should be followed in the spirit in which they are issued and should work on the safe side when there is any room for doubt. This may be impressed on the Railways.

60. (a) In the course of the inquiry, it came to notice that there is large scale theft of permanent way fittings on certain known sections of Eastern Railway including Naihati-Madanpur section where the accident occurred. While the Railway wanted the police to take action to prevent such thefts, the latter wanted the Railway Protection Force to take action. There was, thus, no coordination between the Railway and the Police with the result that thefts continued to persist, creating dangerous conditions for trains to run with reasonable safety.

(b) In case the Railways are unable to prevent thefts of permanent way fittings for any reason whatsoever, there should not be any hesitation in imposing suitable speed restrictions for trains in the interests of the safety of the travelling public. Time Tables must be revised in such cases with lower speeds so that punctuality may not come in the way of safety considerations.

61. The present two way key used with CST9/S.T. sleepers/A.C. bearing plates, etc., is susceptible to easy removal and offers great temptation for stealing since it is handy for making agricultural implements by village black-smiths. It is recommended that a suitable key, the ends of which are split, may be developed so that one of the split ends can be bent in service with a view to make it difficult for miscreants to remove the same. Such special keys may be used in vul-

nerable locations to prevent thefts.

62. After pulling back creep, a closure rail of 115 mm in length was left in the track on main line in the vicinity of point No. 17 at Kanchrapara without any speed restriction. It may be impressed on the permanent way staff that whenever closure rails less than 5.5 m in length are left in track, suitable speed restriction should be imposed. Para 657 of Way and Works Manual may be amended suitably for this purpose.

63. As per Correction Slip No. 108 dated 21-6-75 to Para 1606 of the Way and Works Manual, level-crossings outside the *outer most Stop* Signals shall be under the control of the Permanent Way Inspectors (PWIs). Contrary to these instructions, the double manned level-crossing at Kms. 54/15-17 situated between the Up Home and Up Distant Signals and outside the Up Advanced Starter, i.e., outside the *outer most Stop* Signals of Madanpur station continues to be under the control of the Operating Branch. Had the Gatemen been under the control of the PWI as per the instructions in the Way and Works Manual, they would not have remained indifferent when keys were being stolen in the vicinity of and opposite to the level crossing. The need to implement the amended instructions contained in Para 1606 of the Way and Works Manual may be impressed on Eastern and other Railways.

64. The 90 lb. rail which fractured as a result of the accident was stated to have been imported from France bearing the mark "90-R-MICHE-VILLE R-1958-T/MM". As per the report of Chemist and Metallurgist/Jamalpur "though it satisfied the chemical and physical requirements of the specification, the presence of piping in the web suggested that harmful defects of the ingots before rolling the rail might not have been removed". This defective rail with the presence of piping was, however, not detected when tested by ultrasonic rail flaw detector on 11-4-77, a few days prior to the accident. This casts a doubt whether Rail Flaw Detectors are in good condition and/or are being used with care. Necessary steps may be taken by Eastern Railway to improve the quality of detection by Rail Flaw Detectors and increase the frequency of testing of aged imported rails, which appear to be failing extensively on Indian Railways.

65. Apropos para 32(d), a small stretch of wooden sleeper road exists between the level crossing No. 44/C/T and the Point No 16. for a length of 29.88 metres at Madanpur station. The same was not

properly anchored. The ballast section was also poor. The Railway Board, in their letter No. 71/W6/TK/19 dated 18-1-72, stressed the need to take care of such small stretches of wooden sleeper road in the midst of metal sleeper road. It is suggested that these instructions may be incorporated in the Way and Works Manual, particularly stressing the need to anchor such track on all sleepers when there is unidirectional flow of traffic and to keep it adequately ballasted.

Railway Board's Views

The Railway Board have expressed disagreement with the cause of the accident as established in the Report for reasons elaborated in their Office Memoranda Nos. 77/Safety (A&R)/1/10 dated 16-8-1979 and 14-10-80.

Their views on the other relevant paras of the Report are as under:

Para 52(b): It has been explained by the Railway that on Naihati-Ranaghat section, the maximum, permissible speed for steam locomotives was 96 kmph. The maximum permissible speed for diesel locomotives was 65 kmph. and for electric locomotives was 90 kmph the Railway has also stated that the booked speed of passenger trains (35 paris in all) running on the section was only 72 kmph. and below except in case of one pair of fast passenger train (367 Up and 368 Dn), the booked speed of which was 80 kmph. It is a well known fact that the booked speed of trains is always kept lower than the maximum permissible speed of the section. The lower booked speed of trains cannot be construed to mean that the trains cannot be worked at the maximum permissible speed of the section. Although it is technically correct that ACRS's sanction should have been obtained by the Railway for increasing the maximum permissible speed from 96 kms for steam locomotives and 90 kmph for electric locomotives to 100 kmph, but this increase in speed is considered to be only marginal. As a matter of fact, a speed of 60 miles per hour when converted into kmph is normally rounded off from 96 kmph to 100 kms. The lapse on the part of the Railway administration in permitting a speed of 100 kmph on the section instead of the sanctioned speed of 96 kmphs is, therefore, not considered very serious. The Railway will, however, be advised to ensue that in future the sanctioned speed not be increased without obtaining prior sanction of the ACRS.

Para 54 (a): The push-pull type WAM-2 electric locomotives were originally provided with Hasler type speedo-meters, which are of imported origin. Due to difficulty in getting the foreign exchange, adequate spares could not be procured, which affected the proper maintenance of these speedo-meters and also resulted in some locos running without this equipment. However, with the receipt of the spare speedo-meters, all the locos working Mail, Express and Passenger trains have been provided with speedo-meters and a strict watch is being maintained by the Railway to ensure that the defects, which arise during the course of service, are rectified immediately.

Para 54 (b): The railway administration has explained that the recommendation is too drastic and may lead to many practical problems especially when a speedo-meter may become defective on the run, apart from resultant loss of punctuality of important passenger carrying trains. Since the railway administration have instructed the sheds to keep a special watch on the speedo-meters, the CCRS has noted the position explained by the railway administration.

Para 55: The matter is under examination.

Para 56: In terms of G.R. 111(c), if the railway administration is satisfied that mischievous use of the alarm chain apparatus is prevalent, it may direct the disconnection of the alarm chain for the time being in all or any of the Passenger carriages in any train. Having regard to the law and order situation and activities of the anti-social elements, railway administration are authorised to blank off the alarm chain apparatus on trains/sections where they consider it a unavoidable in order to control the menace of unauthorised chain pulling, when other means to control this practice fail. Extant instructions, however, provide that railway administrations should review the position periodically, and where blanking off the alarm chain apparatus requires continuation, they should approach the Board with full justification and the measures taken to arrest the menace. Instructions have also been issued to the railway, that when a train is running with an alarm chain apparatus balanced off, a Caution Order should be issued to the Guard/Driver of the train to exercise greater vigilance.

Para 57: RDSO advised the Board that for all practical purposes, the behaviour of steel bodied coaches of rivetted design may be taken as similar to all-welded integral coaches so far as protection to passengers in collision accidents is concerned. Moreover, there are large number of steel bodied coaches of rivetted design-built by HAL on IRS underframes, particularly on the metre gauge. Keeping in view the practical difficulties faced by the railways in formation, attaching of sectional coaches, and to eliminate delays to trains, anti-telescopic coaches have been equated with steel bodied coaches. Commissioner of Railway Safety was also advised suitably vide Board's letter No. 76-Chg. II/14/1 dated 26th June, 1979.

Para 58: In the revised instructions No. 76 Coaching II/14/1 dated 4-6-77, the marshalling order of wooden bodied SLRs has been revised in such a way that it is protected by two anti-telescopic coaches. The non-passenger coaches are required to be marshalled as outermost to absorb the collision energy. However, in cases where such non-passenger coaches are utilised to carry passengers regularly, instructions are being issued that they should be treated as regular passenger coaches and marshalled accordingly.

Para 59: Instructions are being reiterated that periodicity of POH prescribed in Railway Board letter No. 72M(W)/14/60 dated 29-4-1972 should be followed strictly and under no circumstances safety aspect should be neglected. The existing rules do not differentiate between the standards of maintenance for slow Passenger or Express trains. Uniform Standards are insisted upon in the interest of Safety.

Even for determining the period of POH, no consideration if given for intensive or non-intensive usage of stock. Instead, POH periodicity is determined by the type of service on which the coach is used. It follows from the existing instructions that the POH date has to be readjusted if the coach is transferred from one service to another.

In the present case, coach No. ER 6107 VP had not completed 24 months after its POH. Therefore, it was fit to run on a Passenger Train.

Para 60: The theft of permanent way fittings is a matter of law and order which mainly concerns the State Government. The Eastern Railway is, however, quite alive to the situation and has been pursuing the matter at various levels with the local Civil and Police authorities with a view to checking the incidence of thefts of permanent way materials and fittings. The Railway administration has no its own provided 6 reverse jaw CST 9 sleepers per rail length instead of 3 reverse jaw sleepers per rail length normally provided. With the provision of 6 reverse jaw CST 9 sleepers per rail length, the possibility of over-turning of rails even where a large number of keys are missing is remote. The Railway has indicated that together with steps taken to prevent thefts, immediate action is taken to replace the missing permanent way fittings.

It is, therefore, felt the imposition of a general speed restriction, as suggested, is not necessary.

Para 61: The use of anti-sabotage two-way keys having a projection at the smaller end for use with ST, CST-9 sleepers and ACB plates, was discontinued vide Railway Board's letter No. 55/W1/172/35 dated 4-9-67 as it was found that these keys could also be removed easily and as such did not serve any useful purpose. The RDSO will be advised to study the problem and evolve a new modified design of a two-way key, which could help prevent thefts of permanent way fittings at vulnerable locations.

Para 62: Para 657 of the *Indian Railways Way and Works Manual* (IRWWM) contains necessary instructions regarding use of rail closures. The Railway has indicated that the rail closure of 115 mm length, which was used in connection with rail renewal and not pulling back of creep, has been removed. Regarding imposition of a speed restriction when a rail closure of less than 5.5 m length is used in the track, it is considered that such a rail closure is normally used in connection with execution of track works which even otherwise require imposition of a speed restriction. Therefore, imposition of a speed restriction just because of the rail closure is not considered necessary. However, in this case the rail closure of 115 mm should not have been kept in the track for a long period. The Railway will be advised in this respect.

An amendment to para 657 of the IRWWM is not considered necessary.

Para 63: It is the duty of every Gateman whether he is under the control of the Civil Engg. department or the Operating department to take prompt action if he observes any tampering of track by an outsider or a miscreant or in case he notices any deficiency in the track which can endanger the safety of a running train. Therefore, just because the Gateman in this case was under the control of the Operating department, he cannot be observed of his responsibility for keeping a close watch on the track in the vicinity of the level crossing and for taking prompt action when he had noticed the keys stolen from the track in the vicinity of the level crossing.

The Railway has, however, taken action to transfer the level crossing at km. 54/6-7 under the control of the Civil Engg. Department.

Para 64: The Railway has noted the ACRS's suggestion regarding improving the quality of detection by ultrasonic rail flaw detectors and increasing the frequency of testing of the aged imported rails. This section was tested 2nd time during the period from 21-3-77 to 16-7-77 when 13 rails found with confirmed defects were replaced.

Para 65: The instructions contained in Board's letter No. 71/W6/TK/19 dated 18-1-72, regarding maintenance of short stretches of wooden sleepers, have been reiterated to the Railways vide Board's circular letter No. 77/W6/PRA/S/17 dated 8-11-78, a copy of which was endorsed to the CRS also.

The incorporation of these instructions in the IRWWM, which is at present under revision, will be considered.

11

GROVER COMMISSION OF INQUIRY, TO INQUIRE INTO CERTAIN ALLEGATIONS OF CORRUPTION, NEPOTISM, FAVOURITISM AND MISUSE OF GOVERNMENTAL POWER AGAINST THE CHIEF MINISTER AND SOME OTHER MINISTERS AND FORMER MINISTERS OF THE STATE OF KARNATAKA, 1977 – FIRST REPORT[1]

One Man Commission A.N. Grover

Appointment

Whereas, the Central Government is of the opinion that it is necessary to appoint a Commission of Inquiry for the purpose of making an inquiry into a definite matter of public importance, namely charges of corruption, nepotism, favouritism or misuse of Governmental power against the Chief Minister and certain other Ministers of the State of Karnataka, hereinafter specified.

Now, therefore, in exercise of the powers conferred by section 3 of the Commission of Inquiry Act, 1952 (60 of 1952) the Central Government in the Ministry of Home Affairs (Department of Personnel and Administrative Reforms) appointed a Commission of Inquiry vide S.O. No. 365 (E), dated May 23rd 1977.

And whereas the Central Government is of the opinion having regard to the nature of the Inquiry to be made by the Commission and other circumstances of the case, that all the provisions of sub-section (2), sub-section (3), sub-section (4), and sub-section (5) of section 5 of the Commissions of Inquiry Act, 1952 (60 of 1952) should be made applicable to the Commission, the Central

---

1. New Delhi, Ministry of Home Affairs, Department of Personnel and Administrative Reforms, 1978, 384 p., (MIMEOGRAPHED)

Government hereby directs, in exercise of the powers conferred by sub-section (1) of said section 5, that all the provisions of the said-sub-section (2), (3), (4) and (5) of that section shall apply to the Commission.

Terms of Reference

(a) to inquire into the following allegations namely:

(i) such of the allegations contained in the memorandum dated 11th April, 1977 received from some Members of the Karnataka State Legislature and addressed to the Prime Minister are specified in Annexure I;

(ii) Such of the allegations contained in the memorandum aforesaid as are specified in Annexure II, but excluding any matter covered by the notification of the Government of Karnataka in the Chief Secretariat No. DPAR 7 GAM77 dated May 18th, 1977;

(b) to inquire into any irregularity, impropriety or contravention of law other than those specified in the said notification of the Government of the State of Karnataka, on the part of any person in relation to any matter referred to in the allegations aforesaid;

(c) to inquire into any other matter which arises from; or concerned with or incidental to any act, omission or transaction referred to in the allegations aforesaid.

Contents

Part I: Introduction and Preliminary Proceedings. Part II: Allegation and facts leading thereto, arguments and findings; Allegation of Nepotism and Misuse of Governmental Powers, etc., Against the Chief Minister, Part A—Kemparaj as Government nominee on the Board of KSFIDC, Part B—Land for Herbal garden allotted to Shri M.D. Nataraj (Chief Minister's son-in-law); Allegation Regarding Shielding of Corrupt Officers; Allegation of Favouritism towards Certain Companies, Firms, etc.; Allegations Against other Ministers; Summary of Findings; Part III--Appendices.

Explanation

In the Annexure to this notification "Chief Minister" means Shri Devaraj Urs, the Chief Minister of the State of Karnataka.

The Headquarters of the Commission will be at New Delhi.

The Commission will complete its inquiries and report to the Central Government on or before the Ist day of December, 1977.

Annexure I

1. Whether the Chief Minister practised favouritism and nepotism by appointing his own brother, D. Kemparaj Urs, as a Director of the Karnataka State Film Industries Development Corporation in place of Shri R.J. Reballo, chief-secretary to the Government, in 1974, and later as Director-in-charge with the powers to exercise all the powers of the Managing Director.

2. Whether the Chief Minister had directed auction of excise shops out of turn in five districts on the eve of the recent Lok Sabha Election in the month of February, 1977, with corrupt motives although the auctions were due in the month of May 1977, and whether this was done with the object of collecting funds for the elections.

3. Whether the Chief Minister, had released Rs. 50.00 lakhs to buy "Understanding Science" from I.B.H. over ruling the decision of the sub-committee constituted for the purpose under the chairmanship of the Chief Minister and also over-ruling the orders of the concerned Minister.

4. Whether the Chief Minister was guilty of shielding corrupt, officers, in particular, two officers of the Public Works Department, namely, Shri Seshagiri Rao, Assistant Engineer, and Shri Shivanna, a clerk, against when persecution orders were passed by the Government on the basis of the recommendations of the Vigilance Commission. Whether the Chief Minister on his own revised the orders and withdrew the prosecution for any consideration.

5. Whether Shri Hanumantha Reddy, Superintending Engineer, was promoted as Chief Engineer by the Chief Minister against the recommendations of the Vigilance Commission that he should be demoted and certain amounts should be recovered from him and whether the Chief Minister also over ruled the orders of the concerned Minister and whether such actions of the Chief Minister

was for any consideration.

6. Whether the following payments were made to M/s Shankaranarayana Construction Co:

(i) An *ex gratia* payment of Rs. 6.37 lakhs in Malaprabha Projects;
(ii) excess payment to the tune of Rs. 12.00 lakhs in Chataprabha Project with an intention to favour the contractors.

7. Whether any misappropriation of funds and fabrication of a accounts of the Social Welfare Departments was made with the connivance of the then Minister Shri B. Rachaiah to the extent of Rs. 30.00 lakhs and whether any fraud was practised in connection with the said matter.

8. Whether appointment was made of fictitious persons as dealers in sandal soap by Mysore Sales International under the orders of the Chief Minister and the Minister for Industry and Payment was made of huge amounts by way of commission.

9. Whether gross misuse of power and position was made by Shri H.M. Channa Bassappa, formerly Minister-in-charge of Public Works Department and Electricity (Now Minister of Health) in converting the residential site which he got allotted to him by the Trust Board into a commercial site and starting a company with his family members as directors.

10. Whether any favourities was shown or whether there was any corruption in the purchase of new tyres and in body building contract for the new chassis by Karnataka State Road Transport Corporation under the undue influence of the Chief Minister and the Minister for Transport Shri Aziz Sait.

11. Whether there was any nepotism and favouritism and misuse of power by the Chief Minister and the Minister of Transport in the matter of nationalisation of contract carriages and wilfully benefiting certain parties with when the Chief Minister's second son-in-law was a partner.

12. Whether any favouritism was shown in the nomination of Shri K.V. Rao as a member of the Karnataka State Road Transport Corporation Board against the provisions of the Act.

13. Whether an undue favour was shown to M/s Balaji Engineering Construction Company by accepting the tender for construction of the Houses under Housing and Urban Development Corporation's Low Income Group Scheme in Dumlur layout by the

Bangalore Development Authority which is under the administrative control of the Chief Minister.

14. Whether allotment of 20 acres of land was made to the three sons of the Finance Minister, Shri M.Y. Ghorpade, in contravention of land grant rules and the provisions of the Land Reforms Act and the land Revenue Acts.

15. Whether any misuse of power was committed, or any corruption, committed, by Shri D.K. Naikar, Minister for Municipal Administration, with regard to the grant of land to Boroka Textile Mills in Hubli-Darwar Corporation Area.

Annexure II

Whether the Chief Minister or any other Minister of the State of Karnataka was guilty of corruption, nepotism, favouritism or misuse of governmental power in connection with all or any of the following matters, namely:

1. Grant of 20 acres of Governmental land, reserve for granting of cattle in Bommanhalli, Nelamangala Taluk, Bangalore District, to the son-in-law of the Chief Minister, Shri M.D. Nataraj, in violation of the provisions of the Land Revenue Code and disregarding the claims of local Scheduled Caste applicants;
2. Allotment of four large valuable house sites in the most posh locality of Bangalore, Raj Mahal Vilas Extension, to Shri Devaraj Urs and his family members in suppression of the rightful claims of other applicants;
3. Undue favours shown to Messrs Nirmala Engineering Construction Company, by releasing Government funds in spite of the fact that the concerned Minister had taken a decision to prosecute the firm on the basis of the recommendations of the Vigilance Commission;
4. Excess payment of Rs. 98.86 lakhs to Messrs Balaji Engineering Company, in Hemavathi Projects in contravention of the terms of the contract with a view to favouring the contractor;
5. Undue favour shown to Messrs Nechipadam Construction Company in Hemavathi Project, by accepting the highest tender with an intent to benefit the contractors and involving

excess payment to the extent of Rs. 3.5 lakhs;

6. Excise payment of Rs. 1 crore to Messrs TICIL Contractors, in Kali Hydel Projects, for the benefit of the contractors;
7. Whether about 5,000 tons of rice, purchased by the Government of Karnataka from the Tamil Nadu Government on government to government basis, was allowed to be marketed by a private party, Shri H.R. Athuq Ahmed, without the knowledge of the knowledge of the Food Department, instead of the Mysore State Co-operative Marketing Federation as was earlier agreed, with the sole intent of benefiting the private party;
8. Undue favour shown to a fictitious cooperative society in regard to conversion of 270 acres of agricultural land called DINSHAW ESTATE into non-agricultural purpose in violation of the mandatory provisions of the Land Reform Act and the Land Revenue Act;
9. Whether undue favour was shown to one Ghanshyam in the sale of 2500 tons of Bajra at the rate of Rs. 73.50p. per quintal without calling for tenders and allowing Shri Ghanshyam to sell the Bajra in the State of Maharashtra at the rate of Rs. 125.00 per quintal during the time drought in Karnataka;
10. Whether undue favour was shown, or concession was made to M/s Karekar & Sundaram Architects, in regard to the preparation of designs for remodelling the K.R. Market in supersession of the order of the concerned Minister;
11. Whether undue favour was shown, or concession was made, to M/s Shah Construction Co., contractors in Upper Krishna Project at Alamatti;
12. Whether undue favour was shown to M/s Krishna Flour Mills in granting valuable land in Bangalore City, which land was meant for children's park, at a nominal rent by over-ruling the orders of the Concerned Minister;
13. Whether there was any misappropriation of funds of the Karnataka State Film Industries Development Corporation, to the tune of Rs. 10.00 lakhs, when the Chief Minister himself was the Chairman of that Corporation and whether the business of the Corporation was conducted with intent to defraud that Corporation, its members, creditors or any other person or otherwise for a fraudulent or unlawful purpose;
14. Whether any undue favour was shown to M/s Poornima

Electronics, Bangalore, in the purchase of electronic equipment (inter-com) by superseding the recommendation of the Head of the Department and orders of the concerned Minister;

15. Whether any misappropriation of the funds of the Karnataka State Co-operative Marketing Federation to the extent of several crores of rupees was made by Shri H.S. Srikantiah, Minister of State for Home when he was the President of that Federation and whether the business of the Federation was conducted with intent to defraud that Federation, its members, creditors or any other persons or otherwise for a fraudulent or unlawful purpose;
16. Whether any undue favour was shown by Shri Satya Pal by the Minister of Transport, Shri Mohammed Ali, by accepting the once rejected tender of Shri Satya Pal in leasing out its building for canteen in Karnataka State Road Transport Corporation Bus Stand, Mysore and whether any undue favour was shown by the same Minister to Shri Satya Pal's son Shri Prem Kumar, in leasing out its retiring rooms of the Karnataka State Road Transport Corporation in Mysore;
17. Whether any undue favour was shown to four firms, namely, All-India Agencies, Vidyut Engineering Co.; Trishul Enterprises and Mysore Woods, in purchasing furniture valued at Rs. 29.00 lakhs in 1973-74 under I.P. Projects by the Minister for Health, Shri H. Siddaveerappa;
18. Whether any undue favour was shown by the Minister of State for Small-Scale Industries, Shri Kaulajgi in 1974, in the issue of Essentiality Certificate to parties many of which were fictitious and bogus;
19. Whether undue favour was shown by the Chief Minister and the Minister for Transport, Shri Aziz Sait, in 1973-74, to M/s Fargo in buying 150 chassis against the advice of the Chief Mechanical Engineer of the Karnataka State Road Transport Corporation;
20. Whether any undue favour was shown by the Minister of Industries, Shri S.M. Krishna, in allotting of paper, cement and steel of the State-owned industries to non-traditional dealers/agents including his kith and kin;
21. Whether an excess payment of Rs. 30.00 lakhs was made to M/s Shankaranarayan Construction Company in regard to the

construction of Combined Board Administrative Building Complex at Bangalore over and above the contract rates;

22. Whether any excess payment was made to M/s Balaji Engineering Company to the tune of Rs. 80.00 lakhs in Harangi Project with an intent to favour the contractor;
23. Whether Shri K.H. Patil, the then Minister for Agriculture and Forest, was guilty of any misuse of power or undue favouritism in relation to Hukkerri Textile Mills or Gadage Co-operative Textile Mills, or both;
24. Whether any undue favour was shown or any Corruption committed by Shri Chikka Gowda, the then Minister for Animal Husbandry and Agriculture in relation to the payment of a sum of Rs. 3.00 lakhs to M/s Navarasa Fertilisers;
25. Whether there was any misuse of power and corruption committed by Shri D.K. Naikar, Minister for Municipal Administration, in connection with the allotment of land and J.C. Road to Shri M.B. Lal and Shri M.V. Venkatappa.

Recommendations

CHAPTER VI

Summary of Findings

1. *Allegation No. 1 of Annexure I:* Whether the Chief Minister practised favouritism and nepotism by appointing his own brother, Shri D. Kemparaj Urs, as a Director of the Karnataka State Film Industries Development Corporation (KSFIDC) in place of Shri R.J. Rebello, Chief Secretary to the Government, in 1974, and later as Director-in-charge with the powers to exercise all the powers of the Managing Director.

Finding

(i) It stands conclusively established that the nomination of Kemparaj as a Director of the KSFIDC by an order of the Chief Minister on 24-12-1973 was an act of impropriety, favouritism and nepotism on the part of the Chief Minister and further that the Chief Minister was deeply interested in favouring his own brother and advancing his cause and he did not observe the norms of propriety becoming the conduct of a Chief Minister.

(ii) The Chief Minister did not appoint Kemparaj as Director-in-charge with powers to exercise all the powers of the Managing Director as alleged; but he made orders which had the effect of continuing Kemparaj as Director exercising the powers of the Committee of Management and these orders were also acts of favouritism and nepotism and, in making them, the Chief Minister departed from well established principles and rules of ethics which are expected to be followed in public administration.

2. *Allegation No. (1) of Annexure II:* "Whether the Chief Minister of any other Minister of the State of Karnataka was guilty of corruption, nepotism, favouritism or misuse of governmental power in connection with all or any of the following matters, namely:

(1) Grant of 20 acres of Government land, reserved for grazing of cattle in Bommanhalli, Nelamangala Taluk, Bangalore District, to the son-in-law of the Chief Minister, Shri M.D. Nataraj, in violation of the provisions of the Land Revenue Code and disregarding the claims of local scheduled caste applications."

Finding

(i) It stand established that 20 acres of Government land reserved for grazing of cattle in Bommanhalli Village, Nelamangala Taluk, Bangalore District, was granted to Shri M.D. Nataraj, in violation of the provisions of the Karnataka Land Revenue Act, 1964, and the Rules made thereunder.

(ii) It is proved that the Chief Minister, Shri Devaraj Urs, who is the father-in-law of Shri M.D. Nataraj, had exercised undue influence in the matter of the aforesaid grant and had thus committed acts of nepotism and favouritism which would undermine confidence in public administration.

(iii) Two ministers of Shri Devaraj Urs's cabinet, viz., Shri N. Rachaiah and Shri N. Hutchamasthy Gowda, the former in all probability and the latter positively, allowed themselves to be influenced by the Chief Minister; but it is not possible to say that they exercised acts of nepotism or favouritism in the matter of grant of land in question.

(iv) It is not correct that the claims of local Scheduled Caste applicants were disregarded. In fact, according to the evidence, four such applicants were also granted land. But other applicants including one Smt. Narasamma who had applied prior to Nataraj, were not granted any land and this was without sufficient ground or reason. In particular, the case of Smt. Narasamma deserved consideration.

3. *Allegation No. 4 of Annexure I:* Whether the Chief Minister was guilty of shielding corrupt officers, in particular two officers of the Public Works Department, namely, Shri Seshagiri Rao, Assistant Engineer, and Shri Shivanna, a Clerk, against whom prosecution orders were passed by the Government on the basis of the recommendations of the Vigilance Commission. Whether the Chief Minister on his own revised the order and withdrew the prosecution for any consideration.

Finding

(i) It stands proved that the order made by the Chief Minister on the letter of Shri R. Gundu Rao, MLA and the telephonic instructions given by him to the Superintending Engineer, had the effect of nullifying the order previously made by the Minister for Public Works which would have led to the two officials being prosecuted. These were done in an arbitrary manner without any justifiable reason, and the Chief Minister's intervention at that crucial stage virtually shielded the two officials from prosecution.

(ii) Although the Chief Minister revised on his own the order of prosecution passed by the Minister for Public Works on 13-9-1973, it has not been proved that he withdrew any prosecution or there was any passing of consideration for any of the acts of the Chief Minister.

4. *Allegation No. 5 of Annexure I:* Whether Shri Hanumantha Reddy, Superintending Engineer, was promoted as Chief Engineer by the Chief Minister against the recommendations of the Vigilance Commission that he should be demoted and certain amounts should

be recovered from him and whether the Chief Minister also over-ruled the orders of the concerned Minister and whether such action of the Chief Minister was for any consideration.

Finding

(i) The Chief Minister went out of this way to favour Shri Hanumantha Reddy in the matter of his promotion as a Chief Engineer. This constituted an act of favouritism on his part.

(ii) The Chief Minister had disagreed with the view of the concerned Minister in the matter of the recommendations of the Vigilance Commission against Shri Hanumantha Reddy, but there was no legal bar to his doing so.

(iii) There is no proof whatsoever that the Chief Minister had promoted Shri Hanumantha Reddy as a Chief Engineer for any "consideration".

5. *Allegation No. 12 of Annexure I:* Whether any favouritism was shown in the nomination of Shri K.V. Rao as a member of the Karnataka State Road Transport Corporation Board against the provisions of the Act.

Finding

(i) It is not proved that any favouritism was shown in the nomination of Shri K.V.R. Rao as a Member of the Board of the KSRTC. It has also not been established that Shri Rao suffered from any statutory disqualifications and, therefore, his appointment as a Member was contrary to the provisions of the Road Transport Corporation Act, 1950.

(ii) The principles on which nominations of Members to the Board of Public Sector Undertakings should be made, and laid down in the Report of the Administrative Reforms Commissioner, 1967, on Public Sector undertakings, should be followed. That would be highly conducive to creating confidence in the public about the bona fides of a nomination by the Government. However, non-observance of such principles will not, by itself, be sufficient to throw doubt on the bona fides of the nomination of a particular member.

(iii) All the circumstances relating to what transpired subsequent to the note made by the Transport Minister, Shri Mohammed Ali, in connection with Shri Rao continuing as a member of the KSRTC after expiry of his term, raise considerable doubt and suspicion that it was an act of favouritism on the part of the Chief Minister by keeping the file with himself and not making any order which cannot inspire confidence in the efficient working of the State Government or administration, but there is not sufficient evidence before the Commission to give a positive finding to that effect against the Chief Minister.

6. *Allegation No. 3 of Annexure I:* Whether the Chief Minister had released Rs. 50.00 lakhs to buy "Understanding Science" from I.B.H over-ruling the decision of the Sub-Committee constituted for the purpose under the Chairmanship of the Chief Minister and also over-ruling the orders of the concerned Minister.

Finding

(i) Although the Chief Minister showed a great deal of interest in the proposal relating to the bulk purchase of the publication "Understanding Science" in Kannada language and gave his approval in a manner which could create an impression that he had not taken stock of all the relevant factors and the necessary implications of the total expenditure that would be involved namely, Rs. 64 lakhs, but it is not possible to find that he was actuated by any motives of favouritism towards the India Book House. It is also not correct to say that a sum of Rs. 50 lakhs was released by him for the aforesaid purpose.

(ii) The Chief Minister did not over-rule the decision of the Sub-Committee constituted under his chairmanship for deciding whether the order for bulk purchase of "Understanding Science" should be placed with the India Book House, but accepted the recommendations of the Sub-Committee.

(iii) The Chief Minister did not over-rule the orders of the concerned Minister (which would mean the Minister of Education). It has further not been established that the subsequent order for the purchase of 15,000 copies of two issues of the value of Rs. One lakh, was placed by the Chief Minister owing to any interest of a special or personal nature which could amount to an act of favouritism.

7. *Allegation No. 14 of Annexure I:* Whether allotment of 20 acres of land was made to the three sons of the Finance Minister, Shri M.Y. Ghorpade, in contravention of the Land Grant Rules and the provisions of the Land Reforms of Act and the Land Revenue Act.

Finding

It is not open to the Commission to convert itself into a civil court which has jurisdiction to adjudicate on question of title to land or to decide disputes of the nature that have been raised. The Commission is bound by the terms of reference and according to the allegation as contained in reference, the only question is whether any allotment of 20 acres of Government land had been made to the three sons of Shri M.Y. Ghorpade in contravention of the relevant statutory laws and the rules. In view of the categorical statement made in the affidavit of Shri V.S. Naik on behalf of the Government of Karnataka that no allotment of any land belonging to the Government had been made to the three sons of Shri M.Y. Ghorpade, the Commission finds that it is not possible for it to proceed further in the matter. It is equally not possible for the Commission to determine whether the sanction of the mutation pursuant to the gift, will constitute allotment of Government land, as has been suggested on behalf of the Memorialists.

This allegation will, therefore, stand disposed of accordingly.

GROVER COMMISSION OF INQUIRY TO INQUIRE INTO CERTAIN ALLEGATIONS OF CORRUPTION, NEPOTISM, FAVOURITISM AND MISUSE OF GOVERNMENTAL POWER AGAINST THE CHIEF MINISTER AND SOME OTHER MINISTERS AND FORMER MINISTERS OF THE STATE OF KARNATAKA, 1977 – SECOND (FINAL) REPORT[1]

One Man Commission Shri A.N. Grover

Appointment

Whereas the Central Government is of opinion that it is necessary to appoint is a Commission of Inquiry for the purpose of making an inquiry into a definite matter of public importance, namely, charges of corruption, nepotism, favouritism or misuse of Governmental power against the Chief Minister and certain other Ministers of the State of Karnataka.

Now, therefore, in exercise of the powers conferred by section 3 of the Commissions of Inquiry Act, 1952 (60 of 1952), the Central Government in the Ministry of Home Affairs, Department of Personnel and Administrative Reforms appointed the Grover Commission of Inquiry vide its S.O. No. 365(E) dated May 23, 1977.

And whereas the Central Government is of the opinion having regard to the nature of the inquiry to be made by the Commission and other circumstances of the case, that all the provisions of sub-section (2), sub-section (3), sub-section (4) and sub-section (5), of section 5 of the Commissions of Inquiry Act, 1952 (60 of 1952) should be made applicable to the Commission the Central Government

1. Delhi, Department of Personnel, Controller of Publications, 1979, LXXIV, 396 p.

hereby directs, in exercise of the powers conferred by sub-section (I) of the said section 5, all the provisions of the said sub-section (2), (3), (4) and (5) of that section shall apply to the Commission.

Terms of Reference

(a) to inquire into the following allegations, namely:

(i) such of the allegations contained in the memorandum dated 11th April, 1977 received from some Members of the Karnataka State Legislature and addressed to the Prime Minister as are specified in a Annexure I;

(ii) such of the allegations contained in the memorandum aforesaid as are specified in Annexure II, but excluding any matter covered by the notification of the Government of Karnataka in the Chief Secretariat No. DPAR 7 GAM 77 dated the 18th May, 1977,

(b) to inquire into any irregularity, impropriety or contravention of law other than those specified in the said notification of the Government of the State of Karnataka, on the part of any person in relation to any matter referred to in the allegations aforesaid,

(c) to inquire into any other matter which arises from, or is connected with or incidental to, any act, omission or transaction referred to in the allegations aforesaid.

Explanation: In the Annexures to this notification, "Chief Minister" means Shri Devaraj Urs, the Chief Minister of the State of Karnataka.

Annexure I

1. Whether the Chief Minister practised favouritism and nepotism by appointing his own brother, Shri D. Kemparaj Urs, as a Director of the Karnataka State Film Industries Development Corporation in place of Shri R.J. Rebello, Chief Secretary to the Government, in 1974, and later as Director-in-charge with the powers to exercise all the powers of the Managing Director.

2. Whether the Chief Minister had directed auction of excise shops out of turn in five districts on the eve of the recent Lok Sabha

Elections in the month of February, 1977, with corrupt motives although the auctions were due in the month of May, 1977, and whether this was done with the object of collecting funds for the Elections.

3. Whether the Chief Minister had released Rs. 50.00 lakhs to buy "Understanding Science" from I.B.H. over-ruling the decision of the Sub-Committee constituted for the purpose under the Chairmanship of the Chief Minister and also over-ruling the orders of the concerned Minister.

4. Whether the Chief Minister was guilty of shielding corrupt officers, in particular, two officers of the Public Works Department, namely, Shri Seshagiri Rao, Assistant Engineer, and Shri Shiranna, a Clerk, against whom prosecution orders were passed by the Government on the basis of the recommendations of the Vigilance Commission. Whether the Chief Minister on his own revised the order and withdrew the prosecution for any consideration.

5. Whether Shri Hanumantha Reddy, Superintending Engineer, was promoted as Chief Engineer by the Chief Minister against the recommendation of the Vigilance Commission that he should be demoted and certain amounts should be recovered from him and whether the Chief Minister also over-ruled the orders of the concerned Minister and whether such action of the Chief Minister was for any consideration.

6. Whether the following payments were made to M/s. Shankaranarayana Construction Co.:

(i) an *ex gratia* payment of Rs. 6.37 lakhs in Malaprabha Project;
(ii) excess payment to the tune of Rs. 12.00 lakhs in Ghataprabha Project with an intention to favour the contractors.

7. Whether any misappropriation of funds and fabrication of accounts of the Social Welfare Department was made with the connivance of the then Minister Shri N. Rachaiah to the extent of Rs. 30.00 lakhs and whether any fraud was practised in connection with the said matter.

8. Whether appointment was made of fictitious persons as dealers in sandal soap by Mysore Sales International under the orders of the Chief Minister and the Minister for Industry and payment was made of huge amounts by way of Commission.

9. Whether gross misuse of power and position was made by

Shri H.M. Channa Basappa, formerly Minister-in-charge of Public Works Department and Electricity (now Minister of Health) in converting the residential site which he got allotted to him by the Trust Board into a commercial site and starting a company with his family members as directors.

10. Whether any favouritism was shown or whether there was any corruption in the purchase of new tyres and in body building contract for the new chassis by Karnataka State Road Transport Corporation under the undue influence of the Chief Minister and the Minister for Transport Shri Aziz Sait.

11. Whether there was an nepotism and favouritism and misuse of power by the Chief Minister and the Minister of Transport in the matter of nationalisation of contract carriages and wilfully benefiting certain parties with whom the Chief Minister's second son-in-law was a partner.

12. Whether any favouritism was shown in the nomination of Shri K.V. Rao as a member of the Karnataka State Road Transport Corporation Board against the provision of the Act.

13. Whether an undue favour was shown to M/s. Balaji Engineering Construction Company by accepting the tender for construction of houses under Housing and Urban Development Corporation's Low Income Group Scheme in Dumlur Layout by the Bangalore Development Authority, which is under the administrative control of the Chief Minister.

14. Whether allotment of 20 acres of land was made to the three sons of the Finance Minister, Shri M.Y. Ghorpade, in contravention of land grant rules and the provisions of the Land Reforms Act and the Land Revenue Acts.

15. Whether any misuse of power was committed, or any corruption committed, by Shri D.K. Naikar, Minister for Municipal Administration, with regard to the grant of land to Boroka Textile Mills in Hubli-Darwar Corporation Area.

Annexure II

Whether the Chief Minister or any other Minister of the State of Karnataka was guilty of corruption, nepotism, favouritism or misuse of governmental power in connection with all or any of the following matters, namely:

1. Grant of 20 acres of Government land, reserved for grazing of cattle in Bommanahalli, Nelamangala Taluk, Bangalore District, to the son-in-law of the Chief Minister, Shri M.D. Nataraj, in violation of the provisions of the Land Revenue Code and disregarding the claims of local Scheduled Caste applicants;
2. Allotment of 4 large valuable house sites in the most posh locality of Bangalore, Raj Mahal Vilas Extension, to Shri Devaraj Urs and his family members in supersession of the rightful claims of other applicants;
3. Undue favours shown to Messrs Nirmala Engineering Construction Company by releasing Government funds in spite of the fact that the concerned Minister had taken a decision to prosecute the firm of the basis of the recommendations of the Vigilance Commission;
4. Excess payment of Rs. 98.86 lakhs to Messrs Balaji Engineering Company, in Hemavathi Project, in contravention of the terms of the contract with a view to favouring the contractor;
5. Undue favour shown to Messrs Nechipadam Construction Company in Hemavathi Project, by accepting the highest tender with an intent to benefit the contractors and involving excess payment to the extent of Rs. 3.5 lakhs;
6. Excess payment of Rs. 1 crore to Messrs TICIL Contractors, in Kali Hydel Project, for the benefit of the Contractors;
7. Whether about 5,000 tons of rice, purchased by the Government of Karnataka from the Tamil Nadu Government on government-to-government basis, was allowed to be marketed by a private party, Shri H.R. Atheeq Ahmed, without the knowledge of the Food Department, instead of the Mysore State Co-operative Marketing Federation as was earlier agreed, with the sole intent of benefiting the private party;
8. Undue favour shown to a fictitious cooperative society in regard to conversion of 270 acres of agricultural land called DINSHAW ESTATE into non-agricultural purpose in violation of the mandatory provisions of the Land Reforms Act and the Land Revenue Act;
9. Whether undue favour was shown to one Ghanshyam in the sale of 2500 tons of Bajra at the rate of Rs. 73.50 P. per quintal without calling for tenders and allowing Shri Ghanshyam to sell the Bajra in the State of Maharashtra at the rate of Rs.

125.00 per quintal during the time of droughts in Karnataka;

10. Whether undue favour was shown, or concession was made, to M/s. Karekar & Sundaram, Architects, in regard to the preparation of designs for remodelling the K.R. Market in supersession of the order of the concerned Minister;
11. Whether undue favour was shown, or concession was made, to M/s. Shah Construction Co., contractors, in Upper Krishna Project at Alamatti;
12. Whether undue favour was shown to M/s. Krishna Flour Mills in granting valuable land in Bangalore City, which land was meant for children's park, at a nominal rent by over-ruling the orders of the concerned Minister;
13. Whether there was any misappropriation of funds of the Karnataka State Film Industries Development Corporation, to the tune of Rs. 10.00 lakhs, when the Chief Minister himself was the Chairman of that Corporation and whether the business of the Corporation, was conducted with intent to defraud that Corporation, its members, creditors or any other person or otherwise for a fraudulent or unlawful purpose;
14. Whether any undue favour was shown to M/s. Poornima Electronics, Bangalore, in the purchase of electronic equipment (inter-com) by superseding the recommendation of the Head of the Department and orders of the concerned Minister;
15. Whether any misappropriation of the funds of the Karnataka State Co-operative Marketing Federation to the extent of several crores of rupees was made by Shri H.S. Srikantiah, Minister of State for Home, when he was the President of that Federation and whether the business of the Federation was conducted with intent to defraud that Federation, its members, creditors or any other person or otherwise for a fraudulent or unlawful purpose;
16. Whether any undue favour was shown by Shri Satya Pal by the Minister of Transport, Shri Mohamed Ali, by accepting the once rejected tender of Shri Satya Pal in leasing out its building for canteen in Karnataka State Road Transport Corporation Bus Stand, Mysore, and whether any undue favour was shown by the same Minister to Shri Satya Pal's son Shri Prem Kumar, in leasing out its retiring rooms of the Karnataka State Road Transport Corporation in Mysore;

17. Whether any undue favour was shown to four firms, namely, All-India Agencies, Vidyut Engineering Co., Trishul Enterprises and Mysore Woods, in purchasing furniture valued at Rs. 29.00 lakhs in 1973-74 under I.P. Project by the Minister for Health, Shri H. Siddaveerappa;
18. Whether any undue favour was shown by the Minister of State for Small-scale Industries, Shri Koulajgi in 1974, in the issue of Essentiality Certificate to parties many of which were fictitious and bogus
19. Whether undue favour was shown by the Chief Minister and the Minister for Transport, Shri Aziz Sait, in 1973-74, to M/s. Fargo in buying 150 chassis against the advice of the Chief Mechanical Engineer of the Karnataka State Road Transport Corporation;
20. Whether any undue favour was shown by the Minister of Industries, Shri S.M. Krishna, in allotting of paper, cement and steel of the state-owned industries to non-traditional dealers/agencies including his kith and kin;
21. Whether an excess payment of Rs. 30.00 lakhs was made to M/s. Shankaranarayan Construction Company in regard to the construction of combined Board Administrative Building Complex at Bangalore over and above the contract rates;
22. Whether any excess payment was made to M/s. Balaji Engineering Company to the tune of Rs. 80.00 lakhs in Harangi Project with an intent to favour the contractor;
23. Whether Shri K.H. Patil, the then Minister for Agriculture and Forest, was guilty of any misuse of power or undue favouritism in relation to Hukkerri Textile Mills or Gadag Co-operative Textile Mills, or both;
24. Whether any undue favour was shown or any corruption committed by Shri Chikke Gowda, the then Minister for Animal Husbandry and Agriculture in relation to the payment of a sum of Rs. 3.00 lakhs to M/s. Navarasa Fertilisers;
25. Whether there was any misuse of power and corruption committed by Shri D.K.Naikar, Minister for Municipal Administration, in connection with the allotment of land on J.C. Road to Shri M.B. Lal and Shri M.V. Venkatappa.

And whereas the Central Government is of the opinion that it is necessary that the scope of inquiry by the said Commission of Inquiry should be extended to include certain additional definite matters of public importance, namely, allegations of excess payments, improper payments, irregularities and undue favour in relation to contracts, grant of land, allotment of sites, purchase of furniture and disposal of food grains, against the Chief Minister and certain other Ministers and former Ministers of the State of Karnataka, specified in the Schedule to this notification: S.O. 760(E) dated 8th November, 1977.

Now, therefore, in exercise of the powers conferred by section 3 of the Commissions of Inquiry Act, 1952 (60 of 1952) the Central Government hereby directs that the said Commission of Inquiry shall also make an inquiry into the allegations specified in the Schedule to this notification and report to the Central Government on or before the date specified in paragraph 4 of the notification No. S.O. 365(E) aforesaid.

And whereas the Central Government is of the opinion, having regard to the nature of the inquiry to be made by the Commission under this notification and other circumstances of the case, that all the provisions of sub-section (2), sub-section (3), sub-section (4) and sub-section (5) of section 5 of the Commissions of Inquiry Act, 1952 (60 of 1952) should be made applicable to the Commissions, the Central Government hereby directs, in exercise of the powers conferred by sub-section (1) of the said section 5, that all the provisions of the said sub-sections (2), (3), (4) and (5) of that section shall apply to the Commission in respect of such inquiry.

Schedule

1. Whether improper or excessive payment was made to Messrs Nirmala Engineering Construction Company, in respect of the contracts awarded to them by the Government of Karnataka and the Karnataka Urban Water Supply and Drainage Board for lift irrigation or water supply scheme?

2. Whether any improper or excessive payment was made to Messrs Balaji Engineering and Construction Works Limited in respect of the contracts awarded to them for—

(i) the construction of the right bank earth dam of the Hemavathy Project from Chainage No. 7890′ to 9510′ ;

(ii) the construction of the right bank irrigation sluice of the Hemavathy Dam;

(iii) the construction of the left bank irrigation sluice of the Hemavathy Dam;

(iv) the construction of the masonry dam of the Hemavathy Project from Chainage No. 4400′ to 5740′ including the overflow section and the protective works;

(v) the construction of the spillway dam of the Hemavathy Project;

(vi) the construction of the masonry dam of the Harangi Project?

3. Whether any improper or excessive payment was made or undue favour shown to Messrs Nechipadam Construction Company in respect of the contract awarded to them for the construction of the Hemavathy right Bank Earth Dam from chainage 2025 m. to 2405 m. and chainage 1750 m. to 2025 m.?

4. Whether any improper or excessive payment was made or undue favour shown to Messrs Shankaranarayan Construction Company in respect of the contract awarded to them for the construction of the combined Board Administrative Division Building?

5. Whether any improper or excessive payment was made or undue favour shown to Messrs TICIL in respect of the contracts awarded to them for—

(i) the construction of the head race tunnel from the Bommanahalli pick up dam to the surge point;

(ii) the construction of the surge tank and the pressure shaft?

6. Whether any undue favour was shown to Messrs Ghanasham Commercial Company Limited, in the sale of 2,500 tonnes of Bajra at the rate of Rs. 73.50 per quintal in 1972?

7. Whether any undue favour as shown to Messrs Krishna Flour Mills in respect of the lease of the land next to its premises, measuring 200′ × 200′ for a period of 30 years?

8. Whether any improper or excessive payment was made or any undue favour was shown to Messrs Shah Construction Company in the settlement of their claims for the contract awarded to them for the construction of the Alamatti Dam?

9. Whether any undue favour was shown to Messrs Poornima Electronics in the placing of orders on them for supply of electronic equipments like Intercom, etc.?

10. Whether there was any misappropriation or fraud in the

dealings of the State Co-operative Marketing Federation during the period 1971-72 and 1972-73?

11. Whether any undue favour has been shown by the Government or the Karnataka Road Transport Corporation in leasing out the building in the Karnataka Road Transport Corporation bus stand at Mysore for a Canteen at Mysore?

12. Whether any undue favour was shown by Government or the Karnataka Road Transport Corporation in leasing out resting rooms in the Karnataka Road Transport Corporation in Mysore to Shri Prem Kumar?

13. Whether the funds of the Agro-Industries Corporation were wrongly diverted to the Gadag Co-operative Textile Mills, Hulkoti Gadag, Dharwar District?

14. Whether undue favour was shown to Messrs Navarasa Fertilizers in purchasing fertilisers and whether payment was made even without receipt of the stock?

15. Whether site on J.C. Road was leased to Shri M.B. Lal and N.V. Venkatappa contrary to the interests of the City of Bangalore Municipal Corporation?

16. Whether the grant of land in S.N. 15 of Bommanahalli Village, Nelamangala Taluk, Bangalore District was made contrary to rules?

17. Whether sites in Rajmahal Vilas layouts were irregularly allotted?

18. Whether the purchase of one thousand tonnes of paddy from Tamil Nadu by Shri Atheeq Ahmed, Proprietor of the Mandya Rice Mills, Mandya at the instance of the State Government and the subsequent disposal thereof were adverse to the interests of the State?

19. Whether the contract for the preparation of models and designs for the remodelling of the K.R. Market, Bangalore was irregularly awarded to Messrs Karekar and Sundaram?

20. Whether the conversion of land owned by Shri C.H. Dinshawa and family in Harasipura Village, Bangalore North Taluk (known as 'Dinshaw Estate') as non-agricultural land was not in accordance with the rules?

21. Whether any irregularities or improprieties have been committed in the administration of the Karnataka Film Development Corporation since 1971?

22. Whether the cement or steel allotted for the construction of

the Government Harijan Hostel building in Bangalore City was diverted to other purposes?

23. Whether orders for the purchase of furniture for the Health Department for the years 1972-73 and 1973-74 were placed at exorbitant rates with firms who were neither furniture dealers nor approved PWD contractors/suppliers?

24. Whether essentiality certificates for stainless steel were issued to bogus firms or fictitious persons during the period 1st March, 1974 to 30th June, 1974?

25. Whether the purchase of Fargo and Bedford Chassis by Karnataka Road Transport Corporation in August, 1972 was against the Corporation's interests?

26. Whether the appointments of the agents, sub-agents and dealers during years 1972-1977 by the Visvesvaraya Iron and Steel Limited, Bhadravathi for the distribution of steel and cement were adverse to the company's interest?

27. Whether the appointments of agents, sub-agents and dealers for the years 1972-1977 by the Mysore Paper Mills Limited, Bhadravathi for the distribution of paper were adverse to the company's interest?

Amendment in the Notification

S.O. 96(E) dated 15th February, 1978. In exercise of the powers conferred by section 3 of the Commissions of Inquiry Act, 1952 (60 of 1952), the Central Government hereby makes the following further amendments in the notification of the Government of India in the Ministry of Home Affairs (Department of Personnel and Administrative Reforms) No. S.O. 365(E), dated the 23rd May, 1977, published at pages 1977 to 1981 of the *Gazette of India*, Extraordinary, Part-II, Section 3, sub-section (ii), dated 23rd May, 1977, namely:

In the said notification, in Annexure II—

(i) in allegation No. 7, for the word "rice" the word "paddy" shall be substituted;

(ii) in allegation No. 24, the following shall be added at the end, namely:
"; and in getting deposited funds of BAFCO and Karnataka Dairy Corporation to the tune of Rs. 50 lakhs in Southern In-

dian Bank against the mandatory rules relating to deposit of funds in nationalised banks; and whether Varalaxmi Cotton Seeds were indiscriminately sold outside the State at the instance of Shri Chikke Gowda for some consideration resulting in heavy loss to the growers; and whether Shri Dwarakanath and Shri Nanjaiah were appointed by the Ministers as Director of Agriculture and Director of Animal Husbandry to suit his motive for making monetary gains; and further whether Shri Chikke Gowda received huge amounts privately as commission from Messrs Vulcan Laval and Larsen and Toubro through their agents Mr. V.V. Parthasarthy, Mrs. Savla and Mr. John, in relation to purchase of machinery by the Agriculture and Animal Husbandry Departments."

(iii) In allegation No. 25, for the words and letters "Shri M.B. Lal and Shri M.V. Venkatappa", the words and letters "Shri N.C. Madhavaraj" shall be substituted.

Contents

Part I – Introduction and Preliminary Proceedings; Part II – Allegations and Facts Leading Thereto, Arguments and Findings: Allegations Relating to Undue Favour, etc., in respect of Private Individuals, Firms, etc.; Allegations Relating to Allotment to Sites, Lands, etc.; Allegations Concerning Semi-Government/Statutory/PublicBodies/Corporations/Undertakings etc; Allegations Regarding Undue Favour, Excess Payments, etc. Relating to Irrigation Projects; Miscellaneous Allegations; General Observations; Summary of Findings.

Recommendations

It is proposed to discuss certain points of general importance which would cover not only the questions which arose in the allegations into which the inquiry was made by the Commission, but also provide material of consideration both for administrative action at the appropriate level and legislative action by the Union Government.

Meaning of Certain Expressions, e.g., Corruption, etc.

2. According to the notifications dated 23-5-1977 and 8-11-

1977 by which this Commission was constituted to make an inquiry into the allegations specified in those notifications, the definite matters of public importance were stated to be charges of corruption, nepotism, favouritism or misuse of Governmental power against the Chief Minister and certain Ministers and former Ministers of the State of Karnataka. It is necessary, therefore, to examine the true ambit and scope as also the meaning of these expressions. The Commission had the benefit of hearing the different views which were put forward by learned counsel appearing on behalf of the Memorialists, the Chief Minister and the Commission itself. One point of view is that corruption does not necessarily mean taking of money of illegal gratification. According to the Santhanam Report, even misuse of Governmental power would amount to corruption. The word 'nepotism' had its origin from the French-Latin word 'Nepos' which meant a nephew. Therefore favouritism shown to nephews and other relatives, would be covered by the expression 'nepotism'. It has come to me now bestowal of patronage by reason of relationship rather than by merit. As regards favouritism, the position is that a person who in the ordinary circumstances could not have had a particular benefit, obtains it because the person who can confer that benefits goes out of the way to give it to him. The nature of the transaction itself can establish favouritism irrespective of whether any connection exists between the person benefited and the person conferring the benefit. The counsel for the Memorialists generally commended the above approach.

3. The other view is that corruption means acceptance of illegal gratification and mere misuse of governmental power cannot amount to corruption. So far as favouritism is concerned, the mental element is most important. While finding out whether favouritism has been exercised, one can look at the direct evidence and also at the circumstances which should lead to no other conclusion but that favouritism was practised. In case of an order passed by a Minister, there can be many possibilities. Firstly, his order can be based on wrong advice given by the departmental officials; secondly, the officers whose duty it is to place all the material before the Minister may have failed to do so; thirdly, there may have been an error of judgement by the Minister and fourthly, it may have just been an act of omission by the Minister. In order to show favouritism to any individual or party, some connection or link must be established between the individual conferring the benefit and the recipient of the

benefit. In other words, favouritism cannot be practised unless the person who is favoured, is known to the Minister or the latter has some personal interest in any concern or organisation with which that person is connected. Moreover, nepotism and favouritism cannot exist and can have no meaning without misuse or abuse of Governmental authority. If a transaction is otherwise regular, there cannot be abuse or misuse of officers. On the contrary if a transaction is irregular and it is made regular, then it would be a typical example of misuse of power. Shri Ramaswamy, counsel for the Chief Minister, strongly supported the above view.

4. Shri S.R. Das, the former Chief Justice of India, in his Report of Inquiry, into the charges contained in the memorandum presented to the President of India on 13-7-1963 made against Sardar Pratap Singh Kairon, Chief Minister of Punjab, dealt with the question whether the charges founded in corruption, must be confined to the meaning given to that expression by the provisions of the Prevention of Corruption Act 1947. The following part of the observations made by Shri S.R. Das may be reproduced:

> "The Commission finds noting on the face of the Memorandum to indicate that the Memorialists did not use the word "corruption" in its ordinary etymological meaning signifying rotten, putrid or impure act or conduct which they, rightly or wrongly, imputed to S. Partap Singh Kairon. The Commission will, therefore have to examine each charge and ascertain the kind of misdeed, corruption or misrule that the Memorialists seek to impute on S. Partap Singh Kairon............"

5. Justice H.R. Khanna in his Report of Inquiry into the allegations against the Chief Minister and Ministers of the State of Orissa, has indicated his approach in such matters. According to him, the most important elements would be *mala fide* intention or ulterior motives. The Ministers have to take a number of bold decisions. The Commission would not go into the questions as to whether those decisions were right or wrong. It is only concerned with the question as to whether they were *mala fide* or influenced by motives of personal gain.

6. It is well settled that the purpose and object of ordering an inquiry under the Commissions of Inquiry Act, 1952 (hereinafter the Act) is to adopt measures for preserving the purity and integrity of

public administration and public life. That shall serve as a beacon light for finding out whether on the material and evidence before the Commission an allegation relating to corruption, nepotism, favouritism or misuse of governmental power stands established or not. These expressions appear to have been used in a wide sense in the notifications by which the allegations have been referred for inquiry to the Commission, and a narrow and restricted meaning cannot be given to them. The presence of some improper or ulterior motive or bad faith would certainly be a very important factor in determining the nature of the act of conduct of a Minister. The standard of proof has to be the same as was applied by the Commission when it made its First or Interim Report. So far as corruption is concerned, the Commission finds it difficult to improve in the observations of Shri S.R. Das, and the said expression must be given its etymological meaning. Favouritism involves treatment showing a marked preference or show of peculiar and unusual partiality. It is manifestation of partiality in the interest of one person or family or of a class to the neglect of others by a person of high rank or authority (see generally the meaning of 'favourite' and 'favouritism' in Websters' New International Dictionary). A direct or personal connection between the person bestowing favour and the recipient thereof is not the *sine qua non* of favouritism. The very act and conduct of the authority committing such an act can demonstrably show an intention to go out of the way to benefit another as it will be lacking in *bona fides*. Although misuse of authority would be invariably involved in an act of favouritism, the converse would not be true. There can be misuse of authority *de hors* exercise of favouritism. Where power is misused but there is good faith, it only makes the act *ultra vires* and not vitiated. Misuse of governmental authority essentially involves misuse or abuse of power in bad faith. (see generally the observations in *Ram Manohar Lohia* v. *The State of Bihar*.*

Position and Powers of the Chief Minister

7. One of the most important and controversial questions has been the role of the Chief Minister in regard to those matters which do not directly pertain to the portfolios held by him and the proce-

---

* A.I.R. 1966 SC. 740 at p. 752.

dure to be followed by him in relation to such matters. Article 166 of the Constitution provides for the conduct of business of the Government of a State. According to clause (3) of that Article, the Governor shall make rules for the more convenient transaction of the business of the government of the State, and for the allocation among Minister of the said business in so far as it is not business with respect to which the Governor is by or under the Constitution required to act in his discretion. In exercise of the powers conferred by the aforesaid Article, the Governor of Karnataka promulgated the Karnataka Government Rules of Business 1964, which will be hereinafter referred to as the Rules of Business. Rule 2 gives the definitions. Clause(fa) of sub-rule (1) defines Minister to mean Cabinet Minister and a Minister of State not attached to a Cabinet Minister is also included in that definition. Sub-clause (g) gives the definition of "Minister-in-charge". He is the Minister appointed to be in-charge of the Department of the Government to which a case belongs. "Case" is defined by sub-clause (f) to include the papers under consideration and all previous papers and notes put up in connection therewith to enable the questions raised to be disposed of. All cases shall be deemed to belong to a Department to which under the Schedule to the Rules, the subject matter thereof pertains, or is mainly related. If in a respect of any case a question arises as to the Department to which the case belongs, it shall be referred to the Chief Secretary who shall decide the question after obtaining the orders of the Chief Minister, if necessary. Rule 5 says that the Governor shall, on the advice of the Chief Minister, allocate among the Ministers the business of the Government by assigning one or more Departments of the Secretariat to the charge of a Minister. Sub-rule(2) of rule 5 provides for allotment to every Minister of State and to every Deputy Minister, such items of work assigned to the Minister to whom he is attached as the Governor may specify. The Minister of State or the Deputy Minister concerned may, subject to the control and orders of the Chief Minister, attend to such items of work allotted to him as the Minister may specify.

8. Ordinarily, all business allotted to a Department under the Rules of Business, is to be disposed of by or under general or special directions of the Minister-in-charge [rule 6(1)]. The Minister in-charge is primarily responsible for the disposal of the business pertaining to the Department [rule 10(1)]. Under rule 29(1) the Minister is empowered to dispose of cases arising in the Department under his

control. These powers of the Minister-in-charge are subject to certain exceptions. He cannot exercise them where the case is required to be submitted either to the Cabinet or to the Chief Minister or to the Governor. The cases which are to be submitted to these authorities have been specified in the Second, Third and Fourth Schedules respectively, of the Rules of Business. Where consultation with the Finance Department is necessary, the Minister-in-charge cannot dispose of the case without the concurrence of that Department except where a decision has been taken by the Cabinet allowing him to proceed in the matter [rule 13(1) and 13(2)]. If there is any difference of opinion between the Departments, the Minister-in-charge has to make an attempt by previous discussion with the Ministers of other Departments concerned to arrive at an agreement. If no such agreement is arrived at and the Minister-in-charge wishes to proceed with the case, it has to be submitted to the Chief Minister for a decision and the Chief Minister may either decide the case himself or refer the case to the Cabinet [sub-rules (3) and (4) of rule 29.]. Item (xxiv) of the Second Schedule may be referred to at this stage. According to item(xxiv) of the Second Schedule cases where Ministers are unable to come to an agreement about the action to be taken, have to be referred to the Cabinet. There appears to be some conflict between rule 29(4) which empowers the Chief Minister to take a decision in case of a disagreement between the Ministers, and item (xxiv) of the Second Schedule which requires the matter to be submitted to the Cabinet where the Ministers are unable to come to an agreement, Rule 16(1)(a) provides that cases specified in the Second Schedule shall be brought before the Cabinet after submission to the Minister-in-charge of the Department. Rule 17 states that subject to the provisions of rule 16, all cases specified in the Second Schedule shall be brought before the Cabinet. Cases other than those specified in the Second Schedule shall be brought before the Cabinet by the direction of the Chief Minister or the Minister-in-charge of the Department with the consent of the Chief Minister. Thus item (xxiv) of the Second Schedule read with the rule 17, seems to indicate that the power conferred by rule 29(4) on the Chief Minister to either decide the case himself or refer it to the Cabinet, is expressly contradicted by rule 17. Rule 11 empowers the Chief Minister to call for papers from any Department. In the same way, the Finance Minister can call for papers from any Department in which financial consideration is involved. Any other Minister can ask to see the papers of any other Department if they are related to, or are required for consideration of any subject allotted to him. Rule 12 requires, every Minister and every Secretary to transmit to the Chief Minister all such information with respect to business of the Government as the Chief Minister may require from time to time to be transmitted to him.

9. Since there is no rule which, in express terms, confers powers on the Chief Minister to make orders superseding or overruling the orders of the Minister-in-charge, it has to be determined what procedure should be followed in case the Chief Minister after exercising his power of calling for papers from any Department under rule 11, wishes to take a contrary view or make an order which is inconsistent with the orders made by the Minister-in-charge. The Chief Minister cannot derive any such power from sub-rule (4) of rule 29 because that is confined only to a case which concerns more than one Minister, and there in difference of opinion and the attempt to arrive at an agreement has failed. The only provision which appears to be applicable in such a situation is item (xxiv) of the Second Schedule. Since rule 2 which gives the definitions, does not define "Chief Minister" separately, he must be included in the definition of a "Minister". Consequently, if the Chief Minister is inclined to take a different view from the Minister-in-charge, the only course open to him is to bring the matter before the Cabinet. The Chief Minister also has the power under rule 16(1)(b) to have the matters brought before the Cabinet in cases other than those specified in the Second Schedule. In any given case, the following situations can arise:

(1) The Minister-in-charge makes a particular order, that order being within his competence under the Rules of Business. The Chief Minister wishes to make a different order in disagreement with him.

(2) A particular person or party makes a direct approach or representation to the Chief Minister and the Chief Minister expresses his own views in the shape of a minute or his own views in the shape of a minute or order, and then the case is sent to the Minister-in-charge who is not prepared to accept the views of the Chief Minister or agree with his minute.

10. In the first case the Chief Minister does not appear under the Rules of Business, to have any power to overrule the decision or order of the Minister-in-charge. If he holds a different view and

wishes to pass an order which comes into conflict with that made by the Minister-in-charge, the only course open to him would be the one provided by item (xxiv) of the Second Schedule, namely the case will have to be referred to the Cabinet. In the second case, if the matter relates to the Department of another Minister, it is only that Minister who is competent to make the order. The Chief Minister's minute can be treated by that Minister more in the nature of a suggestion, expression or opinion or advice. He is free to accept it or not to accept it. If the Chief Minister still wishes his original order or direction to be treated as the final decision, he will have to either persuade the Minister-in-charge to agree with him and, in case of disagreement, the only course open will be that the case will have to be referred to the Cabinet. Rule 74 may also be noticed. According to this rule, the Chief Secretary and the Secretary of the Department concerned, have been made severally responsible for the proper transaction of business and for the careful observance of the rules and when either of them considers that there has been any material departure from them, he has to personally bring it to the notice of the Chief Minister or through the Minister-in-charge as the case may be.

11. While examining the Rules of Business, it is certainly important to bear in mind the position which the Chief Minister occupies in a Cabinet system of Government. By analogy his powers would be practically the same as that of a Prime Minister in England different opinions have been expressed. According to Lord Morley, although the members of the Cabinet stand on equal footing and speak with equal voice, yet the head of the Cabinet, namely, the Prime Minister, is *primus inter pares* and occupies a position which so long as it lasts, is one of exceptional and peculiar authority.[1] Sir William Harcourt thought Lord Morley's estimate of the powers of the Prime Minister was exaggerated. He agreed that though theoretically he was *primus inter pares,* but in reality he should be *inter stellas luna minores*.[2] It has also been said that the Prime Minister is rather a Sun around which all planets revolve.[3] According to Gladstone, "The Prime Minister has no title to override any one of the departments. So far as the governs them, unless it is done by a trick, which is not to be supposed, he governs them by influence only. But the right of the Cabinet to override a Minister cannot be contested and the Prime Minister, who is sure of obtaining support, if necessary, can, in practice, override a colleague's decision. This is done usually at the request of another Minister and particularly where a dispute arises between two

departments".[4] The sum and substance of the various instances and discussions given in the book of Ivor Jennings and that of P. Meckintosh (British Cabinet) is that since the Government is dependent on the leader of the majority in the House, it would seem that the Prime Minister really constitutes the Government and other members of his Cabinet are there mainly to assist him in the discharge of those functions. Depending upon the character and individual temperament, a Prime Minister can control the actions and attitudes of the various members of his Cabinet.

12. In the above background, it is no doubt true that the position of the Chief Minister *vis-a-vis* the other Ministers is predominant and once he calls for an file under rule 11 of the Rules of Business, and expresses his view, it is entitled to great weight. The occasion for expressing his views on a case which concerns the department of the Minister-in-charge, unless the latter has himself invited they opinion of the Chief Minister, is of great importance. As the Chief Minister is bound to act according to the Rules of Business which have constitutional validity, he cannot normally interfere in matters relating to those departments which are not in his charge. There must be strong and compelling reasons for him to differ from the views of the concerned Minister. He is certainly entitled to differ, but in that event the case must be referred to the Cabinet. He can create a very embarrassing situation for a Ministry by expressing his own views first on a mere representation of some person or individual or party without properly acquainting himself or verifying all the relevant facts. That can be subjected to a good deal of criticism as in some cases where Shri Devaraj Urs interfered on mere representation of the parties concerned as has been discussed in allegations No. 3 of Annexure II (M/s. Nirmala Engineering Construction Co.), No. 9 of Annexure-II (Sale of Bajra) and No. 14 of Annexure-II(M/s. Poornima Electronics).

Responsibility in a Cabinet System of Government

13. Some observations may also be made as to how far the principle of collective responsibility in a Cabinet system of Government affects the individual responsibility of the Ministers. The most common political meaning of the word "responsibility" is that certain Minister will answer Parliamentary questions on a given subject. The second sense arises when those in political circles appreciate that a

particular policy is largely the idea of a Minister rather than the traditional policy of the party in power and they may single out the Minister for attack. A third sense is that a Minister is responsible even if a policy is the work of the Cabinet as a whole, but his colleagues choose to place the burden upon him. Our Supreme Court has settled the principles which are apposite for the purposes of the inquiry made by this Commission. Chandrachud J. (now Chief Justice of India), while examining articles 75(3) and 164(2) of the Constitution, stated the true position thus:[5]

> "Articles 75(3) and 164(2) speak of the collective responsibility of the Council of Ministers as a body, to the House of the People or the Legislative Assembly of the State. Whatever may be the findings of a Commission of inquiry, the Council of Ministers, whether at the Centre or in the states, continues to be collectively answerable or accountable to the House of the People or the Legislative Assembly. Indeed, neither the appointment of the Commission nor even the rejection by the Commission of all or any of the allegations referred to it for its inquiry would make the Council of Ministers any the less answerable to those bodies. The object of the two articles of the Constitution on which the State or Karnataka relies is to provide that for every decision taken by the Cabinet, each one of the ministers is responsible to the Legislature concerned. It is difficult to accept that for acts of corruption, nepotism or favouritism which are alleged or proved against an individual Minister, entire Council or Ministers can be held collectively responsible to the Legislature. If an individual Minister uses his office as an occasion of pretence for committing acts of corruption he would be personally answerable for his unlawful acts and no question of collective responsibility of the Council of Ministers can arise in such a case".

In another case, *A. Sanjeevi Naidu, etc.* v. *State of Madras & Anr.*, it has been observed by Hegde J, (now Speaker of the Lok Sabha), that:[6]

> "the essence of collective responsibility of the Council of Ministers is that the Cabinet is responsible to the legislature for every action taken in any of the Ministers. In other words, the principle of collective responsibility governs only those acts which a minis-

ter performs or can reasonably be said to have been performed in the lawful discharge of his official functions".

Role of Secretariat/Civil Service

14. The next point which requires consideration is the role of the Secretariat/civil service in decision making at the governmental level, and the ministerial responsibility for the decisions taken by the Government officials. It is now fully accepted that civil servants should recommend what seems to them to be the correct course of action. The civil servants are, however, bound to act according to the instructions of the Ministers. The role of civil servants falls into two categories one is to investigate and the other is advisory. Civil servants will collect the information by investigation and place them before the Minister after duly processing them with their views on the matter. The policy is to be laid down by the Minister and the civil servants have a duty to carry out the same. Once the policy is formulated, ordinarily, Ministers should not interfere in the day to day decisions. Discussing the *inter se* relationship between Ministers and civil servants, the authors of *Constitutional Law* (eighth edition) have pointed out that while collective responsibility ensures that the Government present a united front to Parliament, individual responsibility in its political meaning ensures that for every act or neglect of his department, a Minister must answer. As the official cannot defend himself in Parliament, it is his Minister alone who must be answerable for his acts. This positive liability of a Minister is essential to the performance by Parliament of its role as a critic of the executive. No Minister can shield himself by blaming his officials[7].

15. It has been suggested in the course of a discussion and arguments before the Commission that certain officials were so appointed in the State of Karnataka to particular posts at higher levels that they would express such views and tender such advice as the Chief Minister desired them to give even though that might not have been in consonance with accepted administrative norms or might have been detrimental to public interest or interests of the State as a whole. It can also happen that if a particular official has not acted according to the wishes of a Minister or Chief Minister, he would be transferred from that Department and replaced by someone else. In some cases, the government servants made notings, etc., on the files anticipating the views of the concerned Minister or the Chief Minister.

16. The Commission does not propose to express any opinion about any individual instances that were given by the Memorialists as the primary function of the Commission is to make in inquiry into the allegations against the Chief Minister, some of the Minister and former Minister of the State of Karnataka as set out in the notifications relating to this Commission of Inquiry. But it cannot be overemphasised that if administrative standards have to be kept at high level of propriety and efficiency, the services must maintain an attitude of strict political neutrality. Legally and constitutionally they have to carry out the policy laid down by the Government in power but that does not mean, nor does it require that impartiality and fairness should not receive dominant and paramount consideration. That can only be done if the members of the services do not get personally involved in various matters on which a decision is to be given by them or advice has to be tendered. There should also be adequate protection for the civil servants if they express their views frankly and in a forthright manner. It would be really unfortunate if in matters of administration, there is constant interference by the Ministers or the Chief Minister even with regard to those matters which do not involve questions of policy.

Constitutional and Personal Responsibility of the Ministers

17. Another matter which arose for discussion in the course of the inquiry was the constitutional and personal responsibility of Ministers in relation to any order passed by the the Government in pursuance of any recommendation made by a High-powered Board or other body which could only make recommendations and give advisory opinion. In particular, the Government orders which were issued on the recommendations of the Major Irrigation Projects Control Board which involved payment of lakhs of rupees to contractors with regard to the various dams and irrigation projects, became the subject matter of considerable debate and controversy. The constitutional position of an order made by the Minister on which finally the Government orders are issued, is quite clear. A minister cannot escape constitutional and individual responsibility according to the principles which have been discussed above. The Memorialists say, whenever a recommendation of a High-powered body which acts in a purely advisory capacity is accepted by the Minister-in-charge, if the advice has not been given *bona fide* and is motivated by extraneous

considerations the Minister who acts on that recommendation are advice, would be equally responsible for the *mala fide* nature of the act and he cannot take shelter behind the fact that the recommendation was made by a High-powered advisory body. This immediately involves the question whether the recommendation made or the advice tendered by that body, was vitiated on account of *mala fides* or motivated by extraneous considerations. If the Minister-in-charge was either the Chairman of that body (in case of MIPCB it was the Chief minister who was also the Chairman and the Minister-in-charge) or if with full knowledge of the *mala fide* advice or recommendation made, he passes an order in accordance therewith, he certainly cannot escape the blame. But in case there is no indication that the recommendation made by the advisory body which was ultimately accepted was so motivated and was not *bona fide,* no responsibility can be laid on the Minister for passing an order based on that advice or recommendation. It may be stated that from the practical point of view it is virtually impossible for any Commission of Inquiry to discover the motives of individual members of a body like the MIPCB when it makes a particular recommendation. Unless from the recorded proceedings of the body or other unimpeachable evidence, some overt act can be discovered of the individual members or of the Chairman, who happens to be a Minister, which influences the decision of the Board and which could be attributed to an intention to show undue favour to anyone or which may involve abuse or misuse of authority, the mere fate that the advice or recommendation given by that Body and ultimately accepted by the Minister is open to criticism in several ways, cannot be regarded as sufficient to give a finding that the Minister was responsible in exercising acts of favouritism or had been guilty of misuse or governmental power.

Ministerial Influence in Government Corporations

18. The question relates to those matters which arise out of the allegations concerning intervention and interference by Ministers in purported exercise of statutory powers conferred on them in the working and functioning of Government Corporations. One of the typical instances is that of purchase of tyres by the Karnataka State Road. Transport, Corporation which forms the subject-matter of allegation No. 10 of Annexure 1. Section 34 of the Road Transport Act, 1950, provides that the State Government may, after consultations

give to the Corporation general instructions to be followed by the Corporation and such instructions may include directions relating to the recruitment, conditions of service, etc. It has been found that regard to that allegation that during the period December 1975 to October 1976, when Shri Mohammed Ali was the Transport Minister, he took under interest in the purchase of tyres from M/s. Modi Rubber Limited and that favouritism was shown by him to that concern. On a true construction of section 34 of the Road Transport Act, the Minister could not interfere in the day to day administration or working of the Corporation. The general instruction with could be given by the Government, meant only policy decisions or such instructions which had a general bearing on the working of the corporation. It could certainly include directions relating to matters contained in section 34, but it was quite clear that the Legislature never intended that the Minister should be concerned with purchase of commodities or articles like tyres from a particular manufacture. It was obvious that where such provisions exit, the Minister-in-charge cannot take upon himself the function of running the day to day administration of the Corporation, nor is he empowered to interfere in such matters as are within the authority of the officers or officials or the Board of that Corporation.

19. Another instance that may be given is of the interference of the Minister-in-charge, Shri S.M. Krishna, in the matter of appointment of dealers, sub-agents, etc., for paper, cement and steel which are the subject-matter of allegation No 20. of Annexure II. He made notings on the applications of certain persons which were virtually orders, to provide them with dealership. It is certainly not the function of a Minister to direct the officers of an independent Corporation or Company to make appointments of particular persons to any office involving pecuniary benefit. One of the major problems that has arisen even in other countries is how to give public undertakings of an industrial or commercial character, a large measure of independence in their day to day activities while reserving for the Government the final decision in matters of major policy. Another problem is how to encourage or promote the management to follow commercial principles while ensuring that social, political and economic goals are pursued when national interest so requires. It has been pointed out in the well known work "Government Enterprise" by W. Friedmann and J.F. Garner that the tendency in Britain, as in other countries, has been for Ministers to intervene in many different ways

regardless of whether they possess the legal power to do so. The Government is usually in so powerful a position and has so many opportunities for inducement at its disposal that it always influences a public enterprise to do what it wants whatever the legal test may say. In the reports of the Select Committee on nationalised industries of Ministerial control, two matters were largely considered. The first was the Governmental structure through which Ministerial control should be exercised. The second was the kind of control which Ministers should exercise and the methods, purposes and objectives which they should use. The Select Committee was highly critical not only of the manner in which Ministers had exercised control but of the whole system. According to the Committee, the Ministers are not aware of the reasons for the powers they possess; that there is confusion about the purposes and methods of Ministerial control; that there is absence of coherent principles among sponsoring departments; that Ministers give little or no guidance on questions of policy but show an increasing tendency to encroach on the details of management. The whole system of sponsoring Ministers has been attacked and rejected by the select committee. According to the view expressed in the aforesaid book it is very doubtful whether Ministers either are or can be responsible for overseeing and ensuring the efficiency of the nationalised industries. The Ministerial powers are explicitly stated in various legislations with regard to public economic corporations their statutes are not always explicit. The provide for a Government "supervision" which cannot imply an overall control of all the acts, even if limited to the grounds of strict legality, ordinary operations should be free from Ministerial control.

20. Nabagopal Das in his book *Public Sector in India* has described the control exercised by the Ministers as going to fantastic lengths. According to him some of the ministers are known to have used the silent methods of informal guidance and pressure, not only on broad matters of policy but also in matters of detail such as personnel management, labour relations, stores purchase policy, etc. In UK the Minister concerned does not interfere in day to day management. But there are many countries management. But there are many countries where despite the autonomy guaranteed to the Board of a Corporation by statute, Ministers have been known to interfere in matters of internal administration either directly or through their representatives on the Board. This has been the experience of the Damodar Valley Corporation in India. It has been argued that in

some under-developed countries, the proliferation of public corporations has been such that they constitute a headless fourth branch of Government. To make them work efficiently it is essential that they should be kept "out of politics". This can be ensured only by giving the Ministers adequate powers to override the Board. But such an argument completely overlooks the fact that Ministerial interference in the name of giving policy directions can become equally "political" and undesirable. The revelations made by the Chagla Commission and the Vivian Bose Enquiry Tribunal in connection with the Mundhra deal of the Life Insurance Corporation of India showed that encroachment over the autonomy of these corporations by the Minister or his Secretary, need not always be in public interest. In the view of the Commission, it would impinge greatly on the independent functioning of the statutory corporations which is the main objective in setting them up, if there can be interference in the normal day to day working and functioning of such corporations. There can be no two opinions about giving power to the Minister in policy matters but the statutory provisions themselves should lay down in clear terms his powers so that in the name of policy directives, he cannot interfere and intervene for political , personal and other reasons.

Ministerial Influence in Municipal Corporations as also Lack of Regulations, etc., regarding Grant of Leases

21. Another matter which engaged the attention of the Commission and which arose out of the allegations relating to J.C. Road (Allegation No. 25 of Annexure II) and Krishna Flour Mills (Allegation No. 12 of Annexure II, together with similar allegations in the schedule), relates to the scope of the interference of the Minister in the working of local bodies like the Municipal Corporation of the City of Bangalore other municipal bodies and the laying down of a proper procedure for allotment of plots or leasing out of public lands so as to avoid arbitrary standards and discriminatory treatment. The finding in the allegation relating to J.C. Road matter is that Shri D.K. Naikar, Minister for Municipal Administration showed undue interest in Shri N.C. Madhuraju in the grant of the lease of land of the city of Bangalore Municipal Corporation on either side of the J.C. Road and that he not only disregarded the norms of propriety becoming the conduct of a Minister but also misused Governmental power in the grant of the said lease. Apart from Ministerial interven-

tion in the matter of grant of lease, it was apparent that no proper rules of guidelines had been framed about fixation of rents for leases of Corporation land. In the allegation relating to the grant of lease to M/s. Krishna Industries, apart from the land leased out to M/s. Krishna Industries, 24 cases of lease of Corporation land had been mentioned in the schedule to the affidavit of the Chief Minister and these had come up for discussion and consideration. It appeared that whereas public institutions had been charged nominal rent, private individuals and institutions had been required to pay higher rent but there was no uniformity even if that classification were to be kept in view. No rules or guidelines appeared to have been followed in the matter of fixing of rents which, admittedly, were determined *ad hoc* and according to the discretion of the authorities concerned, including the Minister-in-charge. The Commission sent a notice to the Corporation to produce the rules or guidelines relating to the fixation of rents for leasing out Corporation lands, but, in spite of more than one attempt having been made to obtain those rules or guidelines, nothing was placed before the commission to throw any light on what bases the rents were being assessed for fixed. It was almost admitted that in such a situation, it was open to the authorities concerned to give leases of lands on such rents as they chose to fix. Similarly, the terms and conditions on which the leases were granted were not regulated by any bye-laws, rules or regulations. It is of paramount importance that in order to avoid any kind of discrimination, proper rules or regulations or bye-laws should be framed not only by the Corporation of the City of Bangalore but by other authorities or bodies which are empowered to make allotment of sites or grant leases of lands vesting in those Corporations or bodies. It was almost common ground that in the absence of proper rules or guidelines no uniformity could be achieved and there could be room for making a discrimination between one party and another while laying down the terms and conditions of the lease including the amount of rent payable by the lessee. It is equally important that there should be Ministerial interference only to the extent it is permissible under the statutory provisions and for giving effect to the policy decisions.

Lacunae in the Commissions of Inquiry Act, 1952

22. It is necessary to point out certain lacunae in the Commissions of Inquiry Act, 1952 which create or are likely to create several

difficulties in inquiry being made a Commission set up under the Act. The suggestions which are being made are purely from the practical and pragmatic point of view so that appropriate amendments may be made in the Act.

23. The first and foremost infirmity in the provisions of section 3 of the Act is that if charges or allegations have been made in the appropriate forum against a State Chief Minister and Ministers who are in office, the State Government can set up a Commission of Inquiry itself. The State Government means virtually the Chief Minister. Thus he can appoint a Commission to make an inquiry against himself. This can lead to many anomalous situations. It will be the State machinery which will be employed to assist in the probe. Moreover, under section 5A, the services of an investigation agency can be availed of for investigating into any matter pertaining to an inquiry. Unless an investigation agency of the Central Government is employed, which is very unlikely, the State officers will be put in a very embarrassing position when they are required to make any investigation against a Chief Minister or a Minister who is holding office and has not admitted it. It is understandable that when a State Government appoints a Commission to inquire into charges against a sitting Chief Minister or a Minister, the Chief Minister or the Minister concerned should immediately resign so as to enable an inquiry to proceed without any fear or inhibitions. But if they enjoy the support of the majority of the Legislature, there is very little chance of their demitting office only because a Commission of Inquiry has been set up. Therefore, apart from the difficulties in the way of any such Commission and the natural reluctance of witnesses coming forward to depose against Ministers in power, the work of the Commission can be greatly impeded and may, in some cases, be reduced to a farce. It will be apposite in this connection to refer to the events preceding and subsequent to the appointment of the present Commission. These have been set out in length in the judgment of the Chief Justice and other Judges of the Supreme Court delivered in the *State of Karnataka* v. *Union of India and another* (1978) 2 SCR 1. A brief resume is also given in the First or Interim Report of this Commission (pages 1 to 3). The Supreme Court upheld the appointment of both the Commissions (the one appointed by the State Government and the present Commission, appointed by the Central Government) on the grounds elaborately discussed in the various judgements. Beg CJ. felt strongly that it was proper for the State Government to

withdraw its own notification if it thinks "that certain members of the State Government will be unduly embarrassed by having to face inquiries by two Commissions on matters which may have some connections or even some common areas. Indeed, to get to the heart of a transaction, its surrounding or superficial shell, which is all that the State Commission can inquire into with regard to some transactions, may have to be pierced, or, to some degree, traversed before the core of these transactions can be reached. As we hold that the two notifications authorise inquires into matters which are substantially different in nature and object, the enquiry by the Grover Commission cannot be said to be barred by reasons of the State Government notification under proviso (b) to section 3(1)........" The further observations at page 39 are noteworthy : "Without doubting the motives of the State Government in appointing its own Commission perhaps we may observe that, in a case involving charges of the kind made against the Chief Minister and other Ministers of the State, it would be better if the State's own Commission did not even remotely appear to have been set up merely in anticipation of a thorough investigation by an outside Central authority which would, presumably, appear more impartial and objective, or, to impede or embarrass the proceedings of the Central Government Commission".

24. It so happened that the notification of the State Government appointing a Commission of Inquiry was struck down for reasons, which need not be stated, by the Karnataka High Court in November 1977. If that Commission had continued to make an inquiry at the same time as the present Commission a host of problems would have been created as most of the same official records would have been required by both the Commissions, and there would have been a lot of overlapping of evidence with consequent inordinate delay. This has been amply illustrated by what has been stated in the First of Interim Report at pages 13 to 26.

25. The weighty observations of Chandrachud J. (now Chief Justice of India) in the above-mentioned case that it is hardly possible, except in utopian conditions, that the State Government will appoint a Commission to inquire into acts of corruption, favouritism and nepotism on the part of its Chief Minister [(1978) 2 SCR 1 at p. 101] have to be kept in view while examining the possibility of two parallel Commissions being appointed. While normally a State Government is not expected to appoint a Commission to look into acts of corruption, favouritism and misuse of power alleged against its Chief Minis-

ter, yet legally as section 3 of the Act stands, there can be no bar to that being done. Indeed, the main argument in the suit field by the State of Karnataka on behalf of the State was that the allegations referred to the two Commissions were the same. That was negatived by the Supreme Court on the grounds given in the judgement of Their Lordships. It is, therefore, essential that a suitable amendment should be made in section 3 by which the possibility of two parallel Commissions being appointed by the State and Central Governments on identical or overlapping allegations involving acts of corruption, misuse of power, etc., alleged to have been committed by the sitting Chief Minister or the Ministers, can be eliminated. It can be made quite clear that when there are allegations involving the personal integrity or honesty of a Chief Minister, the State Government can appoint a Commission only in consultation with the Central Government. Alternatively, in such circumstances only the Central Government should have the power to appoint a Commission of Inquiry. It is likely that the States may object to the Central Government introducing legislative amendment on the above lines owing to political sensitiveness in the matter of Central-State relationship. But if the true position in appreciated, no other alternative is possible in case all the anomalies and infirmities pointed out above have to be effectively removed.

26. Section 5A of the Act requires a good deal of consideration with a view to removing some of the practical difficulties which cropped up, particularly, before the present Commission. It must not be forgotten that when a Commission has to inquire into serious allegations against sitting Chief Minister or a Minister of a State, it can be faced with innumerable hurdles. Firstly, the State Government may not cooperate at all. Secondly, whatever cooperation is extended, it may be given with hesitation and reservations. Fortunately, the present Commission did not have to face those problems after the Commission set up by the State Government ceased to function as a result of the decision of the Karnataka High Court. But when the provisions of an enactment like the Act are being examined, the above aspects cannot be ignored. The biggest hurdle can be presented by the Commission not being able to make much use of the investigation agency as contemplated by section 5A of the Act. The investigation agency can give assistance only if the witnesses it wishes to examine, are prepared to furnish the correct information. The experience of the investigation agency appointed by this Com-

mission which was headed by a D.I.G. belonging to Kerala Cadre, was that witnesses were not willing to spill anything against a powerful Chief Minister or other Ministers in office. The Police officers whose assistance was taken and who were in service of the State were quite frank in requesting that they should not be put in the embarrassing position of having to make an investigation against the Chief Minister of their own State or any other Minister, still in office. The Commission fully realized their difficulties and entrusted only that work which did not put these officers in any compromising position.

27. If inquiries have to be conducted properly and efficiently by Commissions appointed by the State Government or the Central Government the recommendations made by the Law Commission in its 24th report that a machinery similar to that of the Treasury Solicitor in U.K. should be set up in India ought to be implemented. The Treasury Solicitor generally performs the functions of investigation which in a criminal case are usually performed by the Police. Moreover, such an agency would be quite independent and can be of real assistance in making preliminary investigation and sifting facts so that the Commission can make use of the proper material by examining those witnesses whose testimony is relevant and documents which have a bearing on the inquiry.

28. Sub-section (5) of section 5A of the Act is to say the least, ambiguous and not happily worded. It says: (i) the Commission can satisfy itself about the correctness of the facts stated and the conclusion, if any, arrived at in the investigation report, (ii) for the said purpose, it can make such inquiry as it thinks fit, (iii) in that inquiry it can examine any person or persons who conducted or assisted in the investigation. The vexed question is whether the Commission can base its findings on the report of the investigating agency alone if it is satisfied about the correctness of the facts stated and the conclusions arrived at in the report. One point of view (pressed by counsel for the Central Government) is that the entire sub-section (5) would become otiose if the Commission cannot make use of the investigation report as contemplated by sub-section (5). So long as the Commission satisfies itself about its correctness, it can base its findings on the facts stated in the report or the conclusions arrived at by it. Even if the statements of witnesses recorded by the investigation agency are not taken on oath, the Commission can rely on them as substantive material. The opposite view (advanced by counsel for the Chief Minister) is that the Commission can give a finding only on evidence

which according to section 4 of the Act can consist of statements recorded on oath by *viva voce* examination or in the form of affidavits. The Commission cannot act on unsworn testimony. Therefore, the facts found by an investigation agency, from unsworn statements, cannot form the basis for giving any findings by the Commission. All the various aspects relating to the rival contentions have been discussed at some length in the order made by this Commission on 24th October, 1978.[8]

29. The Commission is of the view that sub-section (5) requires a clarificatory amendment. It does appear problematical that the Commission should be able to base its conclusions only on the report of the investigation agency which is meant to assist the Commission and not act as its delegate. Moreover, the inquiry can become more prolonged than curtailed if the Commission is called upon to examine the investigating officers at length and give full opportunity to the parties affected to cross examine them and further to demolish the correctness of the facts and the conclusions stated in the report of satisfy the requirement of the rules of natural justice. The view that the Commission expressed in the above-mentioned order is that the statements recorded by the investigating officer or agency will not be used as substantive material or evidence for basing its findings and that the Commission will not rely on the conclusions in the investigation report alone and use that as substantive material for the purpose of giving its findings. The Commission decided to base its findings mainly on the evidence taken by the Commission itself either by *viva voce* examination or on affidavits. Such evidence certainly included the documents placed on the records of the Commission. In other words, the investigation report would be used for selecting the relevant material for examination by the Commission and not for any other purpose. Thus the machinery contained in section 5A would be utilised for enabling the Commission to do the same work as is being done by the Treasury Solicitor in U.K. What is essential is that all doubts should be removed on the question whether under sub-section (5), the Commission entitled or not to accept the facts and the conclusions in the investigation report without taking the evidence on oath of those witnesses whose statements were recorded by the investigation agency and without allowing and opportunity to the parties affected to cross-examine them.

30. Section 10A provides the penalty for acts calculated to bring the Commission or any member thereof into disrepute. P. Jagan-

mohan Reddy Commission has in its Third Report (regarding Shri Bansi Lal) dealt at length with infirmities in the procedure prescribed by section 10A. According to him, the procedure is long drawn, and by the time a successful prosecution is launched, the Commission may have completed its work, but the Judge, whether retired or sitting, faces the jeopardy of being called as a witness and scurrilously cross-examined in a court in which the complaint is filed. Reference has been made to the position obtaining in England and the views of the Law Commission, as a result of whose recommendation section 10A was inserted by amendment of 1971. There is no need to go over the same ground. This Commission fully shares the view expressed in the Report of the Reddy Commission. It may, however, be pointed out that it is a moot point whether a complaint can be field against a Chief Minister or a Minister who is a public servant without sanction of the State Government owing to the provisions of section 197 of the Civil Procedure Code. That will lead to the astounding result that the Chief Minister may have to sanction his own prosecution.

31. Although the present Commission had to consider the necessity of resorting to the provisions of section 10A only on two occasions, as stated in Part I of the Report, further proceedings were dropped by the Commission for the reasons given therein. But there can be no manner of doubt that section 10A, as it stands, affords very little protection to the Chairman or the Members of a Commission of Inquiry against such attacks either in the press or otherwise, as have been mentioned in the Report of the Reddy Commission. It is absolutely essential that the Commissions appointed under the Act should have the same powers to punish for contempt as the superior courts, even if it becomes necessary to amend Entry 14 of the Concurrent List in the Constitution. Unless that is done, it will become increasingly difficult for High Court or Supreme Court Judges (retired or sitting) to agree to take up an assignment under the Act.

32. Finally, the Commission wishes to emphasise the absolute necessity of a complete review and re-examination of the question how there could be an effective follow-up action on the findings of a Commission of Inquiry. If the expense and labour involved in getting elaborate inquires made by Commissions are only going to add to the numerous reports which have hitherto been given, it will be a most frustrating exercise in futility. The present procedure is neither clear nor leads to any suitable or effective action or result. After the Commission has given its findings, all that can happen is that prosecutions

can be launched on those matters in which it has been found that an offence has been committed which is provided for by some panel statutes, as the Prevention of Corruption Act or the Indian Penal Code, etc. The provisions of the Criminal Procedure Code become applicable for investigation and trial. The police officers having jurisdiction in the State, or the Central Bureau of Investigation in cases which fall within its jurisdiction, have to go through the whole gamut of the various stages of investigation and then initiate proceedings for prosecution in accordance with the statutory provisions. It rests with those officers or agencies to re-assess the evidence which has already been examined by a Commission of Inquiry, and it can legitimately happen that the findings given by a Commission may be set at naught, by the Police making their own assessment as to the chances of success in prosecution, if a trial takes place in court. Meanwhile, even if findings of a serious nature have been given against a holder of high political office, he continues to remain in power and the investigation by the police after the post-Commission stage can be hampered thereby.

33. If the investigation is to be conducted by the State Police against the Chief Minister or a Minister of that State, it will create virtually an impossible situation. The Central Bureau of Investigation, which exercises its powers under the Delhi Special Police Establishment Act, can only hold investigation in those States which have consented, as required by the provisions of that Act, to the members of the Delhi Special Police Establishment exercising powers and jurisdiction in those States. If that consent is withdrawn by a particular State or States, as has been done lately by the States of Andhra Pradesh and Karnataka, the Central Bureau of Investigation will have not authority or power or jurisdiction to carry on any investigation relating to an offence alleged to have been committed in that State. It is, therefore, a matter of urgency that proper legislative measures should be adopted to remove the above anomalous position.

34. Various suggestions have been mooted from time to time as to the consequences which would flow after a Commission of Inquiry set up under section 3 of the Act has given its findings. One suggestion is that proper provision should be made in the Act by which a Minister or Chief Minister against whom findings of a serious nature have been given should be disqualified from being a Member of the Legislature for a specified period, as is the case when in an election

held under the Representation of the Peoples Act a finding is given of Commission of corrupt practice by a candidate at an election. The other suggestion that has been often mooted is that legislation should be made on the same lines as has been done by Sri Lanka by which the findings given by a Commission of Inquiry have to be accepted as final and conclusive, with resultant consequences. It is provided by section 9 of the Special Presidential Commission of Inquiry Law of 1978 that :

> "9. (1) Where a commission finds at the inquiry and reports to the President that any person has been guilty of any act of political victimization, misuse or abuse of power, corruption or any fraudulent act, in relation to any court or tribunal or any public body, or in relation to the administration of any law or the administration of justice, the commission shall recommend whether such person should be made subject to civic disability, and the President shall cause such finding to be published in the Gazette as soon as possible, and direct that such report be published."

All these are matters which deserve the earnest consideration of the Parliament because unless the Act is invested with what may be called some 'fangs' or 'teeth', all the laborious process involved, apart from the heavy expense in the conduct of the inquiry, would lead to no fruitful result. It must not be forgotten that in the present political climate of the country, no person holding a high public office is going to voluntarily resign or demit office simply because a Commission of Inquiry has given a finding against him. In this context, it is note worthy that even with regard to the Lok Pal Bill, the Select Committee is reported to have recommended that the Chief Minister of a State should not be amenable to the jurisdiction of the Lok Pal. In other words, the Lok Pal will have no authority or power to make an inquiry into allegations made against a Chief Minister or Minister in a State, and the only manner in which an inquiry can be held will by means to appointing a Commission of Inquiry under section 3 of the Act. Therefore, if purity and integrity in public life are the main objectives, it would be in the interest of all political parties to evolve by consensus, irrespective of their political alliances or views, a proper mechanism which can be embodied in Parliamentary legislation to ensure that the proceedings of a Commission of Inquiry and the findings given by it do not remain a mere exercise in futility.

Summary of Findings

1. *Allegation No. 1 of Annexure-I* : Disposed of in the First Report of the Commission dated 10-1-1978.

2. *Allegation No. 2 of the Annexure-I* : Whether the Chief Minister had directed auction of excise shops out of turn in a five districts on the eve of the recent Lok Sabha Elections in the month of February 1977, with corrupt motives although the auctions were due in the month of May, 1977, and whether this was done with the object of collecting funds for the Elections.

Findings

There is no material on which it can be found that the Chief Minister had directed auction of excise shops, out of turn, in five districts on the eve of the Lok Sabha election in 1977 with motives which could be called corrupt or with the object of collecting funds for the aforesaid elections, even though the evidence and the material brought on the record may create a suspicion that the said decision was based on extraneous considerations, the nature of which has not come to light.

3. *Allegations No. 3, 4 and 5 of Annexure-I* : Disposed of in the First Report of the Commission dated 10-1-1978.

4. *Allegation No. 6 of Annexure-I* : Whether the following payments were made to M/s. Shankaranarayana Construction Co.:

(i) An *ex-gratia* payment of Rs. 6.37 lakhs in Malaprabha Project;
(ii) Excess payment to the tune of Rs. 12.00 lakhs in Ghataprabha Project with an intention to favour the contractors.

Findings

(i) It has been established that *ex-gratia* payment was made to M/s. Shankar Construction Company in Malaprabha Project amounting to Rs. 6.37 lakhs but it cannot be found that the same was done owing to an intention on the part of the Chief Minister to favour the Contractors.
(ii) It has been established that excess/*ex-gratia* payment was made to M/s. Shankaranarayana Construction Company in Ghataprabha Project amounting to Rs. 12.55 lakhs but that

cannot be attributed to any intention on the part of the Chief Minister to favour the Contractors.

5. *Allegation No. 7 of Annexure-I* : Whether any misappropriation of funds and fabrication of accounts of the Social Welfare Departments was made with the connivance of the then Minister Shri N. Rachaiah to the extent of Rs. 30.00 lakhs and whether any fraud was practised in connection with the said matter.

Findings

(i) It is fully established that Shri Rachaiah who was the Minister for Social Welfare at the material time, was aware that serious irregularities had been committed involving dealings running into lakhs of rupees in the Social Welfare Department, he neither took the trouble of looking into any matter himself nor did he take any action on his own to stop those irregularities which were being blatantly committed.

(ii) There is, however, no cogent material on which it can be found that Shri Rachaiah was either personally responsible for, or wilfully connived at, any misappropriation of funds of fabrication of accounts in the Department of Social Welfare to the extent of rupees 30 lakhs, as also the Commission of any fraud relating thereto.

6. *Allegation No. 8 of Annexure-I* : Whether appointment was made of fictitious persons as dealers in sandal soap by Mysore Sales International under the orders of the Chief Minister and the Minister for Industry and payment was made of huge amounts by way of Commission.

Findings

(i) It has been conclusively established that appointment was made of 51 persons as dealers during the period 30-1-1974 to 12-12-1975, who were paid substantial amount of commission aggregating to about Rs. 5 lakhs. The appointment of these dealers was nominal and in name only and most of them neither had any qualifications from the point of view of business or experience or local influence for being appointed as dealers. The basis on which commission was paid was also quite unusual and had no nexus or connection with the work which was actually done of canvassing by these dealers.

(ii) Although there is a great deal of suspicion that a number of dealers who were well known to Shri S.M. Krishna, the Minister for Industries were appointed as dealers because of the influence exercised by him and on account of his report and understanding with Shri K.M. Shetty, the Managing Director, but it has not been conclusively proved that he alone was responsible for those appointments being made.

(iii) The Chief Minister is not proved to have influenced the appointment of these dealers in any way.

7. *Allegation No. 9 of Annexure-I* : Whether gross misuse of power and position was made by Shri H.M. Channa Bassappa, formerly Minister incharge of Public Works Department and Electricity (now Minister of Health) in converting the residential site which he got allotted to him by the Trust Board into a commercial site and starting a company with his family members as directors.

Findings

Although Shri H.M. Channabasappa might have committed breach of the terms and conditions of the Lease-cum-Sale Agreement as also of the provisions of the Mysore Town and Country Planning Act, etc., it cannot be found that there was any misuse of power or position by him as a Minister in the matter of converting the residential site which had been allotted to him in the Javanagar Extension, into a commercial site.

8. *Allegation No. 10 of Annexure-I* : Whether any favouritism was shown or whether there was any corruption in the purchase of new tyres and in body building contract of the new chassis by Karnataka State Road Transport Corporation under the undue influence of the Chief Minister and the Minister for Transport Shri Aziz Sait.

Findings

(i) It has been established that during the period December 1975 to October 1976, Shri Mohammed Ali, who was the Transport Minister (and not Shri Aziz Sait), took undue interest in the purchase of tyres from M/s. Modi Rubber Ltd. and that favouritism as shown by him to that concern in the matter of purchase of the following new tyres:

(a) 2250 tyres purchased by KSRTC on trial basis,

(b) 6900 tyres purchased by KSRTC on regular basis. (This figure includes 2250 tyres purchased in bulk during the months of October/November, 1976).

(ii) No act of corruption, however, has been established against Shri Mohammed Ali in the matter of purchase of the tyres.

(iii) There is nothing of any consequence that has been established against the Chief Minister and it has not been shown that he had committed any act of favouritism or corruption with regard to the purchase of new tyres by the Karnataka State Road Transport Corporation.

(iv) Nothing could be discovered from the records or from any other material regarding the allegation relating to body-building contracts for new chassis.

9. *Allegation No. 11 of Annexure-I* : Whether there was any nepotism and favouritism and misuse of power by the Chief Minister and the Minister of Transport in the matter of nationalisation of contract carriages and wilfully benefiting certain parties with whom the Chief Minister's second son-in-law was a partner.

Findings

It has not been established that any nepotism and favouritism was exercised or there was misuse of power by the Chief Minister and the Minister of Transport in the matter of nationalisation of contract carriages with the object of wilfully benefiting any private party or parties. It is also not provide that the Chief Minister's second son-in-law, Shri M.C. Mohan, was connected in any way, with the concern of Shri D.P. Sharma, which held majority of the All-India permits, when the legislation for nationalisation of contract carriages was introduced or the Karnataka Contract Carriages (Acquisition) Act, 1966, was enacted.

10. *Allegation No. 12 of Annexure-I* : Disposed of in the First Report of the Commission dated 10-1-1978.

11. *Allegation No. 13 of Annexure-I* : Whether an undue favour was shown to M/s. Balaji Engineering Construction Company by accepting the tender for construction of houses under Housing and Urban Development Corporation's Low Income Group Scheme in Dumlur Layout by the Bangalore Development Authority, which is under the administrative control of the Chief Minister.

Findings

(i) It has not been proved that any undue favour was shown to M/s. Balaji Engineering Construction Company with regard to the tender for construction of houses under the Housing & Urban Development Corporation's low-income group housing scheme in Dumlur lay-out by the Bangalore Development Authority which was under the administrative control of the Chief Minister.

(ii) As a matter of fact, it was the tender of M/s. Bangalore Construction Company which was accepted and regarding which no illegality or irregularity had been committed. There is absolutely no material which establishes that any tender of M/s. Balaji Construction Company was accepted for the construction of any house under the HUDCO LIG Scheme in the Dumlur lay-out either in the first or in the second phase.

12. *Allegation No. 14 of Annexure-I* : Disposed of in the First Report of the Commission dated 10-1-1978.

13. *Allegation No. 15 of Annexure-I* : Whether any misuse of power was committed, or any corruption committed, by Shri D.K. Naikar, Minister for Municipal Administration, with regard to the grant of land to Bhoruka Textile Mills in Hubli-Darwar Corporation Area.

Findings

It has not been established that any misuse of power or that any act of corruption was committed by Shri D.K. Naikar, the Minister for Municipal Administration, in the matter of grant of land to M/s. Bhoruka Textile Mills in the Hubli-Dharwar Corporation Area.

14. *Allegation No. 1 of Annexure-II* : Disposed of in the First Report of the Commission dated 10-1-1978.

Allegation No. 16 of the Schedule to the notification dated 8-11-1977 : "Whether the grant of land in S. No. 15 of Bommenhalli Village, Nelamangala Taluk, Bangalore District, was made contrary to rules?"

Findings

The Commission did not proceed to make any inquiry into this allegation because no specific allegations were filed either by the Memorialists or any party or person in compliance with the Order may by the Commission dated 18-4-1978.

15. *Allegation No. 2 of Annexure-II* : Allotment of 4 large valuable house sites in the most posh locality of Bangalore, Raj Mahal Vilas Extension, to Shri Devaraj Urs and his family members in supersession of the rightful claims of other applicants.

Findings

Although the rules relating to allotment of sites by the City Improvement Trust Board, were not properly and strictly followed and a number of irregularities were committed by the Board in matter of allotment of site No. 15 in Rajmahal Vilas Extension to the daughter or daughters of the Chief Minister, there was no evidence on which it could be found that the Chief Minister or any other Minister of the State of Karnataka had been guilty of corruption, nepotism, favouritism or misuse of governmental power in connection therewith.

Allegation No. 17 of the Schedule to the notification dated 8-11-1977 : Whether sites in Rajmahal Vilas layouts were irregularly allotted.

Findings

(i) There was no material or evidence on which it could be found (and this matter as conceded even by the counsel for the Chief Minister and his daughters) that Shri Kadidal Manjappa, who was the Chief Minister of the erstwhile State of Mysore for a short period in 1956, had been allotted a site in the Palace Orchards in 1960 by contravening the rules and regulations or by use of any political influence by him.

(ii) There was no material showing that any allotment of a site had been made in the Palace Orchards to Shri Virendra Patil. He had only purchased a site in that locality in the year 1972, where he had constructed in a house. As a matter of fact, Smt. Nagarathna withdrew the allegation made in her earlier affidavit with regard to Shri Virendra Patil.

(iii) As regards the allotment of a site to Shri Rama Krishna Hegde, there was no evidence to show that he exercised any political influence as a Minister, in the matter of allotment of a site to him in the Rajmahal Vilas Extension. He had been allotted a site (No. 229) in that locality in exchange for a site which had been allotted to him in the Cambridge Lay-out. The procedural irregularity of making the allotment before he had actually surrendered the site allotted to him earlier, could not be of much consequence as it is abundantly proved from the facts relating to allotment of site No. 15 in Rajmahal Vilas Extension that the Board authorities were not strictly and properly following the requirements of the statutory rules relating to allotment of sites.

16. *Allegation No. 3 of Annexure-II* : Undue favours shown to Messrs Nirmala Engineering Construction Company, by releasing Government funds in spite of the fact that the concerned Minister had taken a decision to prosecute the firm on the basis of the recommendations of the Vigilance Commission.

Findings

It has been conclusively proved that the Chief Minister went out of his way and misused his powers and authority in superseding the orders of the Ministers incharge by making his own orders with the intention of benefiting the firm.

Allegation No. 1 of the Schedule to the Notification dated 8-11-1977: Whether improper or excessive payment was made to Messrs. Nirmala Engineering Construction Company, in respect of the contracts awarded to them by the Government of Karnataka and the Karnataka Urban Water Supply and Drainage Board for lift irrigation or water supply scheme.

No inquiry has been made into this allegation in view of the order made by this Commission dated 18-4-1978 as no one preferred any specific allegations in compliance with that order.

17. *Allegation No. 4 of Annexure-II* : Excess payment of Rs. 98.86 lakhs to Messrs Balaji Engineering Company, in Hemavathi Project, in contravention of the terms of the contract with a view to favouring the contractor.

Allegation No. 2 of the Schedule to the Notification dated 8-11-1977: Whether any improper or excessive payment as made to Messrs. Balaji Engineering and Construction Works Ltd. in respect of the contracts awarded to them for—

(i) the construction of the right bank earth dam of the Hemavathi Project from Chainage No. 7890′ to 9510′;
(ii) the construction of the right bank irrigation sluice of the Hemavathi Dam;
(iii) the construction of the left bank irrigation sluice of the Hemavathi Dam;
(iv) the construction of the masonry dam of the Hemavathi Project from Chainage No. 4400′ to 5740′ including the overflow section and the protective work;
(v) the construction of the spillway dam of the Hemavathi Project.

Findings

It has not been established that excess or improper payment of Rs. 98.86 lakhs was made to M/s. Balaji Engineering Company in Hemavathi Project on account of any favour shown to the Contractors by the Chief Minister.

18. *Allegation No. 5 of Annexure-II* : Undue favour shown to Messrs Nechupadam Construction Company in Hemavathi Project, by accepting the highest tender with an intent to benefit the contractors and involving excess payment to the extent of Rs. 3.5 lakhs.

Allegation No. 3 of the Scheduled to the Notification dated 8-11-1977 : Whether any improper or excessive payment was made or undue favour shown to Messrs Nechupadam Construction Company in respect of the contract awarded to them for the construction of the Hemavathi Right Bank Earth Dam from chainage 2025m to 2405m and chainage 1750m to 2025 m.

Findings

(i) M/s. Nechupadam Construction Company was the second-lowest tenderer and its tender was accepted on the recommendation of the M.I.P.C.B. which involved excess payment to the extent of Rs. 4.33 lakhs as stated in the audit report for the year 1972-73.

(ii) It has not been established that it was the Chief Minister who showed undue favour to M/s. Nechupadam Construction Company in Hemavathi Project in the matter of acceptance of its tender.

19. *Allegation No. 6 of Annexure-II* : Excess payment of Rs. 1 crore to Messrs TICIL Contractors, in Kali Hydel Project for the benefit of the Contractors.

Allegation No. 5 in the Schedule to the Notification dated 18-11-1977 : Whether any improper or excessive payment was made or undue favour shown to Messrs. TICIL in respect of the contracts awarded to them for—

(i) the construction of the head race tunnel from the Bommenahalli pick up dam to the surge point;

(ii) the construction of the surge tank and the pressure shaft.

Findings

It has not been possible to find from the material on record that any improper or excessive payment was made or undue favour by the Chief Minister or any other Minister shown to M/s. TICIL in respect of the contracts awarded to the Company for construction of head race tunnel, surge tanks and pressure shaft.

20. *Allegation No. 7 of Annexure-II* : Whether about 5,000 tonnes of paddy, purchased by the Government of Karnataka from the Tamil Nadu Government on Government-to-Government basis, was allowed to be marketed by a private party, Shri H.R. Atheeq Ahmed, without the knowledge of the Food Department, instead of the Mysore State Co-operative Marketing Federation as was earlier agreed, with the sole intent of benefiting the private party.

Finding

It stands conclusively established that it was owing to acts of favouritism and misuse of governmental power on the part of the Chief Minister that 1,000 tonnes of paddy from out of 5,000 tonnes of paddy allotted by the Government of Tamil Nadu to the Government of Karnataka on Government-to-Government basis was allowed to be marketed by a private party, viz., Shri H.R. Atheeq Ahmed, who sold the same in open market and presumably gained pecuniary advantage thereby.

Allegation No. 18 of the Schedule to Notification dated 8-11-1977 : Whether the purchase of one thousand tonnes of paddy from Tamil Nadu by Shri Atheeq Ahmed, Proprietor of the Mandya Rice Mills, Mandya at the instance of the State Government and the subsequent disposal thereof were adverse to the interests of the State.

Finding

The purchase of 1,000 tonnes of paddy by Shri Atheeq Ahmed from Tamil Nadu in the manner in which it was done and its subsequent disposal were certainly prejudicial to the interests of the State inasmuch as the paddy had been given by the Tamil Nadu Government for the purpose of relieving scarcity conditions in the State of Karnataka, and it was allowed to be utilized by a private businessman for his personal gain.

21. *Allegation No. 8 of Annexure-II* : Undue favour shown to a fictitious cooperative society in regard to conversion of 270 acres of agricultural land called 'Dinshaw Estate' into non-agricultural purpose in violation of the mandatory provisions of the Land Reforms Act and the Land Revenue Act.

Findings

(i) Although it has been established that the Chief Minister recorded a minute in the case of the B.E.L. Cooperative Housing Society, which was bound to influence the statutory authority namely, the Special Deputy Commissioner (and which in fact, did influence him) who had to the power to grant the sanction for conversion of land under section 95 of the Karnataka Land Revenue Act, 1964, no inquiry has been made with regard to any matter relating to that society for reasons which have been set out in the report.

(ii) Even though the Industrial Employees Housing Cooperative Society had been duly registered as a Cooperative Society under the relevant statutory provisions and could not be legally regarded as fictitious, it did not consist of persons who were industrial employees and was managed mainly by private individuals who wanted to make huge profits out of the sale of lands after obtaining the sanction for conversion from agricultural use to non-agricultural uses under section 95 of the Karnataka Land Revenue Act, 1964.

(iii) The Commission is satisfied that one of the main reasons for grant of sanction for conversion to the Industrial Employees Housing Cooperative Society by the Special Deputy Commissioner, was the sanction granted in the case of the B.E.L. Cooperative Housing Society. But there is no document or any other material in the official files that have been made available to the Commission from which it can be inferred that the Chief Minister made any order or interfered at any stage in the grant of sanction to the Industrial Employees Housing Cooperative Society. If the file, which is stated to have been destroyed, had been available, the Commission would have been in a position to find whether the Chief Minister had exercised any influence, as alleged, in the matter.

Allegation No. 20 of the Schedule to the Notification dated the 8-11-1977 : Whether the conversion of land owned by Shri C.H. Dinshaw and family in Narasipura village, Bangalore, North Taluk (known as 'Dinshaw Estate') as non-agricultural land was not in accordance with the rules.

Finding

As at present advised and on the material available to the Commission, it is not in a position to conclusively find that the conversion of land owned by Shri C.H. Dinshaw and family in Narasipura village, Bangalore, known as the Dinshaw Estate, for use as non-agricultural land, had been made in contravention of the statutory provisions and the rules.

22. *Allegation No. 9 of Annexure-II* : Whether undue favour was

shown to one Ghanshyam in the sale of 2,500 ton of Bajra at the rate of Rs. 73.50 per quintal without calling for tenders and allowing Shri Ghanshyam to sell the Bajra in the State of Maharashtra at the rate of Rs. 125 per quintal during the time of droughts in Karnataka.

Allegation No. 6 in the Schedule to the Notification dated 8-11-1977 : Whether any undue favour was shown to Messrs Ghanshyam Commercial Company Limited, in the sale of 2,500 tonnes of Bajra at the rate of Rs. 73.50 per quintal in 1972.

Findings

(i) It is established that the Chief Minister went out of his way and showed undue favour to M/s. Ghanshyam Commercial Company, Bangalore, when he ordered on 28-6-1972 that the offer of that firm for purchase of 14378 quintals of Bajra at the rate of Rs. 73.50 per quintal should be accepted by reversing the orders which had been passed earlier by the Minister of State for Food in consultation with him on 26-6-1972 by which the offer of that firm had been rejected and it had been decided to call for tenders. Even if tenders had not been called, the loss caused to the State Exchequer was to the tune of Rs. 18,943 in view of the firm offer of M/s. T. Venkatachalapathi Setty & Co. to purchase the Bajra at the rate of Rs. 75.40 per quintal.

(ii) The quantity of Bajra which was sold in the State of Maharashtra was 7160 quintals out of 9970 quintals which had actually been lifted by M/s. Ghanshyam Commercial Company, the price realised being Rs. 82.50 per quintal. It is not possible to give the actual rate at which Bajra was sold in that State.

23. *Allegation No. 10 of Annexure II* : Whether undue favour was shown, or concession was made, to M/s. Karekar & Sundaram, Architects, in regard to the preparation of designs for remodelling the K.R. Market in supersession of the order of the concerned Minister.

Findings

(i) From the material and evidence on record of the Commission it is not possible to come to any firm conclusion that the Chief

Minister showed undue favour or concession to M/s. Karekar & Sundaram, Architects, in regard to the preparation of designs for remodelling of the K.R. Market, Bangalore.

(ii) It has not been found that the contract for the preparation of designs for remodelling of the K.R. Market, Bangalore, was awarded to the aforesaid Firms of architects in supersession of the order of the concerned Minister.

Allegation No. 19 of the Schedule to the Notification dated 8-11-1977 : Whether the contract for the preparation of models and designs for the remodelling of the K.R. Market, Bangalore was irregularly awarded to Messrs Karekar & Sundaram.

Finding

No particular irregularity has been found in the matter of the award of the contract for the preparation of designs for remodelling of the K.R. Market, Bangalore, to M/s. Karekar and Sundaram, architects.

24. *Allegation No. 11 of Annexure-II* : Whether undue favour was shown, or concession was made, to M/s. Shah Construction Co., contractors, in Upper Krishna Project at Alamatti.

Finding

It has not been proved that any undue favour or concession was shown to M/s. Shah Construction Company in Upper Krishna Project by the Chief Minister in the matter of removal of machinery from the site.

Allegation No. 8 of the Schedule to the Notification dated 8-11-1977 : Whether any improper or excessive payment was made or any undue favour was shown to M/s. Shah Construction Co. in the settlement of their claims for the contract awarded to them for the construction of the Alamatti Dam.

No inquiry was made into this allegation as no specific allegations were preferred either by the Memorialists or a by any one else in compliance with the order of the Commission dated 18-4-1978.

25. *Allegation No. 12 of Annexure-II* : Whether undue favour was shown to M/s. Krishna Flour Mills in granting valuable land in Bangalore City, which land was meant for children's park, at a nominal rent by overruling the orders of the concerned Minister.

Allegation No. 7 in the Schedule to the Notification dated 8-11-1977 : Whether any undue favour was shown to Messrs. Krishna Flour Mills in respect of the lease of the land next to its premises, measuring 200′ X 200′ for a period of 30 years.

Findings

(i) It stands established that—

(a) a land measuring 200′ X 200′ was granted by the Corporation of the City of Bangalore to M/s. Krishna Industries Private Ltd. on lease for a period of 30 years on the terms and conditions mentioned in the lease deed; and

(b) the above area had been earmarked for an auditorium in the Sports Complex which was to be constructed in Jakkarayanakere tank bed situate in a very important locality and the grant of the lease was made in contravention of the declared and settled policy as well as positive instructions issued by the Government from time to time not to lease out Corporation lands reserved for public purposes to private individuals or institutions.

(ii) It stands proved that it was under the influence or pressure exercised by the Chief Minister that Shri B. Basavalingappa, the Minister concerned, changed his previous order by which he had declined to accord sanction to the resolution of the Corporation dated 31-10-1972 for leasing the land to M/s. Krishna Industries Private Ltd.

(iii) Although the act of the Chief Minister amounted to favouritism as well as abuse of authority, Shri Basavalingappa also allowed himself to be influenced by the Chief Minister which showed lack of that sense of responsibility and propriety which is expected of a Cabinet Minister.

26. *Allegation No. 13 of Annexure-II* : Whether there was any misappropriation of funds of the Karnataka State Film Industries Development Corporation, to the tune of Rs. 10 lakhs, when the Chief Minister himself was the Chairman of that Corporation and whether the business of the Corporation was conducted with intent to defraud that Corporation, its members, creditors or any other person

or otherwise for a fraudulent of unlawful purpose.

Allegation No. 21 in the Schedule to the notification dated 8-11-1977: Whether any irregularities or improprieties have been committed the administration of the Karnataka Film Development Corporation since 1971.

Findings

(i) During the period when the Chief Minister functioned as the Chairman of the K.S.F.I.D.C. there is no material or evidence on which the Commission can give a finding that during his tenure there had been any act of misappropriation of funds of K.S.F.I.D.C., either by him or by any other person with his knowledge or connivance; nor can it be found that the business of the Corporation had been so conducted that there was an intention to defraud the Corporation, its members and creditors or that it was conducted with fraudulent and unlawful purpose.

(ii) Nothing has been established to show that any irregularity or improprieties were committed in the administration of the K.S.F.I.D.C. by the Chief Minister or any other Minister or former Minister, so far as the administration of the Corporation was concerned.

27. *Allegation No. 14 of Annexure-II* : Whether any undue favour was shown to M/s. Poornima Electronics, Bangalore, in the purchase of electronic equipment (inter-com) by superseding the recommendation of the Head of the Department and orders of the concerned Minister.

Finding

The Chief Minister went out of his way and showed undue favour to M/s. Poornima Electronics, Bangalore, in the matter of purchase of 300 sets of electronic equipment. This constituted an act of favouritism on his part.

Allegation No.9 of the Schedule to the Notification dated 8-11-1977: Whether any undue favour was shown to M/s. Poornima Electronics in the placing of orders on them or supply of electronic equipments like Inter-com, etc.

Finding

The Commission did not proceed to make any inquiry into this allegation because no specific allegations were field either by the Memorialists or any party or person in compliance with the Order made by the Commission dated 18-4-1978.

28. *Allegation No. 15 of Annexure-II* : Whether any misappropriation of the funds of Karnataka State Co-operative Marketing Federation to the extent of several crores of rupees was made by Shri H.S. Srikantiah, Minister of State for Home, when he was the President of that Federation and whether the business of the Federation was conducted with intent to defraud that Federation its members, creditors or any other person or otherwise for a fraudulent or unlawful purpose.

Allegation No. 10 of Schedule to the Notification dated 8-11-1977 : Whether there was any misappropriation or fraud in the dealings of the State Co-operative Marketing Federation during the period 1971-72 and 1972-73.

Findings

(i) It has not been proved that any misappropriation of the funds of the Karnataka State Cooperative Marketing Federation (K.S.C.M.F.) was made by Shri H.S. Srikantiah, Minister of State for Home, when he was President of that Federation.

(ii) There is no material or evidence on which it can be found that the business of the K.S.C.M.F. was so conducted by Shri H.S. Srikantiah that there was any intention to defraud the Federation, its members, creditors or other persons, although with regard to the loss of cash receipts amounting to Rs. 11 lakhs which was not realised, fraud might have been committed. But the responsibility for the same cannot be laid on Shri H.S. Srikantiah, President of the Federation.

(iii) As regards the sub-allegation of favouritism in the matter of appointment of Architect as also the acceptance of the tender of M/s. Srinivasa Company, it does not appear to be strictly covered by the Allegations under reference. At any rate, it has not been found that any favouritism was exercised by Shri Srikantiah in these matters.

(iv) As regards the sub-allegation relating to extra payment of transportation rates for transportation of fertilisers, it has not been established that Shri Srikantiah alone was responsible for the payment of the extra amount of 7 paise per tonne.

(v) So far as the *ad hoc* decision to refund recoveries made from contractors for shortages during transit at single and double value of cost is concerned, there is on material on which it can be held that Shri Srikantiah was responsible for favouring the transporters regarding the refund of the amount deducted on account of shortages.

(vi) Regarding the sub-allegation in respect of loss of cash receipts amounting to Rs. 11 lakhs, etc., the responsibility cannot be laid solely on Shri Srikantiah for passing of the consent decree and consequent loss. It may, however, be observed that before approving of the proposal to have a consent decree passed in which the total amount would have been payable in not less than 10 years, Shri Srikantiah did not display or show that wariness and sense of responsibility which is normally expected from a President of a body like the K.S.C.M.F. as he made no attempt to find out any details or particulars from the General Manager or anyone else before agreeing to the consent decree being passed. At the same time, the Board also approved of that action, and therefore, Shri Srikantiah could not be blamed for the loss which resulted from the passing of the consent decree.

29. *Allegation No. 16 of Annexure-II* : Whether any undue favour was shown to Shri Satyapal by the Minister of Transport Shri Mohamed Ali, by accepting the once rejected tender of Shri Satyapal in leasing out its building for canteen in Karnataka State Road Transport Corporation Bus Stand, Mysore, and whether any undue favour was shown by the same Minister to Shri Satyapal's son Shri Prem Kumar, in leasing out its retiring rooms of the Karnataka State Road Transport Corporation in Mysore.

Findings

(i) It has not been established that any undue favour was shown by Shri Mohamed Ali the Minister of Transport to Shri Satyapal in the matter of leasing out of the KSRTC building for canteen at Mysore or that any such favour was shown by him regarding the leasing out of the retiring rooms of the KSRTC in Mysore to Shri Satyapal's son Shri Prem Kumar.

(ii) Shri Mohamed Ali, however, did not exercise due care and caution which should have been normally exercised by him as a Minister while disposing of the representation made by Shri Satyapal dated 8-7-1975.

Allegation No. 11 and 12 of the Schedule to the Notification dated 8-11-1977: Whether any undue favour has been shown by the Government or the Karnataka Road Transport Corporation in leasing out the building in the Karnataka Road Transport Corporation bus stand at Mysore for a Canteen at Mysore.

"Whether any undue favour was shown by Government or the Karnataka Road Transport Corporation in leasing out resting rooms in the Karnataka Road Transport Corporation in Mysore to Shri Prem Kumar."

It is not open to the Commission under the terms of the notification dated 23-5-1977, to inquire whether any undue favour or favouritism was shown either by the Government or the Karnataka State Road Transport Corporation including its Chairman as well as other officers in leasing out the canteen to Shri Satyapal or the retiring rooms to Shri Prem Kumar. It will be for the State Government to take such steps as it may be advised to have an inquiry held in these matters.

30. *Allegation No. 17 of Annexure-II* : Whether any undue favour was shown to four firms, namely, All India Agencies, Vidyut Engineering Co., Trishul Enterprises and Mysore Woods, in purchasing furniture valued at Rs. 29.00 lakhs in 1973-74 under I.P. Project by the Minister for Health, Shri H. Siddaveerappa.

Findings

(i) There is a no material on which it can be found that orders for the purchase of furniture for the Health Department for the years 1972-73 and 1973-74 were placed at exorbitant rates.

(ii) It is not clear whether the P.W.D. (Buildings Division) maintained any approved list of contractors or suppliers from whom purchases of furniture were to be made. At any rate, keeping in view the entirety of the circumstances, the action taken by the various officers concerned and the High-powered Committee in making the purchases, appeared to be justified.

Allegation No. 23 in the Schedule to the Notification dated 8-11-1977 : Whether orders for the purchase of furniture for the Health Department for the years 1972-73 and 1973-74 were placed at exorbitant rates with firms who were neither furniture dealers nor approved P.W.D. Contractors/Suppliers.

The Commission did not proceed to make any inquiry into this allegation because no specific allegations were field either by the Memorialists or any party or person in compliance with the Order made by the Commission dated 18-4-1978.

31. *Allegation No. 18 of Annexure-II* : Whether any undue favour was shown by the Minister of State for Small-Scale Industries, Shri Koujalgi in 1974, in the issue of Essentiality Certificate to parties many of whom were fictitious and bogus.

Findings

It has not been established that any undue favour was shown by the Minister of State for Industries, Shri Koujalgi, in 1974 in the issue of Essentiality Certificates to parties many of whom were fictitious and bogus. However, there is sufficient evidence which shows that he was aware of the complaints relating to the serious irregularities which had been committed in the matter of the issue of aforesaid certificates. But the Minister does not appear to have taken any action in the matter to ensure that these were not issued to bogus and fictitious persons.

Allegation No. 24 of the Schedule to the Notification dated 8-11-1977 : Whether Essentiality Certificates for stainless steel were issued to bogus firms or fictitious persons during the period 1st March, 1974 to 30th June, 1974.

The Commission did not proceed to make any inquiry into this allegation because no specific allegations were field either by the Memorialists or any party or person in compliance with the Order made by the Commission dated 18-4-1978.

32. *Allegation No. 19 of Annexure-II* : Whether undue favour was shown by the Chief Minister and the Minister for Transport, Shri Aziz Sait in 1973-74 to M/s. Fargo in buying 150 chassis against the

advice of the Chief Mechanical Engineer of the Karnataka State Road Transport Corporation.

Allegation No. 25 in the Schedule to the Notification dated 8-11-1977: Whcther the purchase of Fargo and Bedford Chassis by KSRTC in August 1972 was against the Corporation's interest.

Findings

(i) As regards allegation No. 19 of Annexure II to the notification dated 23-5-77, it has not been proved that any undue favour was shown by the Chief Minister and the Minister of Transport Shri Aziz Sait in 1973-74 to any manufacture or dealer in respect of 150 chassis of Fargo make. In fact, ultimately these chassis were never bought.

(ii) The finding in Allegation No. 25 of the Schedule to the notification dated 8-11-1977 is that there is nothing to show that the purchase of Fargo and Bedford chassis by KSRTC in August 1972 was against the Corporation's interest.

33. *Allegation No. 20 of Annexure-II* : Whether any undue favour was shown by the Minister of Industries and Commerce Shri S.M. Krishna, in allotting of paper, cement and steel of the State-owned industries to non-traditional dealers/agents including his kith and kin.

Findings

It has not been found that any undue favour was shown by Shri S.M. Krishna, the Minister of Industries and Commerce, in the allotment of cement and steel produced by VISL to non-traditional dealers and agents including his kith and kin. But he certainly misused his authority as a Minister in making notings which virtually amounted to orders and directions, on the applications of persons whose list is given in the report.

Allegation Nos. 26 and 27 of the Schedule to the notification dated 8-11-1977 : Whether the appointments of the agents, sub-agents and dealers during the years 1972-77 by the Visvesvaraya Iron and Steel Limited, Bhadravathi for the distribution of steel and cement were adverse to the Company's interest.

"Whether the appointment of agents, sub-agents and dealers for the years 1972-77 by the Mysore Paper Mills Limited, Bhadravathi for the distribution of paper were adverse to the Company's interest."

No inquiry was made into these allegations for the reasons stated in para 1 and consequently, no findings can be given.

34. *Allegation No. 21 of Annexure-II* : Whether an excess payment of Rs. 30.00 lakhs was made to M/s. Shankaranarayan Construction Company in regard to the construction of combined Board Administrative Building Complex at Bangalore over and above the contract rates.

Allegation No. 4 of Schedule to the notification dated 8-11-1977 : Whether any improper or excessive payments was made or undue favour shown to Messrs Shankaranarayan Construction Company in respect of the contract awarded to them for the construction of the combined Board Administrative Division Building.

Findings

(i) It has not been found that the Chief Minister or any other Minister in the State of Karnataka was guilty of corruption, nepotism, favouritism or misuse of Governmental power in the matter of any excess payment made to M/s. Shankaranarayan Construction Company relating to the construction of combined Board Administrative building complex at Bangalore over and above the contract rates. The actual amount which was paid in excess was Rs. 14,13,303.00 and that was done pursuant to a decision taken when the State of Karnataka had been placed under what is generally called the President's Rule.

(ii) Another amount of Rs. 3,36,151.02 was paid on account of certain additional items that were executed but which were not included in the original tender. Nothing objectionable has been found against anyone with regard to the payment of this amount. There is no material on which it can be found that any improper or excess payment was made to the Contractors.

35. *Allegation No. 22 of Annexure-II* : Whether any excess payment was made to M/s. Balaji Engineering Company to the tune of Rs. 80.00 lakhs in Harangi Project with an intent to favour the contractor.

Allegation No. 2(vi) of the Schedule to the notification

dated 8-11-1977 : Whether any improper or excessive payment was made to M/s. Balaji Engineering and Construction Works Ltd. in respect of the contracts awarded to them for:

* * * * * *

(vi) the construction of the masonry dam of the Harangi Project.

Findings

(i) The excess cost to the state exchequer which resulted from entrustment of balance works in Harangi Project to M/s. Balaji Engineering Company amounted to Rs. 35.09 lakhs as stated in the audit report for the year 1973-74 and not Rs. 80 lakhs as stated in the allegation.

(ii) The Commission has not been able to find that the aforesaid payment was made owing to any intention on the part of the Chief Minister to favour the Contractors.

36. *Allegation No. 23 of Annexure-II* : Whether Shri K.H. Patil, the then Minister for Agriculture and Forest, was guilty of any misuse of power of undue favouritism in relation to Hukkeri Textile Mills or Gadag Co-operative Textile Mills, or both.

Allegation No. 13 in the schedule to the notification dated 8-11-1977: Whether the funds of the Agro Industries Corporation were wrongly diverted to the Gadag Co-operative Textiles Mills, Hulkoti, Gadag, Dharwar District.

Findings

(i) it is not proved that Shri K.H. Patil, the then Minister for Agriculture and Forests was guilty or any misuse of power or undue favouritism in relation to Gadag Cooperative Textile Mill Ltd., Hulkoti. The Hukkery Textile Mills does not come into the picture at all.

(ii) It is not established that the funds of the Agro Industries Corporation Ltd., were wrongly diverted to the Gadag Cooperative Textile Mill, Hulkoti. The word 'wrongly' can only be understood in the context as meaning wrongfully, which would involve some illegal or dishonest act.

37. *Allegation No. 24 of Annexure-II* : Whether any undue favour was shown or any corruption committed by Shri Chikke Gowda the then Minister for Animal Husbandry and Agriculture in relation to the payment of a sum of Rs. 3.00 lakhs to M/s. Navarasa Fertilizers; and in getting deposited funds of BAFCO and Karnataka Dairy Corporation to the tune of Rs. 50 lakhs in Southern Indian Bank against the mandatory rules relating to deposit of funds in nationalised banks; and whether Varalakshmi Cotton Seeds were indiscriminately sold outside the State at the instance of Shri Chikke Gowda for some consideration resulting in heavy loss to the growers; and whether Shri Dwarkinath and Shri Nanjaiah were appointed by the Minister as Director of Agriculture and Director of Animal Husbandry to suit his motive for making monetary gains; and further whether Shri Chikke Gowda received huge amounts privately as commission from Messrs Vulcan Laval and Larsen and Toubro through their agents Mr. V.V. Parthasarthy, Mrs. Savla and Mr. John, in relation to purchase of machinery by the Agriculture and Animal Husbandry Departments.

Findings

(i) *Re : Purchase of Navaras Foliar Fertiliser*

The facts that have been established may create a good deal of suspicion that Shri Chikke Gowda who was Minister for Agriculture and Animal Husbandry, went out of his way and by-passed the established procedure in the matter of orders which were placed on the Panchjanya Enterprises for purchase of large quantities of Navaras Foliar Fertiliser for "trials", but it cannot be said with absolute certainty that he acted purely out of motive of favouritism and that the merits of the proposal for the purchase of the said fertiliser were not take into consideration by him.

(ii) *Re : Investments of funds of BAFCO and Karnataka Dairy Development Corporation*

It has not been found that any favour was shown by Shri Chikke Gowda, Minister for Agriculture and Animal Husbandry, in the matter of deposit of funds belonging to BAFCO or of the Karnataka Dairy Development Corporation, in South Indian Bank Limited.

(iii) *Re : Varalakshmi Seeds*

(a) Shri Chikke Gowda was primarily responsible for the decision relating to Varalakshmi Cotton Seeds which resulted in a loss which was estimated at Rs. 1,20,14,000 in the case of the seeds which were to be sold by the Karnataka Agro Seeds Corporation and Rs. 1,36,65,082 which were to be sold by the Karnataka Cooperative Seeds Marketing Federation. The final figures about the actual loss incurred cannot be stated with certainty.

(b) It has been established that Parent or Foundation Varalakshmi Cotton Seeds were sold under the orders of Shri Chikke Gowda in a most irregular manner and contrary to the settled policy of not selling parent seeds outside the State of Karnataka so as to avoid substantial loss to the State. It is however difficult to give any estimate of the loss so suffered, if any.

(c) It cannot be found that Shri Chikke Gowda received any consideration in any transaction relating to Varalakshmi Cotton Seeds.

(iv) *Re : Re-appointment of Sarvshri Dwarkinath and Nanjaiah*

It has been fully proved that Shri Chikke Gowda committee acts of favouritism in the matter of the appointment of Sarvshri Dwarkinath and Nanjaiah as Director of Agriculture and Director of Animal Husbandry, respectively.

(v) *Re : Receipt of commission from M/s. Vulcan Laval and M/s. Larson & Toubro Ltd.*

It has no at all been established that any commission was received, as alleged, from M/s. Vulcan Laval and M/s. Larsen and Toubro Ltd., by Shri Chikke Gowda, Minister for Animal Husbandry and Agriculture, and that there were no basis for that allegation whatsoever.

Allegation No. 14 of the Schedule to the notification dated 8-11-1977 : Whether under due favour was shown to Messrs Navarasa Fertilizers in purchasing fertilizers and whether payment was made even without receipt of the stock.

Finding

As regards the first part of this allegation about undue favour having been shown to M/s. Navarasa Fertilizers, the finding is the same as finding No. 1 given under Allegation No. 24 of Annexure II above. So far as the second part of the allegation is concerned, there was no evidence or material on the record of the Commission from which it could be found that any such payment was made in the manner alleged.

38. *Allegation No. 25 of Annexure-II* : Whether there was any misuse of power and corruption committed by Shri D.K. Naikar, Minister for Municipal Administration, in connection with the allotment of land on J.C. Road to Shri N.C. Madhvaraj.

Allegation No. 15 in the Schedule to the notification dated 8-11-1977 : Whether site on J.C. Road was leased to Shri M.B. Lal and M.V. Venkatappa contrary to the interests of the City of Bangalore Municipal Corporation.

Findings

(i) From the entire material on the record it stands conclusively established that Shri D.K. Naikar, Minister for Municipal Administration showed undue interest in Shri N.C. Madhvaraj (also mentioned as N.C. Madhuraju in the files) in the grant of the lease of the land of the city of Bangalore Municipal Corporation, on either side of the J.C. Road and that he not only disregarded the norms of propriety becoming the conduct of a Minister, but also misused governmental power in the matter of grant of the said lease.

(ii) No site on J.C. Road was leased out to Sarvshri M.B. Lal and N.V. Venkatappa.

39. *Allegation No. 22 of the Schedule to the Notification dated 8-11-1977* : Whether the cement or steel allotted for the construction of the Government Harijan Hostel building in Bangalore City was diverted to other purposes.

The Commission did not proceed to make any inquiry into this allegation because no specific allegations were filed either by the Memorialists or any party or person in compliance with the Order made by the Commission dated 18-4-1978.

NOTES

1. Ivor Jennings, Cabinet Form of Government, p. 179.
2. *Ibid,* p. 180.
3. *Ibid*, p. 200.
4. *Ibid,* p. 224.
5. *State of Karnataka* v. *The Union of India.* (1978) 2 SCR, p. 1 (at p. 103).
6. (1970) 3 SCR 505, 512.
7. Wade and Phillips, *Constitutional Law* (eighth edition) pp. 89-90 and 195-196.

13

RAILWAY ACCIDENT INVESTIGATION REPORT ON THE COLLISION OF NO. 20 UP 'TRIVANDRUM CENTRAL-MADRAS/CENTRAL MAIL' TRAIN WITH TWO COUPLED LIGHT ENGINES AT KM. 117/4-5 IN TIRUVALAM STATION YARD ON THE JOLARPETTAI-MADRAS DOUBLE LINE BROAD GAUGE SECTION OF SOUTHERN RAILWAY AT ABOUT 04.07 HOURS ON MAY 27, 1977[1]

May 27, 1977 – September 1, 1977

One Man Commission Shri K.N. Kamath, Additional Commissioner of Railway Safety

Appointment

The Commission was constituted under the Ministry of Tourism and Civil Aviation (Commission of Railway Safety) in accordance with Rule 4 of the Statutory Investigation into Railway Accidents Rules, 1973 vide Notification No. RS. 13-T(8)/71 dated April 19, 1973 on May 27, 1977.

Terms of Reference

To enquire into the collision of No. 20 Up 'Trivandrum Central-Madras/Central Mail' train with two coupled light engines at Km. 117/4-5 in Tiruvalam Station Yard on the Jolarpettai-Madras Double Line Broad Gauge Section of Southern Railway at about 04.07 hours on May 27, 1977.

---

1. Delhi, Controller of Publications, 1983, 17 p.

Contents

Summary; Inspection and Inquiry; Relief Measures; The Train; Local Features; Summary of Evidence; Observations and Tests; Discussion; Conclusions; Remarks and Recommendations; Annexures; Railway Board's Comments on Various Paras of the Report.

Conclusions

25. (a) *Cause of the Accident:* On full consideration of the factual and circumstantial evidence, I have reached the conclusion that the collision of 20 Up 'Trivandrum Central-Madras/Central Mail' train with two coupled light engines at Km. 117/4-5 in Tiruvalam station yard on the Bangalore-Madras Broad Gauge section of Southern Railway which occurred on 27th May, 1977 was caused as a result of 20 Up having been admitted on clear signals on the Up Main line of the station which was already occupied by the coupled light engines.

(b) *Responsibility:* (i) Switchman, Shri V. Raju, of East Cabin, Tiruvalam, is primarily responsible for not correctly setting the route for the common loop line for backing the light engines and for not ensuring that the Main line was clear at the east end before he gave the slot for the Up Main Home Signal. He violated Subsidiary Rules 148*(iii)*.

While adjudging the gravity of his offence, however, the fact that he readily admitted having forgotten to set the cross-over and also that it was not possible for him to see from the Cabin whether the engines were on the loop line or the Main line may be given due consideration.

[*Bio-data of Sh. V. Raju:*

Shri V. Raju was first appointed as a temporary Porter on 30-8-1958 and promoted as Switchman on 6-11-1967 and has been working so since then. His annual increment was withheld on two occasions (without the effect of postponing the future increments) once for failing to book a detention for an express train in July 1968 and inform the Control about the detention and on the other occasion in April 1976 for failing to grant line clear for a goods train in time resulting in detention.]

(ii) Shri T. Veeramuthu, Pointsman, contributed to the cause of the accident in failing to ensure that the route had been correctly set before he had signalled the coupled light engines to back and also in failing to stop the engines before they had passed the Starter Signals. He contravened the provisions of General Rule 163(b)(iv).

[Bio-data of Sh. T. Veeramuthu:

Shri T. Veeramuthu was appointed on 13-7-1963 as a Box Boy. He was temporarily promoted as a pointsman from 2-6-1975 in which position he continues. He was once censured in March 1976 for failing to clear the slide chairs of points.]

(iii) Shri Rajamanickam, Driver, working loco WG 8980 also contributed to the accident by failing to stop the coupled light engines before passing the Up Main Starter Signal by which time he should have come to know that the engines were going back on the Main line and not on the Loop line. He contravened provisions of General Rule 163 (b) (iv).

[Bio-data of Sh Rajamanickam:

Shri Rajamanickam was originally appointed on 10-7-1944 as a temporary Shed Cooly. He worked in various capacities such as Engine Cleaner Shed Khalasi, Fireman 'C', Fireman 'B' Diesel Assistant and Shunter 'B' before he was promoted as Driver 'C' effect from 16-2-1977. He had no punishments during the last five years of his service.]

(c) *Relief Measures:* With reference to Section II of the Report, the relief arrangements were satisfactory.

Recommendations

26. This accident would not have occurred if the Main line at the station had been track circuited. The decision to provide track circuiting on run-through lines at way side stations was taken by the Railway Board as far back as 1966. From information furnished by the Southern Railway it is noted that axle counters are proposed to be provided at Tiruvalam and the work was included in the Works Programme for 1966-67. It is unfortunate that despite the peculiar local conditions obtaining at Tiruvalam were the visibility is restricted on account of the Main lines being on reverse curves, this work was not given a higher priority and completed earlier. The Railway Administration cannot, therefore, escape some blame in this regard.

27. It is seen from information furnished by the Railway Administration that the number of stations programmed for track circuiting has steadily dwindled since 1972-73. Between 1969-70 and 1972-73 more than 40 stations were programmed every year, whereas from 1973-74 onwards the number has steadily come down and was only three in 1977-78. Moreover, of the 46 stations programmed during 1972-73, 23 have yet to be completed of which 16 stations fall on the Bangalore City-Dharmavaram-Guntakal section which are proposed to be completed along with the conversion of the line to BG. As the conversion work has been progressing rather slowly, it is recommended that the track circuiting work, which gives a greater measure of safety to train operation, should not be linked with and should be completed without any further delay. It is also noted that there has been no progress at all on the works sanctioned from 1974-75 onwards. It transpires that the works are held up mainly for want of wooden sleepers. Some special steps need to be taken by the Railway Board for supply of wooden sleepers so that these works may be completed expeditiously. The Railways may also be asked to programme for track circuiting the run through lines at the remaining way side stations on all Trunk routes and Main line sections. It is understood that axle counters are proposed to be provided instead of track circuiting at a few stations on a trial basis in view of the shortage of wooden sleepers. If this proves successful it should be possible to expedite these works.

28. General Rule 124(b) and Subsidiary Rules 124(ii)(a)(1) stipulate that "All right" signals are to be exchanged by the Station Master with the Guards and Drivers of trains. The rules, however, do not indicate the action to be taken by the Station Master if two trains happen to pass through the station simultaneously or a train is stabled between the Up and Down lines when it may not be possible for the Station Master to cross-over and exchange signals with the train which is runinng on the other side of the stabled train. It is suggested that a suitable Subsidiary Rule be incorporated authorising the Station Master to depute a competent Railway servant to exchange signals with the Driver and Guard in such a circumstances.

29. During the Inquiry it came to notice that at Tiruvalam the Station Master and Assistant Station Master had been working on 12 hour shifts since November 1975 though, according to the duty list, they are to work in 8 hour shifts. It is most undesirable to permit staff to work for considerable periods at a stretch for longer hours of duty

than the prescribed hours as this is likely to induce fatigue which could lead to accidents.

30. There was no tail-lamp in the rear of the coupled light engines. According to GR 144(a)(iii) there should have been at least one red tail lamp fixed to the rear engine. The Drivers of the two engines are responsible for not complying with these instructions.

31. According to GR 146 if a train passes without tail lamp the Station Master is to immediately advise the station in advance to stop the train and to see that the defect is remedied. No such action appears to have been taken by the Station Master, Sevur, or the Cabinman of the East Cabin, Katpadi.

32. The emergency lighting equipment which was available on the train could not be utilised because the plug not fit the socket (according toe the Guard's version). It is unfortunate that in case of real need the equipment provided could not be used for some reasons or other. Suitable steps may be taken to ensure that proper sockets are available for using these equipments and that the Guards are also made familiar with the use of the equipment during their refresher course.

33. The Driver of the leading engine of the coupled light engines did not know the maximum permissible speed of WG locomotives. He had also driven the coupled engines at a rather slow speed between Katpadi and Tiruvalam taking about 28 minutes to cover the short distance of about 12 kilometers the average speed working out to about 26 km./h. On being questioned as to why he had gone so slow he stated that this was because there was a "Dead" engine behind. There was no need to observe any speed restriction merely a "dead" engine attached. In this case, had the Driver gone at the permissible speed he would have reached Tiruvalam much earlier and thus given more time to the shunting staff to complete the shunting well before 20 Up had approached Tiruvalam and the accident might have been averted. Suitable action needs to be taken to ensure that Drivers are not only aware of the speed restrictions to be observed but also of the maximum permissible speeds of various locomotives so that they do not take too much time on the run thus upsetting all the calculations of the Section Controller and making the operating staff work under undue pressure.

34. The provisions of the new SR 37(vi) are inadequate and are not strictly in conformity with GR 37(a)(iii) a according to which the Station Master has to ensure that the line over which they train is to

pass is clear and free from obstruction. Moreover, according to this Subsidiary Rule it is only the facing end Cabinman who assures the Cabinman at the trailing end that the nominated line is clear and free from obstruction. As already observed in the previous paragraph this is an impractical provision. Moreover, nothing is mentioned in this rule regarding the trailing end Cabinman ensuring that the line is clear at his end. Nothing is also stipulated as regards the Station Master personally ensuring that the reception line is clear and free from obstruction. The rule as it stood prior to the issue of the Correction Slip introducing the new SR 37(vi) in December 1976, stipulated that the Station Master should satisfy himself that the line on which the train is proposed to be received is clear and free from obstruction. The Station Working Instructions of Tiruvalam also stipulate that the Station Master must decide the line on which the train is to be received and personally satisfy himself that the line nominated is clear and free from obstructions and advise the Switchman at both ends the number of the nominated road and communicate separate Private Number of each Switchman. The Railway Administration may examine the subrule and amend it suitably so that these anomalies are removed.

35. The Station Working Instructions of Tiruvalam were issued as far back as 14-6-1966, i.e., about 11 years ago. As such the issue of fresh Station Working Instructions is overdue and may be expedited.

36. The front SLR of 20 Up was an anti-telescopic coach and was, fortunately, marshalled correctly with the luggage and Guard's portions leading. As a result of the collision it was this front portion which got very badly smashed. Had this SLR been wrongly marshalled the consequences would have been really serious because the passenger portion was over crowded on the day of the accident. This goes to emphasis the great importance of correct marshalling of the SLRs.

37. According to SR 148(i)(a) of the Southern Railway where special shunting staff such as Shunting Jemdars or corresponding officials are employed they must attend to all shunting operations. At all other stations, shunting is to be done in accordance with the instructions issued by the Station Master and must be supervised personally by the Guard. The rules do not stipulate as to who will supervise where no special shunting staff are posted and there is also no Guard as was the case in the case of the coupled light engines which were to be shunted at Tiruvalam. It may be stipulated that in such

cases the shunting shall be supervised personally by a Pointsman in accordance with the instructions instructions issued by the Station Master.

38. There has been considerable increase of traffic on the Railways in recent years and particularly so on some sections like Jolarpettai-Madras section. A number of fast trains have been introduced and several existing Mail and Express trains have been speeded up, mostly by the reduction in the number of stoppages. All this has led to a heavy burden on the train passing staff at stations. Great importance is also being attached to the punctuality of some of the more important trains and any detention to these trains are viewed severely. 20 Up is one such train whose punctuality is carefully watched by the Head Office. In my view, these conditions led to a certain amount of 'fear psychosis' among the train passing staff which causes some confusion in their minds and leads them to commit errors leading to accidents. I had occasion to point this out in the case of the accident involving the collision of 16 Up 'New Delhi-Madras Grand Trunk Express' train with the rear of 'Vijayawada-Madras Diesel-11' Up Goods train at Ongole which occurred on the 8th February, 1977. While punctuality is, no doubt, important it should not be attempted to be achieved by any reduction in the emphasis of safety. I, therefore, reiterate by recommendation made in para 40 of my Report, *ibid* that in depth study be made of this aspects by the Railway Board (perhaps through the Psycho-technical cell of the Research, Designs and Standards Organisation) in order to strike a balance between these two some what conflicting objectives. It is essential that the operating staff should feel assured that in case of detentions due to genuine causes they would not be punished. In the present case the fear that 20 Up might suffer some detention was probably responsible to some extent in making the Switchman and Pointsman work under some pressure and commit mistakes which led to the accident.

39. Until such time either the track circuiting of the Main line or provision of axle counters is completed at Tiruvalam, it is suggested that suitable lighting arrangements may be made in the station yard to improve the visibility of the yard lines from the Station Master's office as well as from the two Cabins.

[Extract of various rules quoted in the Report are at Annexure I].

Railway Board's Comments on Various Paras of the Report

Para 26: Although a decision was taken in 1966 to track-circuit run through main lines at wayside stations with dense and fast traffic, the Railways had necessarily to lay down priorities for execution of this work, keeping in view the limited funds and resources. On the Southern Railway, priority was given to trunk and main lines routes, Arkonam-Jolarpettai is a main line section, through the railway administration while communicating their remarks to CCRS vide letter No. TS/M/185/77-78 dated 1-12-1977, could not spell it out clearly. As a sequel to the recommendations made by RAIC-1968, it was agreed to give first priority to the turn through lines on trunk routes and second priority to lines on the mainline routes. On the Broad Gauge, the sections Madras-Gudur and Madras-Renigunta (forming part of Madras-Raichur), which are trunk routes, were given priority over Arkonam-Jolarpettai section.

Having regard to the priorities laid down for the purpose, run through lines at all way-side stations on the B.G. trunk routes on the Southern Railway (totalling 35) were provided with track-circuit during the period 1966-67 to 1968-69. From 1969-70 onwards BG main line routes were taken up and so far track circuits/Axle counters have been provided at 33 stations. In addition, 53 stations on Guntakal Division (now transferred to South Central Railway) were also provided with track-circuits during the period 1968-69 to 1972-73. Though the railway administration had been proposing provision of track circuiting on run through lines on main lines routes at the rate of 10 to 15 stations per year since the 1969-70, only a limited number of stations could be covered up due to paucity of funds and non-availability of wooden sleepers.

In 1974-75, 10 stations on Arkonam-Jolarpettai section were sanctioned on the basis of availability of wooden sleepers covered under track renewal programme. Since Tiruvalam station was not included under such track renewal, the track circuiting on this station could not be carried out. Due to paucity of funds, the proposal of provision of track-circuiting at this station did not materialise during 1975-76 also. As a measure of expediency, it was decided in 1976-77 to provide axle counters on the run through lines at Tiruvalam station, which work was completed on 4-10-78. However, in view of some failures in the particular design of the Axle counters, it has been decided to make provision of track circuiting at Tiruvalum station by using concrete sleepers with Nylon insets on top priority.

It would thus be seen that the action taken by the Railway to provide tack circuiting at various stations was in consonance with the priorities laid down for the purpose. Under the circumstances, there is no question of blaming the administration who had taken the overall requirements into account in deciding the execution of the work.

Para 27: As explained by the Railway Administration, the execution of the work of track circuiting which was quite fast in the earlier years, had considerably slowed down from 1973-74 onwards. This was due to inadequate supply of wooden sleepers. In fact, it was mainly due to shortage of wooden sleepers that the Railways had to examine the possibility of using Axle Counters as a substitute for conventional track-circuits. The Axle counters are, however, a new development which would take sometime before these can be manufactured in sufficiently large numbers and employed extensively. Further, concreted sleepers are also now being used for track circuiting to reduce dependence on wooden sleepers.

Para 28: CCRS has observed that suitable instructions have already been issued to all the Railways vide letter No. 77/Safety (A&R)/29/31 dated 9-3-78.

Para 29: Suitable instructions have been issued vide letter No. E(LL)/77/ HER/52 dated 26-7-78.

Para 30: Railway has initiated disciplinary proceedings against the drivers of the two light engines. The necessity of ensuring that engines do not run without tail lamps has been reiterated to the railways.

Para 31: Suitable disciplinary action has been initiated by the railway administration against the defaulting staff.

Para 32: Suitable instructions have been reiterated by the railway to all concerned to maintain the Emergency Lighting Equipment in perfect working order and for regular periodical inspection. Instruction have also been issued to ensure that proper sockets are provided for using the emergency Lighting equipment and the Guards are made familiar with the use of the equipment during their refresher course.

Para 33: The matter is under examination.

Para 34: The matter is under examination.

Para 35: The railway administration issues fresh Station Working Instructions whenever the correction slips exceed three, which is a good practice. It is not considered desirable to lay down any periodicity for review of Station Working Rules. Nevertheless, as and when there is any change in the system of working, lay out of yards, signalling arrangements, change in rules, etc., the Station Working Rules have necessarily to be changed which is the extent practice.

Para 36: It is seen that the position explained by the railway has been noted by the Chief Commissioner of Railway Safety.

Para 37: It has been specifically laid down in G.R. 148 that the Station Master shall see that shunting of trains of vehicles is carried on only at such times and in such manner as well not involve danger. It is, therefore, quite obvious that at those stations where no separate shunting staff are provided and in the event of a Guard not being available at a station for this purpose, the responsibility for ensuring that shunting is being performed in a safe and proper manner lies exclusively on the Station Master. It is noted that Chief Commissioner of Railway Safety has agreed with the view point.

Para 38: This Ministry do not agree with this view point. Safety organisations have been set up on the railways with a view to ensuring that the staff work according to rules and no short-cut methods are adopted. The officers and supervisors make surprise inspections both by day and by night to achieve this goal. In fact instructions already exist vide Board's letter No. 77/Safety (A&R)/29/14 dated 6-6-77 (copy sent to CRS under this Ministry's OM No. 76/Safety (A&R)/1/10 dated 27-8-77) that the staff should be educated to develop a balanced outlook and any wrong impression in this regard should be removed. It is also noted that the Chief Commissioner or Railway Safety has accepted the assurance given by the Southern Railway in this regard.

Para 39: Southern Railway has taken necessary steps to improve the lighting of Tiruvalam station yard.

SHAH COMMISSION OF INQUIRY, 1977 – REPORT[1]

Chairman Shri J.C. Shah, Retired Chief Justice of the Supreme Court

Secretary Shri P.R. Rajgopal

Appointment

Whereas there is a widespread demand from different sections of the public for an inquiry into several aspects of allegations of abuse of authority, excesses and malpractices committed and action taken or purported to be taken in the wake of the Emergency proclaimed on the 25th June, 1975 under Article 352 of the Constitution.

And whereas the Central Government is of the opinion that it is necessary to appoint a Commission of Inquiry for the purpose of making inquiry into a definite matter of public importance, that is, excesses, malpractices and misdeeds during the Emergency or in the days immediately preceding the said proclamation, by the political the said proclamation, by the political authorities, public servants, their friends and/or relatives and in particular arrest or detention, maltreatment of and atrocities on detenus and other prisoners arrested under DISIR, compulsion and use of force in the implementation of the family planning programme and indiscriminate and high-handed demolition of houses, huts, shops, buildings, structures and destruction of property in the name of slum clearance or enforcement of town planning or landuse schemes in the cities and towns resulting, *inter alia*, in large number of people becoming homeless or having to move far away from the places of their vocation.

Now, therefore, in exercise of the powers confered by confered by Section 3 of the Commissions of Inquiry Act, 1952 (60 of 1952), the

---

1. New Delhi, 1978, Vol I, 94 p.; Vol II, 147 p.; Vol III, 284 p.; 3 Vols.

Central Government hereby appoints a Commission of Inquiry vide Notification No. II/16011/32/77-S & P (D.II) and S.O. No 374 (E) of *Gazettee of India* dated 28th May, 1977.

Amendment in the Notification

In para 4 of the said Notification for the words and figures "on or before 31st December 1977" the words and figures "on or before 30th June, 1978" shall be substituted.

Terms of Reference

(a) To inquire into the facts and circumstances relating to specific instances of :

(i) subversion of lawful processes and well-established conventions, administrative procedures and practices, abuse of authority, misuse of powers, excesses and/or malpractices committed during the period when the Proclamation of Emergency made on 25th June, 1975 under Article 352 of the Constitution was in force or in days immediately preceding the said Proclamation,

(ii) misuse of powers of arrests or issue of detention orders where such arrests or orders are alleged to have been made on considerations not germane to the purposes of the relevant Acts during the aforesaid period,

(iii) specific instances of maltreatment of and/or atrocities on persons arrested under DISIR or detained and their relatives and close associates during the aforesaid period,

(iv) specific instances of compulsion and use of force in the implementation of the family planning programme during the aforesaid period,

(v) indiscriminate, high-handed or unauthorised demolition of houses, huts, shops, buildings, structures and destruction of property in the name of slum clearance or enforcement of Town Planning or land use schemes, during the aforesaid period:

Provided that the inquiry shall be in regard to acts of such abuse of authority, misuse of powers, excesses, malpractices, etc., alleged to have been committed by public servants, and

Provided further that the inquiry shall also cover the conduct of other individuals who may have directed, instigated or sided or abetted or otherwise associated themselves with the Commission of such acts by public servants;

(b) To consider such other matters which, in the opinion of the Commission, have any relevance to the aforesaid allegations; and

(c) To recommend measures which may be adopted for preventing the recurrence of such abuse of authority, misuse of powers, excesses and malpractices.

The inquiry by the Commission shall be in regard to –

(i) complaints or allegations aforesaid that may be made before the Commission by any individual or association in such form and accompanied by such affidavits as may be prescribed by the Commission, and

(ii) such instances relatable to paragraph 2(a)(i) to (v) as may be brought to its notice by the Central Government or a State Government or an Union Territory for inquiry.

The Commission shall make interim reports to the Central Government on the conclusion of inquiry into any particular allegation or series of allegations and will be expected to complete its inquiry and submit its final report to the Central Government on or before 31st December, 1977.

The Central Government is of opinion that having regard to the nature of the inquiry to be made and other circumstances of the case, all the provisions of sub-section (2), sub-section (3), sub-section (4), and sub-section (5) of Section 5 of the Commissions of Inquiry Act, 1952 (60 of 1952), should be made applicable to the said Commission and the Central Government hereby directs under sub-section (1) of the said Section 5 that all the provisions aforesaid shall apply to the said Commission.

Contents

PART I

I. Notification appointing a Commission of Inquiry and the staff sanctioned, and Categorisation of Complaints; II. Important enactments

and amendments of the Constitution; III. Procedure followed by the Commission explained; IV. Scheme of the Report; V. Circumstances leading to the declaration of Emergency on June 25, 1975; VI. The working of the media of information under the I & B Ministry during the Emergency; VII. Specific cases: (1) The case regarding the reversion of Shri Justice R.N. Aggarwal of Delhi High Court, (2) Refusal by Smt. Indira Gandhi to extend the term of Shri Justice U.R. Lalit of the Bombay High Court, (3) Deviation from established procedure and irregularities in the appointment of Shri K.R. Puri as Governor of Reserve Bank of India, (4) Subversion of lawful processes and well-established conventions in the appointment of Shri T.R. Vardachary as Chairman of the State Bank of India, (5) Deviation from established procedure and irregularities in the appointment of Shri T.R. Tuli as Chairman and Managing Director of the Punjab National Bank, (6) Deviation from established procedure in public sector undertaking in the case of Lt. Genl. Satarawala's appointments as Chairman-cum-Managing Director of I.T.D.C., (7) Deviation from established procedure in the appointment of Air Marshal H.C. Dewan as Chairman, International Airports Authority of India, (8) Misuse of powers and institution of false criminal complaints against four senior official by the CBI at the instance of Smt. Indira Gandhi, (9) Unlawful detention of Textile/Customs employees under MISA by Delhi Administration
and institution of false CBI cases against four of them, (10) Misuse of powers and miscarriage of Justice in the case of Shri Sudarshan Kumar Verma by the CBI officials, (11) Deviation from established procedure by Shri T.R. Tuli, Chairman of the Punjab National Bank in allowing a clean overdraft to M/s. Associated Journals Limited, (12) Deviation from established procedure in sanctioning facility by way of opening three foreign letters of credit by the Punjab National Bank in favour of M/s. KRSMA Chemicals Pvt. Ltd., (13) Concessions by Punjab National Bank in favour of Maruti Limited, (14) Deviation from established procedure in the reconstitution of the Boards of Air India and Indian Airlines Corporations, (15) Decision processes leading to the purchase of 3 Boeing 737 Aircraft by Indian Airlines, (16) Detention of Smt. Gayatri Devi and Lt. Col. Bhawani Singh under COFEPOSA Act, 1974, (17) Detention of Shri Bhim Sen Sachar and seven others, (18) Improprieties committed in regard to Shri Mangal Behari, IAS of Rajasthan cadre and termination of the services of Smt. Chandrawati Sharma, Asstt. Teacher, (19)

Search and seizure operations under the Income Tax Act of two Trade Union leaders

PART II

VIII. Misuse of Media: (i) Translation of the Congress election manifesto by AIR and DAVP Translator, (ii) Design of election posters for Shri V.C. Shukla by the Artists of the DAVP, (iii) Harassment of Shri Kishore Kumar, Playback singer, by I&B Ministry; IX. Cases of Misuse of authority in the Income-tax Department: (i) Search and seizure operations against Baroda Rayon Corporation, (ii) Search and seizure operation in the case of Bajaj Group of Companies, (iii) Special instructions relating to Maruti Ltd.; X. Import of aircraft by Shri Dhirendra Brahmchari of Aparna Ashram and related matters; XI. Arrests and Detentions in Delhi: General Aspects, Specific cases: (i) Detention of Shri Mam Chand, S/o Shri Malkhan, (ii) Detention of Dr. Karunesh Shukla, (iii) Detention of Virendra Kapoor, (iv) Detention of Vaid Guru Dutt, (v) Detention of Shri Prabir Purkayasha, (vi) Use of MISA against ordinary criminals, (vii) Use of MISA against violators of Delhi Administration (Display of Prices of Articles) Orders, 1975; XII. Specific cases of Misuse of authority: (i) Requisitioning of Vishva Yuvak Kendra Building, Delhi, (ii) Appointment of Shri U.S. Shrivastuv as Chairman, Delhi Transport Corporation, (iii) Harassment of M/s. Pandit Brothers; XIII. Demolitions in Delhi: (i) General, (ii) Demolitions in Bhagat Singh Market, (iii) Demolitions in Sultanpur Mazra, (iv) Demolitions in Jahangirpur, (v) Demolitions of Arya Samaj Mandir, (vi) Demolitions in Turkman Gate, (vii) Demolitions in Samalkha, (viii) Demolitions in Kapas Hera, (ix) Demolitions in Arjun Nagar, (x) Demolitions in Karol Bagh, (xi) Demolitions in Andheria Mor, (xii) Conclusions; XIV. (i) Turkman Gate Firing, (ii) Pressurising Magistrates to sign and pre-date the firing order; XV. General Observations

PART III

XVI. Wrongful Confinement and Torture of Shri Lawrence Fernandes by the Police and his Maltreatment in Jail, XVII. Cases from Haryana State: (i) Detention of Shri Murlidhar Dalmia, (ii) Detention of Shri M.L. Kak, (iii) Detention of Cdr. Pritam Dutta, (iv) Detention of Shri Ishwar Lal Choudhary, (v) Detention of Shri

Pitambar Lal Goyal, (vi) Use of force in the family planning programme in Village Uttawar, District Gurgaon, Haryana; XVIII. Abuse of Authority — in Service matters; XIX. Arrests and Detentions — General and Statewise report; XX. Conditions in Jails Statewise report; XXI. Implementation of Family Planning Programme General and Statewise report; XXII. Demolitions General are Statewise report; XXIII. Complaints and the manner of their disposal; XXIV. General Observations; XXV. Conclusion; XXVI. Summary of Findings, Observations and Recommendations; Appendices:

Recommendations

INTERIM REPORT I

CHAPTER I

It contains terms of reference, information regarding the Commission's staff, method followed by the Commission for categorisation of complaints and how the Commission proceeded to start its work.

CHAPTER II

The text of the proclamation of emergency and some important statutory provisions made after such proclamation have been given in this Chapter.

CHAPTER III

The procedure followed by the Commission and the decision given by it on the objection raised regarding the procedure followed have been incorporated in this Chapter. The important findings in this regard are:

(i) The proceedings of the Commission are neither of the nature of a civil suit nor are the proceedings of the nature of a criminal proceeding. (Para 3.4)

(ii) Functions of the Commission under the Commissions of Inquiry Act are of an entirely different nature. The Commission is not concerned with the establishment of any civil rights or the infraction of those rights. The Commission is also not concerned to determine the infraction of any laws involving the imposition of any penalty upon a person charged with the commission of infraction of a law. The proceedings are not of an adversary character. The duty of the Commission is to make an inquiry into the subject matter of the enquiry if the subject-matter is of definite public importance. (Para 3.5)

(iii) The proceedings before the Commission will be of the nature of 'inquisitorial' (meaning thereby that the presiding officer takes upon himself the duty to ascertain, the facts through witnesses after giving opportunity to persons concerned who may be affected by the determination of facts). (Para 3.10A)

(iv) There is no warrant for the view that once a notice under section 8B is issued, there is no obligation on the part of the Commission to issue a notice under rule 5(2)(a) nor that the issuance of the notice under rule 5(2)(a) is dispensed with, when summons under section 8B is issued. (Para 3.14)

(v) The proceedings before the Commission are such in which truth is to be determined by the adoption of a procedure to be devised by the Commission having regard to the nature of the enquiry and which is essentially inquisitorial in character as prescribed by the Act. (Para 3.16)

(vi) The Commission rejected the contention that the appropriate procedure should have been that as soon as a witness appeared before the Commission at the stage of preliminary hearing and made some statement which involved a person in the commission of some impropriety, the Commission was bound to issue summons under section 8B and the Commission had no option to act otherwise. (Para 3.18)

(vii) Under rule 5(2)(a) the Commission is under a statutory obligation to call upon persons who in the opinion of the Commission, should be given an opportunity of being heard, to furnish to the Commission a statement relating to such matters as may be specified in the notice. This obviously could not mean that even though a person is given an opportunity of being heart in an enquiry, he should not be called upon to furnish to the Commission a statement relating to the matters as may be specified in the notice. (Para 3.20)

(viii) Section 8B confers the basic protection to any person that he shall not be condemned unheard by the Commission, i.e., his conduct should not be adversely commented unheard by the Commission, i.e., his version is not true, without giving him an opportunity of being heart. (Para 3.24)

(ix) The proceedings of the Commission are not analogous to proceedings in a civil trial or enforcement of a civil right or obtaining relief for infringement of a civil right nor of a criminal trial in which the conduct of a person or persons for the commission or infraction of the law is sought to be investigated. The function of the Commission is to determine facts relating to matters of public importance and by adoption of a procedure, which is not adversary in character, but inquisitorial in character. (Para 3.28)

(x) Oath of secrecy of office taken by a Minister of the Union does not prohibit a Minister from disclosing the information before a Commission of Inquiry specially when the Central Government has directed the holding of an enquiry for the purpose of ascertaining facts relating to matters of public interest. (Para 3.31)

(xi) The disclosure of information before a Commission of Inquiry held in pursuance to a direction of the Central Government after a person has ceased to be a Minister does not amount to a breach of the oath of secrecy of the Minister concerned. (Para 3.31)

CHAPTER IV

In this chapter the Commission has mentioned the scheme of the report along with brief mention of the types of instances and activities taken up for examination. In this regard, the general principle kept in mind by the Commission has been that the excess complained of must be of a nature which would be capable of creating a crisis of confidence or which is one of national importance. (Para 4.4)

CHAPTER V

Circumstances Leading to the Declaration of Emergency on June 25, 1975

(i) Following the judgment of the Allahabad High Court setting aside the election of Smt. Indira Gandhi, there was a spurt of political activity in Delhi in particular and in the rest of India in general. (Para 5.2)

(ii) Apparently, an effort was made by the followers of Smt. Indira Gandhi to create an atmosphere that she should continue to remain and function as Prime Minister and with that object in view a number of demonstrations, rallies and meetings were arranged by her supporters in Delhi and elsewhere. (Para 5.3)

(iii) Instructions were given in a meeting held at Raj Niwas, Delhi, that full cooperation should be given by the DTC by arranging buses to carry people who were taking part in rallies to be organised to express solidarity to the then Prime Minister. (Para 5.6)

(iv) The practice of making an application in the prescribed proforma for hire by a private party and making of advance payment was not observed by the DTC in the case of the bookings made by the AICC. (Para 5.6)

(v) The number of buses booked during the period June 12 to 25, 1975, on hire was much above the normal booking allowed for private purposes. (Para 5.6)

(vi) On June 13, 1975, the entire fleet of 983 buses plying on the Delhi routes was taken off the road and the buses were diverted to converge on the Prime Minister's house. Residents of Haryana, Punjab, Rajasthan and Uttar Pradesh were sent in vehicles commandeered by the State authorities for the purpose. . . . A large majority of those vehicles coming from the adjoining States did not observe the Route Permit Rules require under the Motor Vehicles Act, and in many cases Government vehicles were used for which no payment was made. (Para 5.7)

(vii) Records of the DTC clearly support the evidence of the witnesses that Government employees were pressed into service for organising these rallies. (Para 5.8)

(viii) Government organisations like Delhi Transport Corporation, New Delhi Municipal Committee and Delhi Electric Supply Undertaking participated in these rallies. (Para 5.9)

(ix) Under the Motor Vehicles Act route permits had to be obtained for sending vehicles outside the Union Territory of Delhi which was not done. . . . The police authorities and the State Transport authorities had been properly briefed and instructed to ensure that the buses crossed the border without any route permits. (Para 5.12)

(x) The State of affairs in this regard was not different in Punjab. (Para 5.19)

(xi) From the State of Rajasthan also, according to the Rajasthan State Electricity Board records, 58 trucks belonging to the State Electricity Board were ordered by the Chief Minister to be placed at the disposal of the Workers Union. (Para 5.21)

(xii) Some of the employees of the DESU who refused to participate in these rallies were allegedly beaten up by the more enthusiastic amongst the supporters of the Prime Minister. (Para 5.24)

(xiii) . . . the law was also discriminately applied to the Congress Party as against the other parties. Enforcement of prohibition of meetings under section 144 of the Cr. P.C. which had become a normal feature in the vicinity of the Prime Minister's house was relaxed when it came to demonstrations and rallies arranged by the Congress Party in support of the Prime Minister. (Para 5.26)

(xiv) The Intelligence Bureau of the Government of India was being used to maintain surveillance on the activities of some of the important Congress leaders and Ministers. This raises a very important issue which has relevance to the assault on the privacy of the individuals and even of Ministers of Government for purposes which are other than those strictly necessary for ensuring the security of the State. (Para 5.27)

(xv) The decision to take certain drastic steps including the declaration of emergency was, apparently, in contemplated even as early as June 22, 1975. (Para 5.29)

(xvi) Efforts were also made to ensure that some important newspapers were prevented from bringing out the morning edition on June 26, 1975. (Para 5.43)

(xvii) In varying degrees the Chief Ministers of several States were taken into confidence as early as the morning of June 25 and they had been instructed to take action on receipt of the advice from the Prime Minister's house that night. (Para 5.46)

(xviii) Some of the special features which could have a bearing on the proclamation of the emergency as gathered from the official records are as follows:

(a) On the economic front there was nothing alarming;

(b) The fortnightly reports regarding law and order showed that the situation was under complete control all over the country;

(c) No reports were received by the Home Ministry from State Governments indicating any deterioration in the law and order situation in the period immediately preceding the proclamation of emergency;

(d) No plans were prepared by Home Ministry prior to June 25, 1975 with regard to the imposition of Internal Emergency;

(e) The Intelligence Bureau had not submitted any report suggesting that the internal situation in the country warranted imposition of internal emergency;

(f) The Home Ministry did not submit any report to the Prime Minister expressing its concern or anxiety about the internal situation in the country;

(g) The senior officers like the Home Secretary, the Cabinet Secretary and the Secretary to the Prime Minister had not been taken into confidence about the intended proclamation of emergency but Shri R.K. Dhawan, the then Additional Private Secretary to the PM had been associated with the preparations for promulgation of the emergency right from the early stage;

(h) Shri Om Mehta, the Minister of State was taken into confidence much earlier than the Home Minister, Shri Brahmananda Reddy. Only some of the Chief Ministers and Lt. Governor of Delhi were taken into confidence regarding the imposition of emergency. (Para 5.60)

(xix) It is not understood how provision (clause da) of the Second Schedule of the Government of India (Transaction of Business) Rules, 1961 read with Rule 7 of these rules could have been circumvented by the application of Rule 12 of the same Transaction of Business Rules. (Para 5.65)

(xx) The work relating to the emergency provisions of the Constitution, relates to Home Ministry and therefore the proposals relating to the proclamation of emergency should have normally originated from that Ministry. The Cabinet Secretariat, however, did not receive any proposals from the

Home Ministry in respect of the proclamation issued on June 25. (Para 5.66)

(xxi) Even in 1971, when a war was being waged with Pakistan, a proclamation of emergency was issued without invoking Rule 12 of the Transaction of Business Rules. A regular meeting of the Council of Ministers was convened and the proclamation was issued thereafter after obtaining clearance from the Home Minister. (Para 5.67)

(xxii) The circumstances leading to the declaration of emergency pursuant to the advice of the Prime Minister leave little room for doubt that the decision to impose emergency ... was exclusively the decision of the Prime Minister. None of her Cabinet Ministers, except Shri Brahmananda Reddy was even aware of the proposal . . . even Shri Brahmananda Reddy, Home Minister, was not consulted; but he was merely informed shortly before the advice was tendered and his assistance was taken only for obtaining a letter from him. . . . (Para 5.68)

(xxiii) The Constitution, in the opinion of the Commission, does not contemplate the proclamation of an emergency upon an emergency already existing, nor prevents the courts from entertaining any challenge to the declaration of this additional emergency. But the provisions of the Constitution were amended by the 39th Amendment of Constitution Act, which prevented a challenge being raised. (Para 5.69)

(xxiv) This was more in the nature of a shock treatment, than a legally permissible emergency, which could be declared according to the law then in force. (Para 5.70)

(xxv) If, however, an internal emergency could be declared apart from the external emergency, the powers which were exercised before any Rules were framed, i.e., disconnecting the electricity connections of newspaper offices were wholly unauthorised, since there was no law which conferred upon any authority such power. Again, the action taken by the authorities under the directions of the Prime Minister to arrest a number of political leaders was not supported by any law. (Para 5.71)

(xxvi) Surveillance of political leaders and others including tapping of their telephones raises a grave issue of public importance .... Such a power, if at all, could be exercised only when authorised by statutory provisions and circumstances strictly necessary for ensuring the security of the State in grave times either of internal disturbance or external aggression or war and not at other times. (Para 5.72)

(xxvii) It would certainly be a travesty of the democratic institutions if the Government constituted by a political party is entitled to watch the activities of other political parties and even of other members of its own party. If, however, such power is to be conferred on this institution (Intelligence Bureau), it must be by a statute or statutory Rules authorising it in that behalf.... This watch of the Intelligence agency on individuals and the materials collected thereby should be open to scrutiny to a Board or a Panel composed of officers or of public men before authorising the continuance of the watch. It should be possible to harmonise the demands of the security of the State with the democratic liberties. (Para 5.73)

(xxviii) Considering the stakes that are involved in the proper and purposeful functioning of the I.B., it is imperative that it gets the benefit of advice, guidance and wisdom of a body of eminent, experienced and patriotic group of individuals drawn from different discipline and whose loyalty and personal integrity cannot ever be called into question. This in turn will generate the requisite faith and confidence of the citizens of the country in this very important institution on the fair, correct and proper functioning of which alone would eventually depend the safety, the security and the liberty of the people of this country. (Para 5.74)

(xxix) The Intelligence Bureau should not be entitled to act as a super-watchman over the activities of politicians to whatever party they belong and the activities of the Intelligence Bureau should be subject to regulation and control insofar as these activities concern some of the clandestine parts which have come to the notice of the Commission, to ensure that this does not degenerate into misuse or abuse of authority. (Para 5.75)

(xxx) The Commission recommends that appropriate safeguards are necessary and should be devised by the Government so as to protect the activities in the Intelligence Bureau being used as an instrument of political spying either by the Government or by some one in the Government. This issue has been raised to concentrate attention and if considered appropriate to generate public debate on the question. (Para 5.78)

(xxxi) It is also necessary to invite attention to the misuse of Air Force aircraft. It appears that for the benefit of individuals for travelling on State duty or for State work Indian Air Force aircraft have been used surreptitiously and, according to the existing Rules, those persons were not entitled to the use of the Aircraft. The Commission recommends to the Government the framing of appropriate Rules in this behalf and also to scrutinise whether the use of the Aircraft on June 25, 1975 in the circumstances was warranted and, if not, whether bills for charges appropriate in that behalf were duly tendered and, if not tendered, to identify those responsible for breach of the Rules. (Para 5.79)

(xxxii) Attention may also be invited to the gross irregularities to which the provisions of Maintenance of Internal Security Act and provisions of the Defence of India Rules were misused to the detriment of political opponents. (Para 5.80)

(xxxiii) The manner in which the provisions of MISA were used was nothing short of perversion and mockery of its provisions and all the safeguards and guarantees that had been promised in the Parliament when the MISA Bill was enacted, were totally disregarded. Many apprehensions, which were expressed by the Members of Parliament, who spoke against conferment of such wide powers when the Bill was enacted, came true. (Para 5.81)

(xxxiv) The safeguards enshrined in the enactment were rendered meaningless by the callous misapplication of this Act by the police and the Magistracy . . . . It needs to be made clear to all those responsible for overseeing the correct application of the powers of arrest/detention by the junior officers, that the senior functionaries at the bureaucratic and political levels would be held directly accountable for any misuse or abuse of the powers of arrest and detention. (Para 5.82)

CHAPTER VI

The Working of the Media of Information under the Information and Broadcasting Ministry during the Emergency

I. *Censorship*

(i) During the two or three days when the censorship apparatus was being set up, power supply to the newspaper offices in Delhi remained disrupted. (Para 6.10)

(ii) The guidelines issued by the Chief Censor exceeded the scope of the Rule 48 of the Defence and Internal Security of India Rules insofar as they prevented editors leaving editorial columns blank or filling them with quotations from great works of literature or from national leaders like Mahatma Gandhi, or Rabindranath Tagore. The Information and Broadcasting Ministry did not attempt to find out whether these guidelines were within the scope of Defence and Internal Security of India Rules or not. (Para 6.14)

(iii) Parliament and court proceedings were also subject to censorship. (Para 6.17)

(iv) Not merely publication of court judgments was censored, but directions were also given as to how judgements should be published. (Para 6.23)

(v) The actual work of censorship on day to day basis went even beyond the scope of the guidelines. Orders were arbitrary in nature, capricious and were usually issued orally without any relation to the provisions of Rule 48. (Para 6.29)

(vi) In practice censorship was utilised for suppressing news unfavourable to the Government, to play up news favourable to the Government and to suppress news unfavourable to the supporters of the Congress Party. (Para 6.30)

(vii) In one instance at least, that of the magazine *'Mainstream'*, pre-censorship orders were issued particularly because of its critical attitude towards Shri Sanjay Gandhi. (Para 6.31)

(viii) Even after the elections were announced and censorship was relaxed, the Government tried to pressurise the Press by giving informally 'off the record' warnings by veiled threats of what would happen to them after the elections if they did not comply with the directions of the Government ....(Para 6.37)

(ix) During emergency, legislation was enacted to make censorship part of the ordinary law of land. Thus the Prevention of Publication of Objectionable Matter Act was passed, the Press Council of India was abolished by an Ordinance and a Bill repealing the Parliamentary Proceedings (Protection of Publication) Act, 1956 was passed. (Para 6.45).

II. *Other Pressures on the Press*

(i) Shri Shukla at a Coordination Committee meeting held on June 29, 1976, had asked the Principal Information Officer to prepare a list of newspapers which were to be categories as friendly, neutral and hostile. (Para 6.47)

(ii) The grading of friendly, neutral and hostile given to a particular newspaper was related to its views on a particular political party. (Para 6.48)

(iii) Political consideration was one of the criteria for giving advertisements. (Para 6.54)

(iv) Contrary to the policy enunciated by the Government on the Floor of Parliament, political considerations were taken into account while releasing advertisements. (Para 6.57)

(v) The Government during this period utilized its advertising policy as a source of financial assistance, etc., in complete variance with the policy which it had enunciated on the Floor of the Parliament. (Para 6.58)

III. *Formation and Functioning of Samachar*

(i) The functioning of Samachar during the emergency both administratively and editorially was supervised by Government. (Para 6.75)

(ii) Accredition of a number of correspondents was terminated and a bulk of these decisions was taken as a part of review. (Para 6.79)

(iii) Shri K.N. Prasad also admitted to having character and antecedents of a number of journalists verified by the Intelligence Bureau at the instance of the Minister. (Para 6.81)

IV. *Functioning of Government media units*

(i) The Government media units had two main functions during the emergency. They were at once a source of patronage and also they were used for building up the image of political party and a few of its leaders. (Para 6.84)

(ii) The D.A.V.P. was used on a large scale for giving advertisements to support the various souvenirs brought out by the Congress Party. Opposition parties were denied any such patronage. (Para 6.85)

(iii) Not merely the Congress Party was given extensive advertising support, but there was an instance when rates per page for souvenirs were increased after they had been agreed upon and the souvenirs printed. (Para 6.86)

(iv) The slant against the Opposition was so obvious that in December 1976, AIR bulletins devoted 2,207 lines to the spokesmen of the Congress Party against 34 lines to the Opposition. (Para 6.90)

(v) After the change of criteria three part-time Correspondents were appointed to AIR, all of whom were office bearers of the Congress Party. (Para 6.96)

(vi) A number of films were produced by the Films Division to project the image of Shri Sanjay Gandhi not only as a Youth leader, but as a leader in his own right. (Para 6.101)

(vii) A number of multi-media campaigns were launched during the emergency to coincide with important milestones in Smt. Gandhi's careers. (Para 6.105)

(viii) The Publications Division was directed to boost the sales of Smt. Gandhi's books and to publish informative and interesting sketches with photographs of Smt. Gandhi in various journals and periodicals. (Para 6.105)

CHAPTER VII

Specific Cases

I. *Case regarding the reversion of Shri Justice Aggarwal of Delhi High Court:*

(a) The order passed against Shri Aggarwal was, *prima facie* in the nature of an order of punishment for participating in the hearing in Kuldip Nayar's case and passing an order which tarnished the image of the Government in the public eyes. (Para 7.13)

(b) A case of misuse of authority and abuse of power is disclosed in this case against Smt. Indira Gandhi. (Para 7.14)

II. *Refusal by Smt. Indira Gandhi to extend the term of Shri Justice U.R. Lalit of Bombay High Court:*

Refusal to extend the term of Shri U.R. Lalit as a Judge of the High Court amounted to subversion of well-established conventions and practices and amounted to abuse of authority and misuse of power by Smt. Indira Gandhi. (Para 7.23)

III. *Deviation from established procedure and irregularities in the appointment of Shri K.R. Puri as Governor of the Reserve Bank of India:*

The normal and established procedure in regard to the appointment of the Governor of the Reserve Bank of India was not followed and that the then Finance Minister Shri C. Subramaniam was virtually compelled to fall in line with the suggestion made by the then Prime Minister Smt. Indira Gandhi. This was yet another case of subversion of established administrative procedure and convention by Smt. Indira Gandhi as the Prime Minister. (Para 7.37)

IV. *Subversion of lawful processes and well-established conventions and deviation from administrative procedures and practices in the appointment of Shri T.R. Varadachary as Chairman of the State Bank of India:*

(i) The Commission gave a ruling that by giving any information before it, Shri Mukherjee would not be violating either the provisions of the Official Secrets Act or the oath of office taken by him. (Para 7.45)

(ii) In the light of the consistent practice and in the light of the nature of the oral testimony of Shri Sen Gupta and Shri Mukherjee, the Commission is of the view that there was no consultation with the Reserve Bank in this case, as was required in terms of sub-clause (a) of sub-section (I) of section 19 of the State Bank of India Act, 1955. (Para 7.45)

(iii) The normal established procedure in regard to the appointment of the Chairman of the State Bank of India was not followed in this case and further that it was not in accordance with the provisions of the State Bank of India Act, 1955, which made consultation with the Reserve Bank of India a condition precedent to the appointment of the Chairman by the Central Government. The Commission is of the view that considerations other than strictly professional and totally extraneous have unfortunately been allowed to operate in arriving at the decision to appoint Shri Varadachary. Shri Pranab Mukherjee has violated established administrative conventions and procedures and misused his position in the appointment of Shri Varadachary. (Para 7.49)

V. *Deviation from established procedure and irregularities in the appointment of Shri T.R. Tuli as Chairman and Managing Director of Punjab National Bank:*

(i) Before arriving at this decision to appoint the Chairman of a comparatively small bank in the Private Sector to the seniormost position in one of the biggest Public Sector banks in the country, no effort was made to consider the suitability for this post, of senior Managers within the public sector banking system itself as had done in several other instances. (Para 7.57)

(ii) This is yet another instance where the then Finance Minister Shri C. Subramaniam was virtually compelled to fall in line with the suggestion made by the then Prime Minister, Smt. Indira Gandhi and that such compulsion amounted to abuse of authority by the former Prime Minister. It clearly resulted in subversion of well established conventions. (Para 7.59)

VI. *Deviation from the established procedure for the selection of officers for top level executive posts in Public Sector Undertakings, in the case of Lt. Gen. J.T. Satarawala, as Chairman-cum-Managing Director, India Tourism Development Corporation:*

It is not a healthy convention to post an officer as a top level executive, who was earlier interviewed and not considered suitable by the Public Enterprises Selection Board to the exclusion of the names in the panel recommended by the P.E.S.B. The better course would have been to request the P.E.S.B., to suggest a fresh panel of names. By ignoring the recommendations of a statutory body, the Government was making an inroad into the relevance and respectability of such a body. (Para 7.63)

VII. *Deviation from the established procedure for the selection of officers for top level executive posts in Public Sector Undertakings, in the case of Air Marshal H.C. Dewan, as Chairman, International Airport Authority of India:*

If the person recommended by the P.E.S.B., in the present case was not acceptable for any particular reason, the appointing authorities could well have asked for a fresh panel of suitable candidates. By not doing this and appointing a person who had been interviewed by the P.E.S.B., and not found suitable, the Government has exposed itself to the charge of, to say the least, injecting into the selection process considerations which may well be extraneous to the requirements of the job. Such a practice does not add to the credibility of established institutions; rather it impaires it. (Para 7.69)

VIII. *Misuse of powers and institution of false criminal complaints against four senior officials by the CBI at the instance of Smt. Indira Gandhi:*

(i) The evidence discloses a gross abuse of the authority vested in Smt. Indira Gandhi. She had taken into her head to act as she did merely because the officers of the Commerce and Industries Ministries had, in the discharge of their duties taken steps to acquire information which was likely to affect the interest of Maruti Limited. She pressurised Shri D. Sen to take proceedings for searching their houses and for filing complaints against them under the Prevention of Corruption Act, which were wholly unjustified and which were eventually dropped. (Para 7.96)

(ii) The conduct of Shri Sen discloses that he has misused his authority in directing that First Information Reports be filed against all the four officers and in starting proceedings against them. (Para 7.101)

(iii) Smt. Gandhi was responsible for institution of criminal proceedings against the four officers concerned, having their houses searched and subjecting then to humiliation; merely because they were responsible for collecting information in the discharge of their duties, which would have been prejudicial to the interest of Maruti Limited, a concern in which Shri Sanjay Gandhi, her son, was vitally interested. (Para 7.102)

(iv) It is imperative for the CBI to realise that in setting afoot a series of actions against individuals – whether officials or non-officials – they irretrievably damaging the reputation and social standing of the individuals concerned. They should not, therefore, be allowed to initiate proceedings against anyone unless it is ensured that the facts on record warrant the type of proceedings that they launch on. (Para 7.103)

(v) Now that we have seen that even the man at the top of the CBI with all this seniority and status can still lend himself and his organisation to serve purposes other than strictly legal, constitutional and moral, it has to be ensured that in future no such individual or organisation should be capable of being rendered a helpless and unquestioning tool in the hands of the powers that be. The Commission feels that certain safeguards need to be provided by making the Director CBI accountable to an independent body. Yet another suggestion can be that the Director CBI may be statutorily rendered independent of the executive Ministry and his term of office be made subject to a tenure. (Para 7.104)

IX. *Unlawful detention of Textile/Customs employees under MISA by Delhi Administration and institution of false CBI cases against four of them*:

(i) Director CBI, Shri D. Sen, showed extra keenness to register cases against these four officers, though the material available on record did not warrant the action that followed. On the other hand, when it came to dealing with Shri Bhatnagar and Shri Suri, Shri Sen adopted a different yardstick. (Para 7.122)

(ii) The Commission cannot help feeling that Shri D. Sen applied invidiously different standards in dealing with the two sets of officers. (Para 7.123)

(iii) Going entirely by the facts available on record, it has nowhere been established that these officers were corrupt or had done any thing which could even distantly be interpreted as improper or incorrect. (Para 7.128)

(iv) Shri Bhinder on his own admission has been the prime mover in the sordid story of these arrests and detentions. (Para 7.130)

(v) The entire action by the CBI under Shri D. Sen was initiated on grounds, which were totally inadequate and imaginary. As against this, he let off without any action, two officials against whom there was adequate material to warrant prosecution under the Prevention of Corruption Act. He has grossly misused his position as the Director, CBI, and abused his authority. (Para 7.133)

(vi) The Commission feels the Smt. Gandhi has abused her authority and misused her power in having caused the arrest and detention of these 12 officers without adequate justification and using the CBI to set in motion criminal cases against four of them, all of which had to be abandoned eventually for want of any material. (Para 7.134)

(vii) Shri Bhinder has been the hatchetman and he went about the arrest and detention of these officers without any justification whatever. He was also responsible along with Shri D. Sen to get the CBI to register cases against four of these officials. He has grossly abused his authority and misused his power. (Para 7.135)

X. *Misuse of powers and miscarriage of justice in saving Shri Sudarshan Kumar Verma, a clerk in the Railways, from legal punishment by the CBI Officials:*

(i) Normally, the Director of CBI handles important cases dealing with high officers, whereas cases involving non-Gazetted officials are dealt with at the Branch level and neither the Director nor the Joint Director is concerned with such cases. But, in this case, shortly after the case against Shri Verma was registered the Director, CBI, Shri Sen called Shri A.P. Mukherjee, DIC, CBI, Delhi Branch and called for the case papers, (Para 7.140)

(ii) Shri A.P. Mukherjee of Delhi Branch sent his comment on the representation of Shri Verma. He was of the view that there was no substance in the representation. Shri A.P. Mukherjee had taken a courageous stand even at this stage when he should have been in no doubt about what this superior officer desired. (Para 7.142)

(iii) The circumstances of the case and the evidence given by Shri Sen leave little room for doubt that someone from the Prime Minister's household contacted Shri D. Sen and asked him to so arrange that Shri Verma was not prosecuted. Accordingly, contrary to the normal procedure, adopted in similar cases, Shri D. Sen himself called for the papers, attempted through his subordinates to retrieve reports from the Railways and having failed to do so, suggested different linc of action according to which Shri Verma should be dealt with departmentally. (Para 7.145)

(iv) It is, thereforc, a clear case in which perversion of the normal process by Shri D. Sen and misuse of power is established. (Para 7.147)

XI. *Deviation from established procedure, misuse of power and abuse of authority by Shri T.R. Tuli, Chairman of the Punjab National Bank in allowing a clean over-draft to M/s Associated Journals Ltd.:*

(i) The bank advancing funds on a clean overdraft would normally try to ascertain the credit-worthiness of the borrower and try to ensure whether the amount advanced would be repaid by the borrower on demand. This would be minimum precaution which a banker could take before advancing even a small amount by way of clean overdraft. In the present case, however, no precautions which would be normal in advancing money on clean overdraft account were taken; but solely because of the intervention of the Minister Shri P.C. Sethi loan was advanced, disregarding the cannons which would ordinarily govern the advancing of such a loan. (Para 7.156)

(ii) The Commission is firmly of the view that Shri Tuli who has permitted the overdraft and was responsible for the decision in this regard had taken it without making the minimum necessary examination of the facts of the case and without exercising a modicum of care or caution and that this conduct on his part is attributable to the fact that he was swayed by collateral considerations. Thus, this transaction was not a normal one in the ordinary course of the Bank's business. The Commission is of the view that Shri Tuli had subverted established procedure in permitting this overdraft without security to M/s. Associated Journals Limited. He has also misused his powers and abused his authority in so doing. (Para 7.157)

XII. *Deviation from established procedure in sanctioning facility by way of opening of three foreign letters of credit by the Punjab National Bank in favour of M/s. Krisma Chemicals Private Ltd.:*

This is a clear instance where the Chairman and Managing Director of the Punjab National Bank, Mr. Tuli, took a decision and gave directions for its implementation contrary to the normal established procedures in such cases. (Para 7.167)

XIII. *Concessions by Punjab National Bank in favour of Maruti Ltd.:*

Taking into account the evidence adduced and the arguments advanced, the Commission is of the view that no subversion of administrative procedures or misuse of power or abuse of authority has been established in this case. (Para 7.173)

XIV. *Deviation from the established procedure and irregularities in the reconstitution of the Boards of AIR India and Indian Airlines Corporations:*

(i) The normal or established procedure in regard to the appointment of the Board of Directors was not followed and Minister Shri Raj Bahadur was practically compelled to fall in line with the suggestions made by the then Prime Minister, Smt. Gandhi, and it was only after the suggestion made by her was carried out that the lists submitted were approved. (Para 7.183)

(ii) The role of oral instructions in the transaction of business of the Government needs to be defined and definite guidelines set down. To the Commission, this seems imperative not only in the interest of healthy administration, but also to protect the junior functionaries acting on the oral instructions of the seniors from the consequences of subsequent denials by the seniors when things go wrong. (Para 7.185)

XV. *Decision Process Leading to the Purchase of Three Boeing 737 Aircraft by Indian Airlines:*

(i) The manner in which this deal was pushed through suffers from several infirmities:–

(a) The Indian Airlines Management sent a letter to the Ministry for permission to issue a Letter of Intent to the Boeing Company without waiting for the report of Interline Committee constituted by the Indian Airlines Board.

(b) The proposal was sent to Government even before it was approved by the Board of the Indian Airlines.

(c) No steps were taken to complete the system study suggested by the Planning Commission's representatives.

(d) The P.I.B. categorically opposed the proposal pending the completion of the system study. The Secretary's recommendations to abide by the PIB's recommendations were turned down by the Minister, Shri Raghuramaiah; apparently because he had been asked by Shri Dhawan to look into the matter urgently and Shri Raghuramaiah took the suggestion of Shri Dhawan as emanating from the Prime Minister.

(e) According to the Finance Ministry, there was no instance of an Administrative Ministry going ahead with the proposal to the Cabinet for a decision against the recommendations of the PIB. This was done in this case.

(f) The decision to sign the contract was given on February 8, 1977. On February 9, 1977 the contract was signed. Actually, the delivery schedule limit given by the Boeing Company had expired on February 7.

(g) The visit of Shri Rajiv Gandhi to the office of the Chairman of the Indian Airlines, where he was shown the financial projections by the Director of Finance, apparently under the instructions of the Chairman, was a procedure, which was totally outside the ordinary course of business. (Para 7.202)

(ii) There has been a certain amount of avoidable haste in rushing through the deal. (Para 7.203)

XVI. *Detention of Smt. Gayatri Devi, Ex-Member of Parliament and Lt. Col. (Retired) Bhawani Singh under COFEPOSA Act, 1974:*

(i) While processing the material that was available with the Deputy Director, Enforcement, against the two individuals, certain significant omissions were made in reproducing the information contained in the two letter of the Reserve Bank of India. (Para 7.210)

(ii) In ordering the detention of these two persons under COFEPOSA Act, the processes and procedures prescribed by the Finance Ministry have not been followed. (Para 7.219)

(iii) It is abundantly clear that in the cases of these two persons, the provisions of the COFEPOSA Act, were not at all applicable and these were resorted to, to give effect to a predetermined decision to arrest these two persons. (Para 7.230)

(iv) Shri Pranab Kumar Mukherjee, the then Minister of Revenue and Banking has misused his position and abused his authority in ordering the detention of Smt. Gayatri Devi and Col. Bhawani Singh on wholly insufficient grounds. It is a clear case of subversion of lawful processes and of administrative procedures. (Para 7.231)

XVII. *Detention of Shri Bhim Sen Sachar and Seven others*:

(i) The practice of issuing warrants of arrest, first and obtaining the pre-dated grounds of detentions thereafter had become the general pattern so far as the detentions of persons under MISA in Delhi during emergency were concerned. (Para 7.240)

(ii) The story of detention of Shri Bhim Sen Sachar and seven others provides a classic example of the misuse of the provisions of MISA .... This and similar cases which have come to the notice of the Commission reveal an undesirable trend in the administration of the MISA. When, as in this case, the Prime Minister felt satisfied about the detention of certain persons, instead of getting the orders issued by the Central Government, small functionaries like the Additional District Magistrates were directed to issue the warrants without they themselves being satisfied either about the need for detention of the individuals concerned or the adequacy of grounds for their detention. (Para 7.245)

(iii) The decision to detain Shri Bhim Sen Sachar and seven others was taken by Smt. Gandhi. She has abused her position and misused her power in ordering the arrest of Shri Bhim Sen Sachar and seven others. (Para 7.250)

XVIII. *Improprieties committed in regard to Shri Mangal Behari, IAS of Rajasthan Cadre, and Termination of the Services of Smt. Chandrawati Sharma, Assistant Teacher:*

(i) Shri Harideo Joshi has conceded that a mistake was committed in the case of Smt. Sharma. He thus misused his position, subverted the established administrative procedures and abused his authority in terminating the services of Smt. Sharma without observing constitutional provisions. (Para 7.280)

(ii) Smt. Indira Gandhi was responsible for (i) causing the termination of services of Smt. Chandrawati Sharma, Assistant Teacher, Government Rajasthan, in violation of the Constitutional provisions; (ii) the prolonged forced leave on which Shri Mangal Behari had to remain for about 16 months; and (iii) for causing the attendant hardships which ensued as a result thereof. She has thus missed her position, abused her authority and subverted well-established administrative procedures and lawful processes. (Para 7.287)

(iii) The services of Smt. Chandrawati Sharma who was only an Assistant Teacher, were terminated without the slightest fuss or protest .... No functionary of the Government put up even as much as a note pointing out that the political activities alleged against her were not correct and that she was being kept out of service for no valid and understandable reason. As against this totally indifferent and callous attitude, the manner in which the State Government officials rallied to the support of Shri Mangal Behari, an IAS officer, is indeed unique and is in striking contrast to the manner in which Smt. Sharma was dealt with. How are we going to ensure that every employee of the Government regardless of their rank and status enjoys full security and protection of services? Until this is done, the manner in which these two functionaries of the Government were dealt with – one a low-placed Assistant Teacher, and the other a high-placed IAS officer – would be considered as an unpardonable and invidious distinction. (Para 7.290)

(iv) Considering the risks involved and the damage that an adverse IB report can cause to an individual, both in terms of his reputation as also of his career prospects, the Commission recommends that the Government should take steps to ensure that every IB report on the activities and material particulars of individual is correct. (Para 7.293)

XIX *Irregularities in Initiating Action Resulting in Search and Seizure Operations under the Income Tax Act in the case of two Trade Union Leaders*:

While the circumstances leading up to the search and seizure operations in these two cases no doubt appear to be somewhat unusual, especially Shri D. Sen's role therein, no subversion of administrative procedure or misuse or abuse of power has been clearly established. (Para 7.30)

INTERIM REPORT II

CHAPTER VIII

Misuse of Media

I. *Translation of Congress Election Manifesto by All India Radio and Directorate of Advertising an Visual Publicity Translators*:

Shri V.C. Shukla has violated the basic norms of administration and has indulged in abuse of authority in getting the translators attached to the All India Radio and D.A.V.P. for translating Congress Election Manifesto. Apart from that, it is also an offence under section 123(7) of the Representation of the Peoples Act of 1951. (Para 8.34 and 8.35)

II. *Design of Election Posters for Shri V.C. Shukla by Artists of the Directorate of Advertising and Visual Publicity:*

Shri V.C. Shukla has violated the basic norms of administration and had indulged in abuse of authority in getting posters for his election campaign designed by the D.A.V.P. artists. Apart from that, his conduct also comes within the mischief of section 123(7) of the Representation of the Peoples Act, 1951. (Para 8.50)

III. *Harassment of Shri Kishore Kumar Play-back Singer, by the Ministry of Information and Broadcasting:*

Apart from the constitutional responsibility, Shri V.C. Shukla is actually responsible for the various disabilities that were inflicted on Shri Kishore Kumar. This was a clear case of vindictiveness and gross misuse of government authority against a film artist of renown, only because the artist did not want to go along with the government sponsored programme due to certain personal reasons. (Para 8.62 and 8.63)

CHAPTER IX

Cases of Misuse of Authority in the Income-tax Department

I. *Baroda Rayon Corporation – Search and Seizure under Section 132 of the Income-tax Act, 1961:*

(i) Shri S.R. Mehta's action in directing Shri Harihar Lal to initiate action under section 132 of the Income Tax Act in this case amounts to subversion of lawful processes and abuse of authority. (Para 9.23)

(ii) As the Head of the Income Tax Department, Shri S.R. Mehta cannot absolve himself of blame for the very grave loss of seized material which should have been returned to the person from whom it was seized, by merely stating that he had left the papers on his Minister's desk. The responsibility for return of these papers to the concerned officers was clearly his and his alone. Shri Mehta's failure or omission in this regard amounts to subversion of lawful processes. (Para 9.24)

(iii) On the uncontroverted statement of Shri S.R. Mehta, that these papers were handed over to Shri P.K. Mukherjee. Shri P.K. Mukherjee's action in obtaining and retaining seized documents and subsequent failure or omission on his part to return them to the Chairman of the Central Board of Direct Taxes or to any other concerned or duly authorised officers in the Income Tax Department also amounts to subversion of lawful processes and abuse of authority. (Para 9.25)

(iv) Shri Harihar Lal was aware of the illegality of his action. However, in the circumstances then prevailing. Shri Harihar

Lal's choice was limited and he chose to render himself a helpless and unquestioning tool of Shri S.R. Mehta. (Para 9.26)

(v) In spite of a wealth of judicial pronouncements and departmental instructions emphasising the need for administrative restraint and strict compliance with the law, the then Chairman of the Central Board of Direct Taxes, Shri W.R. Mehta, was himself instrumental in unleashing this dangerous weapon of search and seizure which could unjustly and irretrievably damage the business reputation and standing of the parties affected. (Para 9.27)

(vi) The extraordinary power of search and seizure under section 132 must be exercise strictly in accordance with law which provides the necessary safeguards and only for the purposes for which the law authorises it to be exercised. (Para 9.27)

II. *Search and Seizure Operation by Income-tax Department in the Case of Bajaj Group of Companies:*

(i) This case illustrates boldly the prevailing misconception that if an authorising officer has, in consequence of information in his possession, reason to believe that action under section 132 should be initiated in the case of a Company or a group of Companies, he will be justified in authorising indiscriminate search and seizure at the business or residential premises of all persons connected with the Company, however, remote the connection may be with these Companies or even with their directors and employees. The conditions justifying the exercise of this extraordinary power did not exist in the case of a large number of 120 places searched or surveyed. (Para 9.41)

(ii) Issue of blank warrants of authorisation is not a mere procedural lapse. Such warrants can be misused so as to cause damage to the reputation of any innocent person. If proper implementation of action u/s 132 is not possible, as suggested, then the solution to the problem lies in seeking to amend the law, consistent with the requirements of adequate safeguards and not in flouting the statutory requirements with impunity. (Para 9.42)

(iii) Judicial decisions and departmental instructions brought to the notice of the Commission appear to have been observed only in their breach. Stern action by the Income Tax Department is necessary to prevent such wanton disregard of the law as well as the privacy of the citizens. (Para 9.40)

(iv) Where a blank warrant of authorisation is issued and the authorising officer has acted without any information on which he could have reason to believe that the statutory conditions for the exercise of the power of search existed, such action is clearly unlawful. (Para 9.42)

(v) The inquiry into search and seizure under section 132 of the Income Tax Act, 1961 in the Bajaj & Mukand Group of Companies have revealed several serious irregularities and the power was not exercised strictly in accordance with law. (Para 9.44)

(vi) The extraordinary power of search and seizure under section 132 must be exercised strictly in accordance with law which provides the necessary safeguards and only for the purposes for which the law authorities it to be exercised. (Para 9.27)

III. *Special Instructions on matters relating to Maruti Limited:*

(i) Shri S.R. Mehta subverted administrative procedures and abused his authority in giving oral instructions to Shri Harihar Lal which had the effect of frustrating or, at any rate, inordinately delaying legitimate enquiries relating to benami share holdings in Maruti Limited, which *prima facie*, indicated evasion of taxes. (Para 9.59)

(ii) Oral orders or instructions involve the danger of being denied, twisted or misinterpreted by either party to suit his convenience. Hence these should be obtained in writing immediately and where it is not practicable to do so, written confirmation thereof should be obtained as soon thereafter as possible and in the meanwhile the recipient should record the oral directions or instructions. (Para 9.61)

CHAPTER X

Import of Aircraft by Dhirendra Brahamachari of Aparna Ashram

(i) Shri S.B. Jain and Shri A.M. Sinha failed to take even the elementary steps and ignored the specific information furnished to them with regard to Brahamachari's proposed trip to New York. (Para 10.30)

(ii) Shri A.M. Sinha has, in not proceeding with the enquiries, failed to discharge his responsibilities. (Para 10.32)

(iii) In this particular case, considering the person involved and the nature of the illegal transaction alleged against Brahamachari, it was a matter for the judgement and direction of a higher functionary than that of Deputy Director. It was a fit case for the exercise of Shri Jain's discretion and guidance. He has, however, tried to shift the onus to the Deputy Director. His conduct becomes yet more blame-worthy in the light of the subsequent note that he recorded in May 1977. (Paras 10.32 and 10.33)

(iv) From the evidence it is quite clear that Brahamachari had obtained the Customs Clearance Permit by misrepresenting that the aircraft was a donation, when it was in fact purchased by him. He also made misrepresentation before the officers in the Office of the Chief Controller of Imports and Exports in the matter of increase in the value of the CCP, which he got increased from Rs. 4,00,000 to Rs. 6,14,000 when there was no evidence to indicate that the aircraft and spares of the value of Rs. 6,14,000 were gifted to him. (Para 10.56)

(v) Brahamachari has fully exploited his association with the then Prime Minister's house in getting the aircraft imported by misrepresenting it as a gift. He has actively abetted the subversion of established procedures. (Para 10.58)

(vi) Not only that the CCP was issued by subverting the well-established administrative procedures, but even the value of the CCP was progressively increased in three different stages by the concerned authority on the request of Brahamachari unsupported by documentary evidence to justify the enhancement . . . . There is no explanation from any of the witnesses either in the course of their deposition before the Commission or from the files that have come to the notice of the Commission for the unusual and extraordinary procedure which the Commission feels is a downright and unpardonable subversion of all the accepted norms and conventions of sound and healthy administration. (Paras 10.21 and 10.65)

(vii) In appears that there had been unduc haste at various levels in processing the application of Brahamachari for the grant of exemption from Customs Duty. In the process, full enquiries regarding the status of the Ashram were not made. (Para 10.40)

(vi) While granting exemption from Customs Duty at the time of the import of the aircraft, the Department of Customs and Central Excise had, *inter alia*, imposed two conditions:–

(1) the aircraft will be used for transportation of the students as well as teachers from plains to Mantalai Ashram and back.

(2) The Yoga training will be imparted free of charge.

From the evidence on record, it appears that both these conditions have been violated. (Para 10.53)

(ix) Brahamachari continued to make misrepresentations for claiming exemption from Customs Duty on the import of the aircraft. His declaration that Aparna Ashram is a charitable institution was also untrue. (Para 10.57)

(x) The evidence before the Commission leads to be conclusion that the initial decision to reject the proposal twice by the Air Headquarters on valid grounds of security and sensitivity of the area was subsequently changed in favour of granting the permission, though with some conditions attached at the instance of the then Defence Minister, Bansi Lal (Para 10.50)

(xi) It is necessary to place on record that various officers of the Ministries showed extraordinary expedition in the processing of this case. For once, the proverbial red-tapism in the functioning of the bureaucrats was nowhere in evidence. While the expeditious functioning of the Government machinery is a desirable objective, expedition in this case was not at all motivated by considerations of efficiency, but on account of extraneous considerations. It is evident from the statements of witnesses before the Commission that almost all of them were aware of the standing of Brahamachari in relation to the Household of the then Prime Minister. Some of the witnesses frankly admitted that they apprehended harm to them should any one obstruct Brahamachari's proposals and projects. The apparently effortless manner in which Brahamachari was able to compel the officials of Ministry after Ministry stands out as a classic example of how an entire administrative system can be subverted by an errant individual if only he has the right contacts at the right places. (Para 10.59)

(xii) For Brahamachari, the entire exercise of securing the CCP, the enhancement of the value of CCP, the Customs exemption, and the grant of landing facilities at Mantalai was effortless . . . . It gives the impression to the general run of the people that rules and laws are intended only for the law abiding citizens and for such of those who wield influence and authority, the rules do not matter and their projects are carried out. (Para 10.60)

(xiii) The Government may examine whether the administrative systems and procedures can be secured in future from the onslaughts of individuals like Brahamachari. (Para 10.61)

(xiv) To protect against misuse of authority at the decision-making levels, the corresponding responsibility to set out their reasons in writing in every case where a major or even a minor infraction of the procedures and rules are sought to be made, should be insisted upon. (Para 10.62)

(xv) The Government must provide for the protect the junior officers from the shifting of the responsibility by the seniors when things go wrong. This salutary principle should not be confined only to the officers but should reach the different levels of Ministers up to the highest. (Para 10.66)

(xvi) While withdrawing papers which have been released earlier as a part of administrative transaction, definite rules and guidelines should be laid down as to how the papers earlier released can be withdrawn or replaced, if at all. (Para 10.67)

(xvii) (a) In dealing with applications for exemption from customs duty, well-defined guidelines should be laid down to enable the decision-making levels to reach the right and uniform conclusions in every case and to safeguard against abuse.

(b) The onus to prove that the exemption sought for well be in public interest, should be on the applicants.

(c) Where exemption has been given subject to certain conditions, the applicant should be required to furnish evidence periodically that the condition imposed continue to be conformed to.

(d) The conditions on which gifts from foreigners may be received even by institutions should be clearly prescribed. (Para 10.69)

(xviii) Security considerations of the country should not be side-stepped to accommodate the demands of individuals like Brahamachari under any circumstances. (Para 10.70)

CHAPTER XI

Arrests and Detentions

I. *Issue of Detention Orders under MISA*

(i) An undesirable feature of detentions in Delhi during the emergency was the misuse of the power under the preventive sections of the Criminal Procedure Code such as Sections 108 and 151, initially to secure the presence of the persons who were subsequently detained under MISA. (Para 11.20)

(ii) Another ugly feature of arrests and detentions in Delhi during emergency concerns the re-arrest of persons released on bail or otherwise by the Courts. (Para 11.26)

(iii) It also came to the notice of the Commission that some MISA warrants were deliberately kept unexecuted. In fact, directions were issued by Shri K.S. Bajwa and Shri P.S. Bhinder to District Superintendents of Police not to execute certain warrants. (Para 11.31)

(iv) Section 14 of MISA read with Section 21 of the General Clauses Act empowers the detaining authorities to revoke an order issued under MISA by the detaining authority. This power was taken away from the District Magistrate/ Additional District Magistrates in Delhi through specific instructions issued from the office of the Lt. Governor under the signature of Shri Navin Chawla on July 4, 1975 . . . . The effect of these instructions was to ensure that whereas detentions could be ordered liberally, revocation of orders was not to be considered by the detaining authorities at all. (Para 11.34)

(v) Though the Law Department was associated with the processing of detention orders at the time of confirmation and review, no legal security was, in fact, done . . . . The initial attempts of the Law Department to scrutinise the grounds of detention and give legal advice were discouraged and they were made to realise the "futility of finding faults with detention orders". (Para 11.37)

(vi) The evidence of Shri J.K. Kohli, Chief Secretary, Smt. S. Chandra, Special Secretary (Home), Shri T.R. Kalia, Deputy Secretary (Home) and Shri Jagmohan, Deputy Secretary to the Lt. Governor, proves beyond doubt the practice of antedating the confirmation orders of the Lt. Governor whenever the papers were not received from the detaining authorities in time. (Para 11.39)

(vii) Though Shri Navin Chawla had no position in the jail hierarchy, he was exercising extra statutory control in jail matters and sending instructions on matters including the treatment of particular detenus. Shri Chawla has suggested the construction of some Cells with asbestos roofs to 'bake' certain persons. (Para 11.47)

(viii) Transfer of MISA detenus presents an excess of its own kind. 200 MISA detenus including some prominent Opposition leaders were transferred from Tihar Jail to jails outside Delhi during the emergency. Shri S.K. Batra has stated that the transfer of such persons involved great discomfort to the detenus because of the additional inconvenience and expense it involved to their relatives. He said that such transfers are always considered as penal measures in Jail always considered as penal measures in Jain Administration. (Para 11.49)

II. *Treatment in Jails:*

Political detention is to be basically preventive in character and not punitive. This aspect seems to have been conveniently ignore during the emergency. (Para 1.52)

III. *Applications for Parole:*

(i) No uniform policy was followed by Delhi Administration in matters relating to grant of parole. (Para 11.55)

(ii) While some deserving cases for parole were dealt with by the Administration in a very callous manner, there were other cases in which the Administration was unmistakably indulgent to the detenus. What governed these different considerations in the attitude of the Administration can only be inferred. (Para 11.56)

(iii) Grant of parole was used by the Delhi Administration as an incentive to promote family planning in the Tihar Jail. (Para 11.57)

(iv) Attitude of Delhi Administration was particularly harsh in dealing with the requests from the student detenus for release on parole to enable them to take their university examinations. (Para 11.58)

(v) Though Section 16 of the Delhi Detenus (Conditions of Detention) Orders, 1976 governing the conditions of MISA detenus in Delhi provided that "student detenus may be allowed to appear in examination only with the permission of the Administrator", the discretion was always used against the applicants.

IV. *Attitude of Delhi Administration towards Ministry of Home Affairs:*

(i) In cases where the Lt. Government did not like to agree with the advice from the Home Ministry, the officials of the Home Department found that invariably the Lt. Governor's views prevailed and the Ministry of Home Affairs had to retrace its stand. (Para 11.61)

(ii) During the emergency, Shri Bajwa used to furnish material to the authorities concerned and used to issue orders to them asking them "to pick up" the persons named in the list. (Para 11.74)

(iii) S/Shri P.S. Bhinder, K.S. Bajwa and Navin Chawla exercised enormous powers during the emergency because they had easy access to the then Prime Minister's house. Their approach to the problems of the period relating to the citizens was authoritarian and callous. They grossly misused their position and abused their powers in cynical disregard of the welfare of the citizens, and in the process rendered themselves unfit to hold any public office which demands an attitude of fairplay and consideration for others. In their relish for power, they completely subverted the normal channels of command and administrative procedures. (Para 11.76)

(iv) Shri Krishan Chand by his various actions and inactions with regard to important and vital matters appears to have abdicated his legitimate functions in favour of an overambitious group of officers like S/Shri Bhinder, Bajwa and Navin Chawla with disastrous consequences to the people. He betrayed his trust and committed a serious breach of faith with the citizens of Delhi and failed to administer the affairs of the territory honestly and justly. (Para 11.77)

(v) Shri Sushil Kumar, in an effort to beat the clock, had also recourse to the issue of a few blank warrants in addition to the warrants that were prepared and issued by him to the police. Since these detention orders were issued without any satisfaction of the detaining authority, the orders were illegal. Since, however, the orders were issued pursuant to the directions of Smt. Indira Gandhi, responsibility for the illegal detentions must primarily rest on her. (Para 11.78)

(vi) . . . . The Commission has to come to the conclusion that in the light of the evidence on record and without the benefit of knowing Smt. Indira Gandhi's version. Smt. Indira Gandhi was responsible for directing the arrest and detention of a number of respected citizens without authority of law motivated solely by a desire to continue to remain in power. (Para 11.79)

V. *Detention of Shri Mam Chand son of Shri Malkhan:*

(i) Both Shri Krishna Chand and Shri Bhinder had misused their position and authority in ordering the detention and continuing in detention a helpless and defenceless individual like Shri Mam Chand. (Para 11.88)

(ii) It was an undesirable act on the part of the Administration to have allowed a poor and innocent man like Mam Chand, the only bread-winner of the family, to remain under detention for 19 long months. (Para 11.89)

VI. *Detention of Dr. Karunesh Shukla:*

(i) Arrest of Shri Karunesh Shukla was a misuse of power by the Lt. Governor of Delhi, Shri Krishan Chand on the advice of Shri Bajwa . . . . Shri K.S. Bajwa as Superintendent of Police

CID apparently wielded enormous powers during the days of the emergency and often misused them. (Para 11.100)

(ii) Shri Krishna Chand and Shri K.S. Bajwa, both misused their powers and misused their authority in the detention of Dr. Karunesh Shukla on grounds which were not covered by the provisions of the MISA. (Para 11.102)

VII. *Detention of Virender Kapoor:*

(i) The initial arrest of Shri Kapoor was in the presence of Shri Bhinder. He as a Deputy Inspector General should have satisfied himself about the necessity of arresting Shri Kapoor. To that extent he had misused his position and abused his authority. (Para 11.118)

(ii) Shri Bajwa has also misused his authority in Shri Kapoor's arrest. (Para 11.119)

(iii) The detention of Shri Kapoor under MISA under the orders of Shri Krishna Chand was in keeping with the general policy of negligence and lack of interest that he had displayed in the general run of detentions numbering over 1,000. He has abused his authority and misused his position in this as in several other cases. (Para 11.120)

(iv) The Commission cannot condemn adequately this type of the use of MISA on fabricated grounds. An Administration which is totally impervious to the awareness of the basic norms of liberty and the provisions of law, and a set of functionaries who are willing to do anything at the bidding of their seniors without application of mind and without realising the consequences of their acts, have in them the makings of a totalitarian society. The Commission is of the opinion that the Government must make appropriate provision for fixing responsibility on the persons issuing written or even oral orders for every detention. (Para 11.121)

VIII. *Detention of Vaid Guru Dutt:*

Shri Krishan Chand misused his position in ordering the detention of Vaid Guru Dutt . . . . In his anxiety to please the ex-Prime Minister he seems to have overreacted to a situation which at best should have been ignored. It is the arrest of an old infirm and respected individual like Guru Dutt which shakes the faith of the people in the fairness and competence of the Administration. (Para 11.133)

IX. *Detention of Shri Prabir Purkayastha:*

The manner in which Shri Bhinder went about the job of arresting Shri Purkayastha believing him to be Shri D.P. Tripathi discloses his callous attitude. This was a gross abuse of authority. The story of arrest of Shri Purkayastha by Shri Bhinder, the manner in which the Magistrate issued the detention orders and the part played by the Lt. Governor illustrate the complete break-down of the rule of law. (Para 11.149)

X. *Use of MISA against Ordinary Criminals:*

A large number of ordinary criminals who could be dealt with effectively under the provision of normal laws were detained under MISA in Delhi during the emergency. This was in defiance of the specific directions of the Ministry of Home Affairs. (Para 11.150)

XI. *Detention of Juvenile Delinquents:*

In these category of cases MISA powers were invoked without adequate grounds and in defiance of the categorical instructions of the Ministry of Home Affairs. Use of the harsh powers under MISA for dealing with such offenders for comparatively unimportant cases which involved no consideration of the security of the State or larger considerations of public order amounts to misuse of the powers and undoubtedly results in denial of the beneficent provisions of law relating to juvenile delinquents. (Para 11.162)

XII. *Use of MISA against violators of Delhi Administration's (Display of Prices of Articles), Order 1975:*

Shri Krishan Chand has misused his position and abused his power by invoking emergency powers including MISA in cases which could well have been dealt with effectively under the normal provisions of law. (Para 11.171)

CHAPTER XII

Specific Cases of Misuse of Authority

I. *Requisitioning of Vishva Yuvak Kendra, Chanakyapuri, New Delhi under the DISIR Act:*

(i) The building of the Vishva Yuvak Kendra was requisitioned by the Delhi Administration at the instance of Smt. Indira Gandhi, in order to pressurize the management of the Indian Youth Centre Trust to agree to re-constitute the Board of Trustees; that Shri Krishan Chand was acting as spokesman of Smt. Indira Gandhi in this regard, and that Shri V.C. Shukla was also making determined efforts to acquire a hold over the Vishva Yuvak Kendra with a view to run it in consultation with Shri Sanjay Gandhi. (Para 12.13)

(ii) Smt. Indira Gandhi unduly pressurized Shri Krishan Chand, the then Lt. Governor, Delhi, to requisition the Vishva Yuvak Kendra building. (Para 12.22)

(iii) Shri Krishan Chand misused his power and authority and so also did Shri V.C. Shukla in this case. (Para 12.23)

II. *Appointment of Shri U.S. Srivastav as the Chairman of Delhi Transport Corporation in 1976:*

This case illustrates how established rules and procedures expected to be followed by the appointing authorities were in fact not observed even though the correct procedures and the problems that were likely to arise from this appointment, were pointed out at different levels. (Para 12.31)

III. *Harassment of the firm Messrs Pandit Brothers: Their arrest and related matters:*

(i) Series of harassments against the firm of Messrs. Pandit Brothers including the arrests of the Manager and the two partners was initiated at the instance of Shri Sanjay Gandhi. (Para 12.60)

(ii) Shri Krishan Chand was the prime mover in getting the raid organised. (Para 12.60)

(iii) It appears that the Administration employed the police for a purpose which did not fall within their legitimate sphere of duties and for which they were not equipped. Such misuse of the police force by the Administration should be a matter for concern. (Para 12.62)

(iv) The association of Commissioner of Income Tax with this case following his visit to Shri R.K. Dhawan in the Prime Minister's house is also disconcerting. Since no summons under Section 8B of the Commissions of Inquiry Act or notice under rule 5(2)(a) of the Commissions of Inquiry (Central) Rules were issued to Shri Luther, the Commission refrains from making any observations on Shri Luther. Yet the Commission is constrained to suggest to the Government that it must lay down certain rules regarding the chain of command through which alone orders from above should be communicated to the officers in the field. If the process of short-circuiting the chain of command is not frowned upon, the system would be exposed to the machinations of unscrupulous operators willing to jump levels in their anxiety to get close to the seat of power. (Para 12.64)

(v) According to Shri Krishan Chand, the decision to launch the Sales Tax and Price Tag raids against Messrs Pandit Brothers was a sequel to the orders that emanated from Shri Sanjay Gandhi. Even so he had a direct responsibility which he failed to discharge. He allowed himself to be used as a willing tool to subserve the designs of Shri Sanjay Gandhi. (Para 12.65)

(vi) Shri Sanjay Gandhi who wielded such enormous power during the emergency did not confine its activities only to the operation of demolition of houses, shops and industrial buildings. He took a hand even in getting some persons whom either he did not like or whom had thwarted him, arrested and detained. In the present case, the evidence brought on record clearly points to him as the source and the motivator of all the harassments that followed the action against Pandit Brothers. On the direct responsibility of Shri Sanjay Gandhi for the harassment that was meted out to Pandit Brothers, the Commission feels no doubt. (Para 12.71)

CHAPTER XIII

Demolitions in Delhi

I. *Demolitions in General:*

(i) After the declaration of the Emergency, demolition operations carried out by the DDA, MCD and NDMC received a spurt. The general policy of caution and concern for the people affected by demolitions gave place to a measure of reckless speed in clearing and cleaning up the areas earmarked without a corresponding concern for the people whose houses were demolished. Alternative arrangements to resettle them were not simultaneously made with the same speed. (Para 13.1)

(ii) An impression had been created that Shri Sanjay Gandhi was actively associated with the demolition programmes in Delhi. . . . The affected people went in deputations to Shri Sanjay Gandhi to seek his assistance in several cases. Shri Sanjay Gandhi used to meet these deputationists and deal with them in his own peculiar way. (Para 13.52)

(iii) In their hurry to implement the demolition programme, neither the DDA nor the MCD took the precaution in a number of cases of following even the basic minimum procedures laid down in the Delhi Development Act, Delhi Municipal Corporation Act and other relevant laws. Some of the features of the demolitions are:–

(i) No notices as required were issued before the buildings were demolished.

(ii) In a number of cases of acquisition of private property, land was occupied before even the proceedings for acquisition were commenced or before the date on which possession could be taken under the law.

(iii) In a number of cases, land use prescribed under the Delhi Master Plan was changed without the concurrence or permission of the Union Government.

(iv) To ensure that the affected people do not approach the law courts for redress, or political leaders, demolitions were carried out without advance intimation. Stay orders, where these could be obtained, were not respected and demolitions were carried out. Persons who approached the law courts were arrested under Section 108 Cr. P.C. on fabricated evidence or threatened with arrest under MISA and complled to withdraw the proceedings initiated by them.

(v) A squad of the Police was permanently attached to the DDA, obstensibly for protection of the DDA officials who used to go on demolition programmes to different areas. Even when the actions were illegal and arbitrary, the Police unit attached to the DDA remained present. The squad used to be supplemented by large contingents of both armed and unarmed police from nearly Policy Stations and the Lines with the object of intimidating and terrorising the aggrieved citizens and to prevent them from offering resistance to the demolitions. This affected the image of the Police also in the eyes of the public.

(vi) When there was criticism against unauthorised demolitions or some affected people had taken the matter to the Court, attempts seem to have been made to fabricate the records or to pre-date orders in an effort to establish that notices were actually issued and served mostly by affixation even when such notices had not been issued.

(vii) The demolition operations were carried out like a blitzkrieg in utter disregard of the human problems involved. Alternative accommodation sometimes was provided, but more often only open plots of land were allotted which were so small that no residential houses could be built on these. Very few built-up quarters were allotted to the affected persons.

(viii) A large number of persons whose residences were demolished, were making a living by performing some services for the residents living in the nearby areas. They belonged mostly to the class of masons, milkmen, domestic servants, watchmen, etc. When alternative sites were given to the persons whose houses were demolished at places far away from their place of work, they had to incur extra expenditure in addition to undergoing additional inconveniences for reaching their site of work.

(ix) In the matter of allotment of alternative accommodation, a

25 square yards of plot was given irrespective of the area earlier occupied by the concerned people and which might have been demolished. Normal price was charged for this plot of land. In many cases no compensations were offered or paid.

(x) In some of the areas of rehabilitation even the basic amenities were wanting, and the houses had been constructed back to back in such a manner that there was no ventilation or even passage between two houses. The rehabilitation areas in some cases presented a picture of hasty planning and indifferent execution. (Paragraph 13.53)

(xi) The demolitions undertaken in Delhi during the Emergency did not conform to the established legal and administrative requirements. The Commission recommends that the Government may take special steps to redress the grievances of the affected citizens on priority basis after considering the cases on merits. (Para 13.54)

II. *Demolitions in Bhagat Singh Market:*

(i) Shri Ailawadi's contention that the demolitions were purely voluntary cannot be accepted . . . . It, therefore, appears from the documentary and oral evidence that New Delhi Municipal Committee had carried out demolitions in Bhagat Singh Mrket and that this was done under the supervision of its Member-Secretary, Shri Ailawadi. (Para 13.79)

(ii) After the verandahs had been declared as a public street under Section 171(4) of the Punjab Municipal Act, the Committee could not proceed to remove encroachments or to demolish any structures unless the proper procedure laid down in Section 172(1) of the Punjab Municipal Act was followed. (Para 13.80)

(iii) Shri Ailawadi had exceeded his powers and misused his authority in demolishing the shops in the Bhagat Singh Market without observing the provisions of the law on the subject. (Para 13.82)

III. *Demolitions in Sultanpur Mazra – Occupation of Land in Village Sultanpur Mazra and Phool Kalan:*

(i) The land was occupied by the D.D.A. in spite of protests of the villagers. The so-called consent of the villagers appears to have been taken after the D.D.A. had already occupied the land and when the villagers had no option but to try and secure the best possible terms from the D.D.A. (Para 13.96)

(ii) At the time land was occupied, even the proposal for the issue of notification under the Land Acquisition Act had not been signed. (Para 13.96)

(iii) From the statements of witnesses, which have not been challenged by Shri Jagmohan or Shri Ranbir Singh, it is apparent that force was used in removing the residents and demolishing their houses. A contingent of police was present and bulldozers were used. (Para 13.106)

(iv) After the structures were demolished, the D.D.A. had no legal right to occupy the land on which these buildings were constructed and the action of S/Shri Jagmohan and Ranbir Singh, Executive Officer of the D.D.A. was illegal as the land was occupied much before the issue of notification on March 2, 1977 (Para 13.107)

IV. *Demolition in Sarai Pepal Thala and Jahangirpur Bhulswa:*

(i) The plea that entire operation carried out was on a voluntary basis cannot be accepted. (Paras 13.121 & 13.126)

(ii) Shri Jagmohan misused his position and abused his authority in ordering the illegal occupation of the land in village Jahangirpur Bhulswa and village Sarai Pepal Thala without proper proceedings under the Land Acquisition Act an also in ordering the demolition of structures in these villages without going through procedure laid down in the Delhi Development Act. (Para 13.128)

V. *Demolition of Arya Samaj Temple:*

(i) Shri Jagmohan has abused his position and misused his powers in ordering the demolition of a building used as place of worship. (Para 13. 144)

(ii) Shri S.M. Dua, the Executive Officer of D.D.A. seems to have played a part in fabricating the record and his denial in this regard is not acceptable. (Para 13.144)

VI. *Demolition in Turkman Gate Area*:

(i) Shri Jagmohan informed his subordinate officers about the proposed demolition operations in Turkman Gate only on April 7, 1976 and did not give sufficient time to them to go through the records and survey the area by making enquiries from the residents about the status of their property. (Para 13.172)

(ii) Shri H.K. Lal and Shri Jagmohan have shown scant respect for the rights of others and have misused their authority on a massive scale. The demolitions insofar as they concerned the unacquired and private properties were done without observing the due processes of law. (Para 13.173)

(iii) Shri Binder's action in requisitioning bulldozers to the Turkman Gate area even before the nots were brought under control is an indication of the extreme and indecent hurry in carrying out the demolition programme. Shri Bhinder thus showed great callousness to the miseries of the people of the area. He has abused his authority and misused his powers. (Para 13. 174)

VII. *Demolition in Village Samalkha:*

The Municipal Corporation of Delhi not only demolished the structures but also took possession of the private land in village Samalkha without any legal authority. Shri O.P. Gupta, the then Zonal Assistant Commissioner(R) who tried to follow the legal procedure was harassed and forced to go on leave. Subsequently he was accommodated in a junior post. The demolition and its illegalities have been admittedly done under the orders of Shri B.R. Tamta. He had misused his power and abused his authority. (Para 13.184)

VIII. *Demolitions in Village Kapas Hera*:

(i) Demolitions carried out in this village allegedly at the instance of Shri Sanjay Gandhi were unauthorised and procedures prescribed by law were not followed either by the D.D.A. or by the M.C.D. (Para 13.186)

(ii) This area was not a development area under the D.D.A. and the D.D.A. had no legal authority to demolish any structures here. However, witnesses stated that it was the D.D.A. which had demolished the structures. (Para 13.208)

(iii) The action of demolishing the house of Lt. Col. Ram Singh Yadav, a retired Army officer in this village was, as per Shri B.R. Tamta, taken on the orders of Shri Sanjay Gandhi. He had also to take disciplinary action against his own officers as he was pressurised by Shri Sanjay Gandhi. (Para 13.214)

(iv) S/Shri Jagmohan, B.R. Tamta, Ranbir Singh and Satya Prakash were all responsible for the demolitions in varying degrees. They had all abused their authority and misused their powers in going about the demolitions in the manner in which the did without observing the requirements of law and procedures. (Para 13.224)

(v) Shri Sanjay Gandhi was responsible for initiating the entire demolition operations in this village and insofar as demolitions were illegal, he has to take his share of the responsibility for the same. (Para 13.230)

IX. *Demolitions in Arjun Nagar:*

Some of the demolitions done by the D.D.A. in Arjun Nagar area were illegal. S/Shri Jagmohan, Satya Prakash and Ranbir Singh have all participated each in his respective field and contributed to the illegal demolitions. (Para 13.270)

X. *Demolitions in Karol Bagh:*

The demolitions in Karol Bagh were done at the instance of Shri Sanjay Gandhi. Among other considerations the political affiliation of the shopkeepers to the party opposed so the Congress was one of the deciding factors which impelled Shri Sanjay Gandhi to order the demolition of the structures in Karol Bagh. The responsibility for these demolitions must rest entirely with Shri Sanjay Gandhi and Shri B.R. Tamta. (Para 13.287)

XI. *Demolitions in Andheria Mor*:

(i) Action for demolition in Andheria Mor could have been taken by the Corporation only under Section 343(1) of the Delhi Municipal Corporation Act. Admittedly the procedure laid down in this Section has not been carried out. There is no other law under which the Corporation could have demolished the structures in Andheria Mor. The fact of demolition and its illegality has been admitted by Shri Tamta and the only plea he has taken is that this was done on the instructions of Shri Sanjay Gandhi. This by itself cannot absolve him of his responsibility. He had abused his authority and misused his powers.

(ii) The demolition operations which took place in Andheria Mor were carried out at the instance and under the directions of Shri Sanjay Gandhi and he was responsible for ordering the properties of the villagers to be demolished and the order was without any authority of law. (Para 13.304)

XII. *Conclusions*:

(i) In a number of cases, the normal and established legal processes were not complied with by Shri Jagmohan and Shri Tamta. (Para 13.306)

(ii) It has also very vividly been brought on record that the Delhi Development Authority indulged in falsification and fabrication of records. (Para 13.306)

(iii) Very often the demolitions were undertaken for considerations which were political and not infrequently whimsical. (Para 13.306)

(iv) Though the Lt. Governor was the head of the Administration and was also the Chairman of the Delhi Development Authority, he appears to have been completely ignored by these functionaries, who for a their actions took orders directly from Shri Sanjay Gandhi. The demolitions of places of worship specifically required the prior orders of the Lt. Governor. The requirements was completely ignored when the DDA demolished the Arya Samaj Temple. The lament of the Lt. Governor, Shri Krishan Chand, that nobody consulted him or listened to him and that they used to take orders directly from Shri Sanjay Gandhi has been heard by the Commission with a feeling of disgust for he admitted that he turned a deaf ear, and a blind eye to every conceivable piece of illegality and impropriety. (Para 13.207)

(v) Shri B.R. Tamta as Commissioner of MCD had the honesty to admit that he had done wrong things because of compulsions particularly the pressure on him of Shri Sanjay Gandhi. This by itself cannot be considered an extenuation of his conduct and he has also abused his authority and misused his power. (Para 13.308)

(vi) Shri Jagmohan grossly misused his position and abused his authority. He, during the emergency, became a law unto himself and went about doing the biddings of Shri Sanjay Gandhi without care or concern for the miseries of the people affected thereby. (Para 13.309)

(vii) Shri Sanjay Gandhi has actually aided and abetted the illegal demolitions undertaken by the DDA and the Municipal Corporation of Delhi and the evidence on record goes to show that he was the prime mover in majority of the illegal operations that took place in Delhi. (Para 13.310)

(viii) In the view of the Commission the manner in which Shri Sanjay Gandhi functioned in the public affairs of Delhi in particular is the single greatest act of excess committed during the period of emergency for which there is no parallel nor any justification for such assumption of authority or power in the history of independent India. While the other acts of the excesses many have been in the nature of act committed by functionaries having some shadow of authority acting in excess of their powers, here was a case of an individual wielding unlimited powers in a dictatorial manner without even the slightest right to it. If this country is to be rendered safe for future generations, the people owe it to themselves to ensure that an irresponsible and unconstitutional centre of power like the one which revolved round Shri Sanjay Gandhi during the emergency is not allowed to come up ever again in any from or shape or under any guise. (Para 13.311)

CHAPTER XIV

Turkman Gate Firing

Turkman gate firing commencement of demolitions:

(i) It is not possible to accept the plea that an operation of the type undertaken in the Turkman Gate locality could have gone on without the Intelligence Wing of the Delhi Police knowing anything about it.

(ii) The uncertainty about the area to be cleared by demolitions and the extension of this area, day after day contributed in no small measure to the tension being built up and which eventually culminated in the tragedy.

(iii) There is confusion about the exact provocation which resulted in the riot. The police placed the responsibility on the public and the public on the police.

(iv) The relevant registers in the police lines did not correctly reflect the actual issue of the arms and ammunition on April 19, 1976. This shows gross carelessness at the concerned levels. These omissions could also be deliberate so that the records would be silent if it is scrutinised in an inquiry.

(v) There is a lot of confusion about the number of rounds that were actuality fired in the course of the riots.

(vi) The police line record did not not even state the exact number of men detailed for duty in connection with the riot on the relevant day in Turkman Gate area.

(vii) A gross and probably a deliberate effort has been made to cover up the whole incident by not getting even an administrative enquiry made into the events leading to the death by police firing of admittedly six persons.

(viii) A report regarding the firing, as required in the Punjab Police Rules, was not drawn up. The report prepared by the Additional District Magistrate and the Superintendent of Police lacked the most important details such as the exact number of persons who died, the rounds fired, etc.

(ix) The magistracy did not fulfil the role expected of it.

(x) The bodies of the persons who had died were taken to the police station and not to the mortuary which was closer to the scene of the incident than the police station.

(xi) Enquiries into complaints and molestation of women and looting of property, ordered in a couple of cases were not pursued.

(xii) A police wireless log book had been tampered with. (Para 14.159)

(xiii) All the important documents such as General Diaries of the Police Stations, the documents of the Reserve Police Lines dealing with the quantum of force on the fateful day, the details regarding the arms and ammunition issued to various police parties and even the one and only report that was sent by the Administration on the events of the day on April 20, 1976 contain no relevant details. Absence of the relevant details and of these vital documents cannot be regarded as mere accidental coincidence. (Para 14.160)

(xiv) Investigation of the FIR No. 189 dealing with the riots was entrusted to a very junior officer of the rank of an ASI when almost all the important senior officers of the Delhi Administration were present and were witnesses to the events of the day. Both the Inspector General of Police and the District Magistrate have stated that they were not aware that the investigation of this important case was being done by such a junior officer. It is not surprising that the prosecution staff who scrutinised the investigation of this case sometime in May 1977 have found the investigation full of defects, many of which were of a grave nature. (Para 14.161)

(xv) The prosecuting officer found a number of defects in the investigation which, in a large measure, was avoidable with a little supervision and guidance of the investigation by the authorities at appropriate levels. This neglect of such an important investigation is a part of design to cover up the events of the day. (Para 14.162)

(xvi) The official communique on the events of the day, prepared at Raj Niwas, issued in the name of Mir Mushtaq Ahmed, sought to give a communal colour to cover up a gross failure on the part of the Administration. (Para 14.163)

(xvii) Though the Family Planning Programme may have contributed to the build-up of tension among all the residents of the area, the firing was a direct and immediate sequel to the decisions of the authorities to proceed with the demolitions regardless of the resistance of the people and the consequences. The subsequent conduct of the authorities, significant silence of several important and relevant records on material particulars, indicates that this was a part of a design to justify the firing by the Police. (Para 14.164)

(xviii) An attitude of vindictiveness by the Administration towards the citizens noticed is indefensible (Para 14.165)

(xix) A pre-dated firing order was not signed through Shri N.C. Ray, after pressure was brought to bear upon him by Shri Sanjay Gandhi at the instance of Shri Bhinder. (Para 14.171)

(xx) Shri Bhinder pressurised the magistrates for doing wholly improper acts and he got the firing order signed and ante-dated through the intervention of Shri Sanjay Gandhi. (Para 14.172)

(xxi) Shri Sanjay Gandhi intervened on behalf of Shri Bhinder and pressurised the District Magistrate and his colleagues and a junior magistrate to sign and pre-date the firing order.

(xxii) It was highly improper and unwarranted interference on the part of Shri Sanjay Gandhi to have called the Magistrates to his residence and ordered them to do a wholly improper and illegal act. (Para 14.178)

CHAPTER XV

Observations of the Commission

(i) With the Press gagged and a resultant black out of authentic information, arbitrary arrests and detentions went on apace. Effective dissent was smothered, followed by a general erosion of democratic values. High handed and arbitrary actions were carried out with impunity. The nation was initially in a state of shock, and then of stupor, unable to realise the directions and the full implications of the actions of the Government and its functionaries.

That the primary and not infrequently the sole motivation in the case of a number of public servants who acted unlawfully to the prejudice of the rights of citizens, was the desire for self-protection-desire for survival, may be regarded as some extenuation of their conduct. Yet, if the nation is to preserve the fundamental values of a democratic society, every person whether a public functionary or private citizen must display a degree of vigilance and willingness to sacrifice. (Para 15.1)

(ii) The circumstances in the which the emergency was declared and the case with which it was accomplished should be a warning to the citizens of the country. (Para 15.30)

(iii) Smt. Indira Gandhi did not consult the Cabinet even though she had plenty of time to do so. There is enough evidence to show that Smt. Indira Gandhi planned the imposition of the emergency atleast, as early as June 22. She had also shared the thought with some of her political confidants as early as morning of June 25. (Para 15.4)

(iv) In the absence of any explanation which would warrant the declaration of an emergency, the inference is inevitable that a political decision was taken by an interested Prime Minister in a desperate endeavour to save herself from the legitimate compulsion of a judicial verdict against her. (Para 15.5)

(v) The nation owed it to the present and the succeeding generations to ensure that the administrative set up is not subverted in future in the manner it was done to serve the personal ends of any one individual or a group of individuals in or near the Government. (Para 15.6)

(vi) Censorship of news and the manner in which the media was manipulated should be a lesson to the Government and to the people that in a vast country like ours Blanketing of news in the way it was done, has serious repercussions on the lives and the thoughts of the people. (Para 15.7)

(vii) The State owes it to nation to assure that judiciary will not be subjected to strains which might even indirectly operate as punitive merely because of pronouncements not to the liking of the executive authority. (Para 15.10)

(viii) In selecting its functionaries the Government should not throw to the winds the rules that have been framed for making such appointments. The Government having framed the rules governing its conduct cannot normally arrogate to itself the discretion to disregard them, unless there are demonstrably compelling reasons and circumstances justifying the side-stepping of those rules. (Para 15.11)

(ix) Forging records, fabrication of grounds for detentions, ante-dating of detention orders, the callousness with which the request of the detenus for revocation of orders for detention or even parole were ignored should be a warning to every thinking man as to how an Act initially intended to serve an extremely limited purpose to deal with the misdeeds of a special category of persons can be given such a wide and comprehensive application so as to embrace all sections of the population to penalise dissent. (Para 15.12)

(x) The collusion between the police and the magistracy in denying the citizens their basic freedoms by arrests and detentions of non-existent grounds is a matter of anguish. (Para 15.13)

(xi) The Government must seriously consider the feasibility and the desirability of insulating the police from the politics of the country and employing it scrupulously on duties for which alone it is by law intended. The policemen must also be made to realise that politicking by them is outside the sphere of their domain and the Government would take a very serious view of it. (Para 15.16)

(xii) The politicians who use a public servant for purely political purpose and the public servant who allows himself to be so used are both basically doing a signal dis-service to the country. (Para 15.18)

(xiii) The vast majority of demolitions were carried out by a complete disregard for the human sufferings of persons in very humble walks of life and the Government could take immediate steps to remedy the wrong and also to ensure that the conditions in the resettlement colonies are rendered safe, clean and convenient. (Para 15.21)

(xiv) The Government has a special responsibility to ensure that extra-constitutional centres of power are not allowed to grow and if and when located, to snuff them out ruthlessly. (Para 15.22)

(xv) Specific instructions should be issued emphasising that the detenus must be treated with dignity and respect due to them and he restraint imposed upon them will be minimal and consistent only with ensuring the safety of the state or interests of law and order and that student detenus will be permitted to take their periodical examinations. For female detenus special provisions should be made for housing them and extending to them appropriate conveniences. (Para 15.23)

(xvi) The practice of continuing in service as Heads of the organisations, retired officers on short-term renewable basis is a pernicious practice and often a source of serious abuse of authority. (Para 15.24)

(xvii) Departments like the Income-tax Department, Intelligence Bureau, CBI, Enforcement Directorate, etc., should be led by strong competent and self respecting individuals who are known for their appreciation of values and their concern for the interests of the country and its citizens. Lesser men as Heads of such organisations which play a vital role in the life of the nation would only be a disaster. (Para 15.24).

(xviii) For the effective and objective functioning of the Intelligence agencies, their activities and achievements should be suitably over seen and evaluated by responsible forums composed of persons specially selected for their integrity and sense of public duty and functioning independently of the Intelligence agencies. (Para 15.26)

(xix) The Commission has drawn the Government's attention to the guidelines dividing the government servants into three broad categories. Only those who had exceeded or misused or abused their powers or authority for securing personal gains or for securing advantage to other individual(s) organisation(s) have attracted the critical attention of the Commission. (Para 15.26)

(xx) The Commission would like to reiterate that it would reckon its achievement not by the number of the seriousness of the punitive actions taken against persons who had transgressed the laws, but by the nature and extent of the remedial and ameliorative actions that follow the labours of the Commission. (Para 15.28)

(xxi) If the Commission's observations generate a public debate on some of the vital issues focused by the Commission with the object of devising corrective machinery and remedial action, the Commission's labour will be amply rewarded. (Para 15.29)

CHAPTER XVI

Wrongful confinement and torture of Shri Lawrence Fernandes by the Police and Maltreatment in Jail

(i) The Commission is of the view that the statement of Shri Lawrence that he was taken away from his house and kept in illegal police custody from May 1, 1976 is true. (Para 16.5)

(ii) The Commission has no hesitation in disbelieving the story of

Inspector Prameswarappa (relating to his visit to K.G. General Hospital Casualty Ward). The study is false and is invented in an effort to save himself and his colleagues from the probable consequences of the illegal police detention and torture of Shri Lawrence. The cumulative effect of his statements leave no room for doubt that they are a tissue of falsehoods. (Para 16.11)

(iii) .....It is established beyond doubt that Shri Lawrence was in the illegal custody of the police from the night of May 1, 1976, and that he had been subjected to physical torture which necessitated his examination by two different doctors on two different dates : on the nights of 3rd and the 7th May, 1976. (Para 16.12)

(iv) The story related by the Police officers that Shri Lawrence was arrested on May 10, 1976 at Devangere at a bus stand bears a clear impress of fabrication and untruth. (Para 16.17)

(v) The circumstances in which Shri Lawrence was reported to have been arrested by Shri Visveshwariah, an investigating officer, is a story which is entirely incredible. (Para 16.20)

(vi) The Commission is inclined to accept the testimony of Dr. Krishnappa and Dr. Nagraj that there was a fracture of the left foot of Shri Lawrence since it is corroborated by the attendant symptoms of severe pain, swelling, inability to stand without support and inability to walk more than a step or two. (Para 16.38)

(vii) On the evidence, the conclusion is inevitable that Shri Lawrence was a physically disabled man when he came into the jail due to the torture and ill-treatment by the police and that within the jail premises Shri Chablani (Senior Superintendent of Jails) colluded with the police by delaying the orthopaedic examination of Shri Lawrence as far as he could and also in keeping him away from the other detenus for obvious reasons. The Commission holds Shri Chablani also responsible for not complying with the order of the court, which had asked for a medical report on the physical condition of Shri Lawrence. (Para 16.40)

(viii) Shri Lawrence was in unlawful police custody from May 1 to May 9, 1976 during which period he was assaulted by the police, which resulted in several personal injuries to him. For this responsibility is of Shri Visveshwariah, Deputy Superintendent of Police and Inspector Prameswarappa. (Para 16.43)

(ix) Shri Vittal Naik was present at the time when Shri Lawrence was produced before the Magistrate on 20th May and Shri Lawrence had complained to the Magistrate about assault on him by the COD people in his presence. Even then Shri Vittal Naik took no steps to make purposeful enquiry. He was under a duty to satisfy himself that Shri Lawrence was not ill treated while he was in the custody of the Police Station which came within his jurisdiction. The Commission, therefore, is of the view that Shri Vittal Naik is as much responsible for all that happened to Shri Lawrence in the police custody and must share responsibility with Shri Visveshwariah and Inspector Prameswarappa. (Para 16.44)

(x) The case diaries of the years of 1975 and 1976, which were purporting to be record of investigations conducted in the years 1975 and 1976 have been found to be written in the forms printed in March 1977. The inference is inevitable that diaries in their original form were found inconvenient and were re-written on the forms printed in March 1977. . . . Considering the importance and the evidentiary value of case diaries in judicial proceedings, the Commission was no doubt that the original diaries were replaced by fresh diaries and the version of Shri Vittal Naik that he did not initially write the diaries and wrote them only when it was necessary to produce them before the investigating officer, is a false statement. (Para 16.45)

(xi) The Commission deems it necessary to draw the attention of the appropriate authorities to the conduct of Shri Vittal Naik which the Commission regards reprehensible. (Para 16.46)

(xii) Shri Krishnamurthi Raju, Superintendent of Police, COD, had deliberately ignored the various lapses in the investigation. The Commission is of the view that as Superintendent of Police, he ought to take the full responsibility for everything that happened to Shri Lawrence while in his charge and on account of the activities of his officers. Shri Raju did not take steps to institute an inquiry even when he was told about the allegations that Shri Lawrence had made before the Magistrate. This is a grave omission on the part of a senior and responsible officer of the rank of Superintendent of Police. (Para 16.47)

(xiii) Shri Krishnamurthi Raju's complicity comes out in yet another context. Presumably, he did not think it necessary to publish any item in the Crime and Occurrence Sheet regarding Shri Lawrence being an absconder because he was already in custody and no further action was indicated in this regard. (Para 16.48)

(xiv) All the four police officers (named earlier) are responsible for illegal detention and torture of Shri Lawrence Fernandes, the primary responsibility resting squarely with Shri Krishnamurthi Raju, Superintendent of Police, Corps of Detectives, who was the senior most amongst them and with whose knowledge and consent everything else appears to have taken place. (Para 16.49)

(xv) Shri Chablani, the Senior Superintendent Jail colluded with the Police officers in gaining time to let the injuries on the person of Shri Lawrence heal by postponing the medical examination of Shri Lawrence by an orthopaedic surgeon. He also failed to comply with the Court's order to submit a medical report on Shri Lawrence. This was a deliberate effort on the part of Shri Chablani with a view to shield the delinquent police officers. The Commission is also of the view that keeping of Shri Lawrence in the corridor of the single cell-barrack was done deliberately with a view to keep all that happened to Shri Lawrence at the hands of the police a secret from the fellow detenus. (Para 16.50)

(xvi) This case highlights not only the illegal detention and torture of an individual by the police but a subversion of an entire legal system including the judicial process by senior and responsible Government officers..... The concerned police officers, have by their conduct, set a very poor example to the members of the Force which they represent. By glibly telling lies on oath, they have attempted to put a premium on perjury. By their conduct they have lowered themselves in the eyes of the public generally and the Police Force in particular and have done more lasting damage to the credibility of the Force as a whole. (Para 16.51)

(xvii) Highly placed officers whether they belong to the administrative branch or the police branch are the custodians of the ideals of the service to which they belong. When the leadership of the highly placed officers fails, it reflects directly upon those whom they represent and result in the erosion of discipline and performance of the rank and file. Examined in that light, the conduct of the police officers, as disclosed by the investigation of the Commission, is bound to leave a dark spot upon the reputation of this Service as an institution. (Para 16.52)

CHAPTER XVII

I. *Detention Under MISA of Shri Murali Dhar Dalmia, Chief Advisor, Technological Institute of Textiles, Bhiwani (Haryana):*

(i) The detention order against Shri Dalmia, passed on November 30, 1975, was based upon trumped-up charges and the grounds of detention fail to stand the test of scrutiny. . . . According to Shri Parmanand CID Inspector his report had to be based on "false and concocted materials". (Paras 17.7 and 17.8)

(ii) Shri R.S. Varma, the District Magistrate Bhiwani, made no effort to satisfy himself on the veracity or the adequate of the grounds of detention and mechanically passed the detention order. (Para 17.9)

(iii) Parole was granted to Shri Dalmia only when Shri K.K. Birla met Shri Bansi Lal and successfully pleaded with him for this. Shri Bansi Lal agreed to grant parole only on conditions that Shri Dalmia would vacate the house that he was occupying and would be away from Delhi for six months. (Para 17.13)

(iv) This case highlights the highhandedness and arbitrary conduct of Shri Bansi Lal in Haryana during the emergency. Various functionaries in the Government fabricated records and concocted grounds to justify an unjusticiable detention order to fulfil the desire of Shri Bansi Lal regarding the arrest of Shri Dalmia. (Para 17.15)

(v) The Chief Minister employed the authority and the resources of the State to wreck his private grudge against a citizen in an unprincipled and unscrupulous manner and Courts felt compelled to hold that they had no power to grant redress. (Para 17.15)

(vi) Shri Bansi Lal, even though he had ceased to be the Chief Ministry of Haryana, and had become Defence Minister in the

Government of India, continued to exercise the same authority and power over the affairs of the State of Haryana as he had done when he was the Chief Minister. . . . The power that he exercised and the manner in which he wielded it would rank him with medieval despots. He grossly misused his position and abused his authority as Chief Minister in ordering the detention of Shri Dalmia. He continued to abuse his position even after he had ceased to be the Chief Minister and became the Defence Minister of the Government of India. (Para 17.17)

II. *Detention of Shri M.L. Kak, Special Correspondent of the Tribune:*

(i) Shri Kak's detention was a part of the large scale MISA detention operations that had been mounted all over Haryana on the night of June 25/26, 1975 at the instance of the Chief Minister, Shri Bansi Lal. (Para 17.19)

(ii) Shri Rudra has admitted that there were no materials against Shri Kak except that he was generally critical of the then Government in his reporting, and that he brought to the notice of the District Magistrate the crucial fact that sufficient materials to warrant detention under MISA against Shri Kak did not exist, Shri Jain, the District Magistrate has, however, denied that Shri Rudra ever told him, before obtaining the detention orders, that sufficient material for detention of Shri Kak was not available. (Para 17.21 and 17.22)

(iii) In the M.H.A. file dealing with the detention of Shri Kak, the then Joint Secretary (I.S.) had noted "This appears to be a case of misuse of MISA." (Para 17.25)

(iv) In the opinion of the Commission Shri Rudra's version seems to be more truthful and correct than that of Shri Jain. The position taken by the District Magistrate that he was told verbally by the Senior Superintendent of Police about the grounds of detention, which he believed to be true and genuine, and he based his detention orders on the version of the SSP, is an attempt to evade his responsibility by shifting the blame on to the SSP Shri Rudra. (Para 17.28)

(v) The stand taken by Shri L.M. Jain that he issued the detention order against Shri M.L. Kak only after the satisfying himself personally about the grounds for detention does not appear to be consistent with the facts of the situation. (Para 17.29)

(vi) ......Commission has no doubt that the story of Shri Jain is false. (Para 17.29)

(vii) In his anxiety to save himself, Shri L.M. Jain seems to have taken recourse to shifting the responsibility on the others. The Commission feels that this officer who was holding the important office of the District Magistrate was a party, under the compulsion of circumstances prevailing at that time, to patently illegal acts, had attempted to Shirk his responsibility and has in that process invented a story, which cannot be accepted. By his unbecoming conduct, he has done a disservice to the traditions of the service and the legitimate expectations that the people and the Government have in the service to which he belongs. (Para 17.31)

III. *Harassment and Detention of Cdr. (Retd.) Pritam Datta of Rohtak*:

(i) The removal of Cdr. Datta from the membership of the District Soldiers, Sailors and Airmen (D.S.S. & A.) Board of District Rohtak was not only improper but also violative of the constitution of the D.S.S. & A. Board. (Paras 17.35 and 17.36)

(ii) Orders for conducting a raid on the business premises of Cdr. Datta at Rohtak were given to Shri J.K. Duggal, Excise and Taxation Commissioner, Haryana, by Shri Sham Chand, the then Minister of Excise and Taxation, Haryana, at the instance of Shri Bansi Lal and the raid was ordered by Shri Duggal even though there was no information with him of the commission of any irregularities or malpractices by Cdr. Datta. (Para 17.38)

(iii) Shri O.P. Taneja, Dy. Excise and Taxation Commissioner, acted with alarming expedition in initiating action against Cdr. Datta and in cancelling his license and closing his godown. No proper warrant was made out and no order in that behalf was recorded. (Para 17.40)

(iv) On November 19, 1975, Cdr. Datta was detained under MISA and he had to remain in detention till December 1975. Shri Mehtani had informed Shri S.P. Mittal, D.C., on a number of occasions that the Chief Minister, Shri Bansi Lal was annoyed with Cdr. Datta and wanted his detention under MISA.

(v) Shri S.H. Mohan, SSP Rohtak has stated that though there were no adverse materials whatsoever to justify Cdr. Datta's detention under MISA, he had to personally prepare a report containing fabricated grounds for detention. (Para 17.43)

(vi) Shri R.C. Mehtani who had commenced his career as an L.D.C. in the Haryana Government and had a meteoric rise when he became O.S.D. to the Chief Minister drawing a salary of nearly Rs. 2,300, wielded extraordinary influence and authority in the State of Haryana....... His relations stood to gain by getting Cdr. Datta in trouble. Towards this end, he appears to have grossly misused his official position. (Para 17.49)

(vii) Shri Bansi Lal had issued verbal instructions to the District Magistrate, Shri Mittal, to detain Cdr. Datta in a move to help one Ram Chander who happened to be very close to him. He also acted under the influence of his official assistant, Shri Mehtani, who had a direct personal interest in promoting the business interest of Messrs. Ram Chander and Sons. In the process he stopped short of nothing including the detention of Cdr. Datta on entirely concocted grounds. (Para 17.53)

(viii) An innocent citizen who had given the best part of his life to the service of the nation suffered irreparable damage to his reputation and social standing by the vindictive operations of Shri Bansi Lal and Shri Mehtani. These two persons have grossly misused their position and authority and were responsible for the illegal detention under MISA of an innocent individual for purely personal reasons. (Para 17.54)

IV. *Detention under MISA of Shri Ishwar Lal Choudhary, District Employment Officer, Bhiwani (Haryana)*:

(i) Shri Ishwar Lal Choudhary, on receiving a message through the D.S.P. met the Chief Minister Shri Bansi Lal at his Bhiwani resident. There the Chief Minister in the presence of various district functionaries as well as members of the public accused Shri Choudhary of registering names of the people of Rohtak District in Bhiwani Employment Exchange and without giving any opportunity to him to explain his conduct ordered his detention under MISA. Shri Choudhary was accordingly arrested by the police. (Para 17.58)

(ii) This case unfolds a sordid tale of abuse of power, misuse of authority and illustrates Shri Bansi Lal's capricious and highly arbitrary style of administration. A straight-forward and honest officer performing his duties according to rules was detained, because he failed to comply with the irregular requests of Shri Surinder Singh son of Shri Bansi Lal. The district authorities of their turn merely and unquestioningly carried out the order of detention of an officer against whom there was nothing on record. (Para 17.65)

(iii) The provisions of MISA were misused in a blatant manner because Shri Bansi Lal wanted it. (Para 17.65)

V. *Harassment and Detention under MISA of Shri Pitambar Lal Goyal*:

(i) Shri Bansi Lal wanted to prevent Shri Goyal from entering the service and so covert efforts were made at his instance to declare Shri Goyal unfit for selection. (Para 17.68)

(ii) Immediately after the proclamation of emergency, orders for detention of Shri Goyal under the MISA were issued. Shri Nakai, the SSP, has admitted that there were no materials available against Shri Goyal but he had fabricated the report against him in view of the clear instruction of the State Government. (Para 17.76)

(iii) Shri R.S. Varma, the District Magistrate, has admitted that he signed the detention order when there was before him no material whatsoever against Shri Goyal. He has also admitted that in the case of Shri Ram Pratap (father of Shri Pitambar Goyal) detention orders were passed without application of mind. (Paras 17.77 and 17.82)

(iv) What Dr. Jain (A.C.) had done....was completely contrary to the conduct expected of a senior and responsible doctor and contrary to medical ethics.... The Commission is of the opinion that he, as the Chairman of the Medical Board, has misused his position and abused his authority in manipulating the medical report on Shri Pitambar Lal Goyal. (Paras 17.87 and 17.89)

(v) The evidence of Shri Harnam Singh, SHO, has not been found by the Commission to be reliable. (Para 17.90)

(vi) .... The Commission does not find Shri R.S. Varma, District

Magistrate, responsible for any improper conduct with regard to the verification of the character and antecedents of Shri Pitambar Lal Goyal. (Para 17.90)

(vii) The Commission finds that Shri S.D. Bhambri, the then Chief Secretary in the Haryana Government had no personal grudge against Shri Goyal. The exercise to change the rules was undertaken by Shri Bhambri pursuant to the wishes of Shri Bansi Lal...... The Commission cannot be oblivious to the prevailing conditions in the State of Haryana during the period of emergency and under those circumstances, it would have been difficult for anyone to act as a hero. Even so, considering the position of trust and responsibility that Shri Bhambri held at that point of time, his conduct did not conform to the best traditions of the Administrative Service to which he belongs. (Para 17.92)

(viii) The Commission finds the conduct of Shri Bansi Lal in regard to this case reprehensible. For purely personal reasons he grossly misused his position as Chief Minister and abused his authority. He went after three generations of a family to satisfy his appetite for vengeance. In the process he got the reports fabricated for the sole purpose of denying a young man an office in the Judicial Service which would have made his career. He got Shri Pitambar Lal Goyal, his father, uncle and grandfather detained also. He appears to have pursued his animosity against the Goyal family even when he was appointed as Defence Minister in the Government of India and got the rules changed so as to disable a detenu and particularly Shri Goyal from taking a competitive examination. There is no evidence before the Commission as to the direct involvement of Shri Bansi Lal, but there is a little doubt, on the evidence, that Shri Bansi Lal was responsible for the change in the rules. (Para 17.94)

(ix) The Commission notes with amazement the statement of Shri B.D. Gupta to the effect that even as Chief Minister, he stood in constant fear of being detained under MISA by Shri Bansi Lal. This typifies the general atmosphere of fear and uncertainty generated by Shri Bansi Lal in Haryana during the period of emergency from the effect of which no one from the highest of the lowest was free. (Para 17.94)

(x) An incumbent to the office of the Chief Minister of a State who should have been the very embodiment of justice and fairplay in all public dealings, has descended in this case to a petty vindictive level to satisfy a personal grudge against the members of a family. (Para 17.94)

VI. *Use of Compulsion and Force in implementation of the Family Planning Programme in village Uttarwar, District Gurgaon*:

(i) This raid on village Uttarwar was, it appears, planned deliberately by the State officials because of the opposition of the local population to submit to the sterilisation programmes of the State Government. (Para 17.96)

(ii) All indications on the basis of oral and documentary evidence are that Shri S.S. Bajwa (I.G.P., Haryana) was fully aware of what was intended and did happen and agreed with the consequential actions that followed the raid. The Commission accepts his plea that he had been rendered considerably ineffective even in the handling of his offices as it emerges from the letter that he had received from the Home Secretary to the Government of Haryana (where he was advised not to initiate action against any Superintendent of Police without prior approval of the Chief Minister). The Commission would like to observed that it cannot be expected on the one hand, the leadership of the Force to function effectively if, on the other, steps are also taken by the Government to undermine the leadership. (Para 17.124)

(iii) Shri M.K. Miglani, the then Deputy Commissioner, appears to have used his position as the Head of the District, to order the disconnection of the electric supply to the village. He was as much a party to the raid as others were and to everything else that flowed from it. Shri Miglani was interested in fulfilling the family planning target that had been set for him from the State HQ. (Para 17.125)

(iv) Shri Tek Chand, as SSP, Gurgaon, was an active participant in the events leading to the raid and following it. The villagers of Uttarwar were carried to the sterilisation centre in trucks under police escort. (Para 17.126)

(v) The three officers were privy to the raid which was planned at the behest of the higher authorities. These officers were powerless to resist the express wishes of the Government of the time. The Commission, therefore, takes a lenient view of the matter as far as the officers themselves are concerned. This is, however, not to minimise the gravity and illegality of what was done to the people of the village both in terms of the raid, sterilisation and the cutting of electricity. (Para 17.127)

(vi) Much concentration of power in the hands of the District Magistrates and the Sub-Divisional Officers with regard to the career prospects of officials belonging to the other departments insofar as these were governed by the favourable confidential reports of the District Magistrates and the Sub-Divisional Officers on the work and conduct of these officials appears to have been, in no small measure, responsible for the willingness of a large body of officials to carry out improper or unauthorised directions emanating from the District and Sub-Divisional authorities. (Para 17.127)

CHAPTER XVIII

Abuse of Authority—Complaints on Service Matters Including Premature Retirements, Dismissals/Removal from Service and Super-sessions During Emergency

In this Chapter, the Commission has set down certain broad aspects relating to abuse of authority and misuse of power in the matter of treatment meted out to public servants insofar as it related in their service conditions generally and with particular reference to their summary dismissal, compulsory/premature retirements and super-sessions.

CHAPTER XIX

Arrests and Detentions

This chapter deals with in a generally way, the detentions under the MISA ordered by the detaining authorities of the respective State Governments. The discussion is intended primarily to compile and set down at one place, on the basis of the records of the respective State Governments, a factual account of the detentions ordered during emergency by the different State Governments as a record of the times.

CHAPTER XX

Conditions in Jails in India with Special Reference to Treatment of Persons Arrested Under the DISIR or Detained under the MISA, etc.

The Commission sent out a questionnaire to all the States requesting information on certain relevant topics. The officers of the Commission also visited Jails in different parts of the country in an effort to make an on-the-spot study of the jail conditions. Information contained in this chapter has been compiled on the basis of such replies and visits. Effort has been made to keep the reports on the Jail Conditions as factual as possible and shorn of any comments whatever except recording a few suggestions for the consideration of the Government.

CHAPTER XXI

Implementation of the Family Planning Programme During the Emergency

This chapter deals with the manner in which the Family Planning Programme was implemented by the Central and State Governments from time to time during the period of emergency.

CHAPTER XXII

Demolitions During Emergency

The Commission had issued a detailed questionnaire on demolition to all State Government and Union Territories seeking information on various aspects of the demolition programme carried out in the States. Some general aspects and the salient points emerging from the replies received from the States have been discussed in this chapter.

CHAPTER XXIII

Complaints and their Disposal with Reference to the Issue of Reference

In this chapter, details have been given regarding the total number of complaints received by the Commission, how these were categorised, classified, investigated and disposed of.

CHAPTER XXIV

General Observations

(i) The one single item which had affected the people most over the entire country was the manner in which the powers under the amended MISA were misused at various levels. (Para 24.2)

(ii) A large number of officers exercising the powers of District Magistrates obediently carried out the instructions emanating from politicians and administrative heads issued on personal or political considerations............... Such conduct on the part of responsible officers is not in consonance with the best traditions of the Service to which they belonged and of the ethical considerations governing the exercise of such powers. (Para 24.3)

(iii) Some Officers did not have the courage to do the right thing during the emergency: they have not the character to face the truth now and own up their past wrongs. (Para 24.4)

(iv) The manner in which the MISA detentions were ordered, should be a lesson to the peoples' representatives in the Legislature as to how a Statute, initially well-conceived, may be misused for purposes totally alien to its object and intentions of its framers. . . . It is time that some mechanism is devised to ensure that such enactments are subjected to a periodical review by the framers themselves. (Para 24.5)

(v) In several cases, large scale fabrication of records has been admitted. Means should be devised to ensure that these concocted records are not used again to the disadvantage or detriment of the individuals concerned. (Para 24.6)

(vi) It is a matter of concern to the Commission that the (then) prevailing acts of impropriety and immorality came to be accepted as a concept of a new propriety and a new morality. (Para 24.7)

(vii) It is necessary to provide certain institutional safeguards to look after the interests of the entire run of officials and particularly those who are involved at the decision making levels of the Government. (Para 24.8)

(viii) Detention of an officer who had reputation for integrity, for not carrying out orders which were plainly unwarranted and which amounted to a flagrant and unpardonable misuse of authority by a politician has a very important and telling lesson for the nation as a whole .... if this instance is projected on the national scale, a political authority may decide to penalize an officer for tendering an advice or taking a decision the operational effect of which, albeit beneficial, transcends the territorial boundaries of the State to embrace the interest of the country as a whole.... Public servants are expected to function in the interest of the country as a whole and not subserve a narrow sectarian or regional interest of politicians. (Para 24.9)

(ix) It is imperative to ensure that the officials at the decision making levels are protected and immunised from threats or pressures so that they can function in a manner in which they are governed by one single consideration.......the promotion of public well-being and the upholding of the fundamentals of the Constitution and the rule of law. (Para 24.10)

(x) It is hoped that the authorities both at the Centre and the States will look at some of the cases in which aberrations have been pin-pointed by the Commission in a spirit of honest inquiry and determine what went wrong not only in each individual case but generally and how a similar situation can and should be averted in the future. (Para 24.11)

(xi) Commitment by the public servants means only and entirely commitment to the policy and programmes of the Government in so far as these are in conformity with the rule of law and fundamentals of the Constitution. . . . Public servants have to be politically neutral at all levels and at all times. . . . It is expected of the Services that they would tender frank, informed and well-considered advice without getting personally involved in their present position or their future advancement. (Para 24.12)

(xii) The Government must encourage its employees to function freely and fearlessly within the framework of established principles, making it clear that deviation from established procedures without justification would be dealt with severely. (Para 24.13)

(xiii) It is necessary for the Government to appreciate the need for defining the various functions and powers of the several lower functionaries who are in close proximity to the seats of power. . . . The circumstances under which the personal staff including special assistants and the private secretaries attached to the Ministers could convey orders be defined precisely and safeguards should be provided for checkback in the event of doubt or difference of opinion. (Para 24.14)

(xiv) The trend in democratic Governments today is in favour of more and more open functioning. The benefit of experience of such working may be availed of for such action as may be feasible, practicable and desirable in the context of our own peculiar needs and conditions. (Para 24.15)

(xv) It is necessary to devise adequate and appropriate safeguards to ensure that powers available to the Government to prematurely retire an employee are not arbitrarily used without any scope for redressal of the employee's grievances. "Droit Administratif" on the French Model can be usefully adopted by the Government. (Para 24.16)

(xvi) What happened during the Emergency was the subversion of a system of administration. To avoid recurrence the system must be overhauled with a view to strengthen it so that it could work in a free atmosphere and in a spirit calculated to promote the integrity and welfare of the nation and the rule of law. (Para 24.17)

(xvii) The events during the Emergency are merely the tragic culmination of the particular trend that had been identified and condemned from time to time by the Commissions of Inquiry in the past. The Commission owes it to the citizens of India to emphasise that appointments of Commissions by themselves are not enough if the Governments concerned do not follow up and implement such of the recommendations as are avowedly accepted by them. (Para 24.18)

(xviii) If administrative machinery in our country is to be rendered safe for four children, the Services must give a better account of themselves by standing up for the basic values of an honest and efficient administration. This alone can resurrect the people's lost faith once again in our Services. If a democratic heritage is to be left for future generations, we should want the truth again to be enshrined in its legitimate place in the social, economic and political scheme of things in our country.

There is a nothing unattainable or profound in this. It is a simple human message. (Para 24.19)

CHAPTER XXV

Conclusion

(i) The Commission had to be selective in the matter of hearing of cases in open session not because the Commission did not appreciate the gravity of the allegations made by aggrieved persons but because of the fact that it would have been impossible to do so in all the cases and complete the job within the foreseeable future. The State Governments have appointed Authorities and the Commission trusts that the proceedings will be disposed of by them expeditiously latest by December 31, 1978. (Para 25.1)

(ii) All the officers and staff of the Commission deserve high praise for the single-minded devotion to duty that they have exhibited in the discharge of functions at various levels. (Para 25.6)

15

COMMISSION OF INQUIRY ON MARUTI AFFAIRS, 1977 – REPORT[1]
May 30, 1977 – May 31, 1979

One Man Commission Shri A.C. Gupta

Appointment

By Notification No. S.O. 375(E) dated the 30th May, 1977 the Central Government appointed a Commission of Inquiry for the purpose of looking into the affairs of the following Maruti concerns:

(i) Messrs Maruti Limited, a company formed and registered under the Companies Act, 1956 (1 of 1956) and having its registered office at Palam-Gurgaon Road, Gurgaon, (Haryana);

(ii) Messrs Maruti Heavy Vehicles (Private) Limited, a company formed and registered under the Companies Act, 1956 (1 of 1956) and having its registered office at 138-B New Colony, Gurgaon (formerly, Palam-Gurgaon Road, Gurgaon);

(iii) Messrs Maruti Technical Services (Private) Limited, a company formed and registered under the Companies Act, 1956 (1 of 1956) and having its registered office at E-49, Kirti Nagar, New Delhi.

Terms of Reference

The terms of reference of the Commission were framed as follows:

(a) to inquire into the matters specified in the Annexure to this notification in relation to the companies and firms specified in the

---

1. Controller of Publications, Delhi, 1979, iv + 141 p.

foregoing paragraph to ascertain whether, in order to show any undue favour, or to cause any undue pecuniary or other benefit to accrue, to one or more Maruti concerns, there was any abuse of power or position or contravention of law or normal official procedure by, or on the part of, any person in authority, or any other person related to, or associated with, such person in authority, or any other high official or public servant in relation to all or any of the matters specified in the Annexure to this notification, and if so, the facts and circumstances relating to, or pertaining to, such abuse of power, position or contravention, the extent of involvement of, or improper pecuniary benefit derived by, any person aforesaid, and the extent of undue favour shown by such person to one or more of the said companies or firms and the undue financial or other benefit accruing to such companies or firms by reason, or in consequence, of such favour; and

(b) to inquire into any other matter which arises from or is connected with or incidental to any act, omission or transaction referred to in the Annexure aforesaid.

The Annexure to the notification lists thirteen matters. The thirteenth item reads:

> "All matters in relation to items 1 to 12 pertaining to the role and part of any Director or Managing Director of the said Maruti concerns, or any friend or associate of such Director or Managing Director, and all the facts and the circumstances relating cases where any direct or indirect advantage was taken of any relationship or connection of any such Director or Managing Director with any Minister or other public servant as well as the role of any person who directly or indirectly aided or assisted in the taking of such an advantage".

Item No. 13 is therefore not a separate matter for inquiry, it really amplifies the scope of the preceding twelve items.

Contents

Introduction; Initiation, processing and clearing of Maruti Car Project: Testing and clearance of the prototype car; Acquisition and allotment of land to Maruti Limited: Location of Maruti complex of buildings at its present site; Raising of capital, working capital and other financial resources and their utilisation by Maruti Limited, Maruti Technical Services Private Limited, and Maruti Heavy Vehicles Private Limited; Appointment of dealers, collection of dealership money and its custody and utilisation by the Maruti concerns; Agreements entered into by and between the Maruti concerns; Transactions regarding sale of mounted cranes, truck tractors, road rollers and building of bus bodies between Maruti concerns and various State Governments, public sector undertakings, statutory corporations, local bodies, etc.; Allotment of controlled commodities — like cement, steel and coal to Maruti Limited and their utilisation/disposal; Securing of loans by Maruti concerns from nationalised banks; Foreign collaboration agreements entered into by Maruti Limited and import licences issued to Maruti Technical Services Private Limited; Conclusion.

Recommendations

CHAPTER I

(a) To consider the feasibility of manufacturing low cost passenger cars in the country, the Central Government had appointed two Committees, one in 1959 and the other in 1960. The project was not implemented even after the committees had submitted their reports as the foreign exchange position at the time was said to be unfavourable. Criticism however grew that the inaction was in the interest of the monopolists in the automobile industry. Replying to a debate in the Lok Sabha on the subject of small car in August 1966 Shri D. Sanjivayya, Minister of Industry, stated that the feasibility of the car project would be considered first in the public sector. Shri Fakharuddin Ali Ahmed, Minister of Industrial Development and Company Affairs, repeated in Rajya Sabha in July 1967 that the endeavour of the Government would be to explore the possibility of manufacturing a cheap car in the public sector. Shri Sanjay Gandhi applied for an industrial licence to manufacture passenger cars on December 11, 1968. The desire expressed by Shri Fakharuddin Ali Ahmed for a new unit in the public sector led to a summary being prepared in September/October 1969 for consideration by the Cabinet. In the summary the Ministry of Industrial Development included a paragraph proposing to seek approval of the Cabinet for the issue of letters of intent to parties who came forward with proposals based on indigenous design and with no request for import or allocation of foreign exchange. From this point the public sector appears to have lost the priority given to it earlier by Shri Sanjivayya and Shri Fakharuddin Ali Ahmed. The trend became more prominent in the note recorded on December 10, 1969 by Shri S.R. Kapur, Under Secretary in the Ministry of Industrial Development, which, after describing Shri Sanjay Gandhi's scheme as completely indigenous, suggested sending all such indigenous schemes to the licensing committee for approval without waiting for the decision of the Cabinet on the summary prepared for its consideration. Besides Sanjay Gandhi's proposal there was then only one more, from Madan Mohan Rao, which claimed to be indigenous. Shri Kapur's anxiety to have the proposals claimed as indigenous sent to the licensing committee without waiting for the Cabinet decision is hard to explain unless the object was to hasten the issue of a letter of intent to Shri Gandhi. If one remembers that it was Kapur who in August 1966 had said that a wholly indigenous car was "inconceivable" "at the present stage of our industrial development" and in January 1967 suggested that the existing manufacturers should be allowed to expand, the change in his view would seem remarkable.

The policy announced in Parliament by Shri Dinesh Singh, Minister of Industrial Development and Internal Trade, on August 10, 1970 contemplated setting up an additional production capacity in the public sector of 50,000 cars per annum based on a proven foreign design concurrently with giving an opportunity to parties in the private sector to manufacture cars based on completely indigenous sources. It thus appears that after the initial assertion of priority in favour of the public sector, Government's policy concerning the manufacture of cars with the arrival of Shri Sanjay Gandhi on the scene was shaped to help Shri Gandhi get an industrial licence for his car project.

(b) The condition requiring the proposals from parties in the private sector to be wholly indigenous was considered impossible to satisfy at that stage of industrial development by many including Shri Sanjivayya, the DGTD and the Tariff Commission. Kapur's note dated August 17, 1966 has already been referred to. The question therefore arises, why such an impossible condition was imposed? Even Madan Mohan Rao who claimed his scheme to be indigenous and who was granted a letter of intent along with Sanjay Gandhi, felt that he could not proceed without having his drawings approved by a foreign expert. Shri Gandhi had an imported NSU engine fitted on the Maruti Prototype that was sent to VRDE for testing which was clearly a fraudulent act. Many of its components were also admittedly imported though some of them were bought out from the local market; use of such components was not permissible according to the notion of a hundred per cent indigenous car as explained by Shri D. Sanjivayya, Shri C. Subramaniam and Shri Dinesh Singh. It seems that Sanjay Gandhi was aware of the difficulty and he never intended to comply with the condition, yet he succeeded in obtaining an industrial licence. Others who were not so bold and resourceful and did not expect to get away with fraud were bound to give up leaving the field clear to Shri Sanjay Gandhi.

(c) Muller, a West German national, who brought the two NSU engines from West Germany was asked by Shri Sanjay Gandhi to join Maruti Limited as technical adviser and Muller had also written a letter to the Foreigners Regional Registration Officer on July 29, 1972 saying that he had entered into a contract with Maruti Limited with effect from July 1, 1972. Then Shri Gandhi changed his mind, presumably because he was advised that Muller's employment with Maruti Limited might be taken as a breach of the first condition of the letter of intent, and Muller was asked to execute a contract with Maruti Technical Services which he did. He was Maruti Technical Services' full time consultant for the Maruti small car project only; he was to advise Maruti Limited through Maruti Technical Services. This was only a device to get round the prohibition.

(d) VRDE's decision to reserve their report on the indigenous character of the assemblies and components of the Maruti prototype car till the strip test stage is difficult to appreciate. Maruti's Chief Executive, Shri R.H. Chawdhry has said that even by looking at it one could tell that the engine fitted on the prototype was an imported one. By reporting this fact earlier VRDE could have avoided all the exercises they had taken which were really useless if the condition insisting on the indigenous nature of car was meant to be taken seriously.

(e) Sanjay Gandhi's car project was treated as a special case. Shri R.V. Subrahmanian admits that this kind of special treatment was not given to any other applicant for industrial not given to any other applicant for industrial licence. Shri Gandhi had his preliminary project report examined by the DGTD and the Planning Commission even before he applied for an industrial licence. This was not usual P.V. Subrahmanian however said that so far as DGPD was concerned it was "not wholly unusual". Shri B.D. Pande, then Secretary of the Planning Commission, asked whether it was customary for the Planning Commission to examine project reports from private parties, replied that it was not "totally unusual". Even before Shri Gandhi applied for a licence the officials of the DGTD had discussions with him regarding the various features of his project. He offered inspection of the Maruti prototype car to the DGTD officials at the residence of the Deputy Minister, Ministry of Industrial Development where Shri R.V. Subrahmanian, Joint Secretary in the Ministry was also present. In the summary for the licensing committee also Sanjay Gandhi's application was treated as a special case. Joint Secretary R.V. Subrahmanian considered Madan Mohan Rao's plan to produce 75,000 cars a year over-ambitious and at his instance the summary recommended in Rao's case an initial capacity of 10,000 cars going up to 20,000 – 25,000 cars a year. The capacity of 50,000 cars a year in the case of Sanjay Gandhi was not disturbed. There appears to be no valid reason for the two cases being treated differently. The licensing committee raised Rao's capacity to 25,000 cars per annum. According to the declared policy, the cars were required to be one hundred per cent indigenous which the DGTD, the Tariff Commission and even Shri D. Sanjivayya thought was an impossible condition. I was therefore hardly of any practical significance whether an entrepreneur was permitted to manufacture 25,000 cars or 50,000 cars a year. To the members of the licensing committee, especially to R.V. Subrahmanian, it seems, no one could be equal to Sanjay Gandhi even in a make believe world.

(f) Shri Sanjay Gandhi tried hard to avoid the tests that VRDE, Ahmednagar, proposed to carry out on the Maruti prototype car, specially the reliability test. The reason was stated by retired Wing Commander R.H. Chawdhry, Chief Executive of Maruti Limited : "that car was not capable of going through the test". Shri S.M. Ghosh, then Joint Secretary in the Ministry of Heavy Industry, admits that in his experience "so much correspondence all round has not been exchanged for testing any other prototype car".

(g) One of the tentative decisions reached in the meetings held in October 1972 between the representatives of Maruti Limited and the officers of the DGTD and VRDE was that "after receipt of the report of the first 10,000 km a view could be taken on the reliability of the vehicle with reference to the condition No. 4 of the letter of intent to Maruti Limited" and "at the same time further running could continue and report submitted at the appropriate time". Even as a tentative decision it was somewhat ambiguous because it did not state who was to take the view. However, the matter was concluded by the recommendation made by Shri V.P. Gupta, Under Secretary, Ministry of Industrial Development, in his note dated January 6, 1973 that in view of the "likely repercussions" the condition regarding the testing of prototype should not be waived "in any one case" and Maruti Limited should be informed that their letter of intent would be converted into an industrial licence only after their prototype had been approved by VRDE, Ahmednagar. Gupta's note was seen by N. Radhakrishnan, Deputy Secretary, Shri S.M. Ghosh, Joint Secretary, Shri R.V. Subrahmanian, Additional Secretary, and finally approved by Shri C. Subramaniam, Minister of Industrial Development. But subsequently another note recorded by Deputy Secretary N. Radhakrishnan on May 3, 1974 at the instance of Secretary, Shri Mantosh Sondhi led to the reopening of the matter which seemed closed with V.P. Gupta's note. For no appreciable reason Radhakrishnan was asked by Shri Mantosh Sondhi to re-examine the point whether on the basis of the interim report received from VRDE the letter of intent issued to Maruti Limited could be converted into an industrial licence. In his note Radhakrishnan said *inter alia* that the interim report "will say whether the prototype is approved for roadworthiness or not". In his deposition Radhakrishnan admits that it was only VRDE that was entitled to give a certificate of roadworthiness but says that in this particular case he thought VRDE might grant a certificate after a run of 10,000 km. It is not clear what made him think so, he must have been aware that VRDE had been insisting on the completion of the reliability mileage test upto 30,000 km.

(h) Maruti Limited received considerable help from Shri S.M. Ghosh, Joint Secretary in the Ministry of Heavy Industry in getting an industrial licence without complying with the fourth condition of the letter of intent. On May 8, 1974 he wrote to VRDE that Government would consider the issue of licence after 10,000 kms run as had "already been agreed"; it was not stated when and between whom this agreement was entered into. On July 4, 1974 he recorded a note in consultation with Shri Sondhi recommending conversion of the letter of intent into a licence saying that continuance of the reliability test up to 30,000 kms "was not considered an integral element of roadworthiness on which the letter of intent was to be converted". In the note he sent on July 22, 1974 to R.K. Tikku, Director, SIA (Secretariat for Industrial Approvals), he said that all the conditions laid down in the letter of intent had been fully and satisfactorily compiled with. All these statements in Shri Ghosh's notes are incorrect. He could not have possibly forgotten that he had earlier endorsed V.P. Gupta's note of January 6, 1973 recommending rejection of Maruti's objection against the tests that VRDE proposed to carry out on the prototype, that he himself had written to Maruti Limited on December 21, 1973 telling them that they must get their prototype tested and approved for roadworthiness and the licence would be issued only on production of a certificate of roadworthiness. In recommending the conversion of the letter of intent into an industrial licence he said in his note dated July 4, 1974 that all major components and assemblies in the Maruti prototype car were of indigenous design. This statement was based on the claim made by the manufacturers of Maruti car. How unwise he had been to accept the statement without making a proper inquiry would be proved by the fact that the prototype had an imported NSU engine.

Ghosh did not make over the main file dealing with the Maruti's letter of intent to SIA as was the usual practice. It is remarkable that so many "not wholly unusual" or "not totally unusual" features have combined in one case. Shri Venkatesan, Under Secretary in SIA, says that they had to act on the basis of the recommendation of the Joint Secretary Shri S.M. Ghosh. If they had the file the SIA could have examined the facts and come to their own conclusion as to whether the conditions of the letter of intent had been compiled with to justify the issue of a licence, though they were not entitled to go behind the views of the administrative ministry.

It seems all the steps Shri Ghosh had taken after December 21, 1973 were calculated to help Maruti in getting an industrial licence without complying with the condition of the letter of intent. Ghosh denies that he had been under any pressure. But there must have been some reason prompting him to act in the manner he did, but it has remained undisclosed. Whatever the reason was it is clear that having known Sanjay Gandhi's reluctance to submit the Maruti prototype to the reliability test, Ghosh did all he could to spare the trouble for Shri Gandhi.

The evidence given by Shri Mantosh Sondhi, Secretary in the Ministry of Heavy Industry, and Shri T.A. Pai who was Minister of Heavy Industry from February 5, 1973 till March 1977, is that the reliability test upto 30,000 km, was not essential in view of the decision taken in the meetings held in October 1972. According to them as a result of this decision the administrative Ministry was entitled to take a view on the roadworthiness of the prototype on the completion of 10,000 km run. On the files however it does not appear that either of them had taken this stand at any time prior to giving evidence before the Commission. Neither N. Radhakrishnan, nor R.V. Subrahmanian nor Shri C. Subramaniam thought that the October 1972 decision gave the administrative Ministry any such power. In any event the controversy on this point was set at rest by Shri V.P. Gupta's note dated January 6, 1973 which was approved by the then Minister of Industrial Development Shri C. Subramaniam. Of course, there is nothing to indicate that Shri T.A. Pai's attention was drawn to Shri V.P. Gupta's note. If it was decided in October 1972, as Shri Sondhi and Shri Pai seem to think, that the Ministry would be competent to take a view as to the roadworthiness of the prototype, the decision was inconsistent with the fourth condition of the letter of intent according to which only the testing agency nominated by the government could take any such view. If Shri Sondhi and Shri Pai were right, the condition required an amendment which normally could not be done without reference to the licensing committee. Even Shri N. Radhakrishnan who thought that a view as to the roadworthiness of the prototype might be taken after a run of 10,000 km only, said that VRDE alone was competent to take this view. Radhakrishnan further said that even if VRDE had taken such a view, it would not have been a decision of general application but restricted only to the case of Maruti. Unless the intention was to do a special favour to Maruti, one could not possibly make an exception only in Maruti's case. The case of Shri Manubhai H. Thakker whose 'Maya' Prototype was made to go through the reliability test for entire 30,000 km and whose request for a licence after the prototype had run for about 22,600 km was turned down, would prove conclusively that no change in the fourth condition of the letter of intent was intended. Shri Sondhi, Secretary, Ministry of Heavy Industry, was also an automobile engineer. Perhaps he was drawing on his expert knowledge when in the course of his deposition he said that reliability test up to 30,000 km was not essential for a car to be considered roadworthy. Whether his opinion was right or not is immaterial, it was the opinion of VRDE that mattered in this case.

It will be relevant in this connection to refer to the answers given to two question asked in the Lok Sabha in 1975. On February 26, 1975 in answer to unstarred question No. 1386 asked by Shri Jyotirmoy Bosu, "whether the prototype Maruti car sent to VRDE at Ahmednagar was approved by the Government and the licence for its manufacture issued to Maruti Ltd.", Shri A.C. George, Minister of State in the Ministry of Industry and Civil Supplies, said : "Licence was issued on approval of the prototype by the VRDE". The facts stated above prove that the reply was incorrect. VRDE never approved the Maruti prototype as roadworthy. The draft reply to the question was prepared by Shri S.M. Ghosh and it was seen and approved by Shri Sondhi. To another unstarred question No. 7335, as to the scope and the nature of the tests proposed by the VRDE for giving a certificate of roadworthiness, "especially the test to which the Maruti prototype was subjected", asked by Shri Madhu Limaye, Shri A.C. George replied on April 23, 1975 : "The tests are uniformly applied to all prototypes. Technical performance trials include tests of maximum speed, acceleration, fuel consumption, brake efficiencies, cooling efficiencies and gradeability". It is to be noted that the answer mentioned only the technical performance trials and did not refer at all to the reliability test. The draft reply was prepared by Shri S.M. Ghosh which appears to have been modified by Shri Sondhi. The office note on the file [File No. 10(61)/75-AEI(1), Department of Heavy Industry] dealing with this question included a statement that the "VRDE has yet to submit a report on the reliability tests after running the vehicle up to 30,000 km". The draft prepared by Shri Ghosh and amended by Shri Sondhi withheld reference to the reliability tests, but the question asked is not correctly answered if all the tests, including the reliability test are not mentioned. The reply given was therefore only half truth. It shows that Shri Ghosh and Shri Sondhi were not willing to disclose all the relevant facts.

Shri Sondhi's contribution to Maruti's success in getting a licence without going through the reliability test cannot be overlooked. There is no apparent reason why Shri Sondhi was so keen on dispensing with the reliability test in violation of the fourth condition of the letter of intent. However, from the facts it also appears that Shri Sondhi was opposed to granting Maruti Limited a capacity of 50,000 cars a year which he considered unrealistic. His attempt to reduce the capacity failed but delayed the issue of a licence for sometime which drew a threat from R.K. Dhawan, Additional Private Secretary to the Prime Minister, that he (Dhawan) would report Sondhi to the "highest". Shri Sondhi has said in his deposition that some of his "actions were not liked by the authorities" and suggested that the delay in the issue of a licence to Maruti Limited might be one of them. It is a fact that Shri Sondhi was harassed. He says : ". . . . not only my family and I were kept under police surveillance, but soon after the declaration of emergency CBI registered a case against me". Another reason why he incurred the displeasure of the "authorities", according to him, was that he tried to protect one of his officers, Shri Krishnaswamy, who was being harassed by the former government. The case registered against Shri Sondhi was dropped in August 1977 because on inquiry no evidence was found to support the allegations made against him.

(i) Shri Sondhi and Shri S.M. Ghosh had taken the view that reliability test could continue after the licence was issued to Maruti Limited. After the issue of licence Maruti stopped the supply of fuel and oil making it impossible for VRDE to continue the test. There was nothing that the authorities could do to compel Maruti to continue the reliability mileage. This was a situation brought about entirely by unauthorised meddling with the conditions of the letter of intent, may be in good faith so far as Shri Sondhi was concerned. One should have expected in such circumstances the Minister or the Secretary to summon the entrepreneur and insist on his completing the test, but Shri T.A. Pai "did not want to deal with" Sanjay Gandhi because Shri Gandhi was "rude" and "absolutely unreasonable". So he had to go to Shrimati Indira Gandhi to tell her to make her son agree to let the test continue.

(j) Shrimati Indira Gandhi did not tell Shri Pai when he went to see her that her son's business was no concern of hers. She assured Shri Pai that she would advise her son to do what Shri Pai had suggested. Shri Sondhi also saw her to convince her that the capacity of 50,000 cars a year granted to Maruti Limited was unrealistic and should be reduced. To him also she said that she would consider what he had told her. If it was legally permissible to reduce the capacity mentioned in the letter of intent, it is difficult to see why that was not done, and if it was not, it is difficult to appreciate why the entrepreneur's mother should be approached to induce her son to be reasonable. The speech Shrimati Indira Gandhi made in Ahmedabad on September 23, 1970 extolling the enterprising spirit of her son Sanjay Gandhi and the virtues of his Maruti car may be recalled. She told the gathering that the car modelled by her son was "fairly comfortable and suitable to Indian conditions" and that "it would suit the middle class". A few weeks before she made this speech she presided over the Cabinet meeting which decided to entertain proposals from the private sector for the manufacture of 'indigenous' cars; she knew at the time that her son was an applicant for an industrial licence to manufacture cars and his proposals claimed to fulfil the conditions which the Cabinet decided to impose in that meeting. Her presiding over the meeting in these circumstances attracts criticism. It is also difficult to believe that she did not know of the inquiries made from her Secretariat about the cause of delay in issuing a licence to her son. From all these one gets an impression that Shrimati Indira Gandhi as Prime Minister was not quite unconcerned in the matter of her son's business enterprise.

CHAPTER II

They bring two prominent features; one of them is the unusual interest shown by Shri Bansi Lal, then Chief Minister of Haryana, in Sanjay Gandhi car project; the other is the stand taken by the Central Government and the conduct of Prime Minister Shrimati Indira Gandhi when Government's attention was drawn by some members of Parliament to the constructions made by Maruti Limited within the clearance zone around the ammunition depot. Shri Bansi Lal directed senior officers of the Government like R.S. Mann, Director of Town and Country Planning and Urban Estates, L.C. Gupta, Director of Industries, and V.S. Ailawadi, Deputy Commissioner, Gurgaon to show Sanjay Gandhi sites around Sonepat and Gurgaon for his car factory. These officers were not sent to select land which could be acquired for industrial purposes of the State, they were asked to take Sanjay Gandhi around waiting for him to choose a site suitable for his purpose which the Government was to acquire and make over to him. Both Mann and Gupta have said that it was unusual for senior officers to be asked to accompany an industrialist to help him select a site for his purpose. The draft development plan for the controlled area in Gurgaon was changed from time to time till Shri Sanjay Gandhi finally made his selection. The Haryana Government was willing to have an industrial zone wherever Sanjay Gandhi decided to have his factory. This is clear from the fact that the Director of Industries reduced the area originally considered necessary for industrial purposes, which was 600 acres, to 400 acres when the defence authorities declined to release the land in their occupation, and also from Mann's attempt to find out from Ailawadi in February 1971 whether Sanjay Gandhi had chosen a new site. Mann himself admits that one factor that "weighed heavily" in preparing the draft development plans was Sanjay Gandhi's choice of site. The site ultimately acquired was fertile agricultural land and those who were dispossessed in consequence were mostly uneducated small land owners depending for their livelihood entirely on agriculture. This was not considered by the State Government a sufficient reason to look for an alternative site.

The Chief Minister also made Shri Mann and Shri R.K. Gupta, Assistant Legal Remembrancer, carry the draft agreement between Maruti Limited and the Government of Haryana to Sanjay Gandhi at New Delhi for his approval. The stamp paper on which Sanjay Gandhi had the draft typed after he had approved it did not bear the stamp vendor's endorsement. Even the Assistant Legal Remembrancer who was expected to detect this deficiency says that he did not notice it, which is surprising. This shows that the officers were concerned only with getting Shri Sanjay Gandhi's signature on the agreement for which they were sent to Delhi, and once he had signed the document they did not apply their mind to any other aspect. It is not impossible that the Assistant Legal Remembrancer did notice the deficiency, but did not dare point it out to Sanjay Gandhi. Having got Sanjay Gandhi's signature on the document on August 9, 1971, Mann and R.K. Gupta who were joined by M. Shankar, Administrator, Urban Estates, at Delhi gave formal possession of the land to Sanjay Gandhi the next day. There is no precedent for senior I.A.S. officers in Haryana being employed for such purposes. Shri Bansi Lal also issued peremptory orders from time to time asking the officers to do something or other in connection with Sanjay Gandhi's car project. He asked the Director of Industries on November 16, 1970 to inform the Central Government on that very day that Haryana Government had no objection to Sanjay Gandhi's proposal for change of the location of his factory from Faridabad to Gurgaon. On April 21, 1971 Shri Bansi Lal told the Director of Industries to write to Sanjay Gandhi on that very day assuring him that 300 acres of land would be allotted to him and accepting his request for payment of the price in instalments. The urgency was due to the fact that Sanjay Gandhi had expressed his annoyance at the delay in allotment of land to him. The Director of Industries was also told not to ask Sanjay Gandhi to justify his requirement of 300 acres on which the Director of Industries was insisting. On June 24, 1971 Shri Bansi Lal telephoned Mann from Delhi directing him to ensure that the acquisition proceedings were completed and possession of the land delivered to Sanjay Gandhi by July 10, 1971 at the latest and to see that a letter was written to Sanjay Gandhi on that very day that he would be given possession of 300 acres of land by July 10. In obedience to the Chief Minister's orders, the letter was despatched to Shri Sanjay Gandhi through a special messenger. Here again what moved the Chief Minister was the fact that Sanjay Gandhi had complained to him about the delay in the allotment of land. In the meeting with Sanjay Gandhi held on July 3, 1971 where the terms and conditions for allotment of the land were settled, it was Shri bansi Lal who took all the decisions giving no chance to the officers present to express their views. The concessions given to Sanjay Gandhi were extraordinary. According to both Mann and L.C. Gupta no other party enjoyed such concessions either before or after. At this meeting Shri Bansi Lal went back on the earlier decision, based on the precedent of Haryana Steel and Alloys Limited, to realise the entire price of the land before possession was given, and agreed to deliver possession on payment of 10 per cent of the price. The decision taken in the meeting was also against the Rules of Business of Haryana Government under which it was the Cabinet and not the Chief Minister alone that was competent to allow transfer of Government land valued over Rs. 75,000; the Ministers whose departments were vitally concerned in the transaction, the Finance Minister, the Industries Minister and the Minister for Public Works were not called to attend the meeting.

When Bansi Lal's attention was drawn to the constructions made by Maruti Limited at gates 1 and 2 in disregard of the provisions of the Punjab Scheduled Roads and Controlled Areas Restrictions of Unregulated Development Act, 1963, he did not take any step on the alleged assurance of Sanjay Gandhi that the illegal constructions would be removed. He took no step even when Sanjay Gandhi gave no indication of keeping his promise. The experience of Building Inspector Ram Lal and Assistant Estate Officer J.N. Bhargava who tried to stop the illegal constructions has been described. The constructions at gates 1 and 2 were started without a sanctioned plan and completed in spite of the demolition order made by Shri Bhargava. Bhargava however did not have the courage to carry out his own order for demolition. When a request for compounding the offence was made to Bhargava on behalf of Maruti Limited he thought it safe to seek the guidance of his superior officer Shri Pritam Singh, Administrator, Urban Estates. Pritam Singh found that the offence could not be compounded under the Act and he reported the matter to his superior officer Shri R.S. Mann because he felt that this was a sensitive issue and apprehended that Sanjay Gandhi might "complain to higher authorities" against him. Mann drew the Chief Minister's attention to this matter who was satisfied with Shri Gandhi's assurance. There was no attempt to stop the construction of the five storeyed Staff Quarters which was completed unopposed. Shri Bansi Lal must have been aware that the Air Force Officers at Gurgaon as well as the Ministry of Defence had been objecting to the erection of structures by Maruti Limited inside the clearance zone around the ammunition depot and within the flying funnel of the adjoining airfield, but he allowed the constructions to be completed.

The extra-ordinary zeal shown by Shri Bansi Lal in Sanjay Gandhi's car project had its effect on the officers. Even Shri R.S. Mann, Director of Town and Country Planning and Urban Estates, and Shri O.P. Yadav, Land Acquisition Collector, who in the beginning refused to be influenced by the fact that it was Shri Sanjay Gandhi, son of Prime Minister Indira Gandhi, for whom the land was being acquired, ultimately had to yield to pressure from the Chief Minister. Mann could not disobey his Chief Minister who asked him to show Sanjay Gandhi sites for his car factory but he declined to take any step for the acquisition of land unless Sanjay Gandhi made a formal application. Mann told the Commission that he now thought that no such application was really necessary, but the point is that at the relevant time he considered a formal application essential and declined to move in the matter until it was made. However, after Bansi Lal fixed July 10, 1971 as the target date for completing the land acquisition proceedings, Mann avoided doing anything which might delay the proceedings. The Land Acquisition Collector's suggestion regarding the availability of an alternative site he rejected out of hand though Land Acquisition Collector Yadav had seen the site for himself before recording his opinion. He also overlooked the recommendation of the Financial Commissioner (Revenue) that the question of funds for paying the acquisition cost should be taken up with the Finance Department; the Minister concerned had also approved the recommendation. Mann told the Commission that it was not really necessary to approach the Finance Department, but, necessary or not, this was the decision taken earlier with the approval of the Minister and any departure from it would be an irregularity. The only reason one can think of why Mann paid out the money without reference to the Finance Departments is that he was able thereby to avoid delay, and this was important in view of the target date fixed for completing the acquisition proceedings. But Mann took about a month after he received Ailawadi's report dealing with the objections raised by the Defence authorities to the Maruti complex of buildings being raised at the present site, to decide to write a letter to the Government of India on the basis of Ailawadi's report. He took another three weeks to prepare a draft of the letter and then further two weeks after the draft was approved by the Chief Minister to issue the letter. In the letter he avoided the question of flight hazard raised by the Air Force authorities. Chief Minister Bansi Lal had made it quite plain that he was determined to let Sanjay Gandhi set up his car factory at Gurgaon as quickly as possible and that he would not tolerate any impediment put in the way. Clearly Mann did not wish to be an obstructionist. He was not keen on dispatch if that would hinder the progress of the Maruti constructions. There is no evidence however that Mann derived any personal advantage out of the indirect assistance Maruti Limited got from him.

O.P. Yadav, Land Acquisition Collector, hearing objections of interested persons under Section 5A of the Land Acquisition Act agreed with the objectors that the Government might acquire the alternative site suggested by the objectors instead of the fertile land notified for acquisition. Later, when informed of the target date set by the Chief Minister for completing the acquisition proceedings, Yadav rushed through the proceedings and made his awards in an unbelievably short time which leaves an impression that the awards had been completed beforehand and kept ready and the exercises prescribed by the Act were taken only as a formality. Yadav himself says that he "had no option but to complete the proceedings" in a hurry because of the time limit fixed. The evidence indicates that what Yadav did was under pressure and not for his personal benefit.

Shri V.S. Ailawadi, Deputy Commissioner, Gurgaon, knew what was expected of him. He showed his anxiety to be of help by suggesting more than once that land in the occupation of Defence authorities should be "got released" for Sanjay Gandhi's car factory. To the problem created by Maruti Limited raising structures within the clearance zone around the ammunition depot, his solution was that the Defence authorities should be asked to shift their fencing line. He also described the airfield adjoining the ammunition depot as abandoned without any reference to the Ministry of Defence, the only authority competent to say if it was really so. Shri Ailawadi had been receiving a series of communications from the Air Force officials since July 1971 expressing their anxiety over the construction of a car factory so close to the ammunition depot and the airfield. In one of the letters his attention was drawn to the fact that Maruti Limited was constructing a wall within 200 yards of the outer parapet of the ammunition depot, but he chose not to take any step. That Ailawadi was well aware of the restriction would appear from an order he himself made on December 17, 1971 in which while permitting a brick kiln to be set up in that area, he added that it must "not be located within 1000 yards of the outer limit of the parapet of the ammunition depot". After Shri M. Shankar, Administrator, Urban Estates, received from Shri Mann a copy of Air Vice Marshal (Retired) Harjinder Singh's letter written to Shri M.L. Batra pointing out the "hazards" for the "defence operations" created by the Maruti constructions, Shankar enquired from Ailawadi if the points made in the letter were valid. Then followed a long spell of inaction during which Maruti Limited proceeded with the constructions unhindered and finally Ailawadi sent his report to Mann on January 28, 1972. The validity of the findings in the report has been discussed earlier. In Ailawadi's case also, there is no material to suggest that he gained personally from what he did.

The other remarkable feature is the stand of the Central Government with regard to the constructions made by Maruti Limited in the prohibited zone, when Government's attention was drawn to it by some Members of Parliament, and Prime Minister Shrimati Indira Gandhi's response to the disclosure. The stand of the Government was that the declaration S.R.O. 6 of 1969 was inoperative and the earlier declaration S.R.O. 315 of 1962 should be considered to have been repealed by implication. The relevance of the rule of implied repeal sometimes applied in interpreting statutes is extremely doubtful to this context. This was a matter concerning the country's security, yet the Minister of State for Defence Production and the Law Minister seemed more anxious to prove the invalidity of the restrictions imposed. Assuming the position was as the two Ministers made it out to be the Defence Minister's letter of April 25, 1973 to Shri Mahavir Tyagi discloses that it was only in December 1972 that the Government was aware that the declaration S.R.O. 6 of 1969 was inoperative. The question therefore remains, why no step was taken to prevent the illegal constructions before December 1972 when there was no doubt as to the validity or the effectiveness of S.R.O. 6 of 1969. And what again did the Government do after December 1972 when the invalidity of the 1969 declaration was known? In July 1973 Shri S.P. Rai, Deputy Secretary in the Ministry of Defence, suggested a meeting "to take stock off the position" and decide upon "the remedial measures". Prime Minister Shrimati Indira Gandhi kept the relevant file with her for about four months taking no action on Shri Rai's suggestion. At the insistence of Shri K.B. Lal, then Secretary, Ministry of Defence, Shri B.N. Tandon, Joint Secretary in the Prime Minister's Secretariat, had a meeting with Shri S.P. Rai. Before the meeting Shrimati Indira Gandhi instructed Tandon to see that the matter was kept pending "for over six months or so". It was been mentioned earlier that all answers by Ministers to questions touching Maruti Limited had to be approved by Shrimati Indira Gandhi. in August 1973 Shri S.N. Mishra by an Unstarred Question wanted to know whether Government had completed the inquiry into the factors responsible for the alleged defects in the notification of 1969, the result of the inquiry, if completed, and the remedial steps taken. The Defence Minister's reply which must have been vetted by the Prime Minister following the usual practice, did not answer the query as to the remedial steps taken by the Government. Ultimately, no remedial measures appear to have been taken.

All that Shri Bansi Lal did, the rules of law and the norms of propriety that he disregarded or caused to be ignored cannot be explained as the natural anxiety of a Chief Minister trying to invite to his State a new and important industry as Counsel for Bansi Lal tried to impress upon the Commission. It was said that this was Shri Bansi Lal's style of functioning, when he wanted to get a thing done for the welfare of the State, he refused to be fettered by red tape. But when Shri Sanjay Gandhi's car project proved a failure and Maruti Limited failed to comply with the terms and conditions of the agreement with the Government of Haryana, the Chief Minister took no steps to recover the dues or to resume the land as provided in the agreement. His inaction was certainly not for the welfare of the State. He did not consider it necessary to act when it was pointed out that the Maruti complex of buildings was a "hazard" to the "defence operations". What then made Shri Bansi Lal act in the manner he did? The following list of dates and events might help in finding an answer to the question:

21-05-1968 Shri Bansi Lal becomes the Chief Minister of Haryana.

According to Shri Mangal Sain, who was then a member of the Haryana Legislative Assembly, soon after Shri Bansi Lal's appointment as Chief Minister there was a "revolt" against him within his own party.

15-09-1968 Three of the Ministers of Shri Bansi Lal's Cabinet write to the President of the All India Congress Party saying that they had "serious doubts" in their minds "about his ability to work as leader".

03-12-1968 About seventeen members of the Haryana Legislative Assembly belonging to the Congress party write to the Governor of Haryana withdrawing support to Shri Bansi Lal.

11-12-1968 Shri Sanjay Gandhi applies for an industrial licence to manufacture motor cars.

18-12-1968 Shri Bansi lal writes to Shri Fakharuddin Ali Ahmed, then Union Minister of Industrial Development and Company Affairs, recommending grant of licence to Shri Sanjay Gandhi and stating that the Haryana Government had offered facilities in respect of land water, electricity and finance for the project.

But neither the officers of the State Government had examined Shri Sanjay Gandhi's project report nor the State Government had decided to offer him the facilities mentioned in the letter.

19-05-1969 A memorandum dated 16-05-1969 containing about 66 allegations against Chief Minister Bansi Lal is submitted to the President of India by Shri Bhagwat Dayal Sharma, Member of Parliament and others praying for setting up a commission of inquiry to consider the allegations.

17-06-1969 Union Home Minister invites comments of Shri Bansi Lal on the memorandum.

06-08-1969 A second memorandum which is really supplementary to the first is presented to the President of India by Shri Bhagwat Dayal Sharma and others.

30-08-1969 Union Home Minister invites comments of Shri Bansi

	Lal on the supplementary memorandum.
23-12-1969	Shri Bansi Lal sends his comments which are received in Home Ministry on 29-12-1969.
27-06-1970	Prime Minister Shrimati Indira Gandhi takes over direct charge of Ministry of Home Affairs and the Department of personnel in place of Shri Y.B. Chavan.
31-07-1970	Shri R.N. Mirdha, Minister of State, Ministry of Home Affairs, states in Lok Sabha that the first memorandum against Shri Bansi Lal and his comments thereon were under examination.
08-08-1970	Prime Minister Shrimati Indira Gandhi sees the first memorandum against Bansi Lal when the Secretary (Services) puts up for her consideration a draft reply to a letter from Shri Rao Birendra Singh, a signatory to the memorandum, requesting examination of the charges against Shri Bansi Lal within a specified period.
2nd week of August 1970	Shri Bansi Lal directs Shri L.C. Gupta, Shri R.S. Mann and Shri S.K. Misra, all senior officers of the State Government, to go to Delhi to help Shri Sanjay Gandhi choose a site at Sonepat for his car project.
17-08-1970	Shri Bansi Lal telephones Shri Ailawadi, Deputy Commissioner, Gurgaon, to select a suitable site near Gurgaon for Shri Sanjay Gandhi.
	The next day Shri Sanjay Gandhi inspects three sites with Shri Ailawadi one of which includes 157 acres of land in village Dundahera in the occupation of the Defence authorities.
22-08-1970	Shri Sanjay Gandhi chooses a tract of land near village Dundahera on Delhi Gurgaon road.
30-09-1970	Letter of Intent is issued to Shri Sanjay Gandhi for his car project.
03-11-1970	Union Home Secretary Shri L.P. Singh finds that there was no case for setting up a commission of inquiry against Shri Bansi Lal but recommends that further information in respect of 14 allegations in the first memorandum be called for from him.
13-11-1970 18-11-1970	Shri Bansi Lal writes to the Defence Minister to release land in the occupation of the Defence authorities at Dundahera for the State's industrial pur-

pose.

14-11-1970 Minister of State, Ministry of Home Affairs, Shri R.N. Mirdha agreeing with the view of the Home Secretary submits the case to the Prime Minister.

On the same day Shri Sanjay Gandhi sends an application to the Director of Industries, Government of Haryana, asking for the allotment of 300 acres of land near Gurgaon for his motor car factory and proposing payment of the price for the land in instalments.

16-11-1970 Copy of Shri Sanjay Gandhi's letter addressed to the Under Secretary to the Government of India, Department of Heavy Engineering, seeking to change the location of the proposed factory from Faridabad to Gurgaon is received in the Directorate of Industries, Haryana. Shri R.C. Mehtani, Officer on Special Duty to the Chief Minister, telephones Shri L.C. Gupta, Director of Industries, telling him to convey the State Government's concurrence to the change of site on the very day.

18-11-1970 Shri R.K. Dhawan, a member of Prime Minister Shrimati Indira Gandhi's personal staff, sends for a map of the land being acquired for Shri Sanjay Gandhi from the office of the Deputy Commissioner, Gurgaon.

24-11-1970 Shri B.N. Tandon, Joint Secretary in the Prime Minister's Secretariat, records on the file relating to the 1969 memorandum against Shri Bansi Lal that "P.M. has seen" meaning that she agreed with the suggestion of Shri L.P. Singh and Shri R.N. Mirdha.

12-01-1971 Shri R.K. Dhawan telephones Shri Ailawadi, Deputy Commissioner of Gurgaon from Delhi asking for copies of correspondence relating to land which was being acquired in Gurgaon.

18-01-1971 A note is recorded on the file of Town and Country Planning Department which discloses that the file had been summoned to Delhi by the Private Secretary to Chief Minister Bansi Lal "for reference".

21-04-1971 Shri S.K. Misra, Principal Secretary to Chief Minister Bansi Lal, conveys to Shri L.C. Gupta, Director of Industries, the Chief Minister's direction that a letter should be sent to Sanjay Gandhi on that very day saying that 300 acres of land would be allotted to him. The Chief Minister also wanted Shri Gupta not to ask from Sanjay Gandhi justification for his requirement of 300 acres on which Shri Gupta had been insisting. Shri Misra further tells Shri Gupta that Sanjay Gandhi has expressed annoyance to the Chief Minister for the delay in allotting land to him.

04-06-1971 Maruti Limited is incorporated under the Companies Act, 1956.

24-06-1971 Chief Minister Bansi Lal telephones Shri R.S. Mann, Director of Town and Country Planning, from Delhi telling him that Shri Sanjay Gandhi had complained to him about the delay in the allotment of land and asking him to ensure that the acquisition proceedings are completed and possession of the land delivered to Shri Sanjay Gandhi by 10-07-1971 at the latest, Mann is also told that a letter conveying this assurance to Sanjay Gandhi must issue the very same day.

25-06-1971 Shri Sanjay Gandhi writes to the Director of Industries indicating in the layout sent to him earlier by the Director of Industries, the plot selected by him for his car factory and asking for immediate possession of the land.

30-06-1971 Shri R.S. Mann writes to Shri Sanjay Gandhi at the instance of the Chief Minister that the price of the land which is being acquired for him would be approximately Rs. 12,000 per acre.

03-07-1971 A meeting is held at Chandigarh between Shri Bansi Lal and some officials of the Haryana Government with Shri Sanjay Gandhi where the terms and conditions for allotment of land to Shri Sanjay Gandhi are settled. The venue of the meeting is not the Chief Minister's office or residence but the Rest House where Shri Sanjay Gandhi was then staying. The terms, according to the Director of Industries and also the Director of Town and Country Planning, are unusually favourable to Maruti Limited and there is no instance of any other run it in Haryana enjoying similar concessions.

10-07-1971 The Land Acquisition Collector makes awards com-

	pleting land acquisition proceedings.
August 1971	File relating to the memorandum against Shri Bansi Lal is again submitted to the Prime Minister with Shri Mirdha's comment that further clarification with regard to the 14 allegations is necessary.
09-08-1971	Shri R.S. Mann goes to Delhi directed by Chief Minister Bansi Lal to have the draft agreement for allotment of land to Shri Sanjay Gandhi approved by him.
10-08-1971	Possession of the land is given to Shri Sanjay Gandhi.
03-09-1971	Prime Minister Shrimati Indira Gandhi agrees with the suggestion that further clarification of the 14 allegations was necessary and Chief Minister Bansi Lal is written to accordingly.
13-10-1971	Chief Minister Bansi Lal furnishes additional clarification on the first memorandum.
27-10-1971	Another memorandum against Chief Minister Bansi Lal, submitted to the President of India by Shri Bhagwat Dayal Sharma, M.P. is forwarded to Prime Minister Shrimati Indira Gandhi. This memorandum contains the following allegations among others: "An impression is being created in the public mind as if the Central leaders are sharing the fruits of misfeasance and malfeasance of the present Government. Shri Bansi Lal even brags about his personal equation with the Prime Minister whom, according to his own statement before responsible persons, he has obliged by acquiring land over 300 acres for the proposed car factory to be started by her son".
20-11-1971	The file relating to the two memoranda submitted in 1969 is put up to Prime Minister Shrimati Indira Gandhi with the finding that none of the allegations has been established. The Prime Minister approves the findings.
27-11-1971	Comments of Chief Minister Bansi Lal are invited on the 1971 memorandum. Prime Minister Shrimati Indira Gandhi records a note on the file relating to the 1971 memorandum : "Ask K. or Dh. to speak with C.M. too". As Shri Tandon has explained, K. refers to Shri Yash Pal Kapoor and Dh. to Shri R.K. Dhawan.

Shri Yash Pal Kapoor was not a member of the personal staff of the Prime Minister at that time while Shri R.K. Dhawan was working as Personal Assistant. Why they are asked to speak to the Chief Minister when a decision has been taken to make a formal reference to him inviting his comments on the memorandum is not stated. The note also does not indicate what Shri Kapoor or Shri Dhawan was supposed to convey to the Chief Minister in this regard. The note thus discloses a parallel personal approach to the Chief Minister by Shrimati Indira Gandhi.

24-02-1972 Another memorandum against Bansi Lal is submitted to the President of India.

28-02-1972 The above memorandum is received at the Prime Minister's secretariat.

01-03-1972 The said memorandum is sent in original to the Secretary, Department of Personnel before Prime Minister has seen it.

27-10-1972 Shri B.P. Bagchi, Secretary (Personnel) having examined the 1971 memorandum suggests a reference to a retired High Court Judge for informal opinion on some of the allegations made in the memorandum.

07-11-1972 Shri Mirdha does not agree with Shri Bagchi's suggestion and recommends that the Chief Minister should be written to asking for clarification Shri Tandon also records a note to the effect that the matter could be examined further after receiving clarification from the Chief Minister.

08-11-1972 Prime Minister Shrimati Indira Gandhi approves Shri Tandon's suggestion.

10-11-1972 Chief Minister Shri Bansi Lal replies to the allegations.

10-11-1972 The file is submitted to the Prime Minister by the Minister of State, Department of Personnel, with his finding that the allegations have not been substantiated.

12-11-1972 Shri Tandon submits to the Prime Minister a 'top secret' hand written note suggesting that the matter be referred to a Committee of Ministers.

13-11-1972 Prime Minister Shrimati Indira Gandhi records a note that she has asked her colleagues, Shri Fakharuddin Ali Ahmed, Shri Swaran Singh, Shri H.R. Gokhale and

Shri Kumaramangalam for advice if there was a case for setting up a commission of inquiry to look into the allegations made in the 1971 memorandum.

12-12-1972 Draft of the report prepared by a Committee of four Ministers is submitted to the Prime Minister for clearance.

15-12-1972 The report is signed by the four Ministers. The report finds that the allegations have not been established.

22-12-1972 In the course of his speech in the Lok Sabha, Shri S.N. Mishra said:

But one thing is abundantly clear, it is almost conclusively proved, that the Chief Minister of Haryana has left nothing undone to place the Prime Minister in a situation of blackmail. He has robbed the peasants to put her in the wrong. He has violated the defence rules which prohibit the setting up of such factories or any construction within a particularly distance to show that he can do anything in the name of the Prime Minister. He has tried to equate public interest with private interest and also tried to say to the world that industrial estate means personal estate.

Now, therefore, this is my submission, that it would be well for the Prime Minister to go into this, because he had been taking all the steps almost at the same time when the charges of corruption against him were being examined. This is no more accident that the failure of the examination of the charges of corruption against him coincides with the period in which he took all these irregular, fantastically irregular, steps.

09-07-1973 Shri S.P. Rai, Deputy Secretary in the Ministry of Defence records a note in the file Dy. No. 4341/JS(A)/73 saying that it would be advisable to take stock of the situation arising out of the constructions made by Maruti Limited in close proximity of the ammunition depot at Gurgaon and within the flying funnel of the adjoining airfield and to decide upon the remedial measures. The note suggests a meeting of the representatives of the Government of Haryana and the Air Headquarters and someone from the Prime Minister's secretariat.

Prime Minister Shrimati Indira Gandhi keeps the file with her for about four months without taking any action on it.

16-08-1973 Answering an Unstarred Question by Shri S.N. Mishra in the Lok Sabha, the Minister of Defence avoids a query made by Shri Mishra as to the remedial steps taken by the Government in the situation brought about by the allegedly defective notification S.R.O. 6 of 1969.

The reply, following the usual procedure, must have been vetted by the Prime Minister.

05-11-1973 A meeting is held between Shri S.P. Rai and Shri Tandon after Shri K.B. Lal, Secretary, Ministry of Defence, requested Shri Tandon to have the matter expedited. In this meeting Shri Tandon on instructions from Prime Minister Shrimati Indira Gandhi tells Shri Rai that the time was not yet ripe to take any action in the matter and it should be kept pending for at least six months.

It has been mentioned that Shri Bansi Lal wrote to Shri Fakharuddin Ali Ahmed in December 1968 sponsoring Sanjay Gandhi's car project and enumerating the concessions offered to him before the Government of Haryana had taken any decision in the matter. This was the time when Shri Bansi Lal's political career was in peril following the revolt in his own party against him. Thereafter as the memoranda against him were being submitted one after another, Shri Bansi Lal went on making large concessions in favour of Maruti Limited attempting, it seems, to please the Prime Minister by making available to her son land for his car factory and other facilities not enjoyed by any other industrialist in the State before or after. Instead of summoning Sanjay Gandhi to his office or residence to settle the terms of allotment of the land, he himself went to the rest house at Chandigarh where Sanjay Gandhi was then staying. What has been stated above also brings to light the calculated inaction on the part of Shrimati Indira Gandhi to enable the Maruti constructions to the completed and her anxiety to keep back the facts from parliament in spite of her knowledge that the constructions were a hazard to the defence operations. It is remarkable that even the report of the panel of Ministers inquiring into the allegations against Bansi Lal had to be cleared by the Prime Minister before it was signed by them. The sequence of events suggests that Chief Minister Shri Bansi Lal sought to protect himself by the services he rendered, and in this situation the former Prime Minister who was aware of Bansi Lal's motive derived for her son the advantages he needed for his car project.

CHAPTER III

The facts disclosed show that the methods by which the Maruti concerns raised capital and the manner in which they utilised their financial resources have not been always proper or regular. Maruti Limited, a public limited company, functioned till the order for its winding up was made without inviting capital from the public by prospectus which was something unique, and though the company was supposed to offer its shares only to the promoters, Directors and their friends, the shares were sold to all and sundry indiscriminately, often thrust on people by coercion, threat or misrepresentation. To get acknowledgement for private issue from the Controller of Capital Issues, Shri Sanjay Gandhi, Managing Director of Maruti Limited wrongly informed the Controller of Capital Issues that the Board of Directors by a resolution passed on June 29, 1972 had decided "to fix the amount of the issued capital at Rs. 7,00,00,000 (Rupees 7 crores)", knowing that no such resolution had been passed on that day and made a series of untrue statements to the effect that the public financial institutions had approved in principle the financial scheme of the company. The way certain public limited companies induced their agents to be dealers of the Maruti car by depositing large sums of money and to buy shares of Maruti Limited for which funds were arranged by these companies, the mysterious coincidence of the Export Manager of J.K. Udyog Limited being released from detention under the Conservation of Foreign Exchange and Prevention of Smuggling Activities Act, 1974 on the day on which J.K. Synthetics Limited stared buying shares of Maruti Limited, their investments in Maruti shares continuing till April 1977 in which period an order of detention under the Maintenance of Internal Security Act against a brother of the Chairman and Managing Director of Straw Products Limited, a J.K. concern, was not executed, the non-existent persons to whom large sums of money were shown to have been returned on the eve of the last General Elections, the manner in which the resources of Maruti Limited were frittered away – all these topics have been discussed in the foregoing pages. What is remarkable is that Maruti Limited got away with every thing. Shri S. Kumar, who has been Registrar of Companies, Delhi and Haryana, since January 15, 1973 repeated several times while giving evidence before the Commission when some irregularity in the functioning of the Maruti concerns was pointed out to him, that if it had come to his notice earlier he would have taken action. He took action ultimately on May 27, 1977 by taking up the technical scrutiny of the balance sheets of these concerns. According to Shri Kumar this could not be done earlier due to the "acute paucity of staff", but the position in this regard had not changed much in May 1977. Shri Kumar added that earlier he thought that "there was no need of technical scrutiny" but "later on when the change of Government was there and a furore was being created about Maruti in the press, I thought in my wisdom that as a special case I should conduct technical scrutiny of these companies and collect whatever material may be for answering further questions if any". It was pointed out to Shri Kumar that after he joined as Registrar of Companies and before the last General Elections were held in the country in March 1977, a number of questions had been asked in Parliament about the irregularities, illegalities and contravention of the law in regard to the affairs of the Maruti concerns which were also published in the newspapers. In fact Shri Kumar himself said that he furnished information to the Department of Company Affairs from the material available on the records with him, obviously for the preparation of answers to the questions asked in Parliament. It is therefore, difficult to understand why in spite of the irregularities alleged in Parliament, which were published in the newspapers, he did not consider it necessary to take any action earlier similar to that he did in May 1977.

Dr. Raj K. Nigam, Additional Controller of Capital Issues, and the Department of Economic Affairs were also extremely helpful to Maruti Limited. Dr. Nigam personally received two of the applications made by Maruti Limited to the Controller of Capital Issues and allowed the company to raise capital by private issue on the verbal assurances of Shri Sanjay Gandhi because he thought that "a man of his status could not go back upon the assurances given to the Government". This suggests that Dr. Nigam acted on the assurances of Shri Gandhi not because he was convinced of Shri Gandhi's integrity as businessman but because of his status as the Prime Minister's son. Ultimately Nigam admitted that he was pressurised by Sanjay Gandhi. In April 1975 Shri C. Subramaniam, Finance Minister, approved the proposal of Shri Pranab Kumar Mukherjee, Minister for Revenue and Expenditure, to allow Maruti Limited the maximum private issue of 40 per cent of the proposed equity capital on the ground that Maruti Limited was pressed for funds. In exercising their discretion the Ministers do not appear to have taken into account that till then the company had filed to make a public issue, and that not even two months earlier, in February 1975, the Public Financial institutions had turned down the company's request for financial assistance. The speed with which the Department of Company Affairs disposed of the file of J.K. Synthetics Limited relating to their investment in Maruti Limited was remarkable. According to Shri V.P. Uppal, Under Secretary in the Department disposed of the file on the same day it was put up to him and he admitted that normally it took about three or four days to dispose of a file at his level Shri Choudhury had to satisfy himself in a few hours that Maruti Limited could "give a reasonable return to the investing company". He could not possibly hold up the file to examine more closely the financial position of Maruti Limited because the Minister incharge had made it known by his telephone call that he was interested in the speedy disposal of Maruti matters. Shri Uppal stated : "while processing and granting approval to the investment by J.K. Synthetics Limited in the share capital of Maruti Limited to the tune of 40 lacs we were aware that we were dealing with a sensitive matter pertaining to Maruti Limited of which Shri Sanjay Gandhi was the Managing Director".

Reference has been made in the previous chapter to the evidence of Shri B.N. Tandon, Joint Secretary in the former Prime Minister's Secrctariat, that "the various Ministries used to refer questions regarding Maruti Limited and allied concerns and members of the Prime Minister's family to the Prime Minister for her approval/clearance", and that even the replies to the letters written by members of Parliament were finalised only after the Prime Minister had seen and approved them. Shri Jyotirmoy Bosu in a letter dated November 4, 1974 addressed to the Minister of Law, Justice and Company Affairs levelled a charge that the Department of Company Affairs levelled a charge that the Department of Company Affairs had been deliberately withholding from him information relating to Maruti Limited. In an unnumbered file of the Department of Company Affairs there are notings by Shri C.M. Narayanan, Director, and Shri K.K. Ray, Secretary, of the Department of Company

Affairs which are reproduced below:

"Shri Jyotirmoy Bosu, M.P., has, in his letter dated 4th November, 1974 levelled a charge that we have been deliberately withholding from him information relating to Maruti Ltd. There has never been an occasion where we have withheld, deliberately or otherwise any information that is available with us. In second para of his letter he wants to know the 'real' value of the assets of the company Schedule VI of the Companies Act prescribes that the balance sheet should indicate the original cost of the fixed assets as also the depreciation. This has been furnished by the company in its balance sheet. We had never any necessity for ascertaining the intrinsic or market value of the assets of the company. The balance sheet of Maruti Ltd., a Public Limited company, is available for public inspection. However, we may furnish full details of the assets as revealed by the latest balance sheet (as at 31st March, 1974) to Shri Bosu.

Shri K.K. Ray marked the file to the Minister of Law, Justice and Company Affairs from where the file found its way to the Prime Minister's Secretariat. Shri B.N. Tandon recorded the following note on the file:

C.M. Narayanan 8-11-1974

"*Prime Minister's Secretariat*

P.M. has seen. She thinks that a reply as in the draft (marked approved draft) enclosed should go to Shri Bosu. It is not necessary to enclose the statement as proposed by the Department of Company Affairs. The latest balance sheet is open for public inspection. Shri Bosu can obtain the required information by inspecting that document.

This shows that the information called for by Shri Jyotirmoy Bosu was communicated to him after the draft reply was shaped as suggested by the former Prime Minister.

Those who had been at any time Directors of Maruti Limited were asked to clarify certain points regarding the functioning of the company. Of them Shri C.B. Saran, Shri Jagdish Prasad, Shri B.C. Jindal, Shri M.A. Chidambram, Shri Vidya Bhusan and Major Kapil

Mohan have replied to the queries sent by the Commission. Shri Raunaq Singh, another Director, was examined as witness and he answered all the material questions in the course of his deposition. Shri Raunaq Singh also filed an affidavit before this Commission in October 1978 wherein he refers to an earlier affidavit sworn by him on July 2, 1977 which was filed with the Ministry of Home Affairs. A copy of this earlier affidavit has been brought on the record of the Commission. In his July affidavit Shri Raunaq Singh States how he came to be a director of Maruti Limited : "I was called by Shri R.K. Dhawan in his office and was requested to serve on the Board of Maruti Limited as according to him Mr. Sanjay Gandhi needed guidance of experienced entrepreneur in his new venture. I also accepted the appointment as a Director as I believed in all sincerity that Mr. Sanjay Gandhi was really a hard working dynamic technocrat who wished to produce a low priced car for the benefit of the middle class people". Shri Raunaq Singh was then asked "to make some contributions towards share capital of Maruti Limited". Accordingly one of Raunaq Singh's companies, namely, Bharat Steel Tubes Limited "purchased shares of Rs. 5 lacs in Maruti Limited". About a year later he was "approached through Mr. R.K. Dhawan" to make an additional investment of about Rs. 25 lacs to which he pleaded his inability. "When I expressed my inability to make any further investment", Raunaq Singh says, "I could smell a feeling of dissatisfaction . . . . I could visualise only later as to what could happen in the event of Mr. Sanjay Gandhi or Mr. R.K. Dhawan not being so happy with someone". Shri R.K. Dhawan when he was trying to induce Raunaq Singh to contribute to Maruti's share capital, he was Personal Assistant to the former Prime Minister Shrimati Indira Gandhi. About the working of the company, Shri Raunaq Singh says : "I had a feeling that the Directors were consulted on formal business at the Board meetings only. No body could question Mr. Sanjay Gandhi as he ran the organisation in the way he liked. . . . In fact the members of the Board were not consulted on any important company policy or details of any contract. All decision were taken by Mr. Sanjay Gandhi as the Managing Director of the company".

Saran, Jagdish Prasad and Jindal were Directors only for a short time. Shri Saran ceased to be a Director on November 30, 1972. He says that he was not present at the meeting of the Board of Directors held on October 18, 1972 which approved the annual report of 1971-72 and the said report was not sent to him prior to October 18, 1972.

As such, he says, he is not responsible for any mis-statement in the annual report of 1971-72. Shri Jagdish Prasad also says that he was not present at the meeting of the Board of Directors held on October 18, 1972 which approved the annual report of 1971-72 and that the report was not sent to him prior to October 18. Accordingly he says that he is not responsible for any incorrect statement that may have been made in the aid report. Shri Jagdish Prasad ceased to be a Director on December 2, 1972. Shri Jindal's statement is that he attended very few meetings before he resigned on October 18, 1972. According to him his "contribution as Director was not purposeful because of lack of knowledge of the English language". He adds that at that stage he had "no basis to suspect the bonafides of Shri Sanjay Gandhi". Shri Jindal says that he was unaware of any part of the land of Maruti Limited being leased out to others and also of any space in the Maruti factory premises being "allowed for other uses".

Shri M.A. Chidambram was a Director from the inception of the company and subsequently made its Chairman. He resigned on May 17, 1977. According to Shri Chidambram, Shri Sanjay Gandhi who was appointed the Managing Director of Maruti Limited was "at all times" fully in management and control of the affairs of the company". Briefly his stand is that the statements in the annual reports were made in good faith upon the information supplied by the Managing Director and responsible officer of the company which he had no reason to doubt. He was not aware of the irregularities like leasing out the factory lands, or that an imported NSU engine was used in the prototype car that was sent to Ahmednagar for test. He had no knowledge of the failure or to refund the dealers' deposits; these were, according to him, routine administrative matters for the offices of the company to deal with.

The statements of Shri Vidya Bhushan and Major Kapil Mohan are similar. Both of them were appointed Directors in 1973. Vidya Bhushan states that the statements in the annual reports were based on information supplied by the concerned offices which he accepted as true because there was no circumstance before him to justify a contrary opinion. Matters like failure to deposit in time the income tax deducted at source or refund of the share application money or the dealer's deposits did not come to his notice. These were part of the routine work of the executives of the company. He was also not aware that an imported NSU engine was fitted on the Maruti prototype car that was sent for test at Ahmednagar. Major Kapil

Mohan's statement is exactly similar. Only he adds that "for all technical and other details of Maruti Limited", he relied on the information supplied to him by the officers of the company and also the Managing Director, Shri Vidya Bhushan does not mention the Managing Director. Both Shri Vidya Bhushan and Major Kapil Mohan assert that the Directors' Reports were intended for circulation to the existing shareholders and not to serve as a prospectus. The facts bearing on this aspect have already been discussed and need not be repeated, but a brief reference may be made to the evidence given by Shri Sitaram Singhania, President of J.K. Synthetics Limited, as to what induced him to but Maruti shares for his company. After discussion with one of his friends. Shri Singhania thought it would be profitable to invest in Maruti, then he met Shri Sanjay Gandhi sometime between September and November 1974. Shri Gandhi gave him "a copy of the balance sheet", ""pertaining to the year 1973-74", he "studied that balance sheet" and found that the prospects appeared to be very bright.

CHAPTER IV

From the evidence discussed it appears that attempts were made to attract prospective dealers and induce the existing dealers not to cancel their dealership agreements by promises of early delivery of the Maruti car. Late L.N. Mishra, when he was Union Cabinet Minister, also tried to get dealers for the Maruti car. The Board of Directors of Maruti Limited left it to Shri Sanjay Gandhi to appoint the dealers on such terms and conditions as he might think proper. To create an impression that the appearance of the Maruti car in the market was imminent, Shri Sanjay Gandhi insisted on the dealers to set up show-rooms even in 1972 and 1973, which many of them did spending large sums of money. Maruti Limited was granted industrial licence in July 1974 and therefore there was hardly any justification for asking the dealers to keep their show-rooms ready in 1972 or 1973. Two of the dealers who were given a car each to exhibit in their show-rooms have narrated their respective experience; one had to push the car to his show-room, and the other who returned the car to the Maruti garage for repairs following a brake failure while he was driving, did not get back either the car or the money (Rs. 22,000) he had paid for it. The dealers have given evidence as to how they were treated by the Maruti management. Some who applied for dealership of the Maruti car were made to but shares of Maruti Limited as a pre-condition under threat. Some of the dealers who terminated their agencies when they found that the car was not available, were made to agree to the conversion of a part of the deposit they had made into Maruti shares. They yielded without raising objection because of fear. One of them said that "the management of Maruti Limited being in power" they had to agree to the proposal. The reference is obviously to Shri Sanjay Gandhi and the suggestion is that he was powerful being a son of the Prime Minister. Another said that "these shares were thrust" on them and that as they "were under some kind of fear', they did not have the courage to tell the management of Maruti Limited that they were not interested in the shares. And the fear was real. One of the dealers, S.C. Aggarwal who terminated his agency was threatened by Shri Gandhi that he would be sent to jail and Aggarwal had to apologise to him by touching his feet. Om Prakash Gupta of Hapur who had asked for payment of interest due to him on his deposit was arrested under the Maintenance of Internal Secruity Act. Shri Chander Bhan Gupta of Bhatinda who also demanded the interest due to him was told by Shri R.K. Dhawan, Additional Private Secretary to the former Prime Minister, that he would be arrested under the MISA if he kept on demanding money. Many did not ask for refund of their deposits or payment of due interest when they came to know of the harassment of those who did. There are only two who appear to have paid some money to one of the Maruti concerns and were not keen on getting it back. One of them, S.N.P. Punj of M/s Dayagen, New Delhi, claims to have paid Shri Sanjay Gandhi Rs. 1 lac by way of a short term loan for six months. But the amount was treated as dealership deposit in the books of Maruti Technical was a Director. The other case of Shri A.P.S. Services Private Limited of which Shri Sanjay Gandhi Arora who deposited Rs. 40,000 for dealership rights of Maruti Petrol Savers. He did not get the dealership and yet he asked the company to retain the money till he made up his mind, which he failed to do in the next three years. In both cases the money was returned but without interest and after the expiry of the period of limitation for the institution of a suit for recovery of the sum. The conduct of both Shri Punj and Shri Arora would strike one as quite unusual for a businessman. What seems likely is that there was more in these transactions than what has been told. Some of the dealers of the Maruti car were forced to buy petrol savers worth thousands of rupees at a considerable loss to themselves but which earned large profits for Maruti Technical Services Private Limited.

CHAPTER V

Agreement dated 21-11-1970 between Shri Sanjay Gandhi and Maruti Technical Services Private Limited: It may be recalled that in his application made on December 11, 1968 for a licence for the establishment of a new industrial undertaking to manufacture motor cars, Shri Sanjay Gandhi had stated that the undertaking was to be a public limited company named 'Maruti Limited'. Before Maruti Limited was incorporated on June 4, 1971, a private limited company, called Maruti Technical Services Private Limited, was brought into existence on November 16, 1970. The authorised share capital of Maruti Technical Services, is Rs. 5 lacs divided into 50,000 equity shares of Rs. 10 each. On November 16, 1970 Shri Sanjay Gandhi and Shrimati Sonia Gandhi, wife of Sanjay Gandhi's elder brother Rajiv Gandhi, who were named as the first and permanent directors in Article 7 of the Articles of Association of the company, held between them twenty equity shares of Rs. 10 each. This was also the financial position of the company on November 21, 1970 when Shri Sanjay Gandhi entered into an agreement with Maruti Technical Services Private Limited under which Sanjay Gandhi agreed to render technical know-how to the company for a consideration of Rs. 3 lacs. It is stated in the agreement that Sanjay Gandhi had "designed, manufactured and assembled in India a wholly indigenous motor car" and that he offered and the company accepted "an option to purchase" the technical know-how acquired by him on the terms and conditions mentioned in the agreement. The agreement defines 'technical know-how' to mean "the existing information, method, design, drawing, material and part specifications, technical documentation including drawings/specifications of required special tools, jigs and fixtures, dies, patterns, core boxes, process sheets, times sheets, calculations, test specifications and records and operating and maintenance manual etc. in possession of the Designer relating to design, fabrication, manufacture, assembly, operation and maintenance of the motor car". The option was exercisable by the company by paying Shri Sanjay Gandhi Rs. 3 lacs within 24 months of the date of the execution of the agreement. It was provided that "forthwith upon the company exercising its option as aforesaid" Shri Gandhi was tc "deliver to the company the technical know-how in his possession". On the date the agreement was executed, the paid-up capital of Maruti Technical Services was Rs. 200 as already stated. On December 15, 1971, 1500 equity shares of Rs. 10 each fully paid-up were allotted to Shri Sanjay Gandhi. On June 2, 1972 an agreement was executed between Maruti Technical Services Private Limited and Maruti Limited according to which Maruti Technical Services was to provide Technical know-how to Maruti Limited and Maruti Limited was to pay in return Rs. 5 lacs in lump sum to Maruti Techincal Services. I shall refer to the agreement between Maruti Limited and Maruti Technical Services Private Limited in more detail later in this chapter, it is sufficient to state here that in terms of that agreement Maruti Limited paid to Maruti Technical Services a sum of Rs. 5 lacs on July 22, 1972. Out of this sum Maruti Technical Services paid Shri Sanjay Gandhi Rs. 3 lacs on January 13, 1973 exercising its option to purchase technical know-how from him, the stipulated period for exercising the option had then expired. Thus it was only after money was available from the funds of the public company that Maruti Technical Services Private Limited of which Sanjay Gandhi was one of the two directors, was able to pay Sanjay Gandhi, the technical expert, the price for the know-how he offered to sell.

According to the agreement between Maruti Technical Services and Sanjay Gandhi, "forthwith" upon the company paying Rs. 3 lacs to Sanjay Gandhi, Shri Gandhi was to deliver to the company the technical know-how in his possession. There is nothing on record to show that Sanjay Gandhi delivered any technical know-how on receiving Rs. 3 lacs. Witnesses examined on this aspect of the matter have said that Shri Sanjay Gandhi did not really possess any technical know-how that he could transfer. The letter this Commission has received from Rolls Royce Motors of England may be recalled. Shri Sanjay Gandhi was with Rolls Royce Motors as special student apprentice for about three years and received an Ordinary National Certificate in mechanical engineering which "was a relatively minor qualification". Shri Gandhi did not complete the special student apprenticeship. Retired Wing Commander R.H. Chawdhry. Chief Executive of Maruti Limited, was examined by the Commission. According to Shri Chawdhry, Sanjay Gandhi "had a very good I.Q. and a very sharp grasp of technical matters but had no practical experience" in the field of car manufacture. Referring to the definition of technical know-how in the agreement between Sanjay Gandhi and Maruti

Technical Services, Chawdhry says, "none of the items constituting technical know-how, e.g., method, design, drawings, materials and part specifications, technical documentation including drawing, specifications of required special tools jigs and fixtures, dies, etc., could have been available at that date as those were not even ready in their totality as on 17th May, 1977, the date from which Sanjay Gandhi stopped going to the factory". Shri Chawdhry has said that till the last the design of the engine had not been finalised and that the results proved that Sanjay Gandhi did not have at his disposal a ready made technical know-how in regard to a definite engine design which he could transfer to Maruti Technical Services.

W.H.F. Muller, the German technician on the staff of the Maruti Technical Services had made certain statements under Section 131 of the Income-tax Act, 1961 on January 23 and February 3, 1978. Copies of these statements have been brought on the record of this Commission. To a question of the Income-tax Officer about Shri Sanjay Gandhi's contribution to the technical side of the car project, Muller's answer was that it was "actually a set of drawings, incomplete set, in respect of the car he had built". According to Muller what Shri Sanjay Gandhi sold to Maruti Technical Services was "the basic concept of a product he had in mind and that the end product of Muller's collaboration with Maruti Technical Services was "a prototype capable of being produced, approximately 80 per cent completed, not including the engine". No car was finally manufactured, "what actually was produced were a few prototypes handmade". The Income-tax Officer asked him. " . . . it is said that some Maruti cars are running on roads. Have you got any idea about this"? Muller's answer was : "these cars were given out to certain people. In all about 10 to 12 – these are all prototypes, not the same in design, etc. They are different from one another. They were changed several times. Engines were modifications of Sun Beam which were also prototypes, made in Maruti Limited. These Sun Beams machines were fabricated (purchased in parts) in Maruti". Muller stated further that "it would be an exaggeration to say that a workable plan or model existed" at the time he joined Maruti Technical Services. The vehicles he then saw were not prototypes suited for production. In Muller's opinion, it was clear that Sanjay Gandhi would not be able to "provide a feasible working prototype, nor the planning required".

The facts stated above show that Shri Sanjay Gandhi had no technical know-how or expertise which he could sell. Though the agreement required him forthwith on receiving the sum of Rs. 3 lacs to deliver to Maruti Technical Services the technical know-how in his possession, nothing in fact was delivered, because there was nothing really to deliver.

Agreement dated 2-6-1972 *between Maruti Limited and Maruti Technical Services Private Limited* : On June 2, 1972 an agreement was executed between Maruti Limited and Maruti Technical Services Private Limited which was signed on behalf of Maruti Limited by Col. V.R. Mohan and Shri Sudhir Kapadia, Directors of the company, and for the private company by its two Directors Shri Sanjay Gandhi and Shrimati Sonia Gandhi. The execution of the agreement was approved in the meeting of the Board of Directors of Maruti Limited held on May 30, 1972 and a special resolution of the shareholders was passed in an extraordinary general meeting on June 29, 1972. Shri Raunaq Singh, a Director of Maruti Limited from September 21, 1971 to May 10, 1977 has told the Commission that this agreement between Sanjay Gandhi and Maruti Technical Services was never brought to the notice of the Board of Directors of Maruti Limited.

This agreement between Maruti Limited and Maruti Technical Services describes Maruti Limited as "the manufacturing company" and Maruti Technical Services Private Limited as "the technical company" and states that the technical company "has capability of imparting technical know-how for the design, manufacture and assembly in India of a wholly indigenous motor car" and the manufacturing company has accepted the offer of the technical company "to acquire on licence basis the said know-how from the technical company". The manufacturing company was to make an initial lump sum payment of Rs. 5 lacs to the technical company for providing technical know-how and also to pay an annual technical fee of 2 per cent on the net sales of the motor cars from "the effective date of the agreement" subject to a minimum of Rs. 2.50 lacs for each accounting year of the manufacturing company. The "effective date of this agreement" has been defined as the "date on which the manufacturing company shall make payment to the technical company of the initial lump sum payment of Rs. 5,00,000 (Rupees five lacs only)". Under the agreement the technical company was to provide technical know-how "on a continuous basis". By this was meant that on receipt of the initial lump sum payment, the technical company was to deliver to the manufacturing company the technical know-how "for the design, manufacture and assembly in India of the motor car" and than on "procuring or developing any improvement of modification in the technical know how" "inform the manufacturing company of such improvement and/or modification, as the case may be". Under the agreement the manufacturing company was also to re-imburse the technical company for the "actuals involved". "Actuals" has been explained to mean "actual disbursements and expenses incurred and/or liable to be paid buy the technical company for or in connection with the provision of the technical assistance". This was to include all printing and publishing expenses, travelling expenses, other out of pocket expenses, etc.

Shri R.H. Chawdhry has said that the technical staff employed by Maruti Technical Services were "very young and inexperienced in the field" and the company had no qualified graduate engineer for design work on their rolls. W.H.F. Muller, the German technician employed by Maruti Technical Services Private Limited, was a specialist in car body welding. As for equipment, Maruti Technical Services had only a few drawing boards and the rest of the plant and machinery and the drawing boards belonged to Maruti Limited. Shri Chawdhry adds that no final car design had been made for mass production. "Whatever was produced had been subjected to thousands of changes rendering earlier achievements completely obsolete" as there was no fixed and finalised design of the vehicles. "The necessary data was produced, changed and condemned as we went on manufacturing and remanufacturing the parts and components". Shri Chawdhry States that Maruti Technical Services "was not in a position to give anything readily available to Maruti Limited". "No research or development work facility was available with M/s Maruti Technical Services (Pvt.) Ltd. as long as I was associated with Maruti Limited", says Chawdhry.

In his affidavit affirmed on December 16, 1977 and filed before this Commission, W.H.F. Muller corroborates Chawdhry that "no research or development work was being carried out by M/s Maruti Technical Services Pvt. Limited and they had no laboratory of their own". Muller adds that 'Sanjay Gandhi had "overestimated his expertise in automobile industry" and, besides lacking the necessary qualification to be able "to design such engines/cars especially those intended for mass production, Shri Sanjay Gandhi lacked experience also".' From a letter addressed to Maruti Technical Services Private Limited by the Department of Industrial Development on November

24, 1975 it appears that the name of the company had been enlisted with that Ministry only for statistical purposes. The relevant part of the letter reads:

> "It may please be noted that this enlistment has been made purely for statistical purposes and does not carry with it any kind of financial benefits or your competence and claim to secure business."

It may be mentioned here that on January 25, 1975 a special resolution was passed at an extraordinary general meeting of Maruti Limited modifying the remuneration stipulated in the agreement dated June 2, 1972. Under the revised terms the payment by the public company of an annual technical fee on the net sales of the motor cars subject to a minimum of Rs. 2.50 lacs for each accounting year of the public company was suspended from the date of the resolution till the company commenced production of motor cars and even after the commercial production started no technical fee would be payable "to the extent of Rs. 110.20 lacs", which is the sum that the public company had already paid.

Shri J.K. Pahuja, Manager, Finance and Credit of Maruti Limited has said that from the books of account of Maruti Limited he found that from August 17, 1971 to March 31, 1977 the total payment made to Maruti Technical Services for technical know-how and reimbursement of actual expenditure was approximately Rs. 16 lacs. Shri P.R. Sasidharan, Accounts Officer of Maruti Limited, supports Shri Pahuja's statement. Shri M.A. Chidambaram who was Chairman of Maruti Limited till May 17, 1977, in an affidavit affirmed on November 9, 1978, has stated that the "agreement was expected to be of benefit to the company" and "there was no intention at all to cause loss to Maruti Limited". The expectation appears to have been belied. The income-tax assessment of Maruti Technical Services Private Limited for the assessment year 1973-74 was re-opened *inter alia* on the ground that inquiries made revealed that "neither Shri Sanjay Gandhi ever had any technical know-how/expertise enabling him to sell any such asset", nor was Maruti Technical Services Private Limited "ever in a position to render any technical services to Maruti Ltd. enabling the latter of manufacture any small car". Referring to Maruti Technical Services Shri R.H. Chawdhry, Chief Executive of Maruti Limited says that "from the very outset" it would seem "that these private companies were being formed only to extract finances from the main public limited company, i.e., Maruti Ltd.". The facts justify Chawdhry's observation.

Agreement dated 25-1-1973 and supplemental agreement dated 17-11-1973 *between Shri Sanjay Gandhi and Maruti Limited* : The Board of Directors of Maruti Limited passed a resolution on March 2, 1972 appointing Shri Sanjay Gandhi, Managing Director, for a period of five years with effect from the said date. His remuneration was fixed at Rs. 4,000 per month as salary plus one per cent commission on the net profits and other perquisites. On the basis of this resolution the company applied under Sections 269 and 198(4)/309(3) of the Companies Act in prescribed Forms 25A and 25C seeking approval of the Central Government to the appointment of Shri Gandhi on the above remuneration and also for protection of his minimum remuneration at the same salary of Rs. 4,000 per month and perquisites not exceeding Rs. 1,000 per month in value in any year when the company would fail to make any profit or adequate profit.

In processing the application the dealing assistant pointed out that the payment of remuneration to the Managing Director had to be considered on merit, i.e., the age, the educational and technical qualifications and the practical experience of the Managing Director in the trade had to be ascertained and that in this case the Department had no information about these details. He added that it appeared to him that in this case the Managing Director had nowhere served as a managing director or a technical director prior to his appointment in this company. He therefore suggested to his higher authorities that information on the above points should be called for from the company. He further observed that the proposed salary, commission and perquisites seemed to be on the "higher side for a company which was still in its infancy stage". The file then went to Shri C.L. Pratham, Section Officer. Shri Pratham who was examined as a witness admitted that he did not verify the age, educational and technical qualifications and practical experience of Shri Sanjay Gandhi but accepted what was stated in the applications in forms 25A and 25C. In column 3 of the form 25A it was mentioned that Sanjay Gandhi was a qualified and experienced technician in the automobile industry and under column 5(i) it was said that he was a mechanical engineer and had considerable knowledge and experience in the design, manufacture and assembly of automobiles. In his note dated August 11, 1972 Pratham also pointed out that the details about the age, educational and technical qualifications and business experience of Shri Gandhi had not been mentioned by the company in the applications. He suggested that the appointment of Shri Sanjay Gandhi as Managing Director for five years from March 2, 1972 on the proposed remuneration might be approved subject to a limit of five per cent of the net profits and the minimum remuneration protected according to the guidelines for one year only. He also stated that considering the present state of affairs of the company the proposed remuneration seemed to be on "very high side". As for the minimum remuneration, Shri Pratham said that as the figure of paid up capital mentioned in column 2 of form 25-A was only Rs. 24,60,700, this had to be taken as the effective capital and, having regard to the guidelines, the effective capital being between Rs. 10 to 25 lacs the minimum remuneration could not exceed Rs. 24,000 per annum, i.e., Rs. 2,000 a month. Deposing before the Commission Shri Pratham stated that he had treated this as an important and sensitive case because Shri Sanjay Gandhi, Managing Director of Maruti Limited, was a son of Shrimati Indira Gandhi, then Prime Minister of India. The file was then submitted to Shri C.R.D. Menon who was Under Secretary in the Department of Company Affairs at the relevant time. Menon has also been examined before this Commission. He found that the applications lacked in certain important particulars like the date on which the paid up capital became effective capital, the educational and technical qualifications of Shri Sanjay Gandhi, his age, etc. The witness dictated a note on the file calling for further details but before he signed it, he had to change the note under pressure. His earlier note on the file was removed and he recorded a fresh note on August 19, 1972 making out the following points : (i) that there was no objection in the absence of any complaint or disqualification to the appointment of Shri Sanjay Gandhi as Managing Director of Maruti Limited on the proposed remuneration subject to the availability of profits to pay such remuneration within the statutory limit of five per cent of the net profits of the company and (ii) that with regard to the grant of minimum remuneration, the maximum of the minimum remuneration admissible under the guidelines should only be Rs. 2,000 per month and perquisites restricted to one third of his annual salary of Rs. 1,000 per month. While computing the effective capital he left out of account the "charges created by the company . . . to the tune of Rs. 441.32 lacs" because he had "no information about the actual amount drawn or the dates thereof in respect of the charges created". Shri Menon indicated in his note that it was possible to relax the guideline on the ceiling on minimum remuneration if there was evidence to show that Shri Sanjay Gandhi was combining in himself the functions of an executive in addition to his responsibility as Managing Director of the company. Menon, however, said that there was no evidence in regard to this on the file. The case was then placed before Shri S.M. Yousuf, then functioning as Secretary of the Company Law Board, who recommended minimum monthly salary of Rs. 4,000 for one year plus perquisites amounting to Rs. 1,000 per month. On the question as to how the minimum salary could be fixed at Rs. 4,000 per month, Yousuf's evidence before the Commission is : " . . . it was a case I made out looking into the overall picture of the company, that it was supposed to be a very big, giant company with some crores of rupees, and with this background I had suggested Rs. 4,000 per month for one year only". He, however, admitted that there was no material on record which could justify fixation of salary at more than Rs. 24,000 a year under the guidelines. When it was pointed out to him that the details of the age, educational qualifications and business experience of Sanjay Gandhi had not been mentioned in the applications, Yousuf only said "I am afraid we did not call for that particular information". He said that "at that point of time there was a certain atmosphere" and it "was always working in everybody's mind" that the "applicant was Mr. Sanjay Gandhi who was the son of the then Prime Minister of India". The recommendation of the Secretary, Company Law Board, was endorsed by Shri C.C. Ganapati, Joint Secretary Department of Company Affairs, who suggested protection of the minimum remuneration for three years in the first instance. This was approved by the Deputy Minister Shri Beda Prata Barua and finally by the Minister of State for Company Affairs Shri K.V. Raghunatha Reddy.

The Department of Company Affairs in its letter dated August 28, 1972 addressed to Maruti Limited conveyed its approval to the company's proposal with this variation only that the minimum remuneration was sanctioned for a period of three years instead of five as asked for by the company.

On receiving the approval Maruti Limited entered into a formal agreement with Shri Sanjay Gandhi on January 25, 1973. The main provisions of the agreement of January 25, 1973 are these. Shri Sanjay Gandhi was to hold the office of the Managing Director for five years. His remuneration was (a) salary of Rs. 4,000 per month, (b) one per cent commission on the net profits of the company subject to a maximum of fifty per cent of the annual salary, i.e., Rs. 24,000 per annum, and (c) perquisites which included (i) medical benefits for self and family not exceeding one month's salary subject to a maximum of Rs. 12,000 for a period of every three consecutive years of service; (ii) leave travel concession; (iii) free use of car the monetary value of which was to be evaluated according to Income-tax Rules, 1962; (iv) subscription to clubs subject to a maximum of two clubs only, etc., it was provided that in the absence or inadequacy of profits in any year, the company would, as and by way of minimum remuneration, pay the same salary but not the commission and the value of the perquisites would not exceed Rs. 1,000 per month.

Thereafter Maruti Limited made another application seeking increase in the remuneration as well as the minimum remuneration of the Managing Director by way of granting bonus and additional perquisites with effect from March 2, 1972. The Company Law Board approved the proposal on July 13, 1973 following which a supplemental agreement was executed between Maruti Limited and Shri Sanjay Gandhi on November 17, 1973. Under this agreement the company was liable to pay the Managing Director bonus "according to Company's rules" and additional perquisites like free telephone facility at company's cost at the residence, free use of company's car with driver, petrol and maintenance cost, the monetary value of which was to be evaluated as per Income Tax Rules, 1962–this was introduced in supersession of the previous term as to the free use of car.

The three years protection of the minimum remuneration expired on March 1, 1975. On March 18, 1975 the Board of Directors of Maruti Limited resolved to extend the protection by two more years, from March 2, 1975 to March 1, 1977 and applied to the Central Government for approval. The Company Law Board approved the proposal on April 3, 1975. The Board of Directors of Maruti Limited on August 26, 1976 passed a resolution re-appointing Shri Sanjay Gandhi as Managing Director on the expiry of his first term as such, subject to the approval of the Central Government and the shareholders, for another period of five years with effect from March 2, 1977 on terms and conditions as before and made an application for approval of the appointment and protection of the minimum remuneration for the said period. Shri B. Prasad, Under Secretary in the Department of Company Affairs, who dealt with the case did not recommend payment of both bonus and commission to the Managing Director because both were incentives and normally it was not the practice to allow two incentives at the same time, it had to be either bonus or commission. The Joint Secretary Shri A. Choudhury agreed with his recommendation. However, Deputy Minister Shri Barua overruled them both and on November 13, 1976 approved Shri Sanjay Gandhi's re-appointment "on the same terms and conditions. . . as was done earlier". But before the agreement for re-appointment of Shri Sanjay Gandhi as Managing Director could be given effect to, Shri Gandhi resigned and ceased to be Managing Director with effect from March 2, 1977.

It is clear that on the basis of the two agreements large sums of money were paid for all these years to Shri Sanjay Gandhi from the funds of Maruti Limited. Clearly Shri Sanjay Gandhi did not possess the requisite qualifications, either technical or managerial to justify the remuneration and the perquisites he was paid. He had no managerial experience and as regards his technical qualification, the letter received from Rolls Royce Motors of England may be recalled. The resolution appointing Shri Sanjay Gandhi, Managing Director with effect from March 2, 1972 was passed by the Board of Directors of Maruti Limited at a meeting held on that day and the appointment was approved at an extraordinary general meeting of the company held on March 31, 1972. It is necessary to state certain facts concerning these two meetings. At the Board meeting held on March 2, 1972 the following Directors were present:

(1) Shri B.C. Jindal (in Chair)
(2) Shri Sanjay Gandhi
(3) Shri Sudhir N. Kapadia
(4) Shri Raunaq Singh

Leave of absence was granted to Shri M.A. Chidambaram, Shri C.B. Saran, Shri Jagdish Prasad and Lt. Col. V.R. Mohan.

In response to a notice issued by the Commission seeking clarification from him on certain matters, Shri Jindal filed an affidavit affirmed on November 15, 1978. In this affidavit he says that he was "not conversant with the English language" suggesting that he did not quite follow the proceedings in the meetings he attended, that he had no personal knowledge of Shri Sanjay Gandhi's qualifications but "believed in good faith that he possessed the requisite qualification to become the Managing Director" and that "at that stage" he "had no basis to suspect the bonafides of Shri Sanjay Gandhi". As regards the extraordinary general meetings held on March 31, 1972 it appears that only six shareholders were present. This meeting which approved Shri Sanjay Gandhi's appointment as Managing Director was presided over by Sanjay Gandhi himself. Those present were–

(1) Shri Sanjay Gandhi (in Chair)
(2) Shri R.K. Dhawan
(3) Shri Bhim Sain
(4) Shri Shealinder Kaintal
(5) Karan Bir Singh Sandhu
(6) Sudarshan Trading Company – Proxy.

In this meeting the resolution approving the appointment was proposed by Shri Bhim Sain and seconded by Shri R.K. Dhawan who was Personal Assistant to the then Prime Minister. From the affidavit dated December 16, 1978 of Shri Digambar Das, Despatch Clerk of Maruti Limited, it appears that notice of this meeting was sent only to twenty six shareholders and that too on March 12, 1972 which was eighteen days' before the date of the meeting though twenty one days clear notice was necessary under the law. Shri A.D. Kolhakar, Manger, Personnel and Factory Administration, Maruti Limited, said: "I can positively say that out of the meetings held between 8th March, 1972 and 15th May, 1974, when I resigned, the extraordinary meeting dated 31-3-1972 was never held. The minutes of the meeting were dictated by Shri Sanjay Gandhi to Shri S.M. Rege before me". This is an uncorroborated statement, but even if the meeting was held, the indisputable facts are that there were only six shareholders present and notice of the meeting was issued to only twenty-six shareholders and the notice again was short. From these facts this at least is apparent that the intention was to avoid a properly convened and largely attended meeting of the shareholders.

It is clear that the authorities did not follow the normal procedure in approving Shri Sanjay Gandhi's appointment as Managing Director or ensuring his minimum remuneration; they were under pressure and afraid to antagonise Shri Sanjay Gandhi. The guidelines issued by the Department of Company Affairs were ignored. The practice of not allowing two incentives, commission and bonus, at the same time was departed from in this case. Shri C.R.D. Menon, Under Secretary, Department of Company Affairs said he had to alter his original note calling for further information. Shri S.M. Yousuf, Secretary, Company Law Board admitted that his recommendation was influenced largely by the atmosphere prevailing at that time.

The two agreements next in point of time are between Shrimati Sonia Gandhi on the one hand and Maruti Technical Services Private Limited and Maruti Heavy Vehicles Private Limited, respectively, on the other. They relate to her appointment as Managing Director of these two companies.

Agreement dated 26-2-1973 *between Shrimati Sonia Gandhi and Maruti Technical Services Private Limited* : Shrimati Sonia Gandhi was appointed Managing Director of Maruti Technical Services Private Limited at the extraordinary general meeting of the shareholders of the company held on January 25, 1973. Shri Sanjay Gandhi and Shrimati Sonia Gandhi, the two Directors of Maruti Technical Services Private Limited were also the only shareholders of the company at the time. A formal agreement was executed on February 26, 1973 under which she was to remain Managing Director for five years from January 25, 1973. The Managing Director was to discharge such duties and services and exercise such powers as assigned by the Board of Directors from time to time. She was to devote such time and attention "as may, from time to time, reasonably be required" of her during the business hours for the discharge of her duties. She was to get a salary of Rs. 2,000 per month plus one per cent commission on the net profits of the company subject to a limit of fifty per cent of her annual salary plus perquisites. As this agreement related to the appointment of a Managing Director of a private limited company, it was not required to be approved by the Department of Company Affairs.

It was a fact known to all concerned that Shrimati Sonia Gandhi was a foreign national. In view of the provision of Foreign Exchange Regulation Act, 1973 which came into force on January 1, 1974 she could neither hold shares of any Indian company nor hold any office of profit in such company from the date the Act came into force without prior approval of the Reserve Bank of India. Ultimately she tendered resignation on January 21, 1975. It is surprising that Shrimati Sonia Gandhi who did not have any technical qualification should be appointed Managing Director of a technical company.

Quite a large sum of money was paid to her on account of her salary and perquisites during the period she remained the Managing Director of the company. Shrimati Sonia Gandhi had shown in her income-tax returns the following income she received from Maruti Technical Services Private Limited:

1.	**For Year ended 30-9-1973**				
	From 26-2-73 to 30-9-73				
	(i) Salary	Rs.	20,484.00		
	(ii) Bonus	Rs.	4,097.00		
	(ii) Commission	Rs.	1,443.00	Rs.	26,022.00
2.	**Year Ended 30-9-1974**				
(a)	(i) Salary	Rs.	30,000.00		
	(ii) Bonus	Rs.	6,000.00		
	(iii) Commission	Rs.	3,393.00	Rs.	39,393.00
(b)	Dividends (Gross)			Rs.	6,030.00
3.	**Year Ended 30-9-1975**				
(a)	Remuneration to Managing Director from 1-10-1974 to 21-1-1975 including commission of Rs. 154	Rs.	9,348.00	Rs.	9,348.00
(b)	Dividends (Gross)			Rs.	1,528.00
			Total	Rs.	82,321.00

Assessing the income-tax of Maruti Technical Services Private Limited for the assessment year 1975-76, Shri A. Banerjee, Income Tax Officer, disallowed a part of the remuneration paid to Shrimati Sonia Gandhi as excessive because she had no qualification to be able to render any technical service to the company. Shri Banerjee's evidence is that he found that the reasonable remuneration admissible to Shrimati Sonia Gandhi could not be more than Rs. 2,000 per month inclusive of bonus and commission. The income-tax assessment of the company for the two preceding assessment years had also been reopened but the proceedings after the re-opening were not concluded at the time Shri Banerjee deposed.

Agreement dated 28-9-1974 between Shrimati Sonia Gandhi and Maruti Heavy Vehicles Private Limited: It is not necessary to discuss the terms of the agreement dated September 28, 1974 between Shrimati Sonia Gandhi and Maruti Heavy Vehicles Private Limited because the agreement was never put into effect and Shrimati Sonia Gandhi did not draw any salary as Managing Director of Maruti Heavy Vehicles Private Limited.

Agreement dated 1-4-1975 between Maruti Technical Services Private Limited and Maruti Heavy Vehicles Private Limited : Maruti Technical Services Private Limited and Maruti Heavy Vehicles Private Limited also entered into an agreement on April 1, 1975 under which the Maruti Technical Services was to render technical know-how to the other company for manufacturing road rollers. The share-holders of Maruti Heavy Vehicles Private Limited passed a resolution approving the agreement on October 30, 1975 long after the agreement was executed. The remuneration that Maruti Heavy Vehicles agreed to pay to Maruti Technical Services for supply of the technical know-how was two per cent of the net sales of road-rollers and spare parts, less all discount. The agreement was to remain effective for ten years from April 11, 1975 and was to continue thereafter on year to year basis until terminated by either side giving the other not less than six months' previous notice.

The difference between this agreement and the one entered into by and between maruti Limited and Maruti Technical Services may be noted. Under the agreement between the two private companies, Maruti Technical Services was to be paid only two per cent of the net sales of road-rollers and spare parts, in this case no payment of any lump sum or any fixed minimum technical fee was stipulated, nor there was any clause for re-imbursement of actuals. The difference presumably was due to the fact that both the private companies were controlled by Shri Sanjay Gandhi. On the day the agreement was executed, Shri Sanjay Gandhi, Shri Rajiv Gandhi, Shrimati Sonia Gandhi and Maruti Technical Services, of which Shri Sanjay Gandhi and Shrimati Sonia Gandhi were the share-holders, held the controlling shares in Maruti Heavy Vehicles Private Limited which had a number of shareholders not belonging to the Gandhi family. From the material available to the Commission a sum of Rs. 82,660/88p. appears to have been diverted from Maruti Heavy Vehicles to Maruti Technical Services. It has been found that Maruti Technical Services was not competent to render technical know-how in respect of motor cars. There is no evidence that it had the know-how in respect of road-rollers. Shri R.H. Chawdhry, Chief Executive of Maruti

Limited, has stated that till he left the company in March 1974 there was no improvement in the technical expertise of Maruti Technical Services, "Upto March 1974 Maruti Technical Services Private Limited did not have any technically qualified person or specialist on roadrollers and whatever little assembly work on roadrollers had started by the time, I had left, was done by Maruti Limited personnel, using Maruti Limited's premises and all the other related services, i.e., electricity, water, telephone, postage, trunk-calls, furniture, tools and vehicles, etc.'.

The officers of Maruti Limited who deposed – R.H. Chawdhry, Chief Executive; S.M. Rege, Secretary; J.K. Pahuja, Manger, Finance and Credit; and A.D. Kolhatkar, Manger, Personnel and Factory Administration, have all stated that the two private companies had been utilising the services of the employees of the public company and also its office space, laboratory, workshop, telephones, vehicles, etc. Rege has said that he himself, J.K. Pahuja and Mohinder Singh, all full time employees of Maruti Limited, were also working for Maruti Technical Services Private Limited and Maruti Heavy Vehicles Private Limited. According to Rege the following members of staff were common between Maruti Technical Services Private Limited and Maruti Limited:

1. Shri S.M. Rege
2. Shri J.K. Pahuja
3. Shri J.L. Varma
4. Shri J.K.K. Afridi
5. Shri A.K. Gulati
6. Shri A.S. Parmar
7. Shri G.L. Kalra
8. Shri P.R. Sasidharan
9. Shri A.D. Kolhatkar
10. Shri Mohinder Singh.

J.K. Pahuja also named the employees of Maruti Limited who were also working for Maruti Technical Services Private Limited and Maruti Heavy Vehicles Private Limited. They were:

1. Shri S.M. Rege
2. Shri A.D. Kolhatkar
3. Shri J.K. Pahuja

4. Shri J.L. Varma
5. Shri A.S. Parmar
6. shri A.K. Gulati
7. Shri J.K.K. Afridi

The employees of Maruti Limited who were working for either or both the private companies were given a nominal honorarium which was not a fixed sum and depended on the discretion of the Managing Director, Shri Sanjay Gandhi. Shri Kolhatkar has said that not only the officers but also the draftsmen and some other employees of Maruti Limited who were workers under the Factories Act were also made to work for Maruti Technical Services Private Limited though they were on the pay rolls of the public company. According to Kolhatkar he pointed out to Shri Sanjay Gandhi that double employment was prohibited under Section 60 of the Factories Act and was punishable under section 93 of the said Act. Kolhatkar suggested to Sanjay Gandhi that he should appoint a separate set of officers for Maruti Technical Services. Shri R.H. Chawdhry also expressed the same view. To that Sanjay Gandhi replied, according to Kolhatkar, that he did not care for the Acts made by Parliament. Kolhatkar added that he had seen the list of employees working with Maruti Technical Services during the year 1972-73 and found that all the 23 employees of Maruti Technical Services figured in the muster rolls of Maruti Limited. Kolhatkar stated further that the employees of Maruti Limited were also utilised by Maruti Heavy Vehicles Private Limited for the assembly of road rollers. He named these employees:

1. Shri Joginder Singh
2. Shri P.N. Raut
3. Shri Alimuddin
4. Shri N.D. Joshi
5. Shri Kishori Lal.

The employment of the staff of Maruti Limited by the two private companies resulted in indirect diversion of a large sum of money from the public company to the two private companies controlled by Shri Sanjay Gandhi. It has not been possible to ascertain the exact amount so diverted. Shri Ram Saroop, Labour-cum-Conciliation Officer of Haryana Government in Gurgaon, deposing before the Commission said that it never came to his notice that the same employees were working for the public company and also for the two private companies. On proper supervision it should not have been difficult to find out the true facts.

CHAPTER VI

On the basis of such evidence as is available in the files, supplemented by the testimony of the witnesses who in their official capacity have dealt with those fields at various stages, the following significant facts have come to light :

1. Shri T.A. Pai, then Minister of Industries and Civil Supplies in the Government of India had addressed d.o letters to the Chief Ministers of State Governments in July 1975 and again in August 1976 requesting them to place orders for road rollers on Jessops and Company, a public sector undertaking, in order to clear the stock accumulated with the company. Jessop road rollers are of reputed make and conform to ISI specifications. They are fitted with M.S. rolls which give better performance.
2. Jessops rollers are normally available on DGS&D rate contract. In 1975-76 period this rate contract was somehow not renewed. Non-renewal of the DGS&D rate contract for Jessop rollers has been mentioned as the reason for inviting direct quotations by most of the purchasing organisations.
3. Garden Reach Workshop (GRW) another public sector unit, is manufacturing road rollers of a reputed make, and conforming to ISI specifications. These road rollers are fitted with cast iron rolls. Under the Government of India orders then in force, the GRW was entitled to a 10 per cent price preference when competitive tenders were invited.
4. Garden Reach Workshop sent their quotations in several cases in response to tender inquiries and the price quoted by them was generally lower than that quoted for Maruti rollers. No business could however be secured by them in these cases. Irrigation Department of Government of Karnataka did not accept their offer. Central Coal field (a public sector unit) did not accept their tender even though it was specifically brought to their notice that GRW was entitled to 10 per cent price preference also. The Municipal Corporation of Delhi ignored

the tender of GRW totally for not furnishing earnest money, a requirement which can be waived in the case a supplier registered with DGS&D. The Delhi Development Authority did not invite any tender from GRW even when the unit had expressed its readiness to supply road rollers.

5. The relative rules of the Government of India for regulating purchase of stores (which are applicable to most organisations like MCD, DDA, NDMC, etc.) have categorised road rollers as 'a centralised item' to be procured only through the DGS&D. All of them, however, procured the Maruti road rollers direct, though in the earlier stages of consideration of the proposals, purchase through the agency of DGS&D was specifically envisaged. In Delhi Municipal Corporation the requisite amount for giving advance deposit was also sanctioned and drawn before a fresh decision to go in for direct purchase was taken.
6. The relative rules also prescribed that even in cases where direct procurement is resorted to, inspection of the equipment should, as far as practicable, be entrusted to the Inspection Wing of the DGS&D. This was ignored by almost all the organisations who bought Maruti road rollers. In the Delhi Municipal Corporation, the draft tender conditions required the material to be inspected by the DGS&D. But this was deleted in the final tender notice by the Executive Engineer. In the case of Central Coal-fields, the purchase order prescribed predelivery inspection by DGS&D. But before this could be undertaken, supply was completed on telegraphic instructions from the Chief Engineer and inspection by DGS&D was later waived. In the Engineering Projects (India) Limited, despite defects appearing during preliminary inspection and despite a specific suggestion by the Adviser, Purchase, Shri Thandani, Inspection by DGS&D was ignored. Inspection by the contracted inspecting agency, General Superintendence & Co., who in 1967 surveyed the stock of engines, transmission, etc., of Agrind Fabricators Limited most of which were later fitted to Maruti road rollers, was also dispensed with, and the road rollers supplied by Maruti Heavy Vehicles Private Limited were shipped to Kuwait without any inspection. In the case of DDA, inspection by DGS&D was not resorted to though DDA itself had no arrangement for carrying it out.

7. The ISI had drawn up standard specifications for road rollers. Maruti road rollers did not confirm to the ISI specifications. These rollers had only three forward and one reverse speed but according to the standard specifications the reverse and forward speeds should be at least three each.
8. Orders for supply of Maruti road rollers were placed without insisting on trial runs in a single case. Certificates issued by Shri V.P. Chetal, Shri A.K. Bhat and the Superintending Engineer, Government of Haryana, were relied upon as technical proof of suitability of the road rollers without verifying whether the certificates had been issued by these persons in their official capacity after carrying out the prescribed tests (including gradient test) and/or after actual use of the equipment. Shri Chetal has stated that he had issued the certificate in his personal capacity.
9. The engines, power packs and some other components used in the assembly of Maruti road rollers were purchased mainly from the Punjab National Bank in an auction. These components originally belonged to a manufacturing unit, Agrind Fabricators Limited, a company which had gone into liquidation, and the court had entrusted the old stock of engines and other components, imported in 1966 to the bank for disposal.
10. The imported engines used by Maruti Heavy Vehicles in their road rollers were out of stock sold by Punjab National Bank. The engine numbers in several cases have been examined and found to tally with those available in bank records. The engine manufacturer's test certificates were not furnished to the buyers of Maruti road rollers.
11. Maruti road rollers had defective brakes and the steering system was also faulty. Maruti rollers had not been subjected to gradient tests. Fitness certificates for Maruti rollers were obtained from Shri V.P. Chetal and Shri A.K. Bhat in their personal capacity but utilised as official documents. The prescribed tests were not carried out before the fitness certificates were issued by them. A certificate of fitness was issued by Superintending Engineer, PWD, Haryana, for Maruti rollers at the instance of the then Chief Minister, Haryana.
12. Maruti Heavy Vehicles Private Limited were liable to pay excise duty from March 1, 1975 on the road rollers assembled by them whereas this duty has been paid by them to the Central

Government only from April 1, 1976.

13. Adverse performance reports have been received from certain users. In some cases road rollers purchased from Maruti Heavy Vehicles have remained idle for long periods. Various technical defects had been reported by Himachal Pradesh, Karnataka, Rajasthan. As against this, the EPI, NOIDA, NDMC and DMC have made no such complaint.
14. R.K. Khadilkar, then Minister for Supply, had put pressure on the officers of DGS&D for granting provisional registration to Maruti Heavy Vehicles as approved supplier of road rollers even though the technical report was adverse.

On the basis of the above facts it is clear that undue favour was shown by the various purchasing departments and organisations in placing orders on Jalan Modi Automobiles for supply of road rollers of Maruti make and allowing in some cases favourable terms of payment, dispensing with inspection before delivery, and failing to take appropriate action for having the defects in the units rectified. The requirement for road rollers was often inflated to increase the sale of Maruti rollers.

Bus Body Building Contract Cases

Bus body fabrication contracts constitute the next important group of cases. The first undertaking to be approached by Maruti Limited, for bus body building work was the Haryana State Road Transport Corporation (HSRTC). The dealings of that corporation with Maruti were specifically excluded from the Terms of Reference of this commission as another Commission of Inquiry headed by Shri Jaganmohan Reddy was looking into them. The other Transport Corporations which gave business to Maruti were Rajasthan State Road Transport Corporation (RSRTC), Delhi Transport Corporation (DTC), Madhya Pradesh State Road Transport Corporation (MPSRTC) and Uttar Pradesh State Road Transport Corporation (UPSRTC), in that order. The DTC case having been investigated already by the Central Bureau of Investigation (CBI), this Commission has not looked into it. The bus body building contracts secured by Maruti Limited, from the remaining three Transport Corporations, namely, RSRTC, MPSRTC and UPSRTC have distinct features of their own in the mode of entertainment of the offer or tender, the accommodation in numbers and also in the fixation of rates. All the three corporations are constituted under Section 3 of the Road Transport Corporation Act, 1950.

Rajasthan Bus Body Fabrication Contract with Maruti

The RSRTC had as many as 152 bus bodies fabricated by Maruti Limited—3 on the Leyland Comet, 75 on Leyland Viking and 74 on Tata chassis, during the period September 1975 to March 1977. From August 1975, when the order for construction of the first prototype bus body was given to Maruti, till March 31, 1977, the total number of bus bodies constructed for the corporation by all the builders was 547. Various types of bus bodies were built by Maruti—three units on Leyland Comet were of RSRTC old model, while 44 units were on Leyland Viking chassis of DTC city type and 21 of DTC Mofussil type. Ten of the Leyland Viking chassis had RSRTC new Mofussil type bodies. All the 74 Tata chassis had RSRTC Mofussil new design.

Maruti Limited first came into picture for bus body building work for RSRTC in June 1975. The RSRTC had floated a tender for the fabrication of 300 bus bodies (for RSRTC old model) on March 21, 1975. The date originally fixed for opening of the tenders was May 26, 1975 which was postponed to June 9, 1975. On June 3, 1975 Maruti applied for the tender documents and soon thereafter filed their tender. The tenders were opened on June 9, but further consideration of the offers received was held up as the then Chief Mechanical Engineer, Shri G.N. Chakrapani, was on leave. After his return from leave in July 1975, Shri G.N. Chakrapani recommended negotiations with the parties for bringing down their rates as the quoted rates were on the high side compared with the previous years' negotiated rates of Rs. 34,000 per unit for Leyland and Rs. 32,500 for Tata and other modal chassis. In the meantime, there was change in the incumbency of the office of Chairman of the RSRTC. The new Chairman, Shri Mohinder Singh, took over on July 14, 1975. He gave a direction that a meeting of the officials should precede the negotiations with the parties and fixed this meeting on July 19. The same day Shri Kalra, an employee of Maruti Limited met Shri Mohinder Singh and had discussions with him regarding the bus body fabrication work. On August 5 Shri Kalra wrote a letter to the corporation seeking allotment of one chassis to Maruti for fabrication of prototype. In this letter he referred to the discussions he had with

Shri Mohinder Singh. Comments of the Deputy General Manager (Accounts) were obtained on this letter and the Chief Mechanical Engineer was not consulted. On the basis of the note recorded by the Deputy General Manager (Accounts), the Chairman, Shri Mohinder Singh, ordered the release of one chassis to Maruti Limited for fabrication of prototype on the same terms and conditions on which other body builders were making bodies for this corporation. Since the new tender for 1975-76 had not been finalised till then, the release of this chassis to the builder (Maruti Limited) in August 1975 had to be reckoned against the 1974-75 tender which was then in operation and the same rate was adopted in this case also. Maruti was not one of the parties who had participated in the 1974-75 tender. The prototype fabricated by Maruti was delivered to RSRTC on January 2, 1976. On the same day, a further allotment of 2 more chassis was made to Maruti Limited on the same rate as on the earlier occasion, in pursuance of their request contained in the letter dated December 6, 1975. In this letter it had been claimed that the prototype job had already been completed to the satisfaction of the Inspectorate of RSRTC. According to the evidence adduced before the Commission, work on the prototype was not completed till December 6, 1975. The allotment of two chassis on January 2, 1976 was also against the 1974-75 tender which was in operation as the tender for 1975-76 had yet to be finalised. Approval of the corporation was obtained for the allotments which were made by the Chairman. According to the delegation of financial powers contained in Order No.F. 4(142)/Accounts/Rules/65-66/7790 dated January 25, 1974, all powers regarding purchases are subject to the usual Tender Rate and Purchase Policy of the corporation and in his deposition before the commission, Shri Mohinder Singh eventually conceded that "tender system and tender rules" could be applicable "to the bus body contracts". While the body fabrication work on the two chassis allotted to Maruti on January 2, 1976 was under way, Shri P.R. Subramanian, Chief Mechanical Engineer, who had in the meantime, left Delhi Transport Corporation had joined RSRTC. He put up a note to the Chairman on February 5, 1976 giving his assessment of the facilities available with Maruti Limited for bus body building work. Shri Mohinder Singh took a decision on this note on February 6 : "It appears from the report of the CME that M/s Maruti Limited, are in a good position to make bus bodies. Accordingly, we could also give them a certain number of chassis for building bus bodies. In the beginning we should keep it restricted to the Mofussil bus bodies and not semi-deluxe or deluxe types". Following this decision a letter was issued to Maruti Limited from RSRTC on the same day, February 6, informing them that RSRTC was prepared to give them chassis at the rate of 10 per month for the year. Shri P.R. Subramanian has said in his statement that "It came to be known for certain that towards the end of 1975 that M/s Maruti was entering the field of bus body building in a big way, evidently after their failure in cheap car production and Haryana Road Transport Corporation had already placed orders and allotted chassis in fairly large numbers.... The emergency atmosphere was very much felt and the general feeling was that RSRTC would have to cooperate with M/s Maruti Limited, to the maximum extent. It was also known that M/s Maruti's case had the backing of Government of Rajasthan".

Between the 8th and 17th April 1976, a further allotment of 15 chassis was made to Maruti Limited. Shri P.R. Subramanian's version is that about the time of finalisation of the tender for 65 bodies, Shri Pant, General Manager of Maruti Limited, "was keen on taking up the construction work of DTC city type buses in as much as, according to him, they were organised for this work and wanted that they should be given chassis for this purpose". According to Shri P.R. Subramanian, he had communicated this request of Shri Pant to the Chairman, Shri Mohinder Singh, "who told me that he will discuss the matter with the Minister and then take a decision. It was in my knowledge that in all important body building matters pertaining to Maruti, the Chairman used to discuss the matter first with the Transport Minister, Shri Chhagani and Chief Minister Shri Harideo Joshi before taking decisions". Shri P. R. Subramanian states that in this case "after discussions the Chairman decided to allot 15 chassis to Maruti Ltd., and 5 to Delhi Automobiles". Shri Mohinder Singh has also admitted this. He has stated : "In view of the known prominence of M/s Maruti Ltd. dealings of the Rajasthan State Road Transport Corporation with that firm were, from time to time, subject of discussion with the concerned Transport Ministers (Shri Mohan Chhagani up to April 16, 1976 and Shri Ram Narain Choudhary thereafter), and with the Chief Minister Shri Harideo Joshi. The Transport Minister and the Chief Minister were of the view that the firm may be accommodated in respect of orders. Maruti Limited was keen for a regular monthly allotment. The request of Maruti Limited for an allotment of chassis on regular basis was first discussed with the Transport Minister Shri Chhagani near about the close of January 1976. Again towards the end of 1976, Maruti Limited wanted to known as to what business it could expect from RSRTC during the forthcoming year of 1977. It was interested in 40 chassis every time more so because of their surplus capacity, with the large U.P. Roadways orders nearing completion. Several discussions were held with them including two meetings at Maruti Limited in December 1976, and January 1977. The matter was discussed by me with the Transport Minister and the Chief Minister. I was advised by them that RSRTC need not enter into any commitment with Maruti Ltd. on this scale, but its request for larger allotment be accommodated".

Fabrication of 29 more bus bodies according to the DTC city model was entrusted by RSRTC to Maruti later in the year. The allotment and release of chassis was as follows:

August 1976	10
October 1976	9
December 1976	10

No tenders were invited for fabrication of bus bodies of the DTC type before giving the job to Maruti Limited, and no prior approval of the corporation was obtained for these allotments. In his statement, Shri Mohinder Singh has given the following explanation for this deal:

> "Having found that Government of India was financing a maximum of 15 Leyland buses and no more, we at the official level reviewed the whole situation probably in the last days of March 1976, or in the first days of April 1976. It was proposed that we may have a minimum of 20 new buses to make a viable unit and that meant putting 5 from our own resources.....CME who had come from DTC advised that as RSRTC had no experience of designing and building specialised city buses, it may adopt *in toto* the DTC city design which he considered as one of the best in India and more suited to our climatic conditions....CME advised that RSRTC may get these 20 built on the same rates as DTC which had an existing tendered rate of Rs. 40,700 for Leyland Comet and was negotiating for the additional amount to be paid for the Viking overhang. Shri Subramanian considered Rs. 40,700

a very attractive rate....CME's advise was accepted and on his informing that Maruti Limited and Delhi Automobiles were building such buses for DTC, 15 were allotted to Maruti and 5 to Delhi Automobiles. The decision taken at the official level was put up to the corporation in the forthcoming meeting on 26th April 1976". The agenda note on the subject not only recommended adoption of the same design as developed by the DTC and payment of the same rate as was to be fixed by DTC to the body builders but a specific recommendation was also made for entrustment of the work to Maruti Limited and Delhi Automobiles only because they had specialised in the fabrication of DTC type bodies. The agenda note did not mention that two Jaipur firms Azad Body Builders and Kamal and Co., who had been having dealings with RSRTC for a long time, had also handled bus body building work for DTC. Shri Mohinder Singh has admitted this omission, but says, "I do not remember whether Shri Subramanian mentioned that the firms of Azad and Kamal of Jaipur were also doing this work. If that had been brought to my notice it is quite possible that these may also have been allotted some. Incidentally the CME has always been favouring fewest possible body builders for specialised bodies on the grounds of standardisation".

On June 7 and July 31, 1976 Maruti Limited were entrusted with the additional chassis, 10 each time, for the fabrication of DTC Mofussil design on Leyland Viking chassis without observing the tender procedure. This decision was taken at the level of the Chairman, Shri Mohinder Singh. These chassis were released from the lot of 65 chassis included in the new tender for 1975-76 for fabrication of RSRTC old Mofussil bodies but the allotment to Maruti out of this lot was for DTC Mofussil design, at rates yet to be fixed by DTC themselves, instead of the RSRTC old Mofussil bodies. By that time DTC had not got any Mofussil design bodies built on their Leyland Viking chassis themselves or by Maruti Limited. On June 18, 1976 a meeting was held between Chairman Mohinder Singh and Chief Mechanical Engineer Shri P.R. Subramanian with representatives of 7 firms who had responded to the tender notice when the issue of fabrication of DTC Mofussil type bus bodies was decided upon. Fabrication for DTC Mofussil bodies was canvassed at this meeting on the ground that delivery of chassis was expected soon, being already in line, and floating of a fresh tender for the fabrication of new design bodies was not advisable as that would mean delay. It was specifically mentioned in the minutes that 10 chassis already released to Maruti and 5 to Delhi automobiles should have Mofussil design bodies.

Maruti also built a DTC Mofussil body on one chassis which was the substitute for another chassis out of the first lot of Viking chassis sent direct to them by Rajesh Motors on September 5, 1976. In fact they were expected to fabricate DTC city type on this unit. This change was, however, condoned by RSRTC.

Work orders subsequently issued in respect of 20 chassis released to Maruti on June 7 and July 3, 1976 mention the tender for 65 bodies of RSRTC old Mofussil design and the negotiations held on April 5, 1976. Thus, against the tender for RSRTC old Mofussil design, allotment were made for body building work for DTC Mofussil type bodies and no fresh tenders were invited for this purpose.

Tenders were invited for body building work on 100 Tata chassis for a new model developed by RSRTC in July 1976. The date fixed for opening the tenders was July 31, 1976. Twelve parties including Maruti Limited and Delhi Automobiles sent tenders. Identical rates of Rs. 44,500 per unit were quoted by Maruti and Delhi Automobiles and these were the highest. On the basis of costing calculation done by RSRTC, the cost of fabrication for this bus body design on Tata chassis was calculated as Rs. 40,000. This figure was higher than the lowest quotation received from one of the tendering firms, M/s Auto Body Centre which had quoted only Rs. 34,240. This lower offer was rejected by Shri P.R. Subramanian on the ground of low capacity and workmanship of the firm and also for the sake of standardisation. The matter was subsequently taken up to the Board on August 20, 1976 and the Corporation's approval obtained. In the provisional allotments of chassis proposed under the tender, the name of Maruti was not included till December 12, 1976. However, a revised allotment was proposed by Shri P. R. Subramanian on December 25 in which 30 chassis were earmarked for Maruti Limited. Subramanian has admitted that this was done in deference to the wishes of Maruti Limited conveyed orally for increased allotment of Tata vehicles. In subsequent letters sent by Maruti on January 7 and 12, 1977 they expressed preference to have 3/4th Tata and 1/4th Leyland for the allotment to be made, and also desired to have monthly allotment of 40 chassis on regular basis. Shri P.R. Subramanian has stated that the Chairman, Shri Mohinder Singh had discussion on this issue with

Shri Harideo Joshi, the then Chief Minister and Shri R.C. Choudhary, the then Minister for Transport and as a result of this discussion Maruti were allotted 30 Tata chassis in January 1977, 20 in February 1977 and 24 in March 1977 at the agreed rate of Rs. 40,000.

RSRTC floated a tender for fabrication of 100 bodies of their new Mofussil design on Leyland Viking which design had been finalised by them towards the end of November 1976. Fifteen firms submitted their tenders, including Maruti and Delhi Automobiles. Maruti Limited and Delhi Automobiles had quoted identical rates of Rs. 46,500 plus taxes. According to the costing done at RSRTC, the cost per unit for this type of body was worked out at Rs. 44,500. In his note on the opening of tenders on December 7, 1976. Shri P.R. Subramanian recomended that the allotment should be restricted to 8 parties, 6 of Jaipur and 2 of Delhi. The noting of Shri Mohinder Singh was in favour of allotting the maximum number of Maruti Limited. In the notional allotment made on the first lot of 22 chassis, the name of Maruti Limited was, however not mentioned. But 10 Leyland Viking chassis were allotted to Maruti Limited against the tender in January 1977 at the agreed rate of Rs. 44,500 excluding taxes.

RSRTC while allotting 15 chassis of Leyland Viking for fabrication of DTC city type of Maruti Limited had, on the assumption that the rate of 40,700 fixed by DTC for DTC city type on Leyland Comet Vehicles was an attractive rate and that the extra amount required for Leyland Viking would work out to only Rs. 2,700, indicated the rate as Rs. 43,400 in their belated work order. Maruti took up the matter with the DTC and in their letter dated May 8, 1976 maintained that the rate fixed by DTC for DTC city, type on Leyland Viking was Rs. 45,000. They stuck to this as far as DTC city type body on Leyland Viking is concerned. But, when it came to the question of DTC Mofussil type they quoted the DTC reference to show that the rate for DTC Mofussil type on Leyland Comet was Rs. 48,700. This was according to DTC's confidential letter dated July 23, 1973, a copy of which was handed over to Shri P.R. Subramanian by Maruti's representative. Subsequently, in their letter dated August 3, 1976 Maruti claimed Rs. 48,500 for DTC Mofussil type on Leyland Comet and Rs. 52,800 for DTC Mofussil type on Leyland Viking. On September 2, 1976 they raised the rate of DTC Mofussil type on Leyland Comet to Rs. 53,000. This was also confirmed by DTC in their letter dated November 2, 1976.

The RSRTC which were advancing only Rs. 40,000 provisionally for each vehicle delivered to Maruti Limited took up the matter for final settlement of the bills on January 7, 1977 on a note by Shri P.R. Subramanian. His recommendation was to accept and pay Maruti Limited at Rs. 53,000 for Leyland Viking, deducting Rs. 3,320 being the difference in using M.S. flooring instead of aluminium flooring. Shri Johri who was the Chief Accounts Officer at that time pointed out the incongruity in this and recommend that payment should be only on the basis of the rate fixed for RSRTC new model on Leyland Viking, i.e., Rs. 44,500. He also pointed out that inasmuch as no tender was floated for the work of such magnitude, corporation's prior approval or at least *ex post facto* approval was necessary. Chairman Shri Mohinder Singh decided to have the *ex post facto* approval of the corporation for the rate recommended by Shri P.R. Subramanian, Chief Mechanical Engineer. However, on February 26, 1977—the day of the meeting—a news item appeared in the *Indian Express* referring to the malpractices resorted to in fixing boosted up rate by DTC for Maruti Limited by no less a person than an ex-Chairman and a member of DTC. A revised agenda note recommending a much reduced rate of Rs. 46,990 was thereafter put up to the corporation and this was approved. The original agenda did not mention the objections raised by Shri Johri nor did the revised agenda refer to the news item.

Investigation has revealed that except in the case of 10 bodies got built on Leyland Viking chassis on RSRTC new Mofussil design in January 1977, and on 74 Tata chassis according to the RSRTC new Mofussil design in the months of January, February and March 1977, where allotments were covered by the regular tender, the allotment of 68 bus bodies in the case of other types in favour of Maruti Limited was made without a tender on even a limited tender enquiry. Nor was the approval of the corporation obtained which was essential as the firm was being accommodated outside the prevailing tender. Fuller details of the various transactions between Maruti and RSRTC can be ascertained from the statement of facts included in the appendix to this report.

Shri Harideo Joshi, former Chief Minister, Rajasthan, and Shri Mohan Lal Chhagani and Shri Ram Narayan Chaudhary, former Transport Ministers of Rajasthan have totally denied their involvement in the dealings between Maruti Limited and the Rajasthan State Road Transport Corporation. In his affidavit Shri Chhagani says "From time to time informal discussions and consultations used to be held by and between the Chairman of the State Corporation and myself. The said discussion and consultations were generally on policy matters. . . . It was very rarely that any specific details as to the day to day functioning of the corporation was ever gone into in depth . . . the corporation was an autonomous corporation and that all matters pertaining to day to day administration were looked after by the officers concerned and the ultimate decisions relating thereto were exclusively the privilege of the Board of Directors of the corporation. At no stage either the Government or myself at the Minister were involved in such specific decisions being taken by the Board or in implementation thereof by the officers concerned. . . . As far as I recollect, it was only once that the Chairman of the corporation had mentioned to me the facts about Maruti Ltd. having a large capacity and plant and their performance and that it would be desirable if some orders are also given to Maruti Ltd. I recollect having told the Chairman that there was no harm in doing it provided there was no detriment to the interests of the corporation or to the local body manufacturers and if placing of the orders with Maruti can help expeditions delivery to cope with the requirements of the Corporation". Shri R.N. Chaudhary has denied that he directed the Chairman or any official of the Rajasthan State Road Transport Corporation to accommodate Maruti Limited in the matter of placing of orders by the Corporation for the construction of bus bodies and thereby giving pecuniary benefit to Maruti Limited. He says that he did not discuss this matter with the Chairman or any other official and that he never asked them to ensure preferential treatment for Maruti Limited. Shri Harideo Joshi, former Chief Minister, Rajasthan, has stated that "except for cursory reference which the then Chairman, RSRTC had once, there had been no discussion, meetings" with him "nor any paper was put up" before him in this connection. The testimony of the witnesses examined before the Commission and the material furnished in the affidavits field before the Commission was sought to be contradicted by a denial.

On a consideration of the available records and evidence it is quite clear that undue favour was shown to Maruti Limited in the placement of orders for bus body fabrication work, allotment of chassis from time to time and in agreeing to pay for the DTC city and Mofussil type bodies at the same rate which was settled by Maruti with DTC without observing the normal financial procedure.

Madhya Pradesh Bus Bodies Building Contracts

Madhya Pradesh State Road Transport Corporation (MPSRTC) entered into two contracts with Maruti Limited for bus body building work. In 1975, the fleet position of the MPSRTC is claimed to have been very bad. About 391 vehicles had become overaged according to the prescribed norms of 10 years for Leyland vehicles and 7 years for TMB vehicles and these were due for replacement during 1976. The cost of operation of the fleet had gone up, due to the bad condition of the vehicles and this had an adverse effect on the income of the corporation. The corporation was also faced with demands for improvement in fleet, expansion of bus services, nationalisation of road transport on new routes and also in uncovered areas along the existing routes, etc. As it was felt that the business of the corporation could no longer be carried on economically and efficiently with an out-moded and depleted fleet, arrangements were made with the Punjab National Bank and IDBI and the Provident Investment Company for loans to the extent of Rs. 327.09 lacs. The financial position of the corporation at the end of the financial year 1974-75 was not sound as the accumulated losses had gone up to Rs. 885.07 lacs. The State Government had advanced a loan of Rs. 50 lacs to the corporation in March 1974 and a further loan of Rs. 50 lacs was advanced by it to the corporation in March 1975, to be adjusted against capital contribution for the next year. Even the loans from the IDBI and the Punjab National Bank were secured on the strength of guarantee from the State Government. While the question of replacement of the old vehicles was still under consideration, a suggestion was made by the Chief Accounts Officer of the Corporation for hiring of privately owned vehicles as an alternative solution. However, this suggestion was not pursued.

The Madhya Pradesh State Road Transport Corporation has two departmental workshops where bus body fabrication work can be undertaken, the Central Workshop at Gwalior and a workshop at Indore. The capacity of both the workshops in 1976-77 according to Shri Krishan Chandra, Chief Accounts Officer, was 275 buses in a year. The capacity of Central Workshop alone was 221 in a year.

MPSRTC had 35 bus bodies fabricated from an outside agency in 1971. This gave rise to an audit objection and in November 1974 the Vice Chairman of MPSRTC Shri Moti Lal Vohra agreeing with the view taken in audit expressed his opinion that these 35 bus bodies could have been constructed more economically at the Corporation's own workshop. In December 1974 the Board of Directors of the Corporation made thereon and referred the matter to the State Government for appropriate action. Final decision in the matter was, however, taken by the State Government only in June 1978.

For road transport operations the most important period in a year when the maximum revenue can be expected is from November to June. The period from July to October is the slack season. The MPSRTC therefore wanted to replace the overaged vehicles during the peak period (i.e., from November to June).

On November 10, 1975 Shri R.S. Khanna, General Manager of the Corporation, submitted a note in file tender No. 1/75/Tech in which he gave justification for getting bus bodies constructed through outside agencies. This note was recorded by him on the suggestion of Shri Sitaram S. Jajoo, who was then Chairman of the Corporation, and in the note it is stated that the Chairman had already been informed about the position verbally by the General Manager Shri Khanna. Shri Khanna stated that new buses were required by the corporation and keeping in view the practical aspects, replacement of 230 buses would take 8 months and this meant that new buses would not be available to the corporation during the best part of the traffic period. He was of opinion that "looking to the construction capability of our workshops, it would be better if we go in for bus body building from outside agencies". This note was put up to the then Chairman Shri Sitaram S. Jajoo. Shri Jajoo marked the note to the Vice Chairman, Shri Moti Lal Vohra, for comments who in his note dated November 13, 1975 stated "the only point which is for consideration is that, if we receive 40 chassis a month, our workshops are in a position to deliver constructed bodies. If this number exceeds then only we should look to outsiders for body building". Chairman Shri Sitaram Jajoo in his note dated November 15, 1975 expressed the view that the bus body work should be done through outside agencies as the Government workshops were not in a position to achieve the target. He directed the General Manager to prepare a precis for the Board meeting. The proposal was discussed on December 1, 1975 at the 85th meeting of the Board of Directors presided over by Shri Sitaram S. Jajoo. The Board approved the proposal for fabrication of 100 bus bodies from outside agencies.

Notice inviting tenders was issued on December 3, 1975, calling for offers from outside parties for construction of 100 bus bodies. It was mentioned in the tender documents that the tender was for construction of bus bodies on TMB chassis only, though the Tender notice mentioned both Leyland and TMB chassis. Tenders from 19 parties were received by January 5, 1976 including Maruti Limited and they were opened on the same day in the presence of members of Headquarters Tender Committee (HQTC) for short. Two more tenders were received on January 6 and these were also opened in the presence of HQTC members on January 7. HQTC's function is to open the tenders received, get the comparative statement prepared and scrutinise it in a meeting. It then recommends the most eligible tender and recommends it for necessary action to the Board. Negotiations with tenderers, if considered necessary, are to be held by the HQTC.

Tenders were tabulated in the Technical Department first and then in the Accounts Department of the corporation. It was found that a valid and current Income Tax certificate had not been furnished by any party which was necessary to be submitted alongwith tender documents according to the purchase policy rules. Maruti Limited had also not submitted the required drawings for TMB chassis. They had instead submitted drawings for bus bodies on Leyland chassis, though the tender documents specifically referred to TMB chassis only. The HQTC of the corporation considered all the tenders in its meeting held on January 9, 1976. The offer of Maruti Limited was not the lowest, six other being lower. These six parties were: M/s Auto Body Centre, Jaipur; Azad Body Suppliers, Jaipur; Rajasthan Commercial Corporation, Jaipur; Rama Body Builders, Delhi; Mehrotra Industries, Calcutta; and Wadia Body Builders, Ahmedabad. These lower offers were rejected on one or more of the following grounds:

(i) Inadequate capacity.
(ii) Designs or drawings not supplied with the tender.
(iii) Earnest Money not deposited.
(iv) No experience of building bus bodies or previous performance with MPSRTC not satisfactory.
(v) Sales Tax on higher side and insurance charges claimed as extra item.

According to Shri Krishan Chandra, Chief Accounts Officer of the Corporation, Maruti Company knew that the said tender was only for construction of bus bodies on TMB chassis and normally a tender could qualify for acceptance only if it was accompanied by the requisite drawings for the model specified in the tender documents. Nevertheless the offer of Maruti Limited was considered acceptable by the HQTC.

It was decided by the Committee to submit the case to the competent authority for consideration. A decision on the offers of other tenders was not considered necessary for the time being till the result of the discussion regarding the delivery schedule, etc., with Maruti Limited was finalised, as the rates of other tenderers (besides the six rejected) were on the higher side. Thereafter, the file was put up by the General Manager to the Chairman who saw it on January 9, 1976 and invited comments of the Vice Chairman, Shri Moti Lal Vohra. Shri Vohra in his note dated November 10, 1976 stated that the rates of Maruti Limited were fairly reasonable, that the tenderer had also expressed his willingness for further discussions regarding the terms, and suggested "As the HQTC has recommended the tender of M/s Maruti Ltd. of Haryana, Chairman may approve the recommendations of the HQTC in anticipation of the sanction from the Board". The file was sent to Shri Sitaram S. Jajoo, Chairman on the same day and he agreed with the note of Shri Vohra and directed that discussions with Maruti Limited be held for obtaining favourable terms. Shri Krishan Chandra, Chief Accounts Officer, has brought out the following facts in his statement: "Subsequently the Chairman, alongwith the Vice Chairman, General Manager and CWM, Shri K.N. Wahi had visited Delhi from 11th to 14th January 1976 for having discussions with Maruti Limited. In the discussions with Shri Sanjay Gandhi it was also decided that Maruti Ltd. would supply us 50 bodies by the end of March 1976. Thereafter, the rate of supply could be more. It could be 30 bodies per month. Neither I nor any other official from the Accounts Department was associated in the negotiations with M/s Maruti Ltd. as provided in the rules". Shri R.S. Khanna, then General Manager, MPSRTC has in the course of his deposition stated: "We found that the Chairman was very much interested in one particular tender. . . . The matter was kept open. We thought that even though there is some interest shown by the Chairman the matter may be kept open because we did not know whether Maruti Limited would be able to fully implement the order for 100 bus bodies or not. . . . The whole thing is that on the first day we visited the factory. On the second day we visited the P.M's residence.

The meeting was held at the P.M.'s residence. And well, first Chairman and Vice-Chairman entered Mr. Sanjay Gandhi's chamber and later on we followed. Well, there it was decided that a rebate of Rs. 1,000 per bus will be given and in order to tempt Mr. Sanjay Gandhi for giving the rebate, the Chairman mentioned, 'well, the order could be for 100–200'. But then I told him later on that 'NIT (notice inviting tender) for 100, I am not going to sign an order for more than 100' and, therefore, the words 'depending upon finances available' was also recorded as a conclusion of the meeting.

Reverting to the statement of Shri Krishan Chandra, he has stated that Shri R.S. Khanna put up the note to the Chairman on January 16, 1976 regarding the discussions which they had on January 13 with Shri Sanjay Gandhi. The General Manager mentioned in the last portion of the note that "the party was asked to depute some person duly authorised to sign the agreement with MPSRTC" Shri Sitaram S. Jajoo, Chairman approved the above note of the General Manager on January 16, 1976 thereby authorising placing of contract for this tender with Maruti Limited. According to Shri Krishan Chandra, rules 43 to 53 of the rules framed by the Corporation regarding tender for purchase of stores and execution of works envisaged that if negotiations were to be done, it should be done by the HQTC with all the parties as far as possible, and that this was not done in the present case when Chairman Shri Sitaram S. Jajoo visited Delhi and Gurgaon for undertaking negotiations with Maruti Limited.

In accordance with the discussions held by Shri Sitaram S. Jajoo the entire lot of bus bodies fabricated by Maruti Limited should have been delivered to the Corporation by the end of May 1976. However, according to the available records, delivery of the bus bodies covered by this tender was completed only September 1976.

In the note recorded by Shri R.S. Khanna it was stated that Shri S.M. Rege was due to arrive at Bhopal on January 7, 1976 for signing the agreement for Maruti Limited. He, therefore, desired that the draft agreement should be prepared urgently. The draft agreement was prepared and vetted by the Law Officer and the agreement was finally typed on the same day January 17, and signed by both the parties. The matter was placed before the Board on February 27, 1976 of ratification. In the meantime in anticipation of Board's approval, 25 chassis were delivered to Maruti Limited, 15 in January 1976 and 10 upto June 14, 1976.

Shri Krishan Chandra has stated that "while placing orders on

M/s. Maruti Ltd. no other officer including myself could have raised objections of any sort because the emergency was on at that time and Shri Sañjay Gandhi, as everybody knows, had attained lot of political power. Moreover, as is borne out from the notings on files, no time was given to us to study the case properly and there was constant pressure on us from the Chairman Shri Jajoo to clear this case on top priority basis without raising any objection, etc., as virtually he had already agreed in Delhi to award this contract to M/s Maruti Limited.

From the records it is quite apparent that within a matter of 4 days the Chairman and the Vice-Chairman not only decided to accept the Maruti tender without placing the matter before the competent authority, which was Board, but also *suo moto* proceeded to negotiate with the contractor, and that too at his residence/factory premises".

As regards delivery of bus bodies Shri Krishan Chandra says, "in fact, no bus body was received in the month of March, 1976 from Maruti Ltd. and only 33 buses arrived in April and May and the majority (67) arrived during the slack monsoon months . . . there was abnormal delay in the supply of the bus bodies by Maruti Ltd. to our Corporation . . . the last lot of 22 bus bodies was received from Maruti Limited by our Corporation as late as September 1976. This means that delivery was late by about four months".

One of the conditions of the agreement was that if there was delay in supply of bus bodies, the body builder was to pay a fine of Rs. 100 per day per chassis and the penalty was to be recovered by the General Manager from the bills and the security deposit of the body builder. The tender was floated mainly with a view to getting the buses in March 1976 so that they could be utilised fully during the peak period between April and June. According to the calculations made by the Accounts Department of the corporation, there was a delay of 414 days and at the rate of Rs. 100 per vehicle per day, the quantum of penalty was worked out at Rs. 41,400. The Technical Department however revised the figure to 328 days delay and the quantum of penalty was reduced to Rs. 32,800. On November 10, 1976 a meeting of the Board was held when the Chairman raised an item outside the agenda and Resolution No. 1774 was passed whereby the Chairman was delegated the power of reducing or condoning the penalty where such penalty had fallen due. No precis was submitted at the Board meeting for this outside agenda item before the resolution was passed and cven the General Manager had not proposed this item for the Board's consideration. According to Shri R.S. Khanna, it was Shri Sitaram Jajoo himself who had proposed this motion at the Board meeting as an outside agenda item. Subsequently, the file regarding levy of penalty of Maruti Limited was put up to Shri Jajoo who recorded a notc on December 21, 1976 and after justifying the waiver of the penalty directed that the entire penalty be condoned.

Even before the last batch of buses was received by the Corporation from Maruti Ltd. on June 7, 1976 Shri Jajoo was contemplating placing a repeat order for another lot of bus bodies on Maruti Ltd. without calling for fresh tenders. This was objected to by some of the officers of the Corporation. Sometime in the first week of September 1976, Shri R.S. Khanna asked Shri Krishan Chandra to accompany him to see Shri S.C. Shukla, the then Chief Minister, who had called him (Shri Khanna) and the Finance Secretary Shri N.V. Krishnan for a discussion. Shri Khanna has deposed before the Commission that he and the Finance Secretary had discussions with the Chief Minister and he (Chief Minister) showed his interest in placing a further order on Maruti Ltd. This was followed by a telephonic call on September 14, 1976 from Shri Shukla to Shri Khanna asking him to send 20 chassis to Maruti Limited. However, as the first contract had just been completed, Shri Khanna put up a note on the same day mentioning that this could be done only if the Board gave its sanction or the Government issued a direction in that regard.

Thereupon the Chairman asked the General Manager to prepare a precis whereby a case could be made out for placing a further order of 100 bus bodies on Maruti Ltd. The General Manager put up a note dated September 23, 1976 which was signed by Shri Jajoo on the next day. It was to be put up before the Board meeting on October 4, 1976. The precis was finalised without getting the comments of Chief Accounts Officer. According to the provision of Section 15(2) of the RTC Act, 1950, all precis/proposals having financial implications should be shown to the Chief Accounts Officer for his views/ comments before putting the same before the Board. In the precis it was stated *inter alia* that it was "considered desirable to go in for outside contract as last year. M/s Maruti Limited have expressed their willingness to construct another 100 bus bodies on the terms and conditions as was done last year. In fact inviting of tenders may take a long time. The rules may probably require calling fresh tenders, but as time is an important factor, getting bus bodies constructed by Maruti Ltd. may be considered proper. Prices have gone up in the meantime and therefore, tenders may entail a higher cost also". Protest against this procedure was made by some of the Board members, including Shri M.N. Buch, the then Secretary, Town & Planning. As a sequel to this there was meeting with the Chief Minister Shri S.C. Shukla on October 5, 1976. This meeting was attended by M.N. Buch, Secretary, N.V. Krishnan, Finance Secretary, R.K. Tikku, Secretary to the Chief Minister and R.S. Khanna, General Manager. In that meeting Chief Minister ordered that tenders should be floated for further 70 bus bodies to be constructed for the corporation from outside agencies. Shri Khanna then put up a note on October 6, 1976 in which he stated *inter alia* that "in order to obviate calling tenders afresh, in case requirement goes beyond 70, approval may be obtained for getting 100 bus bodies constructed from outside". Shri Khanna in his deposition before the Commission has said that it was Shri Jajoo who had ordered him to change the figure of 70 to 100.

A revised precis was prepared for floating tenders for 70–100 bus bodies which was approved by the Board on October 15, 1976, Shri Krishna Chandra in his state says "I remember that when the Chairman was bent upon giving a repeat order to Maruti Ltd. for construction of another 100 bus bodies, the then Chief Minister Shri S.C. Shukla was also vitally interested in this matter. Some time in the first week of Sept. 1976, Shri Khanna, G.M. told me that Shri Shukla, C.M. had called him, *viz.*, G.M. and Finance Secretary for a discussion. Shri Khanna requested me to accompany them as some matter involving financial implications was to be discussed by C.M. . . we then, three of us, went to Vidhan Sabha. Shri Krishnan and Shri Khanna met the C.M. in his chamber. I remained outside. After the meeting Shri Khanna and Mr. Krishnan came out from the chamber. Shri Khanna told me that the C.M. wanted us to approach the nationalised banks for agreeing to reimburse the amount of loan drawn by our Corporation from the State Govt. as an interim arrangement as and when the case for term loan was finalised by the Banks where our request was pending. I also learnt from Shri Khanna that the Chief Minister was also very much interested to place an order on Maruti Ltd. for the second contract for fabrication of bus bodies".

Shri R.S. Khanna and Shri N.V. Krishnan have corroborated the statement of Shri Krishan Chandra about the meeting they had with the Chief Minister, Shri S.C. Shukla. Shri Khanna in his deposition has stated that all the time there was pressure on him from the Chairman for placing a repeat order and calling for the second tender was mere formality as it had already been decided by the Chief Minister and the Chairman to award the second contract also to Maruti Limited. However, a notice inviting tender was issued on November 11, 1976 calling for tenders from outside agencies for construction of bus bodies on about 70–100 TMB chassis. Sealed Tenders were received from 13 parties including Maruti Limited, one of them late by one day. These were opened on December 16 and 17, 1976 in the presence of HQTC members. HQTC in its meeting held on December 20, 1976 considered the tenders. It rejected the lowest tenders, 9 in number, for reasons like non-submission of earnest money and drawings. After that the other lower tender was of M/s Rama Body Builder, but it was not accepted as according to HQTC the terms quoted by the part were not in accordance with the terms and conditions prescribed in the tender. The HQTC found the tender of Maruti Limited in order. The tenders in respect of other parties were not considered as their rates were higher than Maruti's offer. The matter was then put up to the Board. In this case also Maruti had not submitted drawings which were a pre-requisite according to the terms and conditions of the tender. According to Shri Krishan Chandra, Chief Accounts Officer, the tender of Maruti Limited should have been rejected straightaway on this ground. In this tender also Maruti Limited had offered to negotiate; however, no negotiations were held.

A draft precis was prepared, which was seen by Chief Accounts Officer and General Manager and approved by the Chairman Shri Jajoo all on the same day, December 20, 1976. The matter was then put up before the Board in its meeting held on December 24 and the Board approved the award of this contract to Maruti Limited.

Shri Sitaram S. Jajoo, former Chairman of the MPSRTC, and Shri R.S. Shukla, former Chief Minister, have denied that any pressure was put by them on the officers in the matter of award of these contracts. Shri Jajoo has taken up the position that it was absolutely essential in the interest of the corporation to get the funds utilised and place a new fleet on the road as early as possible so that the corporation could start getting better return. There is no other evidence in rebuttal of the testimony of Krishan Chandra, R.S. Khanna and other witnesses.

On the basis of the material before the Commission, it is clear that undue favour was shown to Maruti Limited in the award of the two contracts and confining negotiation of the rate of first contract only to them and also in condoning the delay in supplying the built vehicles.

Uttar Pradesh Bus Body Building Contracts

Uttar Pradesh State Road Transport Corporation (UPSRTC), a public undertaking established by the State Government of Uttar Pradesh under the Road Transport Corporation Act, 1950, also placed bulk orders with Maruti Limited for fabrication of bus bodies in 1976-77. The Corporation have their own Central workshop at Kanpur with a production capacity of 50 chassis per month. In December 1975, the Board had occasion to review the production capacity of the Central workshop. In the course of discussions regarding the ways and means of clearing the backlog of 250 chassis lying the yard, it was pointed out that at the rate of 50 per month, the Central workshop could provide only 150 buses by the end of March leaving 90 chassis on which bodies had to be built only by April 1976. Since peak traffic season normally commences from April, both loss of revenue and public criticism would follow, if the remaining buses were not ready before April. The idea of getting atleast 75 bus bodies built on Tata chassis through the agency of private builders was therefore mooted. In the Board Resolution No. 392/75, this suggestion was accepted by the Corporation and fabrication of bus bodies on 75 chassis through private agencies on the lowest rate accepted in 1974-75 was sanctioned. Along with this it was decided to augment capacity of the Central workshop as also to develop Allen Forest Workshop to raise its capacity for renovation work to about 50 buses per month. This mater was also discussed on December 24, 1975 at the third meeting of the Corporation. In March 1976, the position was reviewed at a meeting held in the office of the General Manager and Chairman. At this meeting Shri K.R. Ramanujam, Deputy General Manager (Mechanical Engineering) pointed out that according to the budget provision only 400 chassis were to be purchased during the year and, therefore, tenders should be invited from private body builders for fabrication of only 400 bodies. The then General Manager and Chairman Shri Anand Swarup, however, was of the view that tenders could be invited for fabrication of 1000 bodies. Shri K.R. Ramanujam has explained that this view was taken in order to put on the road additional vehicles to meet the *Kumbh Mela* requirements. Based on this decision a tender was floated for fabrication of bus bodies on 1000 chassis and necessary publicity was also arranged. In response to the tender notice 31 tenders were received. The tenders were opened by the Purchase Committee in the presence of the representatives of several tenderers. Tenders invited were for fabrication of both Mofussil type and City type bus bodies on Tata LWB chassis, hill type bodies on Tata WSB chassis and Mofussil type buses on Leyland Viking LMB chassis. Eighteen firms had quoted lower rates than Maruti for Mofussil bus bodies and hill type bodies on Tata chassis the number of tenders lower than that of Maruti was 14 and 4 respectively. In respect of Mofussil design on Leyland Viking, 14 tenders with rates lower than that of Maruti were received.

The rates of Maruti Limited and Delhi Automobiles were not the lowest in terms of landed cost. In his statement, Shri K.R. Ramanujam has clarified that originally Maruti had quoted for bodies of one specification only and they were asked to send their rates for bodies for other specifications also, and the required information was sent by Secretary, Maruti Limited in letter dated May 29, 1976. There were other firms also besides Maruti which had omitted to quote correctly for the different specifications and therefore a letter was sent to all the tenderers for furnishing the rates for different specifications on May 7, 1976. A tabular statement of the various rates quoted by the firms for the different bodies was prepared. Among the firms whose quotations were lower than those of Maruti were reputed firms such Hindustan Steel Industries, Lucknow, Utkal Automobiles, Jamshedpur, Kamal & Co., Jaipur, Azad Body Builders, Jaipur and Hyderabad Allwyn, for different types. At this juncture, Shri S.K. Modwel, the then General Manager received a telephone call from Shri A.B. Malik, Resident Commissioner, Government of Uttar Pradesh at Delhi, to the effect that the then Chief Minister, Shri N.D. Tiwari, desired that the maximum number of chassis be allotted to Maruti Limited for fabrication. Shri Modwel who was to proceed on leave from May 31, 1976 assured Shri Malik that he would look into the matter on his return from leave. Shri Modwel remain leave upto June 20, 1976 and during this period Shri Fazle Ahmed Khan, the then Transport Commissioner held charge of the post. Shri Ramanujam in his statement has said that "on 2-6-

1976 (forenoon) Shri Maheshwar Prasad, Secretary, Transport/Chairman, called me to his office and I was asked by him to go to Delhi immediately and meet the Resident Commissioner for U.P. at Delhi, Shri A.B. Malik the same evening and on the following day to meet Shri Sanjay Gandhi for discussions regarding bus body fabrication. A little later, I was informed on phone by the Secretary that the Chief Minister (Shri N.D. Tiwari) had desired that he (the Secretary) should also go to Delhi and meet Shri Sanjay Gandhi. Accordingly myself and the Secretary, Transport, both travelled by the same plane on 2-6-1976 afternoon from Lucknow to Delhi and in the evening met Shri Malik at U.P. Niwas. The following morning we again met at U.P. Niwas. Shri Fazle Ahmed who was the acting G.M. in the absence of Shri S.K. Modwel on leave, also joined us at U.P. Niwas on 3-6-1976. We, all the four of us, Shri A.B. Malik, Shri Fazle Ahmed, Shri Maheshwar Prasad, the Transport Secretary, and myself went to Maruti Limited at Gurgaon at 9.00 a.m. It may be mentioned that the previous evening on 2-6-1976 when we met Shri Malik, he had indicated that discussions with Shri Sanjay Gandhi would be, more or less one sided and, therefore, one has to be cautious while conversing with him. So it was decided that only the Secretary Shri Maheshwar Prasad would conduct the discussions, being the senior-most officer in the group. We met Shri Sanjay Gandhi in the office of the G.M. Shri Pant, Maruti Ltd. During the discussions, on behalf of Maruti, Shri Rege and Shri Pant were also present besides Shri Sanjay Gandhi. At the outset Shri Sanjay Gandhi asked us as to how we had come to visit Maruti. Shri Maheshwar Prasad expressed that we were directed by the Chief Minister to go and meet him (Shri Sanjay Gandhi) as he (Sanjay Gandhi) had desired to discuss on bus body fabrication tender. Shri Sanjay Gandhi said that he had nothing to discuss. He mentioned that regarding bus body fabrication he had seen that tender was issued by UPSRTC and Maruti Ltd. had also tendered. In case UPSRTC required Maruti Ltd. to fabricate bus bodies, they would be in a position to fabricate bus bodies against a planned programme. Shri Sanjay Gandhi was then informed that on a rough tabulation made on the tenders received, Maruti stood at Serial No. 11 on basic rates and 16 on landed cost. Shri Sanjay Gandhi immediately pointed out that the tabulation could not be final and UPSRTC would be calling the selected firms for negotiations. He indicated that at the time of negotiations, their rates would be brought down to match with other firms selected for entrusting with bus body work. He also mentioned that though Maruti would be prepared to reduce the rates, it would do so only to the level of the rates offered by reputed firms. During the course of discussion, Shri Sanjay Gandhi asked as to when the tenders were opened. He was informed that the tenders were opened on 15-5-1976. On hearing this, he sharply reacted and remarked that it was already 3-6-1976 and the tender was yet to be finalised. He also made a sarcastic remark that perhaps work in U.P. was done in this fashion. After this the meeting closed and the Transport Secretary asked me to finalise the tender as soon as possible and in any case within the tender as soon as possible and in any case within the next 15 days. He also asked me to inspect Maruti workshop then and there and during the course of the day see as many bus body fabricating firms who had tendered as possible at Delhi also and to visit Jaipur following day to inspect the body builders there. Accordingly all of us along with Shri Sanjay Gandhi inspected the Maruti Ltd. workshop before leaving the place. I subsequently inspected two workshops at Delhi that day and also visited Jaipur on 4-6-1976. On 6-6-76 the tenders received were considered by a Committee comprising of Chief Accounts Officer and myself. The Committee broadly considered entrusting of bus bodies for fabrication to the firms based on the rates tendered, location, area, equipment, production capacity, etc., as revealed from the tenders received, the inspection note of workshops by different officers and other factors which are explained in the note dated 6-6-76. . . . It was recommended in the same note that the following 11 firms could be called for negotiations in order to determine uniform basic rate:–

1. M/s Azad Body Builders, Jaipur
2. M/s Royal Body Builders, Rohtak
3. M/s Maruti Limited, Gurgaon
4. M/s Hindustan Steel Industries, Lucknow
5. M/s Utkal Automobiles, Jamshedpur
6. M/s Kamal & Co., Jaipur
7. M/s Sanghi Engineers, Jaipur,
8. M/s Harish Industries, Meerut
9. M/s Sukhanand Jain, Meerut
10. M/s Jullunder Body Builder, Delhi
11. M/s Delhi Automobiles, Faridabad

The note was duly approved by the Chairman on 7-6-1976. The Negotiation Committee meeting was to be held in the office of the UPSRTC, Ajmeri Gate, Delhi, on 14-6-1976. The meeting was proposed to be held at Delhi because most of the firms selected for negotiations were located at Delhi and around Delhi."

As a result of the negotiations it was decided to arrive at the following uniform rates:

Tata Mofussil (District) type	Rs. 42,500
Tata City type	Rs. 41,000
Tata Hill type	Rs. 38,500
Leyland Viking Distt. (Mofussil).	Rs. 46,000

The Committee recommended acceptance of the rates arrived at and recommended the allotments of chassis as under:

Maruti Limited

(i) Tata Hill bodies	105
(ii) Tata Rural bodies	105
(iii) Tata city type bodies	50
	260

Hindustan Steel Industries

Lucknow	50	
Delhi Automobiles, Faridabad	90	
Azad Body Builder, Jaipur	65	
Sanghi Engineers	35	
Central Work Shop, UPSRTC	60	
Harish Industries	1	(prototype)
Sukha Nand Jain	1	(prototype)

The note prepared by the Negotiation Committee after their sitting on June 14, 1976 was included in the Agenda for the 26th Board meeting which was put up to the Chairman, Shri Maheshwar Prasad on June 15. The Chairman discussed the note with Shri Ramanujam orally and approved the inclusion of the item in the Agenda. When the matter came up for consideration before the Corporation at the meeting held on June 23 a revised note was submitted on the ground that the previous note contained clerical and other errors which had inadvertently crept in. According to the revised note Maruti Limited was proposed to be allotted 280 chassis instead of 260 chassis while others were proposed to be allotted chassis as follows:

Delhi Automobiles	75	
Hindustan Steel Industries	110	
Central Workshop, UPSRTC	105	
Harish Industries	1	(prototype)
Sukha Nand Jain	1	(prototype)

Two firms of Jaipur, M/s Azad Body Builders and Sanghi Engineers, were omitted in the new allotment proposed. In the Board Resolution No. 431/76 it was specifically noted that hill type vehicles should be allotted only to Maruti Limited and Delhi Automobiles. One chassis was thereafter allotted to Maruti Limited for construction of a prototype. Shri Ramanujam thereafter visited Maruti Limited on July 24, 1976 along with Shri Diwale, Chief Accounts Officer, and Shri Rajinder Singh, Service Manager, Meerut. During this visit Shri Sanjay Gandhi suggested some alterations in the body specifications in order to make the structure of the body as a whole look elegant. The changes envisaged replacement of aluminium outer framework with treated mild steel for strength and stability; reduction in the number of roof sticks, reducing the size of the window glass according to the DTC design and also the size of the window to 46" and certain other changes. Shri Sanjay Gandhi assured them that the revised costing based on these changes in the specifications would be intimated to UPSRTC. Shri Ramanujam has in his statement given the following facts:

> "The G.M. in his observations on page 6 of the note had enquired if the changes involved any difference in cost. Since the Managing Director, M/s Maruti Ltd. had assured during the discussions that variations in the costs would be worked out and intimated later, this matter was not pursued in routine course. Further there was always a fear complex persisting in the minds of the officers while dealing with Maruti Ltd. It was known too well, how deeply interested were the Chief Minister, the Transport Minister, the State Minister for Transport, in Maruti Ltd. as evidenced in the allotment of vehicles and especially in view of their indication to

us to see that Shri Sanjay Gandhi was not displeased at any stage, it was considered quite unsafe to take up this matter of cost variations with the firm on urgent basis. It was left pending to be taken up at the time of final settlement of accounts. Moreover, it was during this period that Shri Sanjay Gandhi had once spoken to me on telephone and expressed his annoyance over the delay in the delivery of chassis to Maruti Ltd. He accused that on the previous visit of General Manager and myself to Maruti Ltd. We had furnished incorrect information and that all the files had also been manipulated. As a result G.M. and myself had to seek an appointment with Shri Sanjay Gandhi on telephone and had to rush to Delhi on the same day by car for want of accommodation either by train or by plane from Lucknow or Kanpur and explain the position to him in person".

On July 19, 1976 Shri S.P. Singh, Minister for Transport, had proposed at a meeting that the UPSRTC should go in for purchase of 2,000 additional buses by the end of 1976, in addition to renovating 1,000 buses. This was also stressed by Shri N.D. Tewari, the very next day at a review meeting on the working of Transport Department and Road Transport Corporation. However, the Corporation approved the purchase of only 560 new chassis and its meeting on July 28, 1976 mainly due to the paucity of funds. It was also decided to make the allotment only to such of the private bus body manufacturers who had responded to the tender floated in May 1976.

In view of this decision to allot extra number of chassis to the private builders, Shri K.R. Ramanujam, visited Maruti Limited on August 10, 1976 for assessing the additional capacity of the firm. He was told by Shri Pant that Maruti Limited would be in a position to augment their capacity to 65 bodies from October to December 1976 and 85 from January 1977 onwards. While UPSRTC officials were preparing the notional allotment to Maruti Limited and other bus body builders on this basis, they were pressurised by Shri S.P. Singh, Minister for Transport to think in terms of increased allotment to Maruti Limited. In deference to his wishes and the directions of Shri Maheshwar Prasad, then Chairman, who had received a similar direction from the Minister, General Manager Shri S.K. Modwel visited Maruti Limited on September 25, 1976 with Shri K.R. Ramanujam for further discussions with Shri B.M. Pant. Shri Sanjay Gandhi also joined the discussion. He told them that Maruti Limited could fabricate 100 or even 150 buses per month.

Before the revised notional allocations of chassis could be finalised by UPSRTC officials, Shri Sanjay Gandhi personally rang up Shri K.R. Ramanujam on phone on September 29 and expressed his annoyance that Maruti were not being allotted any chassis despite their availability and accused the UPSRTC officials of giving false data and information and manipulating records. About the same time, Shri S.P. Singh, Transport Minister, spoke to Shri Modwel, General Manager, UPSRTC and told him (as stated in Shri Modwel's affidavit) that the Chief Minister was extremely upset over the delay in giving increased allotment of chassis to Maruti Limited and that he desired that action should be taken immediately in this regard. He directed Shri Modwel to seek an appointment immediately with Shri Sanjay Gandhi and rush to Delhi to settle the matter. Thereafter, the General Manager rang up Shri Sanjay Gandhi and sought an appointment to explain to him the correct position. Appointment was given by Shri Sanjay Gandhi at 9.30 a.m. on September 30, 1976 and the General Manager Shri Ramanujam had to leave for Delhi on September 29 in the evening. On September 30 they met Shri Sanjay Gandhi and explained the position of availability of chassis and their allotment to Maruti. On return from Delhi a note of the discussion held was prepared by Shri K.R. Ramanujam and both the General Manager and the Chairman approved the revised proposal made in this note.

According to the new proposal Maruti Limited was to get 125 chassis in October, 110 in November and 41 in December 1976. Shri Ramanujam has stated that, "This of course has to be at the expense of other private body builders". In his affidavit Shri S.K. Modwel, General Manger, has corroborated this statement. Shri S.K. Modwel on return from Delhi apprised Shri N.D. Tewari, Shri S.P. Singh, Shri R.P. Gupta, then State Minister for Transport, and also the Chairman, Shri Maheshwar Prasad, of the talks he had with Shri Sanjay Gandhi and the revised allotment proposed to be made. An agreement was thereafter executed between UPSRTC and Maruti Limited by which Maruti were to get 170 chassis over and above 280 chassis already allotted. In December 1976, a further move was made to increase the flow of chassis to Maruti. On December 13 Shri S.K. Modwel was instructed over phone from Delhi by Shri R.P. Gupta, the then State Minister of Transport, not to make any further allotment of chassis to M/s Azad Body Builders and M/s Sanghi Engineers, both of Jaipur, till further orders. Shri S.K. Modwel has recorded a note to this effect in the relevant file. Shri Modwel was also instructed to meet Shri Sanjay Gandhi in this connection and to ensure that allotment to Maruti Limited was kept at the maximum possible level. Shri S.P. Singh, Transport Minister also gave similar instructions to Shri Modwel from Delhi and desired that final outcome should be reported to him and the Chief Minister. Shri Modwel in his affidavit has averred that Shri Maheshwar Prasad, Chairman, UPSRTC, has also received similar instructions from the Chief Minister and had conveyed them to him. On December 17, 1976, Shri Modwel along with his Assistant General Manager (ME) met Shri Sanjay Gandhi. Shri Modwel says that Shri Sanjay Gandhi found fault with him for diverting chassis to other firms in spite of clear instructions from the Chief Minister, Transport Minister and the State Minister of Transport and directed him to divert all chassis to Maruti Limited. Shri S.K. Modwel pointed out that it was necessary to keep the Central workshop of UPSRTC engaged in bus body building work. Besides, there was difficulty in securing loans from Banks for purchase of chassis. It has been further stated by Shri Modwel that the Managing Director of Maruti Limited became very stern and told him in clear terms that no further diversion of chassis to other body builders should be done and it should have been clear to him that the highest officials of the U.P. Government had already given direction that all chassis should be diverted to Maruti Limited for bus body fabrication. Two remedial measures were suggested by Shri Sanjay Gandhi to overcome the difficulties mentioned by Shri Modwel. He suggested firstly that the Central workshop could be kept fully engaged with the renovation and re-renovation of old buses in order to lengthen the service span of the bus bodies beyond 4 lac km. Secondly, he said, Maruti Limited would use its influence with Punjab National Bank to provide credit facilities to the UPSRTC on suppliers credit basis. Discussions which Shri Modwel had with Shri Sanjay Gandhi were duly conveyed to Chief Minister, Minister of Transport and State Minister of Transport by Shri Modwel immediately on return. As a result a further allotment of 60 Tata chassis of small wheel base was made in favour of Maruti Limited for fabrication of hill bodies and 80 LWB Leyland chassis at at 40 per month in January and February 1977, subject to Maruti Limited arranging credit facilities through Punjab National Bank. The Transport Minister Shri S.P. Singh, according to Shri Ramanujam, again spoke to Shri Modwel and desired that all vehicles except those intended for the Central workshop should be allotted to Maruti Limited. A note was recorded by Shri Modwel on January 7, 1977 in this connection which was submitted by him to the Transport Minister through the Chairman. The Transport Minister thereafter had discussions with the Chairman, Shri Maheshwar Prasad, and agreed to modify his direction to the extent that the commitments already entered into with small scale industries could be honoured. These facts have been mentioned in the noting in the relevant file. The proposal to make further allotment to Maruti Limited was brought to the notice of the Ministers including the Chief Minister in a note prepared by Shri K.R. Ramanujam on January 12, 1977.

The proposal mooted by Shri Sanjay Gandhi at the time of the discussions he had with General Manager, UPSRTC, on December 17, 1976 to arrange credit facilities through Punjab National Bank on suppliers' credit basis for the purchase of 80 Leyland Viking chassis did not however materialise. Both Shri S.K. Modwel and Shri K.R. Ramanujam have stated quite clearly that at every stage in the bus body fabrication programme ever since Maruti entered the field there was interference and pressure exerted by the Chief Minister, Shri N.D. Tewari, Transport Minister, Shri S.P. Singh and the State Minister of Transport, Shri R.P. Gupta, for the allotment of maximum number of chassis to Maruti Limited. Shri S.K. Modwel has stated in his affidavit:

> "That in view of what has been stated above, it is evident that at various stages the Chief Minister, Transport Minister and the State Minister for Transport had told me and the Chairman of the Corporation that the chassis to the maximum possible extent may be given to the firm for bus body fabrication, and subsequently there were clear orders that all contracts for bus body fabrication should be entered into with one good party".

Shri K.R. Ramanujam has stated:

> "While dealing with M/s Maruti Ltd., in the matter of bus body fabrication, I have been under constant fear of being put under MISA for any lapse which would cause annoyance to Shri Sanjay Gandhi. On 17th December 1976 when I was on leave in Delhi, I

was called by the Transport Minister who was also in Delhi in U.P. Niwas. He told me that Shri Sanjay Gandhi was extremely annoyed with me but that he had explained to him that there was perhaps some misunderstanding and it was within his personal knowledge that I was not putting any impediment with regard to the payments or allotment to the firm. It was, however, suggested by the Minister that the matter be explained to Shri Sanjay Gandhi personally".

In the statement submitted in response to the notice under Section 8B of the Commissions of Inquiry Act, both Shri S.P. Singh and Shri R.P. Gupta have denied the role attributed to them and so did Shri N.D. Tewari by a telegram.

On the basis of the material available to the Commission it is quite clear that undue favour was shown to Maruti Limited in the matter of consideration and acceptance of their offer which was not the lowest, changes in the body design as suggested by Shri Sanjay Gandhi without checking the cost variations involved, and allotment of additional chassis from time to time beyond the limit envisaged in the original tender. It appears Maruti Limited dictated terms. A bus body builder in the normal course of business cannot summon the top management of any Transport Corporation to his business premises to tell them how much business he must get. The UPSRTC, a statutory Corporation, is an autonomous body and the frequent interferences by the former Chief Minister, Transport Minister and the State Minister for Transport were wholly unjustified and only indicated their desire to help Maruti at the expense of the other body builders including the Central Workshop of the Road Transport Corporation itself.

CHAPTER VII

The tenth item in the list concerns "all facts and circumstances relating to allotment of controlled commodities and materials, like steel and cement, to the said (Maruti) concerns and their utilisation or disposal otherwise". The controlled commodities concerned here are steel, cement and coal which were allotted to Maruti Limited.

Steel

Maruti Limited got the letter of intent on September 30, 1970 and the industrial licence on July 25, 1974. As in the case of other industrial units holding letters of intent or industrial licences, the Directorate General of Technical Development (Automobile Directorate) became the sponsoring authority in respect of steel for Maruti Limited. During the period 1971-75 supplies of iron and steel materials were regulated and allocated to the consumers from the following sources:

(i) Steel Priority Committee (assisted by Joint Plant Committee);
(ii) Billet Re-rollers Committee; and
(iii) Discretionary Quotas as the disposal of

(a) Iron and Steel Controller,
(b) Regional Iron and Steel Controller, and
(c) Stockyards of the main producers.

Allocation of steel was normally made to the various sponsoring authorities leaving it to them to sub-allocate different quantities among the the individual indentors. To the units sponsored by the Directorate General of Technical Development (DGTD for short), however, the sub-allocations were made by the Iron and Steel Controller at the instance of DGTD. Altogether 6066 tonnes of steel were allocated to Maruti Limited.

On March 24, 1972 the Chief Executive of Maruti Limited wrote to the Iron and Steel Controller in Calcutta the following letter:

"Dear Sir,

You may have already heard that we are setting up a very major industrial complex to mass produce "Maruti — The People's Car" at an annual rate of 50,000 pieces under the Government permission being granted to Shri Sanjay Gandhi our Managing Director.

We have already applied for the requisite steel requirements to the J.P.C., but the processing of the application form submitted to the J.P.C., will take sometime. As we have to complete our project in 6 months' time, we will request you to allot some quantities of steel through the stockyard on priority basis.

In this respect we are also attaching the certificate of our architects for the immediate need of the steel quantities to start the construction programme.

Thanking You.

Yours Faithfully,
for Maruti Ltd.
Sd/-
Wg. Cdr. R.H. Chawdhry (Retd.)
Chief Executive"

On the next day, March 25, 1972 the DGTD received an undated request on a plain white sheet of paper from Shri Sanjay Gandhi, Director, Maruti Limited for exemption from payment of 15 per cent advance with the order of 6000 tonnes of structural steel, placed by the company with Joint Plant Committee and Billets Re-rollers Committee at Calcutta. The request was based on the ground that Maruti Limited was still a new company with limited resources. On this undated letter a telephone, 617477, and a name "R.K. Dhawan, P.A. to P.M." are written in ink in a corner. It is not known who wrote this, but 617477 was number of one of the telephones in Prime Minister Shrimati Indira Gandhi's residence. As Maruti Limited had not yet been granted an industrial licence, DGTD sought the advice of the Ministry as to whether the request should be processed further. The Ministry decided that in the circumstances of the case the request for allocation of structural steel should be accepted in principle. In a note recorded on April 10, 1972 Shri R.V. Subrahmanian, Additional Secretary in the Ministry of Industrial Development (Department of Heavy Industry), said ". . . the request of Shri Sanjay Gandhi for allocation of structural steel for the construction of factory building should be accepted in principle. The actual quantity of structural steel to be recommended for allocation by J.P.C. (Joint Plant Committee) should be decided by DGTD in accordance with the accepted norms. Being a new unit. . . the case should be recommended for exemption from payment of earnest money". Shri R.V. Subrahmanian deposing before the Commission sought to justify the decision by saying that "since the production of prototype was a primary condition of the letter of intent, I thought that we should enable them to produce prototypes and give them such facilities needed for the purpose", Shri Subrahmanian agreed with Counsel assisting the Commission that at that stage the object was not mass production of cars but only the production of prototypes and that for this limited purpose the same quantity of steel was not required. It was pointed out to Shri Subrahmanian that for the production of prototypes it might be necessary to construct a research and development block but not a full-fledged factory, and 6000 tonnes of steel was certainly not required for constructing a research and development block. Shri Subrahmanian admitted that he did not indicate in his note that the requirement of steel at that stage was for the limited purpose of production of prototypes. But did the company require any steel at that stage? The progress report sent February 26, 1972 by Maruti Limited to DGTD discloses that they had already constructed a research and development shed, an office block, and a design office and in addition had set up a tool room, a jig boring shop, a small foundry and small forge shops. The report to DGTD also stated that the first ten production models of the car were "well near completion" and that out of these first three were soon to be offered to the government for trials. Thus Maruti Limited seems to have already completed construction of such structures as were necessary for the production of prototypes. When Maruti wrote to the Iron and Steel Controller, Calcutta or to DGTD it held only a letter of intent and the grant of industrial licence depended on the prototype car being declared roadworthy, yet in its letter of March 24, 1972 to the Iron and Steel Controller, the company stated "we are setting up a very major industrial complex to mass produce Maruti–the people's car at an annual rate of 50,000 pieces". The company appears to have been in no doubt that an industrial licence would be granted and obviously its requirement of steel was calculated on that basis. If the success of Maruti's application for an industrial licence appears predetermined, so it seems was Maruti's demand for 6000 tonnes of steel. The telephone number and the name noted on Sanjay Gandhi's undated letter to DGTD acquires a significance in this context.

DGTD was directed to process the case on the basis of the Ministry's decision. Another problem arose at this stage. An industrial unit sponsored by DGTD for the grant of steel had to be registered with DGTD. On August 29, 1972 the Joint Plant Committee asked for a photo copy of Maruti's DGTD registration number for their record. Maruti Limited approached DGTD for allotment of a registration number. Shri B.S.V. Rao, Development Officer, DGTD examining the position recorded a note on September

12, 1972 that normally registration was allotted to a unit after the issue of an industrial licence. The Ministry was therefore again requested to advise. In the Ministry Shri N.R. Krishnan, Deputy Secretary, recorded the following note on December 18, 1972: "Two courses are open without waiting for the fulfilment of the conditions of the letter of intent or authorise the DGTD to issue the registration number in anticipation of the grant of an industrial licence. I understand that the prototype of the vehicle has not yet been despatched to VRDE, Ahmednagar. It may not perhaps, therefore, be desirable to grant an industrial licence at this stage. It is therefore for consideration whether the DGTD should be authorised to issue the registration number". On the same day Shri R.V. Subrahmanian made his recommendation that the "DGTD may be authorised to issue the registration number". This was approved by the Ministry of Industrial Development, Shri C. Subramaniam on December 30, 1972. Examined before the Commission on this aspect Shri R.V. Subrahmanian said that according to the "general policy and practice" "a unit is allotted a controlled commodity like steel only after either it has industrial licence or registered with the DGTD". Shri R.V. Subrahmanian however added, "I did feel at that point of time that in order to enable the holder of the letter of intent to be able to fulfil the terms of the letter of intent and in order to make the prototypes, they would require certain facilities in the shape of some sort off factory buildings and some other equipment. . . ." R.V. Subrahmanian however failed to recall any other case where "the general policy" was departed from as was done in the case of Maruti Limited. Shri C. Subramaniam was also questioned on this point. He said "two courses were open to us. . . though as fact we may either issue the industrial licence without waiting for the fulfilment of the conditions of the letter of intent or order the DGTD to issue the registration certificate for certain specific purposes for the allotment of steel etc. So we had opted for the second alternative". Really no two courses were open. It was not possible to issue the industrial licence disregarding the conditions of the letter of intent. I do not think Shri C. Subramaniam was suggesting that the Ministry could have made an exception in the case of the Maruti and issue licence just to enable the company to get a quota of steel. The only course open therefore was to deviate from the general practice, and direct DGTD to issue a registration certificate in favour of Maruti Limited, if this was necessary for the purpose of enabling the company to produce prototypes.

Shri R.V. Subrahmanian's note did not mention that Maruti's requirement of steel was for this limited purpose only. I have already dealt with the question whether at the stage Maruti Limited really needed any steel even for this limited purpose.

Reference may be made to one other feature relating to the allocation of steel to Maruti Limited. Chapter 8 of the guide book for iron and steel indentors issued by the Joint Plant Committee in 1972 empowers the Iron and Steel Controller to issue allotment letters from time to time for small quantities, not exceeding twenty tonnes, to a party which were to remain valid for ninety days from the date of issue. It appears that Shri Shivender Singh Sidhu, Iron and Steel Controller, issued allotment letters for 643 metric tonnes of steel on 28/29 March, 1972 apparently in violation of the procedure laid down in chapter 8 of the guide book. Section 5 explanation is that in practice twenty tonnes was always taken as twenty tonnes per section/thickness of a category of steel. Shri Sidhu elaborated this as follows. Allotment letters issued by the Steel Controller were registered as demands with the stockyards and it was the policy "to keep the stockyards adequately loaded with these registration of demands so that they are not able to misuse". According to Shri Sidhu the "general experience has been" that of these allotment letters not more than ten per cent or fifteen per cent "ultimately materialise". He added that in this particular case though the allotment was for 643 tonnes, the party concerned received with a period of three months only forty-six tonnes i.e. seven per cent, and the allotment letters became invalid after ninety days from the date of issue. "So we were deliberately liberal with these allotment letters" which were "not like formal allotment orders or firm allotments", said Sidhu. His attention was drawn to an order he recorded on March 28, 1972 on the letter dated March 24, 1972 addressed by Maruti Limited to the Iron and Steel Controller, Calcutta, for allotment of "some quantities of steel through the stockyard on priority basis". While assenting to the release of "some material from the stockyards of the main producers" he mentioned in the order apparently in justification of it that "industrial Development Ministry has already issued the licence" for Maruti's car project. That was an incorrect statement. Maruti Limited got industrial licence in July 1974 and Shri Sidhu admitted his mistake before the Commission.

From the evidence of several traders and some of the employees of Maruti Limited it appears that a part of the controlled steel allocated and despatched to the company was sold to private parties in violation of the Iron and Steel Control Order, 1956. Some of these traders have filed affidavits before the Commission and one of them was examined as witness, Shri Vishwanath Nanda, a partner of the firm M/s Prem Nath Nanda and sons of Hauz Kazi, Delhi, states in his affidavit (affirmed on 16-12-78) that they used to purchase steel from registered stockists or from the open market and offer the same for sale, and that between November 1973 and May 1974 they bought steel materials from Maruti Limited. This firm used to sell mill stores and tool items to Maruti Limited. In November 1973 one of the employees (Shri M.M. Puri) of Maruti Limited informed Shri Nanda that the company had iron scrap for sale. After a discussion with Shri Sanjay Gandhi, Shri Nanda purchased the first lot of Iron scrap from the company on November 24, 1973. Nanda also "came to know that there were other parties of Delhi who were buying steel materials from Maruti Limited". He adds: "we were also sold the steel materials at rates mutually settled between us. But mutual settlement I mean that the rates were quoted by Shri Sanjay Gandhi in respect of particular items and they were accepted by me. There was no question of a counter offer from my side. . . while taking out the materials from the premises of the Maruti Limited they used to give a gate pass allowing the materials to be taken out of their premises. They used to give only one copy which we surrendered at the gate to the security staff of Maruti Limited". Shri Nanda says that the steel materials purchased from Maruti Limited were all sold by his firm in the open market to various parties. He produced the book of account of his firm recording the transactions and his affidavit includes a statement setting out the dates of transactions, the quantity and description of material and the amounts paid.

Shri Ved Prakash, partner of firm M/s Chaudhary Ram Chuni Lal & Company of Loha Mandi, Naraina, Delhi also filed an affidavit, affirmed on December 18, 1978. The business of this firm "consists of sale and purchase of iron and steel materials". They "specialised in the sale and purchase of items like M.S. plates, T. Iron, angles, squares etc. The iron and steel materials purchased from rerollers and others were sold by retail to factory owners and small/large scale industries and steel dealers". Ved Prakash came to know that M/s Prem Nath Nanda & Sons of Delhi from whom his firm purchased 31,900 kgs. of M.S. angles got these materials from Maruti Limited. Thereafter, he contacted M.M. Puri whom he describes as purchase supervisor of Maruti Limited. "He showed me the angles and plates that they were offering for sale and he also got my offer of the rates. After this he took me to Shri Sanjay Gandhi, Managing Director, Maruti Limited, in his factory office at Gurgaon. This should have been on February 22, 1984 or a day or two earlier". As a trader in steel he knew that "iron and steel was in short supply and was a scarce commodity in those days for most of the items, particularly M.S. angles and plates", but he was not aware whether these were controlled items or not. Ved Prakash sets out in his affidavit the dates, the quantity and description of the material and the amounts paid. He also says that gate passes were issued to them for taking the material out of the Maruti factory which had to be surrendered at the gate.

The business of M/s S.N. Steel Corporation was also purchase and sale of iron and steel materials. Shri S.N. Beriwal, a partner of the firm, affirmed an affidavit on December 15, 1978 in which he states that one of his employees Shiv Kumar Sharma had met Shri Sanjay Gandhi and got an offer of sale of iron scrap. Beriwal accompanied by Shiv Kumar Sharma met Shri Sanjay Gandhi in the third week of January 1974. Shri Sanjay Gandhi said that "there was no scrap available then for sale and he offered to sell M.S. Plates and angles and asked us to quote. . . I knew that M.S. plates were not easily available in the open market". This firm sold all the materials purchased from Maruti Limited to other parties in Delhi. Beriwal's affidavit also contains a statement containing the details of the transactions between his firm and Maruti Limited, Shiv Kumar Sharma has filed a supportive affidavit.

Shri Santosh Kumar of Narela, Delhi, carried on business of purchase and sale of iron and steel in the name and style of M/s Santosh Kumar. In his affidavit (affirmed on December 16, 1978) he says that he purchased M.S. steel materials from Maruti Limited on different dates, the details of which were annexed to his affidavit. "I used to arrange my own trucks to take the steel materials from their premises to Delhi. . . steel materials purchased by me were sold to various steel merchants in the market". He produced the books of accounts of his business recording the transactions.

Rama Nand, a partner of M/s Rama Industries of Rewari (Rajasthan) with branch office at 21, Industrial Estate, Gurgaon, deposed before the Commission. His firm used to supply machinery, namely deep drawing boards, wooden patterns, iron castings etc. to Maruti Limited. Rama Nand says: "We started construction of our own factory at our branch at Gurgaon from 2-2-74. We needed steel materials of various types for construction purposes on coming to know that some steel materials are available with Maruti Limited with whom I have already doing business, I approached Mr. Gulati, Accountant, and discussed the rates etc. in respect of those items which I required and asked him if they were available. . . I purchased the steel items from Maruti Limited on ten occasions". The details of the purchases such as bill number, dates and the amounts paid have been mentioned by Shri Rama Nand. According to him Shri Gulati told him that "they can sell these materials since they had purchased the steel from open market also apart from the steel mills and most of their construction work was over".

It is incorrect to suggest that what Maruti sold to these parties were all steel purchased from "open market". Shri Trilochanjit Singh who was Store Keeper in Maruti Limited from August 1972 till February 15, 1975 has filed an affidavit affirmed on December 29, 1978. As Store Keeper his "duties were to look after the receipts and issues of the building materials and maintain the records thereof". His records contain entries of all receipts of cement, and steel materials from the stockyards as well as from the local market. He says that the sale of steel to private parties commenced from the middle of 1973 and continued upto about the end of 1974. "These sales were affected because they (steel materials) were considered surplus after the completion of the various phases of the factory building". Some steel materials purchased from the local market were used in the construction of the Maruti Complex. On the basis of the available records Shri Trilochanjit Singh has compiled charts in respect of five items namely, M.S. angles, M.S. plates, M.S. channels, M.S. flats and R.S. joists, showing the receipts of these five items by Maruti Limited during 1972-73 and 1973-74 from stockyard as well as from the local market. These charts are a part of his affidavit. Shri S. Venkataraman joined Maruti Limited as Cost Accountant in April 1973 and from November 1973 he was asked also to look after the day-to-day work of the purchase department under the supervision and control of the Managing Director Shri Sanjay Gandhi. In his deposition he said that he knew that steel materials were being sold to some local parties of Delhi. He was asked whether he could on the basis of the available records trace the origin of the steel materials sold by Maruti Limited " to the controlled steel items purchased from the government stockyards". Shri Venkataraman worked out the answer on the basis of the records including the charts prepared by

Shri Trilochanjit Singh in respect of three items, (i) R.S. Joist, (ii) Tor steel-18 mm and (iii) M.s. Plates 8 mm. The statement prepared by him "showing the minimum amount of stores materials whose sales can be traced to government purchase is as follows:

"R.S. Joists

In M. Tonnes

31-3-1973 Closing balance of stock		Nil (as per the inventory list dt. 16-5-1973)	
Purchases from 1-4-1973 to 31-3-1974 (as per the Building Material Receipt Register			
HSL	25.085		
TISCO	5.955		
IISCO	9.994	41.034	
Local purchases		Nil	
Return from Contractors (as per the Store Return Register)		33.009	75.043
Sale during 1973-74 (as per the Issue Register)			
Returned to Steel Sales Syndicate		41.034	
Others		27.536	68.570
Stocks as on 31-3-1974			6.473
Physical balance recorded as on 31-3-1974 (Building Material Inventory List 31-3-1974)			7.118

From the statement as shown above, it is seen that 68.570 M. Tonnes of RS Joists all of which can be traced only to Government purchases have been sold in the local market. This I say on the basis that firstly there has been no purchases from local markets in the year 1973-74 and secondly the return from the Contractors of materials presumably purchased in 1972-73 were all Government purchased materials as seen from Shri Trilochanjit Singh's statement.

TOR Steel (18 mm)

In M. Tonnes

Closing balance as on 31-3-1973	Nil
Purchased during 1973-74	
Local	Nil
Government	91.730
Sales	59.395
Returned to Steel Sales Syndicate	9.980
Total Sales	68.375

From the above chart it is seen that 69.375 M. Tonnes of Tor Steel 18 mm were sold in local market and there was no purchase of this material from the local market during the year 1973-74 and also there was 'NIL' Closing Balance as on 31st March 1973. Thus all the 69.375 M. Tonnes are clearly traceable to Government stockyards purchases.

M.S. Plates (8 mm)

	M. Tonnes	M. Tonnes
Closing Balance as on 31-3-1973	79.411	
Purchases during 1973-74		
Local	Nil	
Government	35.069	
Sale during the year 1973-74		47.385
Steel Sale Syndicate		23.240
Total Sales		70.625

The Closing Stock of 8 mm MS Plates as on 31st March 1973 was 79.411 M. Tonnes as shown above. From Shri Trilochanjit Singh's statement it is seen that 69.532 M. Tonnes of 8 mm MS Plates was purchased from Government stockyards and only 6.628 M. Tonnes from the local market (in 1972-73). Therefore, it is clear that the bulk of stock in hand as on 31st March 1973 consisted of Government purchased materials. Therefore, the sale of 70.625 M. Tonnes during the year 1973-74 was from the Government's stocks since no local purchases had been resorted to in the same year". Even if the entire quantity of MS Plates (8 mm) sold to or transferred otherwise during 1973-74 did not come out of the government stock, the bulk of it must have, because the quantity of locally purchased steel in stock was only 6.628 Tonnes. Venkataraman added that he prepared the statement "within the limits of time" meaning it was hurriedly done and therefore was not comprehensive, however, the statement puts it beyond doubt that Maruti Limited sold considerable quantities of steel despatched to them from the stockyards.

Trilochanjit Singh says: "if any material were to be taken outside the factory I would generally act on a written requisition from heads of various divisions. . . no head of any division would direct me to issue the same to outside parties unless the matter had the concurrence of Shri Sanjay Gandhi, Managing Director".

It is found from the figures supplied by the Ministry of Steel and Mines that altogether 6066.082 metric tonnes of steel had been allocated and despatched to Maruti Limited. Apart from the evidence of witnesses to the effect that the company sold a part of this quantity to private parties, the investigation agency attached to this Commission also made an attempt to find out the actual quantity of steel that went into the construction of Maruti factory building which would indicate approximately the total quantity of steel misutilised by the company. Owning to the limitations of time and resources it has not been possible to make a thorough probe into the matter, the total quantity of steel bought from the open market by the company is not known but the results yielded by such investigation as the Commission has been able to make would justify having more time and resources at its disposal. It may be recalled that Maruti Limited in their report dated February 26, 1972 to DGTD stated that the company had completed the construction of research and development wing and office block, tool room, jig boring shop, a small foundry and forge shops by February 1972 which was before the allotment of steel was made to the company. That being so, the steel used for these buildings has not been taken into account by the Commission's investigation team. Roughly the total utilisation of steel for the company's main factory building has been calculated as follows:

(a) Normal bays roofing	2800	Tonnes
(b) High bay roofing	489	Tonnes
(c) Steel columns	140	Tonnes
(d) Crane Girders	89	Tonnes
(e) Bracing of columns in High bay	20	Tonnes
	3538	Tonnes

To that must be added 50 tonnes which on a rough estimate was used for miscellaneous purposes making the total 3588 tonnes. This quantity includes M.S. angles, plats, flats, joists, and channels. Central Public Works Department's analysis of rates allows five per cent wastage. This quantity added to 3588 tonnes would make the total 3767.4 tonnes.

M.S. sheets have been used for covering the channels provided in the factory building and also for making cable ducts which are provided inside the channels. 123.824 tonnes of CR and HR sheets were despatched to Maruti Limited. The quantity of M.S. sheets used for gate, the gauge of which cannot be measured easily, is likely to be about one tonne. The total quantity of M.S. sheets used works out, again on a rough calculation, to 7.64 tonnes against 123.84 tonnes received.

64,839 tonncs of angle 200 X 200 X 20 MM were also despatched to Maruti Limited. From the Company's profit and loss control ledger volume II, 1973-74, it appears that 57,935 tonnes of 200 X 200 X 20 MM has been sold.

Cement

As regards cement, Maruti Limited appears to have sold large quantities of it almost openly. A.D. Kolhatkar, Manager, Personnel and Factory Administration of Maruti Limited, says in his affidavit (affirmed on December 19, 1978) that "a substantial portion" of the "stocks of cement which they had secured from the cement controller", "became surplus because of over-estimation of their actual requirements". There is no dispute that in 1973-74 there was acute shortage of cement and the evidence indicates that industries in Gurgaon were in great difficulty because of the shortage, and even the requirements of municipal bodies could not be fully met. Shri S.M. Goyal who was Sub-Divisional Magistrate of Gurgaon as well as District Food and Supplies Controller at the time has filed a statement supported by an affidavit in which he says that he was informed towards the end of 1973 or early 1974 by Shri V.S. Ailawadi, Deputy Commissioner of Gurgaon, that Maruti Limited had substantial quantity of surplus cement and that "it might be possible to arrive at a suitable arrangement" with them for distribution of cement "amongst the public". Shri Goyal met Shri Gandhi who "stipulated two conditions: one was that whenever Maruti Limited themselves required some cement, the District Food and Supplies Administration should be willing to make the cement available from the district quota without delay. The second condition was that permits should be addressed to Maruti Limited favouring parties who were interested in collecting the cement from them (Maruti Limited)". According to Shri Goyal the first condition could not be accepted "because in the scarcity conditions prevailing then no Controller could have anticipated the supply position during the coming months to be able to say that he would meet the requirements of a big factory like Maruti

Limited. Also no time limit was indicated by Shri Sanjay Gandhi as to when he would require the cement which again complicated matters even more. . . . The second condition could also not be met because permits could only be addressed to licensed dealers and neither Shri Sanjay Gandhi nor Maruti Limited was registered as a dealer in cement with the District Food and Supplies Controller", Goyal adds, "I am not aware of the intention behind the second condition but it was not possible under the Regulations to address a permit to anyone other than a licensed dealer". He therefore came away and "reported the matter to the Deputy Commissioner". Shri Satish Chander Virmani, a partner of M/s Akash Industries of Gurgaon, in his affidavit (affirmed on December 26, 1978) says that he and several other industrialists were summoned by telephone to the office of Shri Dhanpat Singh, Assistant District Industries Officer, Gurgaon, where Shri S.N. Goyal was also present. They informed the industrialists, according to Virmani that surplus cement was available will Maruti Limited and that the company was "willing to sell it to the industries of the town to the extent that was required by each party". This information conveyed by the industrialists present to others. Virmani says Maruti Limited later went back on the promise made and declined to part with the cement in their stock for reasons unknown to him. A probable reason is suggested in the affidavit of Shri Dhanpat Singh (affirmed on December 22, 1978),". . . they (Maruti Limited) took this decision because of the prohibition under the Haryana Cement (Sale and Licensing) Control Order which was in force at that time under which only licensed dealers were authorised to sell cement. It would have been an offence for M/s Maruti Limited to have sold any surplus cement within being a licensed dealer and if they had granted cash memos, that would have created documentary evidence against them". Dhanpat Singh however, denies that the Industries Department of Haryana sponsored Maruti's proposal to sell controlled commodities like cement his version is that the representatives of the District Industries Association brought it to his notice that Maruti Limited was in a position to distribute cement to the industries. Shri Goyal could not recall having met the industrialists. But Dhanpat Singh admits that he "ascertained that M/s Maruti Limited had approximately 3,000 to 4,000 bags of surplus cement with them which they were prepared to dispose of" and that the company ultimately did not sell the cement to the industries in spite of an assurance given earlier.

Maruti Limited however, did sell cement to private parties and even municipal and local authorities, only the transactions were labelled as loan. The company realised from the transferees the value of the cement made over to them with a condition that whenever asked for they would return the quantity of cement they had received. No time limit was fixed for such re-transfer and the value realised from the transferees in most cases, as would appear from the statements of these parties, was Rs. 15 per bag which was in excess of the controlled rate. From the evidence it appears that except in two cases, in no other the cement transferred was returned. The two parties who returned the cement bags were Tiger Locks Limited and Ansal Housing and Estates Private Limited, Gurgaon. From the affidavit (affirmed on December 16, 1978) of Shri A.R. Verma who was the Public Relations Officer of Tiger Locks Limited at the relevant time, it appears that the cement bags returned by Tiger Locks came from the Regional Cement Officer, New Delhi. Such use of the controlled cement was also not permissible as would appear from the statement of Shri L.R. Julka, Joint Cement Controller, New Delhi. It is not known from which source Ansal Housing and Estates Private Limited returned the quantity of cement which they received from Maruti Limited.

Shri Trilochanjit Singh, Store Keeper in Maruti Limited, who prepared in the course of his duty vouchers "to show on a day-to-day basis and transactionwise all issue of building material" under instructions from his superiors, has drawn up a chart showing the relevant transactions which is as follows:

Of the parties mentioned in the above chart, the following– A.R. Verma, Sales Executive of Tiger Locks Limited; Rajinder Sharma, Store Keeper in Ansal Housing and Estates Private Limited; Mai Chand, ex-Sarpanch, Mullahera Village Panchayat have filed affidavits before the Commission admitting the transactions. Shri Rama Nand, Partner of Rama Industries, and S.D. Diwan were examined and they affirmed the transactions mentioned in the chart against their names. However, Shri G.S. Aneja, Proprietor of Surin Engineering Works, Faridabad, who was also examined denied that he received any cement from Maruti Limited and stated that the signature appearing in the records of the company against receipt of the 20 bags of cement was not his. Evidence has been adduced in respect of one more transaction which does not figure in Trilochanjit Singh's chart. This was the transfer of 500 bags of cement to Gurgaon

S. No.	Voucher No.	Name of the party and date of issue	Description of item issued with qty.	Remarks
1.	17839	Rama Industries 2-3-74	Cement (150 bags)	
2.	17836	Om Surin Engg. Works 1-3-74	Cement (20 bags)	Gate Pass No. 2827—Party's sig. available
3.	17812	Shri S.D. Diwan, DSP, Gurgaon 23-2-74	Cement (150 bags)	Gate Pass No. 2183—Party's sig. available
4.	17811	Rama Industries 22-2-74	Cement (100 bags)	Gate Pass No. 2175—Party's sig. available
5.	17810	-do- 21-2-74	-do- (100 bags)	Gate Pass No. 2174—Party's sig. available
6.	9992	-do- 13-2-74	-do- (50 bags)	Gate Pass No. 2149—Party's sig. available
7.	9989	Tiger Locks Ltd. 12-2-74	Cement (600 bags)	Gate Pass No.s 2128-30—Party's sig. available
8.	9985	-do- 11-2-74	-do- (200 bags)	Gate Pass No. 2127—Party's sig. available
9.	9984	Tiger Locks Ltd. 11-2-74	Cement (200 bags)	Gate Pass No. 2126—Party's sig. available
10.	9956	Mr. Chaman Lal Arora 25-1-74	Cement (20 bags)	Gate Pass No. 1976—Money Receipt No. 395
11.	9952	Surpanch, Mullahera, 17-1-74	Cement (60 bags)	Gate Pass No. 1933—Money Receipt No. 379
12.	9948	Tiger Locks Ltd. 14-1-74	Cement (800 bags)	Gate Pass No. 1907, 1909, 1910 & 1911—Money Receipt No. 373
13.	9945	-do- 12-1-74	Cement (200 bags)	
14.	9902	Ansal Housing & Estates P. Ltd. 21-12-73	Cement (150 bags)	Party's signature available

Municipality, R.S. Duggal formerly Administrator, Gurgaon Municipality and Bhim Singh, an Overseer, Gurgaon Municipality, have filed affidavits before the Commission stating that the municipality received 500 bags of cement from Maruti Limited, in May and June 1973. A.D. Kolhatkar, Manager, Personnel and Factory Administration, Maruti Limited, also refers to this transaction in his affidavit. Trilochanjit Singh has said that these bags of cement could not have been taken out of Maruti's store and transferred to the different parties without the concurrence of Shri Sanjay Gandhi.

The steel and cement sold by Maruti Limited were purchased by the company out of advance taken from the Punjab National Bank against hypothecation of these materials and the conditions of the loan did not permit the company to remove the hypothecated materials except against proportionate payment.

Coal

Coal the remaining controlled commodity relevant in this context.

On December 23, 1971 Maruti Limited was granted a brick kiln licence by the District Food and Supplies construction of the company's factory building. On or about March 16, 1972 Shri L.C. Gupta, who was Director of Industries, Haryana at the time, handed over to Shri H.D. Bansal, then Director, Food and Supplies Haryana, a copy of letter dated January 31, 1972 addressed by Maruti Limited to the Director of Industries requesting him to allot to them "slack coal to the tune of 12 wagons per month (i.e. 288 tonnes)", Bansal made over the letter to S.P. Bhasin, Deputy Director in the Food and Supplies Department, Government of Haryana, to deal with. On the copy of the letter Shri Bansal made the following endorsement: "Given to me personally by Director of Industries, Shri L.C. Gupta, please take action urgently". Shri L.C. Gupta has deposed that the original of this letter was not received in his Directorate though the letter is supposed to have been addressed to him. He has stated how he came in possession of the copy that he handed over to Bansal: "I recall that this letter was received by me from Shri Mehtani (Officer on Special Duty to the Chief Minister Shri Bansi Lal) Shri Mehtani rang me up one day sometime in the forenoon stating that he had sent through a messenger a letter of Maruti Limited addressed to me as Director of Industries requesting for allotment of slack coal. He also told me that the C.M. had desired that action should be taken on the letter very urgently. I told him that the matter concerned the Directorate of Food and Civil Supplies and that I in my capacity as Director of Industry was not concerned with it. Shri Mehtani told me that since he (Mehtani) was going to Delhi and as Shri Bansal, Director of Food and Supplies, was located in the same building as the Director of Industries, I may pass it on to Shri Bansal for doing the needful. I accordingly handed over the letter personally to Shri Bansal and told him about the message received from Shri Mehtani". However, the original of the letter is found in the file of the Directorate of Industries, Haryana. It also appears from the file that on February 24, 1972 a reply was sent to Maruti Limited by Assistant Director for Director of Industries advising the company to take up the matter with the Director, Food and Supplies, Haryana, Chandigarh.

Shri Bhasin drew up a proposal on the same day in which he stated:

(i) That the Chief Engineer, P.W.D. had informed the Director, Food and Supplies, a few days earlier that P.W.D. did not require any slack coal in Gurgaon district and therefore the company's requirement could be met out of the "incoming supplies" without any difficulty;
(ii) That one rake of slack coal had been included for Ballabgarh for the month of March 1972 out of which 12 wagons could be directed to be allotted to Maruti Limited for March 1972; and
(iii) That a telegram be sent to Calcutta for the Allotment of 12 wagons to the company for the month of April 1972 and that 12 four wheeler wagons be included for the company from 1972 onwards till the company's requirements were satisfied.

Shri Ishwar Chand Gupta, Chief Engineer, P.W.D. has denied in an affidavit that he gave any such information as alleged by Bhasin to the Director, Food and Supplies. In fact, according to Gupta, P.W.D. did require slack coal in Gurgaon because "during the relevant period viz. 1971-72 the P.W.D. was experiencing great difficulty to accomplish the programmes for the construction of roads and buildings in the State of Haryana for want of bricks all over the districts including the district of Gurgaon".

Bhasin has filed an affidavit, affirmed on December 21, 1978. He says that the system of sponsoring slack coal had been in force since the creation of Haryana State and that for several years since then "coal was being brought to the State by coal agents who undertook to invest the entire cost of the coal as well as movement from the collieries and the State helped them by recommending to the railway authorities allotment of railway rakes in their favour so that the requirements of the brick kiln owners could be met without any difficulty. The railways themselves would not allow any wagons to the coal agents without necessary recommendations from the States". He adds that "such recommendations were being made only in favour of coal agents who in turn would declare the arrival of the coal to the District Magistrate as well as the District Food and Supplies Controller for arranging their further distribution. The coal agents were not free to dispose of the coal directly. The District Magistrate/District Food and Supplies Controller would allot the slack coal to the brick kiln owners on a rotational basis. . . ." Bhasin admits that there was "no direct sponsorship of any brick kiln owner to the railways for allotment of coal wagons" and the recommendation to the railways to allot wagons in favour of Maruti Limited was a "departure" from the normal policy and practice. But that was what he proposed. Bhasin's proposal for the allotment of 12 wagons for the month of March 1972 out of the incoming supplies was approved by Shri Bansal. According to Bansal he "reserved the decision on his (Bhasin's) proposal to sponsor the firm directly to railway authorities for allotment of wagons" until he discussed the matter with the Secretary of the Department. Later, after a discussion with Shri Din Dayal Sharma, Secretary to the Department of Food and Supplies, Government of Haryana, Bansal approved the proposal to sponsor Maruti Limited directly to the railways. When Shri Din Dayal Sharma was confronted with Bansal's statement, he first stated that the matter was several years old and that he did not remember anything about it, but later he admitted that Bansal had mentioned to him "something about the party being important and the need for caution in dealing with the matter". All of them, Shri Din Dayal Sharma, Shri Bansal, and Shri Bhasin have admitted that there was no other instance of a party who was not a coal agent being allotted wagons as done in the case of Maruti Limited. On the same day, March 16, 1972, Bhasin wrote a letter to Maruti Limited requesting the company to intimate their total requirement of Bricks. On March 16, Bhasin also wrote to District Magistrate, Gurgaon, informing him about the allotment of 12 wagons of slack coal to Maruti Limited during March 1972 and requesting him to arrange the supply out of the incoming slack coal to Gurgaon District. On April 1, 1972 Maruti Limited replied to Bhasin's letter stating that their total requirement of bricks upto December 1974 was 2 crores and 60 lacs. District Magistrate, Gurgaon, Shri V.S. Ailawadi received Bhasin's letter on March 20, 1972.

Ailawadi ordered supply of 178 tonnes of slack coal to Maruti Limited out of the dumped coal at Ballabgarh although the decision had been to allot coal to Maruti out of the stocks to be received. However, after Ailawadi's attention was drawn to this decision, he directed that the quantity allotted should be deducted out of the future allotment to this company. Thereafter, Ailawadi appears to have made an allotment of five box wagons of coal to Maruti Limited by his order April 11, 1972 out of the coal received by the Executive Engineer, P.W.D. (E&R), Palwal through M/s Khas Khajura, coal agents, Calcutta. This order was again revised two days later, on April 13, and the allotment was raised to eleven box wagons. Eleven box wagons work out to roughly 28 wagons (four wheelers). Thus the allotment ordered by Ailawadi in favour of Maruti Limited in April 1972 was much in excess of the authorisation sent by the Directorate of Food and Supplies. Shri Bhasin is unable to say what considerations prevailed with Shri Ailawadi in making this allotment. It appears from the evidence of Shri S.L. Behl, District Food and Supplies Controller, Gurgaon, that the increase in the number of wagons from five to eleven in favour of Maruti Limited was made possible by reducing the allotments made to six coal agents, and the result was that "some of the original allottees were now given reduced quantity, the only party who gained substantially in this process was Maruti Limited". Asked to explain Shri Ailawadi first tried to hedge by saying that he did not know how the allotment to Maruti Limited came to be revised from five to eleven box wagons. He then took up the position that "it was certainly within the power of the District Magistrate to exceed the allotment", but he did not say that Maruti Limited approached him for raising the quota. Asked why he allotted box wagons instead of four wheelers as contemplated in the decision of the Directorate of Food and Supplies, Ailawadi tried to argue that the quota of twelve wagons fixed by the Director of Food and Supplies did not indicate the type of the wagon. It is too much to accept that when only 'wagon' was being mentioned without anything more, Ailawadi had any justification to take it as a box wagon. Even Maruti's application mentioned twelve wagons per month and not box wagons.

The supply of excess quota of slack coal to Maruti Limited and sponsoring Maruti Limited, not a coal agent, directly to the Railway authorities for allotment of coal wagons are clear instances of undue favour shown to the company. What Maruti Limited, a brick kiln owner and not a coal agent, gained by being directly sponsored to the railways for allotment of coal has been stated by S.P. Bhasin: "This had the effect of enabling only this party to get bricks at subsidised rates. . . . It also had the effect of sparing them of the obligation to pay sales tax and other incidental charges which they would have had to pay if they purchased bricks from the open market".

CHAPTER VIII

This chapter deals with the eleventh item specified in the terms of reference which includes:

> "All matters relating to the securing of accommodation, loans or other assistance from nationalised banks and other financial institutions by the said Maruti concerns, including the eligibility of the said concerns to obtain the financial assistance sought for, the standard of care which the applications were considered and the measures of conformity to the policies, practices, rules and directives for the time being in force in regard to grant of such assistance."

The unsuccessful attempt made by Maruti Limited to get financial assistance from the public financial institutions has been described in a previous chapter. The Maruti concerns succeeded in getting financial assistance from two nationalised banks, Punjab National Bank, Parliament Street Branch, New Delhi, and the Safdarjang Enclave and Mullahera branches of Central Bank of India.

PUNJAB NATIONAL BANK

Maruti Limited

Of the Maruti concerns only Maruti Limited approached Punjab National Bank for assistance. In August 1971 Maruti Limited opened a current account with Punjab National Bank, Parliament Street branch, New Delhi. In the first week of December 1971 the branch manager received an undated letter signed by Shri Sanjay Gandhi on behalf of Maruti Limited asking for an interim loan of Rs. 35 lacs required for construction of their factory premises and purchase of machinery. About repayment it was said that "this may be paid out of the funds to be received from the public issue", and the company expected "to issue the capital. . . to the public by the end of April 1972". On December 6, 1971 Shri O.P. Mathuria, Manager, Parliament Street branch, forwarded the loan application to the District Manager recommending sanction of inland letter of credit with a limit of Rs. 25 lacs and term loan limit of Rs. 40 lacs against hypothecation of machinery and equipments and suggesting adjustment of the loan from the share capital to be raised by the company by June 1972. He also recommended that pending sanction of the proposal, the Parliament Street branch might be permitted to establish letters of credit upto Rs. 10 lacs. On December 13 the District Manager of the bank recommended to the Assistant General Manager sanctioning a cash credit-cum-inland letter of credit with a limit of Rs. 30 lacs against hypothecation. On the same day the Assistant General Manager put up a proposal to the Custodian of the Bank, Shri S.C. Trikha, endorsing the recommendation of the District Manager. Shri D. Sharma, Officer on Special Duty, discussed the proposal with the General Manager and the Custodian after which Shri Sharma returned the proposal to the Assistant General Manager on December 14, 1971 with the remark "We should wait for some time". The reason behind this advice is not apparent on the record. Shri Trikha who was given evidence could not remember what the reason was after the lapse of time.

On December 30, 1971 Shri Mathuria wrote to the Manager, Loans Department informing him about the "latest development", which was that "the Central Bank of India have since opened L/Cs amounting to Rs. 10 lacs on behalf of the aforesaid company for purchase of machinery and also reported to have assured the company of any other accommodation that they may require before the share capital is duly raised". Shri Mathuria in his deposition stated that he got information from Shri J.K. Pahuja, Manager, Finance and Credit, of Maruti Limited and that his object in writing the letter was to see that such an important client was not lost to the bank. It may be mentioned here that on November 12, 1971 Shri K.L. Kalra, Manager of Safdarjang Enclave Branch of Central Bank of India, while forwarding to the Chief Agent of the Bank a loan proposal from Maruti Limited had said, "Punjab National Bank have approached the party and assured them such facilities at the earliest and thus they are offering every competition. Since it is a highly remunerative account with huge potentialities, we cannot afford to lose it". Ultimately on January 3, 1972 the Assistant General Manager of Punjab National put up a proposal to the Bank's Board of Directors through the Officer on Special Duty, The General Manager, and the Custodian for consideration whether the bank might accommodate Maruti Limited for their interim requirements. The proposal suggested an inland letter of credit-cum-term loan of Rs. 30 lacs on hypothecation of tool room plant, machines and equipment with a margin of 25 per cent and interest 5 per cent over bank rate with a maximum of 11 per cent per annum for a maximum period of one year. The "deficiencies in the proposal at this stage" were also pointed out which indicated that the project report had not so far been completed and the share capital had not been issued. The proposal suggested three conditions:

"(i) The facility to be guaranteed by at least two of its (company's) Directors;
(ii) The company to undertake that the account will be adjusted from the share capital; and
(iii) The company to furnish to the Bank its project report by the end of February 1972."

The proposal was considered by the Board on January 3, 1972. The Board sanctioned inland letter of credit-cum-fixed loan facility of Rs. 30 lacs on the terms and conditions suggested in the Assistant General Manager's note of January 3, 1972.

While the company was yet to avail of the facility, the Branch Manager and the District Manager recommended conversion of the term loan into cash credit facility. The Assistant General Manager put up a proposal to the Custodian on March 3, 1972 accordingly. The Custodian on March 8, made the following order: "We may agree to allow the inland letter of credit-cum-fixed loan facility by way of inland letter of credit-cum-cash facility as recommended subject to the observance of all other terms and conditions of the sanction as laid down by the Board. . ." The facility was allowed without an examination of the viability of the Company's car project for which the loan was asked for. On March 5, 1972 the hypothecation agreement was executed in which the goods hypothecated were mentioned as "tool room plant, machines, equipment etc. to be purchased out of the loan proposed". The charge was registered with the Registrar of Companies on May 9, 1972.

It appears that in the meantime Maruti Limited had approached the Branch Manager to reduce the rate of interest from 11 per cent to 10.5 per cent. On March 14 the Branch Manager wrote to the District Manager recommending acceptance of the company's request and all the intermediate authorities having endorsed the recommendation, the Board of Directors accorded necessary sanction to the proposal by resolution No. 10 dated March 19, 1972. The project report which Maruti Limited was to have submitted by the end of February 1972 had not yet been submitted. The Board's resolution therefore added: "the Bank should insist upon getting Project Report from the company by 15-4-1972. In the meantime 50 per cent of the sanctioned loan may be disbursed and the balance amount only after the company furnished the Project Report". Shri S.C. Trikha has said that the "restriction on disbursement of the credit facility to 50 per cent was imposed by the Board in order to bring pressure on the borrowing company to submit project report urgently". The project report was submitted on April 18, 1972.

On April 14, 1972 the Chief Executive of Maruti Limited wrote to the Branch Manager asking for another loan of Rs. 60 lacs against "hypothecation of iron, steel, cement and other basic building materials". It was said that out of Rs. 60 lacs, Rs. 40 lacs was required for purchase of iron and steel only. The letter added that the company proposed to "come in the share market sometime in August-September when we shall pay off all the outstanding loans against this proposal. . . ". The Branch Manager, Shri Mathuria forwarded a copy of the letter to the District Manager on April 21, 1972 recommending a fresh inland letter of credit-cum-cash credit limit of Rs. 60 lacs. On the same day the District Manager sent his recommendation to the Assistant General Manager put up a proposal to the Board through the Deputy General Manager, the General Manager and the Custodian for sanction of an inland letter of credit-cum-cash credit limit of Rs. 60 lacs against hypothecation of iron and steel materials, cement and other building materials. Two of the Directors of the company, V.R. Mohan and Sanjay Gandhi, were required to be guarantors. Some of the other conditions suggested were "(1) The advance against cement and other building materials shall not exceed

Rs. 10 lacs each and bank charge will be got registered with the Registrar of Joint Stock Companies, (2) Advance to be adjusted within a period of six months out of the capital issue". On examining the Assistant General Manager's note, the Deputy General Manager observed that it was incomplete in certain respects; these were clarified later. The Statement of Advances bearing date April 28-29, 1972 which was placed before the Board shows the net means of the two guarantors, Shri V.R. Mohan and Shri Sanjay Gandhi, as Rs. 52,06,000 and Rs. 1,00,000 respectively and mentions the following six conditions for sanction:

"1. The advance against cement and other building materials shall not exceed Rs. 10 lacs each.
2. Bank's charge to be registered with the Registrar of Joint Stock Companies.
3. Advance to be adjusted within a period of six months out of the capital issue.
4. The limit to be released after the company gets extension from the Government for getting its (Government's) approval of Prototype of the small car.
5. The company to give us an undertaking that the security offered to us will be excluded from the charge of any other Bank/Financial Institutions with which the company might make arrangement for working capital/long-term loan.
6. Total under Inland letter of credit-cum-cash credit limit not to exceed Rs 60 lacs and total under all the facilities including the existing letter of credit-cum-cash credit limit of Rs. 30 lacs not to exceed Rs. 75 lacs."

The proposal was sanctioned by the Board on May 15, 1972 for 6 months only and the decision was conveyed to the Loans Department on May 19 and on the same day the Loans Department issued the letter of sanction to the Branch Manager. This letter mentions seven conditions for allowing facility. Conditions 1 to 5 are the same as mentioned in the Statement of Advances placed before the Board. Condition No. 6 of the Statement figures in this condition No. 7 and a new condition No. 6 was incorporated in the letter which reads as follows:

"The limit is sanctioned subject to the additional condition that if any stocks are required by the borrowers for use during the period of six months for which term the limit has been proposed, that can be taken delivery of only against proportionate payment".

From the available records, it does not appear who introduced this condition and at what stage. The hypothecation agreement was signed by Shri Sanjay Gandhi as Managing Director of Maruti Limited on June 2, 1972. The charge was registered with the Registrar of Companies on July 28, 1972; the details of the materials actually hypothecated were not however commented to the Registrar. This facility was also allowed without an appraisal of the viability of the company's car project.

With the sanction of the loan of Rs. 60 lacs, Maruti Limited became entitled to avail of two cash credit facilities:

(a) Rs. 30 lacs for a maximum period of one year. The letter allowing this facility was sent to the Branch Manager on January 6, 1972. The validity there expired on January 5, 1973; and
(b) Rs. 60 lacs for six months. The letter sanctioning the advance was sent to the Branch Manager on May 19, 1972. In this case the validity period expired on November 18, 1972.

A ceiling of Rs. 75 lacs was imposed on total withdrawals under both facilities. Both the accounts were however, allowed to continue beyond the stipulated period, even beyond the whole of the following year 1973 and no one raised any question about it. The main guarantor V.R. Mohan died on January 28, 1973, yet the operation of the accounts was not stopped, the reason being that it would 'create unnecessary unpleasantness" as Shri B.S. Puri who had succeeded Shri Mathuria as Manager of the Parliament Street Branch explained to the Regional Manager in his memorandum dated February 27, 1973 adding "we shall stop the operation is so instructed by you". A fresh guarantee by Shri Sanjay Gandhi and Shri M.A. Chindambaram, Chairman of the Company was furnished in November 1973.

On November 16, 1973 Maruti Limited had already drawn Rs. 80.88 lacs i.e. Rs. 5.88 lacs in excess of the ceiling of Rs. 75 lacs. On November 20 the Branch Manager wrote to the Regional Manager saying that Maruti Limited had approached him to remove the stipulation that the advance against both the facilities was not to exceed Rs. 75 lacs at any time (condition 7) and to permit them to avail the limits to the full extent (90 lacs). He recommended waiver of the restriction. The Regional Manager's office endorsed the Branch Manager's recommendation. The Credit Administration Division, when the matter was put up to them, pointed out to the Branch Manager that he had not given any justification for removal of the ceiling of Rs. 75 lacs and referring to the fact that the account was overdrawn by Rs. 5.88 lacs asked him to submit his remarks for allowing unauthorised accommodation to the company. The Credit Administration Division further advised the Branch Manager to "assess the genuine requirements of the company and submit a complete renewal proposal in its favour with your comments/recommendations, through your Regional Manager". It has been already stated that the validity period of both the facilities had long expired. On December 27, 1973 the Branch Manager wrote to the Manager, Credit Administration, stating that "this case does not require submission of renewal facilities" and it was enough "to let this gap loan continue till it is adjusted out of the share capital. According to the present expectations", he said, the company "will go to the market to raise the capital. . . sometime by the middle of the next year". Seeking to explain why he allowed the company to overdraw, he said: "Both the C/C-*cum*-L/C limits were being conducted in terms of the sanction. In the first week of November the company had to meet certain commitments and he had to accommodate them thus exceeding the permissible limit of Rs. 75 lacs. Instead of putting the accounts in order, we were requested by the Co. to get the restriction of Rs. 75 lacs removed. The case was accordingly referred to you. Our action in letting the Company cross the limit of Rs. 75 lacs was motivated out of the commercial consideration as returning the cheque unpaid would have compromised the company's position. Normally such an action is avoided in case of good parties". On February 9, 1974 the Credit Administration advised the Branch Manager to move through his Regional Manager for (i) confirmation of his action in accommodating the company beyond the sanction limit; (ii) extension of the facility beyond the sanctioned period stating clearly the period by which extension was required, and (iii) removal of the present stipulation requiring outstanding not to exceed Rs. 75 lacs under the two limits.

On May 10, 1974 Shri Sarwan Singh who succeeded Shri Puri as Branch Manager submitted a proposal for renewal of both the facilities for consideration of the Credit Administration. For the second facility of Rs. 60 lacs he suggested as security "existing and future machinery acquired by the company" in addition to the original security in iron and steel, cement and other building material. On May 14, 1974 a proposal prepared by the Chief, Credit Administration on the lines suggested by the Branch Manager was placed before the Board recommending (i) for the first cash credit account a limit of Rs. 30 lacs, (ii) for the second Rs. 60 lacs and (iii) inland letter of credit with a limit of Rs. 20 lacs; the total withdrawals were not to exceed Rs. 80 lacs. In cash credit account No. 2 "machinery installed or to be installed" was recommended as additional security. The inland letter of credit for Rs. 20 lacs was for establishing letters of credit relating to building material and/or machinery." The following conditions were also specified:

(1) Advance to be adjusted either out of proposed public issue or loans received from financial institutions whichever is earlier.
(2) Bank's charge to be got modified with the registrar of companies in respect of additional securities.
(3) The company to submit statement of hypothecated stocks each month which should be checked by the Branch Manager regularly.
(4) All the machinery hypothecated to the Bank, should be adequately insured with agreed Bank clause.
(5) The company to undertake that the security offered to the Bank will be excluded from the charge of any other Bank/Financial Institutions with which the company might make arrangement for working capital/Term Loan.
(6) Margin may be stepped up in terms of L&A Circular No. 106/73.
(7) The advance against cement and other building material not to exceed Rs. 10 lacs.

The Board considering the proposal on May 23, 1974 decided to renew the limits but at the existing level and suggested that the position may be reviewed in December 1974. The Board was particularly interested to know if the net means of the guarantors had been verified and, if so, how. One of the conditions of the renewal proposal was that the bank's charge was to be modified with the Registrar of Companies in respect of the additional security i.e., machinery installed or to be installed. No step however, appears to have been taken in this direction. The result was that in the case of cash credit facility of Rs. 60 lacs, the charge registered continued to be iron and steel, cement and other building material whose value could not be adequate security against facility.

On January 14, 1975 Shri Sanjay Gandhi, Managing Director of Maruti Limited, wrote to the General Manager, Punjab National Bank informing him that the company would go for public issue of share capital in the second half of 1975 and requesting him to remove the condition that the total withdrawals should not exceed Rs. 75 lacs. On February, 1975 Chief, Credit Administration put up a proposal to the Board that "as the company's need is only by way of bridge finance and is repayable out of public issue, we may agree to the removal of the ceiling of Rs. 75 lacs subject to the condition (a) that the outstandings be adjusted out of public issue when subscribed or on release of term loans when sanctioned by financial institutions whichever is earlier; (b) under facility No. 2, advance against hypothecation of iron and steel material should not exceed Rs. 5 lacs instead of allowing advance to the full extent". This proposal was approved in the Board meeting held on February 18, 1975. Condition (b) is significant because it shows that the charge registered with the Registrar of Companies was not modified following the inclusion of the additional security in machinery. After the Board's approval was obtained, the Chief, Credit Administration, wrote to the Reserve Bank of India on February 26, requesting them to accord necessary authorisation. The authorisation came from the Reserve Bank of India in their letter dated March 31, 1975 which stated *inter alia* "We have no objection to your bank allowing the proposed bridge finance of Rs. 15 lacs to the above mentioned company for a period of six months only or till the proposed public issue of shares, whichever is earlier, provided the bank is fully satisfied on merits. The bridge finance should be disbursed after the company has made firm arrangements for the underwriting of the proposed public issue of its shares. Our authorisation is also subject to the condition that the bridge finance should be utilised by the company for the purpose for which it had been allowed". On April 29, 1975 Punjab National Bank addressed a letter to the Reserve Bank of India, the relevant portion of which is set out below:

"We have now been informed by the company that they had applied to the Controller of Capital Issues who has sanctioned them issuance of securities privately for the value of Rs. 1,15,39,300 and in such a case underwriting arrangements are not required to be made. A copy of letter dated 16-4-1975 from Controller of Capital Issues to the company is enclosed for your kind perusal.

However, the company is expected to go to the market for capital issue during 2nd half of the year 1975 after getting the necessary clearance certificate from Financial Institutions and permission from Controller of Capital Issues.

Since there is sufficient gap and the finalisation of underwriting arrangements at this stage would be too early, they have stated that the necessary arrangement shall be made about two months prior to the Public Issue. They have requested us to release the bridging loan as the funds are needed by them for genuine needs.

Please reconsider your decision and allow us authorisation at an early date to release the bridging loan, as requested earlier."

Reserve Bank of India replied to this letter on May 15, 1975 saying ". . . we advise that we have no objection to your bank disbursing the bridge loan before the company has made firm arrangements for underwriting of the proposed public issue of its shares. Your bank should, however, ensure that the bridge loan of Rs. 15 lacs is repaid by the company out of the private issue of its shares of Rs. 1,15,39,300 for which the Controller of Capital Issues has given his approval in April 1975".

The General Manager for Maruti Limited wrote to the Chairman, Punjab National Bank, on September 15, 1976 offering to regularise the cash credit accounts by payments of monthly instalments of Rs. 1 lac and also down payment of Rs. 5 lacs provided the penal interest amounting to Rs. 67,302.17p. already charged was refunded to them and waived for future and the rate of interest reduced to the maximum extent possible. It was said that the irregularities in the accounts were mainly due to the accumulation of interest. The Bank's Board in the meeting held on October 6, 1976 approved refund of the penal interest charged and waiver of the demand in future. The rate of interest was also reduced from 15.5 per cent to 14 per cent. The company paid Rs. 5 lacs and several monthly instalments of Rs. 1 lac and then discontinued payment from April 1977.

In October 1976 the Bank had formulated a scheme for promoting family planning by industrial and commercial establishments. Under this scheme a higher rebate in the rate of interest at 1/2 per cent per annum was allowed to Maruti Limited for a period of one year from November 1, 1976. Maruti Limited had claimed that out of 100 employees eligible for sterilisation operation, 96 had already undergone the operation and therefore they were entitled to the reduction in the rate of interest. The claim was allowed for five months from November 1976 to March 1977 amounted to Rs. 19,000 whereas according to the terms of the scheme sanctioned by the Board it should not have exceeded Rs. 10,000 for 96 employees of the company.

The liabilities of Maruti Limited in the two accounts amounted to more than Rs. 94 lacs in May 1977.

Summary of Reserve Bank of India's Inspection Reports: Shri D.N. Samrath, Assistant Chief Officer in the Department of Banking Operations, Reserve Bank of India, who prepared summaries of the reports of inspection conducted by the Reserve Bank of India in relation to the loan accounts of Maruti concerns in Punjab National Bank and Central Bank of India, has given evidence, and the summaries he prepared have been brought on record as evidence. The irregularities observed regarding the sanction, supervision and conduct of the two accounts of Maruti Limited in Punjab National Bank have been summarised as follows:

(1) The credit limits were sanctioned to the company without proper pre-sanction appraisal or a study of viability aspects of the company's car manufacturing project.

(2) Initially it was stipulated by the Board that the company should furnish its 'project report' to the bank by the end of February 1972. Subsequently, the then Chairman (Shri S.C. Trikha) authorised to release of 50 per cent of the sanctioned amount although the company had not furnished the 'project report', stipulating that it should furnished by April 15, 1972; the residual 50 per cent of the sanctioned amount was to be released only after the report was made available to the bank.

(3) The above credit limits were sanctioned by way of 'bridging finance', the first sanction being valid for 12 months and the second one for six months. The relative advances were expected to be adjusted out of the proceeds of public issue of the company's shares. However, the company has not been able to go in for such an issue so far and the advances have remained unadjusted. The bank, however, has not considered the

desirability of taking effective steps for recovery/regularisation of the advances.

(4) The reasons and circumstances explained by the company from time to time for its failure to execute its project and raise its share capital have been accepted by the bank without an independent analysis of the bottlenecks and problems stated to have been faced by the company.

(5) The aggregate outstandings in the two accounts have been allowed to exceed the limit of Rs. 75 lacs continuously since 1973, the maximum amount outstanding at any time being Rs. 105.17 lacs in October 1976.

(6) The bank did not take adequate steps to ensure during the period prior to November 1975 that the aggregate borrowings of the company from it and its other bankers (viz. Central Bank of India) did not exceed Rs. 1 crore without prior reference to Reserve Bank of India, as required by the Credit Authorisation Scheme. (This ceiling was raised to Rs. 2 crores only in November 1975).

(7) The concerned branch of the bank did not exercise proper supervision over the operations of accounts. The company was highly irregular in the submission of the monthly statements of hypothecated stocks. On several occasions drawings were allowed in excess of the drawing power, much beyond the discretionary powers of the branch manager and such overdrawings were not reported by him to the appropriate higher authorities for ratification; during June-October 1976, the outstandings exceeded even the value of securities charged in the accounts. There are indications that the company had borrowed from/lent to other companies in which its director/s were interested as directors.

(8) The supervision and control exercised by the branch over the securities charged to the bank was also not satisfactory. There was no record to indicate that the branch official had carried out inspections of securities at periodical intervals. The invoices relating to the machinery hypothecated to the bank could not be matched with the list of hypothecated machinery available with the branch.

Apart from the above irregularities, the summary specifically mentions the following concessions given to Maruti Limited:

(a) The rate of interest was reduced from 15.5 per cent per annum to 14 per cent per annum as from October 1, 1976; and
(b) Penal interest aggregating Rs. 0.67 lac charged in the accounts uptil then was refunded and levy of such interest in future was waived.

As regards the rebate in the rate of interest allowed to Maruti Limited under the Bank's scheme for promoting family planning, it has been said:

"The bank's then Chairman (Shri T.R. Tuli) authorised in November 1976 a further rebate of 1/2 per cent per annum in the rate of interest, under the bank's Family Planning Incentive Scheme approved by the Board in August 1976 for all industrial/commercial concerns. While authorising this, Shri Tuli did not ensure that all the terms and conditions of the Scheme were duly satisfied. It is also observed that the benefit of the Scheme was availed of by/given to only Maruti Limited and no other borrower of the Bank."

CENTRAL BANK OF INDIA

All the three Maruti companies namely, Maruti Limited, Maruti Heavy Vehicles Private Limited and Maruti Technical Services Private Limited figure in the transactions with Central Bank of India. I shall start with Maruti Limited.

Maruti Limited

Shri Sanjay Gandhi as Director of Maruti Limited made an undated application to the Manager, *Central Bank of India*, Safdarjang Enclave Branch, New Delhi for an interim loan of Rs. 10 lacs against hypothecation of "machines and equipments". From other materials on record the application appears to have been made on or about November 12, 1971. The loan, it was said, to be "utilised to meet part of the expenditure likely to curred towards implementation" of the company's car manufacturing project "for installation of machinery and equipment". As to the mode of repayment of the loan, the letter said: "may be determined mutually. This may be paid out of the funds to be received from the public issue". It was also stated that all the

Directors of the company were "prepared to provide guarantee against their personal assets for the repayment of the said loan". Shri K.L. Kalra, Manager of the Safdarjang Enclave Branch, processed the application on November 12 not on the prescribed proposal form but on bank's letter head. Shri Kalra explains this by saying that Safdarjang Enclave Branch being a new branch, the proposal form was possibly not available, but he does not say why he considered the matter so urgent that he could not wait and send for the prescribed form from the Regional Office or some other branch office of the Bank in Delhi. He forwarded the proposal to the Chief Agent (subsequently this post was designated as Zonal Manager) on the same day recommending that sanction of the Head Office to the proposal be obtained by telex. This also suggests that he treated the proposal as very urgent. Shri Kalra did not make any appraisal of the loan proposal according to the guidelines provided in the circulars issued by the Bank's Head Office from time to time. These circulars were consolidated in the Manual of Advances published in 1972. In his forwarding letter he mentioned among other points that "Punjab National Bank have approached the party and assured them such facilities at the earliest and thus they are offering stiff competition.

From the Chief Agent's office the proposal was forwarded to the Head Office on the next day, November 13, with a request to convey their decision by telex. There was also no appraisal of the loan proposal by the Chief Agent. As it was mentioned in the loan application that all Directors of the Company would offer guarantee in their personal capacity. Shri Bhalla, Chief Agent, had written to the respective bankers of six of the Directors of the company; Maruti Limited had then seven Directors including Shri Sanjay Gandhi. Nothing was done to verify his financial status. In the Head Office the proposal was put up before the Custodian of the Bank Shri B.N. Adarkar who became its Chairman and Managing Director from December 11, 1972. On November 19, the Custodian informed Shri Bhalla by telex that he would agree to sanction the proposal subject to Bhalla's submitting a report on certain points. One of the points was "willingness of at least some Directors to furnish guarantee and an indication of additional bridge finance they are going to provide". Bhalla clarified the other points after a discussion with the Directors of the company but as regards the guarantee by the Directors he informed Head Office that the other Directors wanted their personal guarantee waived and only Shri Sanjay Gandhi was prepared to furnish guarantee. On December 9, 1971 an interim loan of Rs. 10 lacs on personal guarantee of Shri Sanjay Gandhi and hypothecation of machinery purchased and to be purchased was sanctioned by the Head Office for three to four months subject to confirmation from Shri Sanjay Gandhi and Shri V.R. Mohan, another Director of the company, that the small car project would be implemented according to the time schedule despite the state of emergency that was prevailing in the country at the time. For this loan the interest was 10½ per cent per annum and margin 25 per cent. Shri Sanjay Gandhi confirmed in writing that the car project was going to be implemented according to the time schedule.

On January 10, 1972 Shri Sanjay Gandhi executed a document hypothecating in favour of the bank "existing and future machinery to the extent of Rs. 10 lacs purchased out of the said loan of Rs. 10 lacs provided by Central Bank of India". The document contains the statements: "A list of existing machinery worth of Rs. 10,10,782.54 is enclosed herewith duly signed by Shri Sanjay Gandhi". Along with this document of hypothecation Shri Sanjay Gandhi signed a guarantee form for payment to the bank the sum advanced and a letter declaring that the machinery hypothecated "were free from any encumbrance whatever". No list of machinery however appears to have been enclosed with the document. Shri K.L. Kalra told the Commission that Shri Sanjay Gandhi had furnished a list of machinery but he could not say what had happened to this list. It is not possible to accept Shri Kalra's statement in view of the following facts. A list of machinery worth Rs. 10,10,782.54 was sent by Shri Sanjay Gandhi to Safdarjang Enclave Branch of the Bank of February 23, 1972 which shows that the company had machinery worth Rs. 8,76,455.2 only in their possession on January 10,1972 when the document of hypothecation was signed and, further, that the machinery of the value of Rs. 1,34,327,29 was procured by the company after January 10, 1972. It seems clear that Kalra accepted the document without insisting on the list and his statement that the list was enclosed with the hypothecation agreement is not correct. Also, having regard to the condition of the loan requiring a margin of 25 per cent, machinery worth Rs. 12.5 lacs should have been hypothecated.

This loan which was sanctioned for three or four months only was opened by Shri Kalra as a C.C.M. (Cash Credit Mercantile) account. Shri G.K. Narula who was the Accountant in Central Bank of India,

Safdarjang Enclave Branch, at the relevant time explains the difference between a C.C.M. account and a term loan account. The term loan is sanctioned for a fixed period and it is to be adjusted within the stipulated time. "C.C.M. loan is a sort of continuous account and it fluctuates within the limit mentioned". Shri Narula further says that by treating this loan as C.C.M. account the advantage that accrued to Maruti Limited was that they got the facility of availing it for a long period beyond the stipulated time. Kalra's explanation is that as the Head Office had not classified it as a term loan, he opened it as C.C.M. account. He admits he did so without consulting the Zonal Office or the Head Office but seeks to justify his action by saying that "nomenclature of the loan" was not material but the terms and conditions according to which the loan should have been adjusted after three to four months and that it was the duty of the Branch Manager who succeeded him to recall the dues from the company. His successor Shri F.C. Khatri is dead. According to Shri Adarkar it was wrong to treat this loan as if it was a cash credit limit. Shri Adarkar says that it was enough that the transaction was classified as a loan: "a loan for three months is all the classification on earth that is required. Mr. Kalra does not require any further classification. This is a matter of common sense". According to Shri Adarkar "changing the basic character of the loan from a loan into a cash credit is a very material change" and that a man who does not understand this "does not understand banking". Shri D.V. Taneja who became Chairman and Managing Director of Central Bank of India after Shri Adarkar has also said that conversion of the loan into cash credit arrangement "was not in order", and "if the Branch wanted to convert the loan into cash credit, they should have asked the sanctioning authority for such as arrangement". Normally C.C.M. limit is sanctioned against stock in trade without any fixed period of payment and it is subject to review and renewal every year. Maruti Limited repaid this loan to the extent of Rs. 9.90 lacs on January 24, 1973 about nine months beyond the stipulated time, but as the loan had been opened as C.C.M. account the company against availed of this arrangement to the fullest extent by June 1973 and this sum was never realised from the company. On September 7, 1973 Shri Khatri who was then the Manager of Safdarjang Enclave branch wrote to Zonal Manager requesting him to have the C.C.M. account of Maruti Limited renewed till the public issue of their shares. Shri T.N. Dastur, Zonal Manager at the time, did not, however, refer the matter to the Head Office and allowed the account to continue as it was on some assurance given by Shri Pahuja, Manager, Finance and Credit, Maruti Limited.

In February 1972 Maruti Limited had approached the bank for issuing a deferred payment guarantee for Rs. 25 lacs on its behalf. The Bank's Board rejected this request in June or July 1972 on the view that the company should approach a term lending institution for the purpose. In the meantime in April 1972 Maruti Limited had applied for a loan of Rs. 6 lacs for purchasing steel, cement, etc., required for the construction of its factory and other buildings. Shri Adarkar who was then Custodian of the bank rejected the demand on April 19, 1972 but the next day when the Chief Executive Officer of the company approached him. Shri Adarkar sanctioned a key loan of Rs. 6 lacs against pledge of steel for three months only. But this was not availed of by the company as it was not considered convenient.

In August 1973 the company approached the bank for a 'bridging' loan of Rs. 1.5 crores required for financing its project and this proposal was forwarded by the bank's Mullahera branch which was opened in September 1973 and was housed in a room in the Maruti complex of buildings near the company's factory. Although the banks's Head Office processed the proposal after obtaining certain additional information from the company, it was never placed before the Board of Directors, perhaps in view of the Board's earlier direction that the company should approach the term lending institutions for such finance.

In April 1974 the company approached the Safdarjang Enclave branch of the bank to convert the key loan of Rs. 6 lacs granted to them in April 1972 which the company did not avail of, to hypothecation loan against machinery. On that day the loan of Rs. 10 lacs sanctioned in December 1971 for three to four months was still outstanding. R.L. Grover, Manager of Safdarjang Enclave Branch, recommended to the Zonal Manager conversion of the aforesaid key loan of Rs. 6 lacs to C.C.M. open loan against imported machinery. Zonal Manager Shri A.B. Wadia in his turn recommended the proposal to the Head Office on May 18, 1974. Shri Wadia has explained a key loan as follows: "The principle of key loan is that the stock should remain under the effective possession of the bank and the stock should move out of the godown with the full knowledge of the bank and either on replacement by fresh stock or by payment there against". On May 23, Wadia received a letter from Shri R.M.

Pradhan, Assistant Manager, Advances, Head Office, Bombay, where the loan proposal of Rs. 1.5 crores was pending consideration, stating that the bank should not make any commitments even by way of short term finance which might lead to giving the company further finance in future. This letter written on May 18, 1974 was followed by a telex on May 27 saying that the facility sanctioned in April 1972 should not be kept open for a long period and it should be treated as cancelled. Wadia says that on May 27 Pahuja of Maruti Limited saw him and pressed for immediate release of Rs. 6 lacs which, Pahuja said, was required for purchase of machinery. Wadia informed him of the direction from the bank's Head Office, Pahuja then saw Shri D.V. Taneja who was then the Chairman and Managing Director of the bank who happened to be present in the Zonal Office at the time. Shri Taneja asked Wadia to put up a note which he did without mentioning anything about Shri Pradhan's letter or telex. Shri Taneja sanctioned a fresh loan of Rs. 6 lacs with 25 per cent margin against machinery for a period of six months. In his order the Chairman gave the following directions:

(i) the Chief Internal Auditor should depute a Godown Inspector to check about the state of machinery;
(ii) the original invoices should be taken on account;
(iii) the machines should bear the note that they were hypothecated to the Central Bank of India; and
(iv) the bank's charge for additional machinery should be registered with the Registrar of Companies.

On June 28, 1974 Shri Sanjay Gandhi, Managing Director of Maruti Limited, applied to the Safdarjang Enclave branch of the bank for another loan of Rs. 6 lacs required, it was said, for making urgent payments. Shri R.L. Grover, Branch Manager, forwarded the application to the Zonal Manager with his recommendation. The Zonal Manager held up the proposal for a discussion with the Chairman of the bank who was expected in Delhi on July 19, 1974. Shri Taneja must have visited the Maruti factory some day around this date as would appear from a telex received by the Zonal Manager, Delhi on August 7, 1974 from Head Office saying that during Chairman's last visit to the Maruti factory, the company had requested the Chairman to release a sum of Rs. 5 to 6 lacs to enable them to take delivery of some machinery and that the amount should be released, if not released already, after completing the necessary formalities. The Zonal Office was also advised to send a comprehensive proposal for the sanctioned limits aggregating Rs. 22 lacs for being placed before the Board for obtaining its confirmation.

On August 13, 1974 Shri A.B. Wadia, Zonal Manager, sanctioned a loan of Rs. 6 lacs for three months with 25 per cent margin. The Zonal Manager also directed the Branch to put up a consolidated proposal of Rs. 22 lacs for consideration. The consolidated proposal could not, however, be sent for want of required information which the company did not furnish.

It does not appear from the files that any appraisal was made of the company's requirement before the two loans of Rs. 6 lacs each were sanctioned respectively on May 27 and August 13, 1974. The loans were sanctioned on the ground of urgency pleaded by the representatives of the company. Shri R.L. Grover, Manager of Safdarjang Enclave branch, who had processed the aforesaid loan proposals has said that although it was necessary to examine the past performance and repaying capacity of the party, it was not done in this case. He admits that while sending his recommendation to the Zonal Manager he did not mention the fact that Maruti Limited was a defaulter in respect of Rs. 10 lacs loan sanctioned in 1971. He explains the reason: "the Managing Director of the Company was so important a personality in those days and he was so close to the Head Office and the Regional Office. I dared not highlight the past performance of this company in my recommendation". Grover has also said that Sanjay Gandhi and V.R. Mohan refused to enclose the list of machinery along with the document of hypothecation. Shri Grover "dared not withhold disbursement to the party because such action against this party could have invited troubles for me. . . . because this was not an ordinary party, its Managing Director being the son of the then Prime Minister". He has said further that Shri Sanjay Gandhi refused to allow the name plate of the bank to be placed on the machine indicating that these were hypothecated to the bank.

Shri Sanjay Gandhi had certified before the above three loans were disbursed that the machinery hypothecated to the bank was free from encumbrance. It may be recalled that the Government of Haryana held first charge on the machinery installed on the basis of the agreement dated August 9, 1971 between the Government of Haryana and the company.

Shri R.L. Kapahi, Inspector of Godown, inspected the hypothecated stock of Maruti Limited with reference to the C.C.M. accounts of the company in Safdarjang Enclave branch of Central Bank of India on different dates in 1974 and 1975. He did not find the name plate of the bank displayed or painted on the machinery to indicate the bank's lien. On inquiry Shri Sanjay Gandhi informed him that this condition had been waived. There is, however, nothing on record to support Shri Gandhi's statement. Shri Kapahi found that the company had included the installation charges and cartage in the valuation of the machinery which was not proper, the valuation of the hypothecated stock should have been the actual value mentioned in the invoices. The borrower had not calculated the depreciation while valuing the securities which were purchased three to four years back. In view of the fact that Punjab National Bank had also sanctioned loans to this party against machinery. Shri Kapahi suggested that the lists of machinery hypothecated to the two banks should be exchanged for a clear indication of the securities hypothecated to each bank. Shri Kapahi's inspection notes were sent to all concerned including the Branch Manager and the Zonal Manager, but no corrective measures were taken.

In April 1975 the company's accounts at Safdarjang Enclave branch were transferred to the Mullahera branch. In early May 1975 Shri P.F. Gutta took over as Chairman of Central Bank of India. A note indicating the position of the bank's advances to Maruti Limited was submitted for his sanction. On May 7, 1975 Shri Sanjay Gandhi, Managing Director of Maruti Limited, applied for cash credit limit of Rs. 15 lacs and bill discounting facility of Rs. 5 lacs for financing certain 'job works' undertaken by the company under its diversification programme. Since the company's aggregate dues to Central Bank of India then amounted to about Rs. 25 lacs and it was enjoying limits aggregating Rs. 90 lacs with an overall ceiling of Rs. 75 lacs with the Punjab National Bank, grant of any additional facility would have required prior approval of the Bank's Board and the Reserve Bank of India. For this complete data was not available from the company and the Head Office therefore did not sanction this facility. The Head Office asked the Zonal Office to explain the position "tactfully" to the company.

On June 16, 1975 the Zonal Office recommended a cheque discounting limit of Rs. 1.75 lacs stating that the branch concerned (Mullahera) had already allowed the facility in anticipation of the sanction. While the matter was pending with the Head Office, Shri

A.B. Wadia, Zonal Manager, advised that Rs. 1.7 lacs was inadequate and recommended consideration of a cheque discounting limit of Rs. 3 lacs and clean overdraft limit of Rs. 1 lac with the stipulation that the aggregate outstandings under these two facilities should not exceed Rs. 3 lacs. On July 11, the Head Office sanctioned cheque discounting limit of Rs. 3 lacs but the clean overdraft limit was rejected. However following persistent requests by the company and recommendations from the branch and the Zonal Offices, the Chairman sanctioned clean overdraft limit of Rs. 1 lac on August 30, 1975 for "occasional use". The Head Office advised the Zonal Office to ensure that the total advances to the company made by Central Bank of India and Punjab National Bank did not exceed Rs. 1 crore violating Reserve Bank of India's credit authorisation directives. On September 4, 1975 Mullahera branch wrote to the Zonal Office saying that according to its information the company's total borrowings had already exceeded Rs. 1 crore. The overdraft limit for Rs. 1 lac was therefore not released. It was released after the aggregate limit requiring prior approval of the Reserve Bank of Indian under the credit authorisation scheme was raised from Rs. 1 crore to Rs. 2 crores in November 1975. Even thereafter Shri H.S. Chawla, Manager of the Mullahera branch often accommodated Maruti Limited beyond the sanctioned limits for clean overdraft or for discounting cheques and not always with the prior approval of the Zonal Office.

In May 1975 the Zonal Office recommended enhancement of cheque discounting and clean overdraft limits to Rs. 5 lacs and Rs. 3 lacs respectively which were sanctioned by the Chairman. In June 1976 the company approached Mullahera branch of the bank for sanction of an overdraft limit of Rs. 15 lacs against dues from the State Transport Undertakings. The Zonal Office sanctioned a limit of Rs. 3 lacs and forwarded the proposal to the Head Office. The Head Office examined the proposal and sanctioned a limit of Rs. 10 lacs. Subsequently in October 1976 the Zonal Office recommended enhancement of this limit to Rs. 15 lacs. The Chairman approved this subject to the condition that the advance would be limited only against the dues from the State Government undertakings and a margin of 25 per cent should be maintained. The Chairman also directed a full review of the facilities sanctioned to the company to be placed before the Board. A comprehensive note was placed before the Board at its meeting held on December 27, 1976. No additional limits for advances were sanctioned thereafter. By the end of May 1977, except the initial loan of Rs. 10 lacs sanctioned in December 1971 and Rs. 12 lacs in May and August 1974, other facilities were adjusted. For recovery of the dues amounting to Rs. 22 lacs, Central Bank of India instituted a suit in April 1978.

Shri Sanjay Gandhi demanded reduction of the rate of interest from Central Bank of India on the ground that Punjab National Bank had already agreed to reduce the rate. Although the conduct of the aforesaid cash credit/loan limits aggregating Rs. 22 lacs was never satisfactory, the company was granted concession in the rate of interest which was reduced from 16 per cent to 14 per cent with effect from September 17, 1976 under the orders of the Chairman subject to the production of a letter from Punjab National Bank confirming the reduction of the rate of interest by them. When the Manager of Mullahera branch approached Shri Sanjay Gandhi for a written confirmation, Shri Gandhi refused to producc any confirmatory letter. That however did not stand in the way of the rate of interest being reduced. Punjab National Bank reduced the rate about two weeks later, from October 1, 1976 after the bank's Board of Directors approved the proposal.

Summary of Reserve Bank of India's Inspection Reports

The Reserve Bank of India noted the following irregularities in regard to the sanction, supervision and conduct of the above facilities as would appear from Shri D.N. Samrath's summary:

(1) The various credit facilities were sanctioned from time to time on an *ad hoc* basis without a critical assessment of the company's genuine requirements over a period of time.

(2) The cash credit/loan limits against hypothecation of machinery aggregating Rs. 22 lacs were sanctioned for periods of three to six months but when the stipulated period was over, adequate measures were not taken by the Branch/Zonal Office/Head Office to ensure the repayment of the advance. In the case of the limit of Rs. 10 lacs sanctioned in December 1971 which was to be repaid in 3 to 4 months out of the proceeds of public issue of the company's shares, it is observed that the outstanding balance was reduced to Rs. 0.10 lac in January 1973 on account of moneys received from private issue of shares but the company was subsequently al-

lowed to again avail of the limit to the full extent.

(3) Part of the machinery in respect of which the above limits were granted was all purpose machinery and it appears that such machinery was mainly utilised for the manufacturing and other activities of Maruti Heavy Vehicles Private Limited, an allied concern.

(4) On several occasions the company was accommodated for large amounts (upto Rs. 10 lacs) by way of overdrawings beyond sanctioned limits or advance granted under different heads without any sanction of regular limits, particularly at the Mullahera branch. However, this branch did not ensure that all such accommodations were duly reported to higher authorities for obtaining confirmation thereof.

(5) The company was extended credit against cheques by way of both purchase thereof and/or allowing overdraft there against by the Mullahera branch. Although many of the cheques were drawn by the same party and in round sums, the branch did not make enquiries about the nature of transactions in respect of which they were drawn. In the case of overdrafts allowed against book-debts, it did not observe the usual safeguards of obtaining statements of outstanding debts at regular intervals, deleting long outstanding dues from the drawing power, verification of company's books, etc.

(6) While sanctioning the additional cash credit limit of Rs. 6 lacs in August 1974 (raising the aggregate limits against machinery to Rs. 22 lacs) the Head Office had instructed that a comprehensive proposal should be submitted for being placed before the Board. However, this was never compiled and submitted. A note reviewing the various facilities was placed before the Board only in December 1976, when the various advance limits aggregated Rs. 45 lacs. Certain adverse comments made by the internal auditors/godown inspectors about the conduct/supervision of the accounts were not brought out in this note, and in the paragraph provided for bringing out such features, it was indicated that there were no such comments.

(7) The company has availed of advances against hypothecation of machinery from Central Bank of India as well as Punjab National Bank. The internal auditors of the former bank had reported, *inter alia*, that the machinery charged to the two

banks were not clearly demarcated and hence it was not possible to verify all the machinery charged to the Central Bank, the invoices relating to the machinery available on the bank's records could also not be matched with the list of hypothecated machinery.

Apart from the aforesaid irregularities, the Reserve Bank summary refers to the various concessions granted to Maruti Limited in the rate of interest, charges for collection of cheques and issue of drafts, etc., which have been mentioned already.

The summary also cites instances of the "company's indifference towards the normal requirements of the bank":

(a) In connection with the company's request made in May 1975 for additional cash credit limit of Rs. 15 lacs and a bill discounting limit of Rs. 5 lacs, it was requested by the bank to furnish certain data but it refused to do so, stating that sufficient data had been given in connection with its application for 'bridging' loan; but that was given prior to August 1973, i.e., nearly two years ago.

(b) In July 1974, in connection with the proposal for a cheque's discounting limit of Rs. 3 lacs, the Head Office desired to know the nature of the transactions in respect of which the cheques were received by the company. The company refused to furnish these particulars stating that it was an internal matter of the company and that its sources of funds were disclosed on the face of the balance sheet.

(c) The limits sanctioned in December 1971 and May 1974 were guaranteed by the company's Managing Director and some of the other directors. However, the Managing Director refused to extend his personal guarantee in respect of the limit of Rs. 6 lacs sanctioned in August 1974. The matter was not pursued by the bank.

Maruti Heavy Vehicles Private Limited

This company was incorporated on February 22, 1974 with Shrimati Sonia Gandhi, Shri Sanjay Gandhi, Shri Kishan Lal Jalan and Shri Om Prakash Modi as its Directors. The company was formed with share capital of Rs. 20 lacs divided into two lacs equity shares of Rs.

10 each for the purpose of assembling/manufacturing road rollers. M/s Jalan Modi Automobiles, a firm of Calcutta which used to deal in motor cars, automobile spare parts, etc., was one of the dealers of the Maruti car and later became the sole selling agents of Maruti Heavy Vehicles Private Ltd. In October 1973 the firm offered to pay Rs. 28 lacs of certain imported road-roller parts and components advertised for sale by the Receiver of a company in liquidation. The offer was accepted by the Receiver on December 5, 1973. Shri Sanjay Gandhi approached Mullahera branch of Central Bank of India with a request for financial assistance of Rs. 24 lacs to be disbursed in the name of Shri Kishan Lal Jalan. This was before Maruti Heavy Vehicles Private Limited was incorporated. M/s Jalan Modi Automobiles also requested Shri D.V. Taneja, who was then Deputy General Manager at the bank's Head Office in Bombay, to grant them interim finance of Rs. 15 lacs for paying the Receiver for the road-roller parts and components. This request was conveyed to the Zonal Office at New Delhi with instructions to consider it on merits. In March 1974 Shri Jalan on behalf of Maruti Heavy Vehicles discussed the proposal with Shri Taneja and on his instruction the Zonal Manager Shri A.B. Wadia sanctioned on March 12, 1974 a C.C.M. Key Loan of Rs. 5 lacs. The conditions of the loan were that the payment should be made direct to the Receiver and original receipts issued by the Receiver should be kept on record, the company should take delivery of the pledged goods within six months from the date of advance, all the Directors of the company must furnish personal guarantee and the progress made by the company from time to time in regard to the assembly of road-rollers should be informed every month end.

On March 26 Shri Sanjay Gandhi, Director of Maruti Heavy Vehicles, requested the Mullahera Branch Manager to release the balance of Rs. 19 lacs out of the original proposal of Rs. 24 lacs. This was followed by a telephonic request from Shri Kishan Lal Jalan to Shri D.V. Taneja to sanction the limit. Shri Taneja approved the release of an additional sum of Rs. 5 lacs on cash credit pledge basis on April 1, 1975 on which date Shri Taneja succeeded Shri Adarkar as Chairman of Central Bank of India. Eight days later, on April 9, Shri Sanjay Gandhi again approached the Branch Manager to release another sum of Rs. 5 lacs "for taking further delivery of road-roller components and parts". The Branch Manager forwarded the request to the Zonal Manager on the same day. In the meantime the Head

Office of the Bank sought information on certain points relating to the original proposal of Rs. 24 lacs. While the Branch Manager was in correspondence with the company on this subject, Chairman Shri Taneja sanctioned a further release of Rs. 5 lacs on April 15, 1974 on key loan basis with 35 per cent margin with a rider that any further increase in key loan facility would be considered only when the paid up capital of the company was raised to Rs. 20 lacs. It was further indicated that stocks should start moving as soon as assembly of road rollers started and the movement of stock must be reflected in the operation of the account. Three days later, on April 18, Maruti Heavy Vehicles requested the Mullahera branch for sanctioning a part limit of Rs. 5 lacs on hypothecation basis out of the sanctioned limit of Rs. 15 lacs in key loan and also for reducing the margin of 35 per cent to 25 per cent. This also was sanctioned by the Chairman adding that hypothecation facility would be allowed only in respect of goods which could not be stored in the godown.

On May 3, 1974 Shri Sanjay Gandhi requested the Manager of the Mullahera branch for release of another instalment of Rs. 5 lacs assuring him that the paid up capital of the company would be increased from Rs. 13.74 lacs to Rs. 15 lacs "in near future". The Branch Manager forwarded the request to the Zonal Manager and before the Zonal Manager's recommendations could go to the Head Office, the Chairman sanctioned thc proposal on May 17, 1974 with the instruction that the money should be disbursed only after the paid up capital of thc company was raised to Rs. 20 lacs and on the personal guarantee of the four Directors. But after a week the Head Office sent a telex to the Zonal Office authorising release of Rs. 5 lacs without insisting on the enhancement of thc paid up capital.

On June 25, 1974 Shri Sanjay Gandhi as Director of Maruti Heavy Vehicles again applied to the Branch Manager to sanction a loan of further Rs. 4 lacs making the aggregate Rs. 24 lacs which was the company's original proposal. The Branch Manager forwarded the request to the Zonal Manager for consideration but in the meantime the Branch Manager allowed the company to overdraw to the extent of Rs. 2.60 lacs in excess of the sanctioned limit of Rs. 20 lacs. This was subsequently confirmed by the Zonal Manager. The Zonal Manager asked the Branch Manager on August 19, 1974 to send a quarterly report on the monthwise schedule of production and sale in number and value, credit and debit summations in the cash credit account, position of the account, etc., as on July 31, 1974. The Branch

Manager's reply was that in spite of several attempts he had not been successful in obtaining the necessary information from the company. The company subsequently intimated that efforts were being made to collect the information asked for. On September 30, 1974 the Head Office reminded the Zonal Manager and the Branch Manager that the paid up capital of the company should be raised to Rs. 20 lacs and a certificate of the auditors of the company should be obtained. In response to the Branch Manager's query the company informed him on November 23, 1974 that its paid up capital was Rs. 15,04,000 and that the Board of Directors had decided not to raise the paid up capital to Rs. 20 lacs "due to obvious reasons".

From July 1974 Mullahera Branch had allowed the limit to be overdrawn and by December 17, 1974 the company availed of Rs. 4,20,895,03 in excess of the sanctioned limit of Rs. 20 lacs only. When the Branch Manager asked the company to regularise the account, Shri Sanjay Gandhi wrote directly to Shri Taneja stating that the Company was sanctioned limits aggregating Rs. 20 lacs as against the company's requirement of Rs. 24 lacs and therefore the Bank could sanction enhancement in limit to regularise the account. Shri Gandhi also stated that the company was experiencing difficulty on account of the facility being allowed only on a pledge basis and requested for its conversion into a hypothecation limit. The Head Office increased the cash credit key loan limit from Rs. 20 lacs to Rs. 25 lacs with increase in the open loan sub-limit of Rs. 5 lacs to Rs. 10 lacs on the existing security and conditions on February 3, 1975. The Directors of the company however declined to sign the letter of guarantee for the enhanced limit of Rs. 25 lacs. The Head Office instructed the Branch Manager that in the event of the Directors failing to offer guarantee for the enhanced limit, the limit should be reduced to Rs. 20 lacs. The Branch Manager reported his helplessness to the higher authorities saying that neither the company's Directors were offering their guarantee for the enhanced limit nor were they in a position to reduce the limit. Even thereafter the enhanced limit of Rs. 25 lacs was allowed to be exceeded, the maximum outstanding during the period upto December 1975 being Rs. 27 lacs. In March 1976 the Chairman approved the extension of temporary enhancement of the cash credit limit from Rs. 25 lacs to Rs. 28.50 lacs upto April 1976. This additional facility had been earlier allowed by the Zonal Manager in January 1976 for a period of one month and reference was made to the Head Office only when the company failed to regularise the account.

Though out of the sanctioned limit of Rs. 25 lacs, Rs. 15 lacs was key loan and Rs. 10 lacs was on hypothecation, it appears from the report of the Godown Inspector Shri R.L. Kapahi that the company availed almost the entire limit on hypothecation basis. Shri Kapahi who inspected the hypothecated and key loan godowns in December 1974 found that the bank's boards were not displayed on the godowns of the hypothecated stock. The godown of the pledged stock remained unlocked from 10 a.m. to 5 p.m. and the workers were found carrying their job work on the pledged stock. Ford Super Gear Box assemblies numbering 123 valued at Rs. 8,88,000 of the pledged stock were all found dismantled and there were no details of other items of the pledged stock Many items of the pledged stock were fitted with the road-rollers of the hypothecated stock and the value of such items was counted in both.

The account was however adjusted in full in 1977.

Summary of Reserve Bank of India's Inspection Reports

The following irregular features in regard to the sanction, supervision and conduct of the credit facilities were noticed by the Reserve Bank of India:

(1) The credit limits were sanctioned without critical assessment of the company's long term requirement. In fact, during March – May 1974 limits aggregating Rs. 20 lacs were sanctioned in four instalments of Rs. 5 lacs each as and when approached by the company. The enhancement of the limit to Rs. 25 lacs was sanctioned in February 1975 mainly for enabling the company to regularise the account which was overdrawn by over Rs. 5 lacs. The condition that the company should raise the capital of Rs. 20 lacs which was first stipulated in April 1974 and again reiterated in May 1974, was waived soon thereafter. The company's paid up capital as on the 31st March 1976 was Rs. 15.04 lacs only.

(2) No invoices in respect of the parts/components pledged with the bank were obtained. Similarly, original receipts issued by the Receiver for Agrind Fabricators Limited were not obtained by the branch although it was required to do so in terms of sanctions. The control over storage/movement of

stocks was lax. The bank's internal auditors could not verify some of the stocks because of dismantling of various materials and haphazard storage. They had also reported, *inter alia*, that no record was maintained of many items, which were taken by the company (for the remodelling of designs) without issue of Delivery orders and that certain parts pledged with the bank were fitted in the road-rollers without making payment therefor; yet, their value was included in the value of the road rollers hypothecated to the bank.

(3) In January 1975 the internal auditors reported that there was no movement of stock since March 1974. Up to June 1975 not even a dozen road-rollers were assembled, although the project envisaged assembly/sale of about 80 rollers by that time; the bank, however, does not appear to have taken up the matter with the company. The sales picked up only after August 1975 on account of orders received from various Government Departments/bodies.

(4) The bank is not aware of the terms of agreement between the company and its sole-selling agents M/s Jalan Modi Automobiles. Sizeable amounts in round sums have been paid from the company's account to this firm and Shri Kishan Lal Jalan, but to this firm and Shri Kishan Lal Jalan, but the branch is not aware of the nature of transactions involved. At times cheques drawn by M/s Jalan Modi Automobiles were discounted by the branch on behalf of the company to regularise its cash credit account. Shri Kishan Lal Jalan was operating the company's account and signing delivery orders stock statements, etc., since the beginning but the branch obtained the necessary authority only in June 1975.

Maruti Technical Services Private Limited

This company was incorporated in November 1970 with the share capital of Rs. 5 lacs and Shri Sanjay Gandhi and Shrimati Sonia Gandhi as Directors. The object of the company was to provide technical know-how and other services connected with automobile and engineering industries. The bank granted to this company loans of Rs. 35,000 and Rs. 34,000 for acquiring motor vans in July 1974 and August 1976 respectively. These loans were repaid in June 1976 and April 1977 respectively. In January 1975 the company had approached the bank for a loan of Rs. 25 lacs for purchasing 'general purpose' machinery but did not pursue the matter after it was called upon to furnish essential data in the forms prescribed under the credit authorisation scheme. In November 1976 the Zonal office at New Delhi sanctioned a 'packing credit' limit of Rs. 5 lacs to the company for financing the export of petrol savers developed by the company. This limit was availed of to the extent of Rs. 3.25 lacs in February/March 1977 and was repaid in April 1977 through exports effected under the relative letter of credit.

From the above account it appears that Maruti Limited and Maruti Heavy Vehicles Private Ltd. were got almost whatever they asked for from the two banks. Shri H.S. Chawla, Manager of Mullahera branch of Central Bank of India from August 1973 to April 1978, who was responsible for giving some undue facilities to the Maruti concerns admits that "all requests made by Maruti Limited and its allied companies were considered at all levels at a comparatively quick speed". He says : "since Maruti Limited and Maruti Heavy Vehicles Private Limited big projects having high connections inside and outside the bank, it always worked on my mind that they should not be given any opportunity of making complaints such as delayed processing of their proposals . . . . I thought it better to leave the matters to the better judgment and discretion of my higher bosses by sending their proposals quickly to them". He adds that he could not "resist meeting the demand of the party with whom our higher authorities were directly in touch". Shri R.L. Grover, Manager of Safdarjang Enclave branch from October 1973 to the end of March 1977, "dared not" raised any objection to the disbursement of the loans "because such action against this party could have invited trouble for him"; he was very much conscious that Shri Sanjay Gandhi was the Prime Minister's son and an "important personality in those days". Even the Head Office of Central Bank of India finding itself unable to sanction a further cash credit limit of Rs. 15 lacs asked for by Shri Sanjay Gandhi as Managing Director of Maruti Limited, advised the Zonal Office to convey their inability 'tactfully' to the borrower. The Reserve Bank of India has listed the irregularities in regard to the sanction, supervision and conduct of the accounts of Maruti Limited and Maruti Heavy Vehicles Private Limited with the two banks. None of the officers of Punjab National Bank and not all the officers of Central Bank of India who have been examined have made any such admission as Shri Chawla or Shri

Grover have done; some of them must have been responsible for the irregularities pointed out. The fact that so many irregular features are present in the accounts of the same borrower (treating Maruti Heavy Vehicles as an allied concern of Maruti Limited) would suggest that these officers went out of their way to help the two Maruti concerns for which they must have had some motive, if it was not fear that made them act as they did.

Shri D.V Taneja was appointed Chairman of Central Bank of India but his term was not renewed after one year. The way he was chosen for the office and then got rid of gives an indication of the trend of things of the time. Shri Taneja was appointed as Chairman with effect from April 1, 1974. In November/December 1971 he was associated with the deliberations over the Rs. 10 lacs interim loan proposal of Maruti Limited when he was posted at the Head Office of the Bank in Bombay. Before the proposal was put up to Custodian of the bank Shri Sanjay Gandhi met Shri Taneja in October/November 1971. Thereafter in January 1974 Shri K.L. Kalra who was then Development Officer in Central Bank of India, introduced Shri Taneja to Shri Kishan Lal Jalan and Shri J.K. Pahuja. On January 23, 1974 Shri Kalra arranged a meeting between Shri Taneja and Shri Sanjay Gandhi at the Maruti factory. At this meeting Shri Gandhi told Taneja that "his machinery was lying idle and he wanted to utilise it" by manufacturing or assembling road-rollers in collaboration with Shri Jalan. Shri Gandhi also wanted to know when his proposal for a loan of Rs. 24 lacs to be disbursed in the name of Kishan Lal Jalan would be sanctioned. Taneja replied that he as Deputy General Manager had no sanctioning power. To that Shri Gandhi said that Shri Adarkar, Chairman of Central Bank of India was due to retire shortly and that "search for a suitable person was on". On Taneja's next visit to Delhi on March 11, 1974 Kalra again took him to Sanjay Gandhi saying that Shri Gandhi wanted to "discuss his proposal for road-rollers" with him. At this meeting Shri Gandhi informed Shri Taneja that he had floated a new company called Maruti Heavy Vehicles Private Limited.

Shri Adarkar's term as Chairman of Central Bank of India was due to expire on March 31, 1974. From some papers which this Commission received from the Prime Minister's Secretariat it appears that on January 19, 1974 Shri P.N. Dhar, Secretary to Prime Minister, Indira Gandhi, recorded an internal note on the subject of a successor to Shri Adarkar as Chairman of Central Bank of India. The note runs as follows: "P.M. had mentioned to me the name of Shri Taneja in connection with the Chairmanship of Central Bank of India. As P.M. knows the Central Bank is not in a good shape. Much will, therefore, depend on the new Chairman. . . The proposal is to appoint Shri Gupta of the Union Bank as the Chairman, Shri Gupta is a very able banker and enjoys a high reputation. Shri Taneja is at the moment No. 3 in the Central Bank . . . As I have told P.M. I have checked on the relative merits and demerits of the two candidates from several sources including the Auditor-General, some officials and bankers. The proposal for Shri Gutta's appointment has already been made formally to the A.C.C. [Appointments Committee of the Cabinet] and is being submitted to P.M. by J.S.-1 separately. I would respectfully submit that this proposal may be accepted." Prime Minister Shrimati Indira Gandhi recorded the following observation on a slip of paper bearing the date March 14 (the year which is not mentioned should be obviously 1974) : "I have expressed my firm views regarding this matter. I think Taneja (underlining is 'Shrimati Gandhi's) should be given the post".

It is a fact that during Shri Taneja's tenure as Chairman he granted a number of facilities to Maruti Limited and Maruti Heavy Vehicles Private Limited. Shri Taneja has described before this Commission his experience in dealing with the Maruti concerns as Chairman of Central Bank of India. "The Maruti group of companies were not normal borrowers" according to him. The opening of a branch of the bank in the Maruti complex of buildings in Mullahera "was an invitation to pressures from a person who enjoyed wide government patronage. It meant an announcement of the bank's mind that it was closely identifying itself with Maruti business" After a couple of meetings with Shri Sanjay Gandhi, Shri Taneja found that Shri Gandhi "was wanting everything to be done immediately and had no patience for rules, procedures and formalities". Shri Taneja found that Shri Gandhi "was wanting everything to be done immediately and had no patience for rules, procedures and formalities". Shri Taneja states that Kalra who had developed a close friendship with Shri Sanjay Gandhi was exerting great pressure on him [Taneja] to "keep on releasing funds for Maruti Heavy Vehicles Private Limited". Taneja had known Kalra since the time he was posted in Delhi when Kalra also was working in the Delhi Office. During the period between April and September 1974 Shri Sanjay Gandhi started putting pressure on him regarding various matters, one of which was that Shri

Taneja "must immediately sanction the Rs. 1.5 crores loan for which proposal had been sent in December 1973". Another point on which Shri Gandhi insisted was that Kalra must be promoted Taneja states that "the more pressure Mr. Gandhi put regarding promotion of Mr. Kalra, the greater pressure Mr. Kalra would bring on me for Mr. Gandhi", Shri Taneja admits being "quite in a dilemma whether I could take the courage of transferring Mr. Kalra" but "felt that this would not be prudent at that stage". According to Shri Taneja from September 1974 till almost the end of the year, Shri Gandhi repeatedly telephoned him or sent messages to him through Kalra that "something immediately should be done to finance his car project". As the pressure from Sanjay Gandhi continued to amount, Taneja "could not bear it any longer" and he made up his mind "to take a decision one way or the other". He got the proposal for a loan of Rs. 1.5 crores examined by various people in all its aspects and their reaction convinced him that this was not a viable project. Taneja felt that "a stage had come when I must tell him that so far and no more". Before conveying his decision to Shri Gandhi, Taneja saw the Finance Minister Shri C. Subramaniam fully agreed with him and "also added that a snap election was round the corner. In any elections that would he held in that atmosphere, Maruti would turn out to be a millstone round the neck of the Congress party". While Shri Subramaniam was being examined before the Commission Shri Taneja's statement was put to him for his comments Shri Subramaniam admitted having met Shri Taneja but said "I cannot recollect all those things he had stated". Shri Taneja himself conveyed his decision to Shri Sanjay Gandhi on January 5, 1975. Shri Gandhi "was very upset" and told Taneja that if Taneja put up the proposal to the Board, he "would have arrangements made to ensure that it would passed". Finding Taneja hesitant, Sanjay Gandhi asked him to "think it over". When Shri Taneja was next in Delhi on January 24, 1975 Kalra conveyed to him that Shri Sanjay Gandhi was very angry and wanted Taneja to see him at once. Possibly this being a case of not a "normal borrower", Taneja went to see Sanjay Gandhi that night at the Prime Minister's house. Shri Gandhi who was "rude, insulting, haughty, and demanding" said that "if this was the way important clients were treated and commitments not honoured, proper people would have to be brought to head banking institutions". "This was a direct reference to me", says Taneja, "as my one year term as Chairman and Managing director was expiring on March 31, 1975". On

February 8, 1975 Shri Sanjay Gandhi spoke to him on telephone, it was "a monologue of complaint spoken in haughty and demanding language" ending with the threat that he would "deal with him [Taneja] properly". Taneja says that on the same day Kalra also conveyed to him a message from Sanjay Gandhi which Taneja noted down in his diary; the messages was, "unforeseen and dire consequences would follow for not helping Maruti".

Taneja's term was to expire on March 31, 1975. On March 22 a proposal was sent by the Secretary, Department of Banking, Ministry of Finance, recommending extension of the term of the Chairmen of six nationalised banks including Central Bank of India. For Shri Taneja the recommendation was for extension of his term for a period of four years. The recommendation was made in consultation with the Governor, Reserve Bank of India, with the approval of the Finance Minister Shri C. Subramaniam. On this proposal Shri P.N. Dhar, Secretary to the Prime Minister, recorded a note on March 31, 1975 that the file containing the Finance Ministry's proposals regarding the extension of the term of office of the six Chairman expiring that very day "was received only this morning". The note said "P.M. is unhappy that such important proposals should be submitted for approval at the very last moment". Prime Minister directed the term of the Chairman to the extended by one month for the time being. Thereafter Taneja's case was discussed between Finance Minister Shri C. Subramaniam and the Prime Minister. Shri Subramaniam has described the substance of the discussion in his deposition : "She said there were certain complaints against Mr. Taneja which required inquiry and therefore his term may not be continued". While Shri Subramaniam was giving evidence he was asked whether it was not unfair to drop Shri Taneja merely on the basis of some complaints made to the Prime Minister without an inquiry. Shri Subramaniam's reply was "you should realise that she was the Prime Minister'. It is not clear what this meant; she herself had told the Finance Minister that the allegations called for an inquiry and not that the allegations had been proved. Shri Gutta was appointed Chairman and Managing Director of Central Bank of India with effect from May 1, 1975.

On April 25, 1975 the senior executives of Central Bank of India made a written representation urging "the Reserve Bank of India and the Government of India to consider the re-appointment of Shri D.V. Taneja as Chairman and Managing Director as we all feel that such re-appointment would be in the best interest of the institution". Shri

R.C. Pochkhanawala, General Manager, was authorised to approach the "authorities and also, if possible, to place this representation personally before the Hon'ble Minister for Finance as well as before the Prime Minister with a view to conveying to them our unanimous feeling and as expressed through this representation". From the papers received from the Prime Minister's Secretariat it appears that Shri N.K. Seshan, Private Secretary to the Prime Minister, recorded a note on a sheet of paper on April 26, 1975 which reads : "Shri P.A. Narielwala sent Mr. R.S. Pochkhanawala, General Manager, Central Bank of India with the attached memorandum. The executives of the Central Bank of India wanted to see P.M., if it was possible. I told them that P.M. was very hard pressed for time and they could leave their memorandum with me and I shall place it before her. Apart from the points made in the memorandum, the only point he was making was Taneja had been a Chairman only last year. He was a Deputy General Manager and was picked up by the Government to head the Central Bank of India. To drop him suddenly only after a year will have a demoralising effect on the entire institution. He made it very clear that they were not questioning the right of the Government to appoint any body to the post of Chairman of a nationalised bank". Below this note Prime Minister Shrimati Indira Gandhi added in her own hand on the same day: "There were many doubts about Shri Taneja, F.M. himself was reluctant. I overruled him in order to give Shri Taneja a chance but reports about his activities are not good. His patronising of a particular union has naturally brought him some support from the employees. But it does [not ?] auger well. There is no point in my seeing Mr. Pochkhanawala. Also I have no time". She marked her note 'secret'. Thus she again overruled the Finance Minister and, on this occasion, the Reserve Bank of India as well. On April 29, 1975 at a meeting of the Bank's Board the Directors (Taneja was absent) decided to call on the Finance Minister to press for Taneja's continuance as Chairman and Managing Director. Shri Balasubramanian, Additional Secretary, Ministry of Finance, after speaking to the Finance Minister informed Shri Taneja that the "Finance Minister could not meet the Directors in the foreseeable future".

The inquiry against Shri Taneja was ultimately dropped for want of evidence. From the facts the conclusion seems inescapable that Prime Minister Shrimati Indira Gandhi opposed the renewal of Shri Taneja's term as Chairman of Central Bank of India overruling the recommendations of the Reserve Bank of India and the Finance Minister because Taneja did not find it possible to approve Sanjay Gandhi's proposal for a loan of Rs. 1.5 crores to help maruti Limited.

CHAPTER IX

The twelfth item in the list of matters specified for inquiry in the terms of reference relates to—

> All matters pertaining to foreign collaboration agreements, contracts with foreign parties and all foreign exchange transactions entered into by all or some or any of the said Maruti Concerns, including the capacity and execution capabilities of the Indian collaborating party to the agreement, the merits and fairness of such agreements, the *modus operandi* of securing such agreements and the degree of conformity of law, prescribed conditions, policies, practices, rules and regulations in relation to the entering into and/or approval of these said agreements, contracts and transactions.

Only two transactions arise for consideration in this context on the evidence received by the Commission; they are the two foreign collaboration agreements entered into by Maruti Limited, one with International Harvester of Chicago, U.S.A., and the other with Machinenfabrik Augsburg-Nurnberg (MAN for short) of West Germany, both for the production of heavy duty trucks. In fact, Maruti Limited cancelled the agreement with International Harvester to enter into an agreement with MAN. Apart from these two agreements Maruti Technical Services Private Limited applied for and obtained licences to import a number of scientific instruments from abroad but there is no evidence that this company utilised these licences to enter into an agreement with any foreign party to import these instruments.

It may be recalled that the letter of intent issued to Sanjay Gandhi and the subsequent industrial licence granted to Maruti Limited for the manufacture of passenger cars were subject to conditions forbidding foreign collaboration or foreign consultancy agreements, and import of capital goods, components of raw materials. There was a marked fall in the demand for passenger cars and certain other types of consumer goods in 1974. The Central Government in 1975 sought to meet the situation by allowing the affected industries to diversify. Maruti Limited was allowed to manufacture Heavy Duty Vehicles, and the foreign collaboration agreements entered into by the company were treated as incidental to diversification.

The facts concerning Maruti Limited's diversification plan and the collaboration agreements may now be stated. On October 8, 1975 Finance Minister C. Subramaniam wrote to Shri T.A. Pai, Minister of Industry and Civil Supplies, stressing the "urgent need to make a critical study of the possibilities of diversification" in regard to the industries affected by the slump. Shri Pai in reply suggested setting up a study group to examine the problem and to make appropriate recommendations for the rehabilitation of the industries. On November 19, 1975 a study group headed by Shri Mantosh Sondhi, Secretary, Department of Heavy Industry, was set-up. Shri S.M. Ghosh, Joint Secretary in the Ministry of Industrial Development, Department of Heavy Industry, was its Member Secretary. One of the decisions taken by the study group in a meeting held on December 30, 1975 was that passenger car units should be allowed to diversify to other vehicles, industrial machinery, and machine tools. However, even before the study group met, Joint Secretary, Shri S.M. Ghosh, recorded a note on the departmental file on December 19, 1975 that "the following passenger car units *viz.* Premier Automobiles Ltd., Hindustan Motors, Standard Motor Products of India and Maruti Limited may be allowed this concession (diversification) immediately", but on condition that "they will not need any imported equipment or foreign collaboration and there will not be any substantial addition to capital equipment barring balancing equipment". Shri Mantosh Sondhi, Secretary, Department of Heavy Industry, saw this note on December 22, 1975 and added his own comment "I would suggest that we should issue a notification to cover diversification so far as the passenger car manufacturing units are concerned. A notification couched in general terms should be adequate; it is not necessary to specify each car unit by name". The Minister Shri T.A. Pai approved the note on December 25, 1975. On the file, when it was on its way back to Shri S.M. Ghosh the next day, Shri Sondhi added: "please let me have a look at the notification before it is released". After the file reached Shri Ghosh, he summoned Shri Kannan, Under Secretary in the Department of Heavy Industry working as Officer on Special Duty to the Minister of Industry and Civil Supplies Shri T.A. Pai, and asked him to put up a draft press note. Shri

Kannan accordingly drafted a press note which was put up to Ghosh no December 30, 1975 for approval. Ghosh saw Kannan's draft on the same day and marked it to Mantosh Sondhi in deference to his request, before sending it to the Department of Industrial Development whose job it was to issue the press note. Sondhi found the draft press note to be in order and marked the file to Ghosh also on the same day, December 30. Next day Ghosh sent the file to D.K. Saxena, Joint Secretary, Department of Industrial Development. Accordingly Shri Kannan put up a draft on December 30, 1975 which I marked to the Secretary. After Secretary had seen, I sent it to the Industrial Development for issuing the press note. However, the press note that was issued on January 3, 1976 did not contain the conditions barring imported equipment foreign collaboration and substantial addition to capital equipment. The versions of Shri Kannan and Shri S.M. Ghosh differ as to how this happened.

According to Kannan he lost touch with the case after the file was sent by Ghosh to D.K. Saxena, Joint Secretary, Department of Industrial Development, for issue of the press note until Shri Bharat Bhushan, Under Secretary, Department of Industrial Development, who was dealing with the matter came to see him three or four days later. Bharat Bhushan informally showed him a draft press note which had been cleared by S.M. Ghosh, D.K. Saxena and R.V. Raman, then Secretary, Department of Industrial Development. This draft did not contain the conditions mentioned in S.M. Ghosh's note dated December 19, 1975 which Kannan had incorporated in his draft. Bharat Bhushan told him that a decision had been taken by the aforesaid senior officers to omit these conditions. It appears from the file that Bharat Bhushan recorded the substance of the discussion that Ghosh had with Saxena on the subject of the press note on January 2, 1976, and this shows that Ghosh suggested that the conditions need not be incorporated in the press note. Kannan says that at the request of Bharat Bhushan he scrutinised the draft that Bharat Bhushan had brought and made certain corrections therein but these are not relevant for the present purpose.

The account Shri S.M. Ghosh has given to explain the deletion of the conditions from the press note as published makes Kannan largely responsible for it. This is what Ghosh says in his statement before the Commission: "After the orders of the Secretary and the Minister were obtained I gave it (file) to Shri S. Kannan. . . to draft the notification. Shri Kannan came back to me to say that the conditions suggested by me (in the note dated 19th December 1975) did not figure in any of the press notes issued earlier allowing diversification to machine tools, industrial machinery, electrical equipments and foundry industries. He enquired of me if it would be correct to incorporate these conditions in a particular industry when these conditions did not figure in any of the earlier notifications. I asked him to check up again if the earlier relevant notifications did have these conditions. He came back to me after checking up that they did not. Then I told him that in that case it will be better if the press note was drafted on the lines the earlier press notes were framed and I would show it to the Secretary before it is sent to the Department of Industrial Development. Accordingly Shri Kannan put up a draft on December 30, 1975 which I marked to the Secretary. After Secretary had seen, I sent it to the Industrial Development for issue of press note. After the receipt of the press note I was asked by the Joint Secretary Shri D.K. Saxena to come over to his room for a discussion. As I went there, Shri Saxena pointed out that the draft press note did not contain the conditions. . . . He also said that the earlier notifications for diversification prescribed much simpler procedure. I said that if the notifications issued in respect of industrial machinery, machine tools and other industries did not prescribe these conditions, they should not be prescribed for this notification also. A note of these discussions was recorded on 3rd January, 1976 and routed through me to the Secretary, Industrial Development. On approval by the Secretary, Industrial Development, the press note was issued".

Thus Shri Ghosh suggests that he allowed himself to the persuaded by Kannan who first questioned the propriety off incorporating in the press note the conditions mentioned in Ghosh's note dated December 19, 1975. According to Ghosh the press note drafted by Kannan did not contain these conditions. In fact the draft press note which is now in the file does not contain the conditions. Kannan, however, has stated that the draft now found in the file was not the one prepared by him. Kannan denies that there was any such discussion as alleged by Ghosh regarding the absence of similar conditions in the previous notifications. Kannan asserts that the draft he prepared contained the conditions included in Ghosh's note of December 19, 1975.

It is not possible to accept Shri Ghosh's version of the affair. Shri Sondhi has told the Commission that the draft press note which he saw on December 30, 1975, contained all these conditions and that the draft press note which is now in the file was not the one which he had seen and approved. No reason is suggested why Sondhi should approve a draft that was not in accordance with the policy which both he and the Minister concerned had earlier approved; it is also a little difficult to accept that Kannan, an Under Secretary, who was given the work of drafting the press note on the basis of that policy would propose to the Joint Secretary to deviate from it. It seems that the draft made by Kannan had been removed from file and was replaced by another which had not been seen by the Secretary. Shri Ghosh's claim that there was only one draft which is the one that is now in the file cannot be accepted in the circumstances stated above. The draft now found in the file was not the one prepared by Kannan, there is, however, no evidence how it found its way into the file. Shri Sondhi pointed out the hollowness of the attempt to justify the exclusion of the conditions from the press note on the ground that the previous notifications issued in respect of similar other industries did not contain such conditions. Sondhi explained that there could be no uniform pattern for all press notes, and the claim that the previous press notes did not contain the conditions, even if it were true, was hardly any justification for not incorporating them in the notification issued in this case, specially when both Sondhi and the Minister concerned had approved the conditions as part of the diversification policy. It was not within the rights of either Shri Ghosh or any other officer to change the draft to deviate from the policy decided on. "It is an accepted practice" Sondhi said "that whenever a draft notification is put up on a file, it has to be strictly in conformity with the policy decision taken on the file. If the officer was to make a departure from the policy-decision taken on the file and that too at the level of the Minister, it is his duty to bring it out very clearly in his note giving reasons why a change is necessary and seeking my approval as well as that of the Minister". Shri T.A. Pai, then Minister of Industrial Development, has said that the notification that was issued excluding the conditions had not been brought to his notice and did not have his approval.

Shri S.M. Ghosh also sought to defend the exclusion of the conditions by saying that the "substantive decision of the Minister was to allow diversification to the passenger car industry and that decision remained unchanged" and that the conditions subject to which diversification was allowed was only "the procedural part of it" which was not incorporated in the press note as ultimately published "to bring it in line with similar other press notes relating to other industries". This is a wholly untenable argument. When a thing is permitted to be done subject to some conditions, the conditions are an integral part of the decision, and it seems absurd to call them the "procedural part". The defence strikes one as an afterthought which further affects the credibility of Shri Ghosh's version.

The press note, as edited by S.M. Ghosh, was published on January 3, 1976. On May 6, 1976 Shri S.M. Rege, Secretary of Maruti Limited, in a letter to the Joint Secretary, Ministry of Industry and Civil Supplies, Department of Industrial Development, said that "taking advantage of the press note" Maruti Limited had "decided to take up the manufacture" of heavy trucks of the capacity of 50 tonnes GVW and above in collaboration with M/s International Harvester of Chicago, USA. A formal application dated May 4, 1976 accompanied the letter from which it appears that the details of the project were still being worked out. A few days later, on May 10, 1976 Maruti Limited applied in the prescribed form for approval of their collaboration with International Harvester of Chicago. Next day, May 11, the Secretary of Maruti Limited wrote again to the Joint Secretary, Ministry of Industry and Civil Supplies, conveying some additional information in connection with their application for diversification. "We hereby confirm that the production of cars at present per year is to the tune of 50 lacs"; this obviously was a reference to the value of the cars produced. It was further stated that the demand for the heavy trucks which they proposed to manufacture would be 500 in number per year. Out of which "Government orders will be to the tune of 250 trucks per year" and the "balance demand will be from the public undertakings and private sector".

Before proceeding to describe how Maruti's applications were dealt with, it is necessary to state how an application made by Unimac Corporation of Ahmedabad for industrial licence to manufacture a similar item in collaboration with certain American firms, was disposed of a few months before Maruti applied. On February 10, 1975 Unimac submitted a composite application for an industrial licence for the manufacture of:

(i) Heavy Duty Truck chassis of 200 HP to 500 HP, highway and off highway type, for rated capacities 14000 kgs. (14 tonnes) to 60000 kgs. (60 tonnes);
(ii) Heavy Duty Axles and Transmissions, with foreign collaboration.

It was stated in the application that vehicles of the aforesaid type were being used "for such purposes as haulage vehicles, fire crash trucks, mobile crane mounting purposes, aerial ladder use, truck tractor combinations, oil field equipment mounting and various and numerous other purposes for organisations like ONGC (Oil and Natural Gas Commission), Priority projects, Air Force, Civil aviation, Fire departments and, particularly, Defence". These requirements, it was stated, were being met through "an aggregate import of average 500 to 600 such type of special duty vehicles". In the preliminary survey report that accompanied the application Unimac said that their "proposed scheme is aimed at making the industry self-sufficient in a phase programme of four years". The applicant also undertook a commitment of 20 per cent of output for export which was proposed to be stepped up later.

The procedure normally followed when such applications were received from the parties has been described by E.V.L. Prasada Rao, Section Officer in the Department of Industrial Development, in his affidavit dated February 2, 1979: "Copies of the application when received from the parties are initially dealt with in the Central Receipt and Despatch Section of the SIA (Secretariat for Industrial Approvals). That section after initial scrutiny sends the copies to various scrutinizing agencies" who are "expected to forward their comments within a period of one month approximately to SIA and administrative Ministry". The case is thereafter considered by the Screening Committee which is headed by the Joint Secretary of the administrative ministry, and in this case it was Shri S.M. Ghosh, Joint Secretary of the Department of Heavy Industry. After the matter is considered by the Screening Committee a summary is prepared in SIA for consideration of the Project Approval Board. After the Project Approval Board has considered the matter the minutes of the meeting are submitted to the Minister and after he has recorded his final decision the minutes are forwarded to the administrative ministry. Unimac's application was referred by SIA to the scrutinizing agencies on March 26, 1975 and April 16, 1975 was the date fixed for the Screening Committee meeting. However, on April 16, Shri R. Krishnaswamy, Director, Department of Heavy Industry after a discussion with Shri S.M. Ghosh, Joint Secretary, recorded a note saying that the meeting was postponed and that the Joint Secretary had stated that this was a case "for rejection". Shri Krishnaswamy in his affidavit dated February 5, 1979, says that on May 21, 1975 he discussed the next date for the Screening Committee meeting with Shri S.M. Ghosh. Shri Ghosh told him that there was no need for a meeting of the Screening Committee but a note should be prepared and sent to SIA recommending the case for rejection mainly on the ground that there was no market for the type of vehicles proposed. Shri Krishnaswamy recorded a note accordingly on the basis of which Shri V.P. Gupta, Under Secretary in the Department of Heavy Industry prepared an Office Memorandum on May 31, 1975 which was sent to SIA. The Office Memorandum said: "It is felt that there is no market at present for the type of vehicles proposed to be manufactured by the above applicant. It is also learnt that the applicant has submitted another proposal to the Ministry of Commerce for setting up an assembly plant in the Kandla Free Trade Zone on 100 per cent export basis and it has been approved by that Ministry. It will, therefore, be seen that setting up of a unit for he proposed items of manufacture for internal sale alone will offer no scope for a viable unit. In the circumstances, this Department recommends rejection of the proposal". At the time Shri Ghosh is said to have indicated that there was no market for the type of vehicles proposed to be manufactured, he had before him the views of DGTD, Council of Scientific and Industrial Research (CSIR) and also of the Development Commissioner, Small Scale Industries. All these scrutinizing agencies had recommended the proposal. DGTD in particular touched upon the demand aspect fairly extensively: "Heavy duty truck chassis is, at present, being imported for various applications such as a pulling unit for heavy duty trailers, chassis for crash fire tenders, heavy duty drilling rigs, oil field trucks, heavy duty recovery vehicles etc. The total annual requirements would be of the order of 100 Nos. to 150 Nos. These vehicles can also be made suitable for off the highway duties". Contrary to the views expressed by these scrutinizing agencies, Shri S.M. Ghosh held that there was no market for such vehicles. No exercise of any sort appears to have been conducted in the Department of Heavy Industry to support the view expressed by Shri Ghosh. It appears from the affidavit of Shri V.P. Gupta, affirmed on February 7, 1979, that the "sources of demand" referred to by the applicant *viz.* Defence, Civil aviation, ONGC etc. were not asked whether they had any requirement for such vehicles before Shri Ghosh decided that there was no demand for them. Shri Krishnaswamy in his affidavit dated February 5, 1979 says: "In the specific case, although it would appear that no examination was made, the decision which Shri Ghosh gave must have been based on his knowledge for need for a unit as applied for. . . ". Thus it was mainly Ghosh's idea that Unimac's application should be rejected and it was he alone who offered the view that there was no demand for such vehicles in the face of the views expressed by DGTD which, as Ghosh has himself admitted, was the "principal technical adviser to Government on Technology and Capacity".

On July 21, 1975 the Project Approval Board also recommended rejection of Unimac's proposal. Shri T.A. Pai, Ministry of Industry and Civil Supplies approved the recommendation on August 6, 1975. Shri Khasgiwale of Unimac made a representation against the order of rejection on October 9, 1975. In this representation he attempted to meet the two points on which the rejection of his proposal was based. As to the question of demand he said: "The Defence alone needs around 400 to 500 vehicles of this type which I have suggested, and the recent requirement indicates that immediately they need 60 fire crash chassis of 400 HP for airport operations, and 400 vehicles with wrecker attachments for desert and off highway operations. . . . Their present requirement of [chassis of] 15 tons and above is therefore in a vicinity of 500 vehicles a year. Organisations like International Airport Authority, Director General, Civil Aviation, Oil and Natural Gas Commission and so many other buyers need vehicles of this regularly. . . . The requirement of present mobile crane manufacturers is also handicapped due to non-availability of a suitable crane carrier chassis". As regards the proposal of assembly plant at Kandla Free Trade Zone he clarified that his application was cleared by Ministry of Commerce for setting up the plant on 100 per cent export basis for 50 vehicles only. This representation was also rejected by the Department of Heavy Industry on December 24, 1975.

On May 12, 1976 Shri S.M. Ghosh handed over the application for diversification received from Maruti Limited and the two letters of the 6th and the 11th May, 1976 to Shri V.P. Gupta, Under Secretary, and asked him to process the matter personally, normally such applications used to be passed on to the concerned section for processing. The procedure for processing the applications for diversification in the passenger car industry at the relevant time was laid down in circular No 4 (1976 series) of the Department of Industrial Development according to which the applicants had to submit five copies of the application in the prescribed form, one copy each for the Directorate General, Technical Development, Development

Commissioner (Small Scale Industries), and the Department of Company Affairs who were required to send their comments within two weeks. Even the press note that was issued required the applicants to file five copies of the application. Maruti Limited, however, submitted only one application in the prescribed form. Shri V.P. Gupta, Under Secretary says that having regard to "the sensitive nature of the case", he "felt that calling for additional copies of the application before processing it was not be insisted on". In terms of the aforesaid circular, applications for diversifications from large business houses registered under Monopolies and Restrictive Trade Practices Act (hereinafter called MRTP Act) where to be considered by a Task Force; other applications, the Joint Secretary was competent to dispose of. Maruti Limited was not registered under MRTP Act but Shri S.M. Ghosh decided in consultation with Shri V.P. Gupta that it would be advisable to consult the Task Force before taking a decision. Accordingly Shri Ghosh asked Shri Gupta to prepare a note for circulation to the Task Force in consultation with Shri K. Sankaranarayan, Development Officer in the Automobile Division of the Directorate General of Technical Development.

Why did Ghosh think it advisable to consult the Task Force though it was not necessary? He has said that it was the "sensitive nature" of the case which prompted him to involve the Task Force in the decision. It may be noted that the Task Force had six members including S.M. Ghosh as its Chairman and Sankaranayan and V.P. Gupta as members. The note prepared by V.P. Gupta for the Task Force with the help of Sankaranarayan whom Ghosh had asked Gupta to consult, reflected the views of Gupta, Sankaranarayan and, it is reasonable to think, also of S.M. Ghosh, and they constituted half the numerical strength of the Task Force. There seems to have been no doubt as to the opinion the Task Force was likely to express. In these circumstances, it seems the motive in involving the Task Force in the decision was only to allay suspicion by apparent sharing of responsibility.

V.P. Gupta's note for the Task Force was ready the same day Shri Ghosh had asked him to prepare it – May 12, 1976. The note justified the proposal for diversification on the ground that there was considerable demand for heavy trucks of 50 tonnes GVW and above that Maruti Limited intended manufacturing. Paragraph 3 of V.P. Gupta's note said: The heavy trucks of 50 tonnes GVW and above are off the highway vehicles required by project authorities for transportation of heavy materials and equipments. They can be used as tractors for heavy trailors required by various projects. They are also required by Defence for use as as Recovery Vehicles and Carriers. With the emphasis on off-shore drilling for oil exploration in the country, there would be increased demand for these vehicles of higher pay-load capacity. These types of vehicles are also used by ONGC for their drilling rigs equipments. Presently vehicles in this range are not manufactured in the country. The entire requirements for such vehicles, are therefore, met by import. The manufacture of these vehicles in the country will, therefore, result in direct import substitution from the very beginning. . . . It is, therefore, essential that a beginning should be made with the manufacture of heavier off the highway vehicles as early as possible". What V.P. Gupta did not mention in his note was that the demand for vehicles in the higher GVW ranges 50 tonnes and above, which Maruti proposed to manufacture was comparatively low. Shri K. Ramakrishna Rao who was Development in the Office of DGTD at the relevant time in his affidavit dated February 3, 1979 states: "with reference to the nature of the demand for the various organisations envisaged, the demand for vehicles below 50 tonnes would be about 75 per cent and for those above 50 tonnes GVW, it would be 25 per cent."

A meeting of the Task Force was held on May 17, 1976 where it was unanimously agreed that Maruti's proposal for diversification should be approved. The extract from V.P. Gupta's note for the Task Force quoted above appears to be a restatement of the points made in Unimac's application and their subsequent representation both of which were rejected. A thing which was said to have no demand, in a matter of months became a much needed commodity. V.P. Gupta's note does not mention the relevant fact that only a few months earlier they had rejected a similar proposal from Unimac Corporation of Ahmedabad. By way of explanation Gupta says in an affidavit affirmed on February 7, 1979 that he was "not able to connect the two cases presumably as GVW was not specifically mentioned" in Unimac's application and "being a non-technical person" he "did not co-relate the axle rating and GVW rating". If this is true, then he did not know what he was writing about in his note, but the explanation does not seem to be at all convincing. Gupta admits in his affidavit that the "sources of demand" mentioned in both cases were the same, *viz.*, Defence, Civil Aviation, ONGC etc. and there was also no difference in the use to which the vehicles could be put as stated by the either party. Even as a "non-technical person" the similarities between the two cases could not possibly have escaped him. What finally demolishes the explanation is that in the second paragraph of the representation submitted on October 9, 1975 by Shri Khasgiwale for Unimac Corporation, it is said that there proposal "covers manufacturing programme for Heavy Duty Truck Chassis 200 HP to 500 HP for haulage purposes. This covers 500 nos. of various types of chassis with GVW ratings of 14,000 kgs [14 tonnes] to 60,000 kgs [60 tonnes] capacities". In any case, Shri S.M. Ghosh could not have possibly forgotten the view he himself had expressed a few months back that there was no demand for such type of vehicles. Quite obviously the entry of Maruti Limited on the scene accounts for this volte face. Why Unimac's application rejected on the ground that there was no demand when various organisations were in need of such type of vehicles remains unanswered. Maruti applied about 9 months after the rejection of Unimac's application. It seems all facts touching this aspect have not come to light.

In approving Maruti's proposal for diversification, the Task Force assumed as correct the claim made in the company's letter to the Joint Secretary, Ministry of Industry and Civil Supplies, written on May 11, 1976 that they were producing passenger cars of the value of Rs. 50 lacs every year. Shri V.P. Gupta has told the Commission that the value stated meant about 200 cars a year. The two half-yearly returns that Maruti Limited submitted in the prescribed form to the Department of Heavy Industry however disclose quite a different picture. According to the return for the period ended December 31, 1975, the company had made a number of prototypes. It was also stated in this return that production on moderate scale had commenced and it was expected to increase in the near future. The return for the period ended June 30, 1976 was a replica of the earlier one. The 5th Annual Report of Maruti Limited for period 1975-76 shows that the "actual production" of motor cars till March 31, 1976 was only 21 in number. The claim that Maruti Limited was producing cars of the value of Rs. 50 lacs a year, made apparently to impress the authorities who, would consider the company's diversification proposal, was therefore quite untrue.

Shri Shankaranarayan, Development Officer in the Automobile Division of the DGTD had visited the Maruti factory along with his colleague Shri K. Sharma, another Development Officer, on February 15, 1975 to assess the progress made by the company in the production of passenger cars. They submitted a joint report on February 26. The report expressed doubts as to the ability of Maruti Limited to step up production of cars on commercial scale with the various limitations they had. In reply to a question put to him as to whether it would have been possible for Maruti Limited to manufacture heavy duty vehicles with the equipments already installed, his answer was that though some of the equipments already installed "could be utilised for the manufacture of some components and sub-assemblies of the heavy duty vehicles, it would have been necessary to add significantly to the capital equipment or alternatively go in for heavy sub-contracting for components, sub-assemblies etc.". Shri Mantosh Sondhi has told the Commission that he did visualise any manufacturing unit of passenger car to go in for manufacture of such heavy duty trucks by way of diversification because the manufacture of heavy duty trucks would involve substantial expansion. Shri Sondhi's view is of course based on the policy approved by the Minister and reflected in S.M. Ghosh's note dated December 19, 1975. Ghosh admitted that for Maruti Limited switching over to the production of heavy vehicles implied substantial expansion of its capacity, but he said that in his opinion the diversification press note "comprehended it and covered such expansion implicit in diversification". Shri Ghosh added: "the press note was issued by the Department of Industrial Development and my presumption has been that it has been competently issued. We were implementing the press note in terms of specific request". The significance of deleting the conditions from the draft press note prepared by Kannan is now apparent. The policy approved by the Minister concerned as appearing from Kannan's draft press note would not have permitted Maruti Limited to diversify to the manufacture of heavy duty vehicles which implied substantial expansion of its capacity. Shri S.M. Ghosh first removed from the draft press note the impediments to diversification and then took his stand on the press note to claim that it "comprehended and covered such expansion". According to the Minister, Shri T.A. Pai, the press note as published did not have his approval and was therefore "out of order" and accordingly "whatever was done on the basis of that press note was also out of order". It may be mentioned here that the application for diversification made by Maruti Limited was the only application received from the passenger car industry after the press note was published.

On May 20, 1976 Maruti Limited wrote to the Under Secretary,

Ministry of Industry and Civil Supplies (Department of Industrial Development), acknowledging the letter approving its proposal for diversification: in this very letter Maruti also asked the Government to increase the capacity from 500 to 2,500 heavy duty vehicles per year. The request for increased capacity was made on the ground that ". . . the demand that we envisaged for these vehicles at present was 500 vehicles per year, however, this may increase in the future and as such we request you to kindly increase the licensed capacity from 500 nos. per year to 2,500 nos. per year. The demand for this type of vehicles is going to increase and hence this request". It is a little difficult to understand why only nine days earlier, on May 11, 1976, when Maruti Limited mentioned 500 as the number of heavy trucks which the company intended to manufacture, this likely increase in demand could not be anticipated. The letter of May 20, does not disclose any fact that was not known on May 11. The Department of Heavy Industry supported the proposal for increase of licensed capacity and so did DGTD and the Development Commissioner, Small Scale Industries. Shri V.P. Gupta, Under Secretary, Department of Heavy Industry, who dealt with this matter says that he was requested by Shri S.M. Ghosh, Joint Secretary to process the proposal immediately "as it was a sensitive matter". He put up a note on May 27, 1976 suggesting that the proposed enhancement in the capacity be approved: "There is no gain-saying the fact that the demand for the above types of vehicles [50 tonnes GVW and above] may increase sizeably in the future". S.M. Ghosh, Joint Secretary, accorded his approval on the same day and a letter conveying the approval was issued to Maruti Limited also on the same day, May 27, 1976. In his affidavit Shri V.P. Gupta has admitted that there was no fresh material before him on May 27 to support the conclusion that the demand would go up five times–from 500 to the approved capacity of 2,500 in number.

In the meantime the application for foreign collaboration made by Maruti Limited on May 10, 1976 was also being processed. The Secretariat for Industrial Approvals endorsed copies of the application to the Department of Heavy Industry, DGTD, Development commissioner, Small Scale Industries, CSIR and several other authorities for comments. The application mentioned only the product proposed to be manufactured, the name of the foreign collaborator — International Harvester of Chicago, U.S.A., and the terms of collaboration. It lacked information on many relevant particulars such as the estimated value of annual production, proposed capital cost of the project including cost of imported and indigenous capital equipment estimated requirements of raw material and components, phased manufacturing programmes for import substitution, effect on balance of payment with foreign exchange earning and foreign exchange outgo and net foreign exchange inflow, and percentage of royalty computed as a proportion of the ex-factory value of annual production. The foreign collaboration agreement was "finally for a period of five years". No export was "proposed at present" and "no commitments" were "made at present" for exports. The terms of foreign collaboration proposed were:

(i) Royalty of "5 per cent of the net difference between the U.S. net export price of a licensed product less the value of components purchased from International Harvester. This fee will not apply to any Indian sourced components which International Harvester does not supply drawings or other technology".

(ii) "Maruti will pay International Harvester 5 per cent on International Harvester's distributor net price of all service parts manufactured by Maruti or produced from sources other than International Harvester, except that such fee was not applied to service parts for which International Harvester does not supply either the design or application drawings or manufacturing or engineering research or other data developed by International Harvester".

CSIR found that it was not possible for them to technically examine the application in the absence of the aforesaid data. They wrote to Maruti Limited and also asked SIA to furnish them with further information. DGTD considered that the technology involved being highly sophisticated it would be necessary to go in for proven technology and that the International Harvester enjoyed a very high reputation. According to DGTD, five per cent royalty was reasonable. The lack of technical data in the application, DGTD explained on the ground that unless the foreign firm was assured of government's concurrence to the proposal, they would be willing to part with necessary information. The Department of Heavy Industry was also of the same view.

A summary for the Foreign Investment Board (FIB) was thereafter prepared incorporating the details of the application and the comments received. The summary was considered by the Board at its meeting held on June 30, 1976. The Foreign Investment Board agreed with the recommendations of the administrative Ministry and approved the proposal on the terms specified above. On July 12, 1976 a letter was issued from SIA to Maruti Limited approving their proposal for collaboration with International Harvester of U.S.A. The terms of collaboration approved appeared to have excluded the following standard condition governing foreign collaboration:

> "The duration of the agreement shall be for a period of five years from the date of agreement or five years from the date of commencement of production provided production is not delayed beyond three years of signing of agreement, i.e. a maximum period of eight years from the date of signing of agreement. Within this period, the Indian company should develop and set-up their own design and research facilities so that continued dependence on foreign collaboration beyond this period will not be necessary."

A copy of the approval letter sent to Maruti Limited which is found in the file [No. 1(24)76-AEI(1) of Department of Heavy Industry] shows that in the annexure containing all the standard terms this one which figures at serial No. (vi) has been crossed out.

On December 15, 1976 Maruti Limited wrote to the Secretary, Department of Industrial Development, Secretariat for Industrial Approvals (Foreign Collaboration Unit) informing him that the "proposal (collaboration with International Harvester] could not materialise because we were offered better terms and conditions by an equally renowned company of West Germany – Machinenfabrik Augsburg-Nurnberg, commonly known as MAN". In fact Maruti Limited had already entered into an agreement with MAN on December 14, 1976 initially for a period of ten years subject to the approval of Central Government. The request made by Maruti Limited in their letter was : "treat our previous foreign collaboration with International Harvester as cancelled and accord your approval to our present collaboration proposal with MAN at the earliest opportunity". As in the case of Maruti's application for collaboration with International Harvester, this letter also not furnish details on many relevant items. Unlike the previous agreement, the agreement with MAN involved initial lump sum payment of Deutsche Marks (DM) 5,00,000 for transfer of technical know-how followed by payment of 3.5 million DM for transfer of know-how of the proprietory items in instalments proportionate to the value of items. The know-how for the manufacture of axles was not to bc transferred before the end of 1982. A two per cent royalty payment on the value of the proprietory items to be manufactured under the licence was also to be paid. The deal with International Harvester involved payment of royalty for five years, the agreement with MAN envisaged payment of royalty for ten years. MAN would also charge technical know-how fee of DM 1 million for the engine. It was added, however, that "MAN has presently a requirement of about 1000 engines per year or the equivalent amount of sparcs, which could be procured from Maruti within a period of 2 years", but it is apparent from the words used that this was not a firm commitment. The technical know-how fee and the royalty would be subject to taxation under Indian laws. The agreement with MAN covers the following types of vehicles:

Model	Drive	Gross vehicle weight in 1000 kg.
32.320 DFT	6 X 4	32
32.320 DFAT	6 X 6	32
19.320 FT	4 X 4	19
19.320 FAT	4 X 2	19

Maruti's letter of December 15, 1976 was addressed to the Secretary, Department of Industrial Development but the Secretary being away on tour it was marked to Joint Secretary Shri A.F. Couto in the Department of Heavy Industry. The application which was in the form of a letter was thus taken on the records of the Department of Heavy Industry and a copy of it was sent to DGTD for comments on December 20. Copies of Maruti's application were not circulated to different authorities by Secretariat for Industrial Approvals, as was the usual procedure. Shri K. Sankaranarayan of DGTD examined the application on the same day and found the terms of collaboration reasonable. A comparative assessment made by DGTD indicates that the foreign exchange outgo under the agreement with MAN was slightly lower, but this was based on the following assumptions:

(i) In a period of ten years it would be possible to market at least 4000 vehicles at an average cost of Rs. 7,00,000 each.

(ii) The proportion of bought out components would be around 40 per cent and imported components 30 per cent with the result that royalty would be payable only on 30 per cent of the output. On this reckoning the flat royalty of 5 per cent for International Harvester would work out to Rs. 4.2 crores without tax deductions. In the case of MAN the 2 per cent royalty worked out to Rs. 1.68 crores without taxes. The lump sum payment of 5 million DM (0.5 million down payment plus 3.5 million for transfer of know-how plus 1 million for technical know-how of engines) would be Rs. 1.75 crores without taxes. After deducting the taxes it was found that payment to International Harvester would be Rs. 2.52 crores and to MAN Rs. 2.41 crores.

DGTD also mentioned the following in favour of MAN:

(a) The lump sum payment to MAN was related to indigenisation programme, and

(b) MAN would take from India 1000 engines or its equivalent as exports from India which would mean about Rs. 600 to 700 lacs during the ten year period of agreement. It has been pointed out earlier that this could not be taken as a firm commitment.

As regards the longer duration of the MAN agreement, according to DGTD, it was unlikely that any Indian firm would be in a position to absorb the technology in a period of five years. On December 21, the very day on which the comments of DGTD were received in the Department of Heavy Industry, Joint Secretary Shri S.M. Ghosh recommended to the Minister that Maruti be permitted to substitute MAN as collaborator in place of International Harvester. All this was done without reference to the Foreign Investment Board. In his note Shri Ghosh stated among other things that collaboration for ten years for items of high technology had been a practice and not an exception and emphasized the aspect of progressive indigenisation of components envisaged in Maruti's agreement with MAN. An examination of the foreign collaborations approved during the period July 1975 to June 1977 however, reveals no case where a foreign collaborator of a private firm had been allowed royalty for ten years without the export condition. Maruti did not undertake any export commitment. As regards indigenisation, it is surprising that Shri Ghosh should have been so enthusiastic about this aspect of MAN's proposal without probing it a little deeper in view of his past experience. What happened was this. A proposal to set up a public sector unit for manufacturing heavy commercial vehicles was already under consideration when the Department of Heavy Industry started processing Maruti's applications for foreign collaboration. In fact a negotiating committee had been appointed with Shri S.M. Ghosh as Chairman, who were negotiating with various parties including MAN of West Germany. The Committee in their interim report stated as follows:

> "M/s MAN have left the Committee with a distinct impression that they would prefer not to be involved in the responsibility relating to indigenisation of vehicle and component design. In spite of long arguments with the firm's representatives, they continued to harp the view that, at best, they would make available the services of one or more of their specialists to guide Indian engineers in the problems attached to indigenisation but without any commitment or responsibility for such adjustment."

One should have thought that after this Ghosh would prescribe sufficient safeguards so that the condition of 'transfer of technical know-how' in terms of indigenisation was spelt out beyond any ambiguity.

The Minister of Industry Shri T.A. Pai cleared the proposal also on the same day, December 21, 1976. This meant that Maruti Limited was permitted diversification for the production of heavy duty trucks of 19 tonnes and 32 tonnes GVW. Originally Maruti was allowed diversification for heavy duty vehicles of 50 tonnes GVW and above, it appears that when they applied for change of collaborator on December 15, 1976 they also wrote to the Additional Secretary, Ministry of Industry and Civil Supplies (Department of Heavy Industry) asking for permission to diversify "by taking up manufacture of heavy duty vehicles of 40 tonnes GVW and 100 tonnes GCW and above" in collaboration with MAN. [Department of Heavy Industry File No. 1(23)/76-AEI(1)]. Shri V.P. Gupta, Under-Secretary, Department of Heavy Industry, wrote to Maruti Limited on December 22, 1976 conveying approval to Maruti's proposal for "taking up manufacture of heavy duty vehicles of 40 tonnes GVW/100 tonnes GCW and above. The position therefore was that while Maruti Limited was permitted to collaborate with MAN for the production of vehicles of 19 tonnes and 32 tonnes GVW, the permission given to them to diversify was for the manufacture of vehicles of 40 tonnes GVW/100 tonnes GCW and above. This anomaly was too glaring to have escaped the notice of the authorities. But nothing was done about it. One has no doubt that the approval accorded to collaboration with MAN would not have been cancelled and matters would have been regularised somehow if the irregularity was detected, but from the fact that the authorities did not take any steps, it seems they did not attach any importance to it. Whatever Maruti wanted they had granted, and there was nothing more to do. Secretariat for Industrial Approvals wrote to Maruti Limited on December 23, 1976 conveying Government of India's approval to the change of collaborator. It may be recalled that Shri T.A. Pai told this Commission that the press note on the subject of diversification (to which foreign collaboration was incidental) had been issued without his approval and that everything done on the basis of this press note was out of order. On March 17, 1977 SIA submitted a note regarding this matter to Foreign Investment Board "for its information and concurrence".

I have earlier referred to a proposal to set up a public sector unit for manufacturing heavy commercial vehicles. How the proposal originated and what happened to it ultimately, which is relevant in this context, may now be told. In March 1973 Shri Mantosh Sondhi, Secretary, Heavy Industry, suggested expansion of the vehicles factory at Jabalpur, which had been set up under the control of the Director General of Ordnance Factories, to bridge the gap between the output and the projected requirement of heavy duty vehicles by the end of seventh decade. The draft Fifth Five Year Plan (1975-79) assigned Rs. 50 crores for the purpose. In June 1974 a decision was taken in the Department of Defence Production, Ministry of Defence, to de-link the manufacture of vehicles of 10 tonne pay load and above from the expansion off the vehicle factory at Jabalpur. The National Industrial Development Corporation was asked to prepare a feasibility report on the basis of a new plant for manufacture of 12,000 such vehicles in the first phase and 24,000 vehicles in the second phase. They submitted a report in September 1974. After examination of the report the Department of Heavy Industry wrote to five reputed foreign manufacturers of whom Volvo of Sweden, MAN of West Germany, International Harvester of U.S.A. and, later, Berliet of France replied. The first three firms submitted their proposals by June 1975. To examine the proposals and negotiate with the parties a negotiating team of three persons with Joint Secretary, Department of Heavy Industry, Shri S.M. Ghosh as leader was formed in October 1975. The negotiating committee held discussions with the representatives of MAN, International Harvester and Volvo in December–January 1975/76. A draft interim report of the negotiating committee appears to have been prepared. However, no papers relating to the deliberations of the committee with the foreign collaborators or of its own internal meetings are available in the Department of Heavy Industry except a carbon copy of an unsigned draft interim report. It appears from this draft that the negotiating committee recommended ". . . of the four proposals received those of M/s MAN, M/s. Volvo may now be dropped. Representatives of M/s. Berliet and M/s. International Harvester should now be invited for a final round of negotiations making it clear to them that the choice has now been reduced to one of the two depending upon the adjustments they are willing to make further in their proposal as they stand today". In a meeting held on May 14, 1976 for finalisation of the Fifth Plan, the Planning Commission agreed to make an allocation of Rs. 10 crores during 1977-79 for the public sector vehicle project. For the Annual Plan of 1976-77, the Department of Heavy Industry proposed an outlay of Rs. 1 crore for the heavy vehicle public sector project. The project report was still to be prepared, but to meet the expenditure on preliminary studies. Planning Commission agreed to make a token provision of Rs. 10 lacs and the entire amount was provided as budgetary support. On May 10, 1976 Maruti Limited applied for approval of their collaboration agreement with International Harvester. On October 2, 1976 the Chief Minister of Andhra Pradesh enquired of the Industry Minister about the stage to which the Public-sector Heavy Vehicle project had progressed. The Secretary, Heavy Industry, to whom the letter was forwarded directed Shri S.M. Ghosh, then an Additional Secretary, on October 8 as follows:

> "Please put up a draft reply stating that due to financial constraints it has been decided not to pursue this project."

Shri Ghosh, however, put up a draft stating "investment sanctioned for this project has yet to be obtained. In view of competing claims on scarce investment resource, it is difficult to say when such a sanction will be forthcoming". This draft was endorsed by the Secretary and a reply was sent to the Chief Minister of Andhra Pradesh accordingly on October 21, 1976. At that point of time the project had been included in the Fifth Plan with the budgetary allocation of Rs. 10 lacs for preliminary studies during 1976-77 and Rs.10 crores for the project during 1977-79.

It appears that on December 20, 1976 Shri S.M. Ghosh informed the foreign parties that the Government had "decided not to pursue the project for the present". However, only two days earlier, on December 18, an application of Punjab State Industrial Development Corporation Limited seeking approval to their proposal for manufacture of commercial vehicles in Sangrur District, which had earlier been rejected, came up for consideration before the full Licensing Committee when the representative of the Department of Heavy Industry, Shri V.P. Gupta, Under Secretary, informed the Committee that "his Department would not support the scheme", apart from other reasons, on the ground that "his Department was actively pursuing a proposal to set up a public sector project for the manufacture of commercial vehicles". On January 7, 1977 Andhra Pradesh Minister for Small Scale Industry wanted to be appraised of the progress of the public sector project. A draft reply was put up by the Section endorsed by Shri V.K. Mathur, Private Secretary (Technical) to Minister of Industry, and Additional Secretary S.M. Ghosh. The Andhra Pradesh Minister was informed that "Government have decided not to pursue the project for the present".

After the general elections held in March 1977, at the instance of the Industry Minister an explanatory note was prepared in May 1977 which was approved by Additional Secretary Shri S.M. Ghosh on the subject of the public sector project for heavy vehicles. This note states *inter alia*: "After two rounds of discussion the firms were requested to complete their proposals and these were submitted by them over a period of time, the last of which was received from M/s Berliet of France on 30th June, 1976. Subsequently the Planning Commission indicated that budgetary constraints precluded inclusion of this project in the Vth plan. On their advice, further processing of this proposed (sic.) was abandoned and the foreign bidders for a collaboration, informed accordingly". No papers are available with the

Department of Heavy Industry about the deliberations of the negotiating committee. On January 5, 1978 Shri J.M. Lalvani, Secretary of this Commission wrote to Shri Majumdar, Secretary, Planning Commission requesting him to make available to the Commission of Inquiry all files and papers with the Planning Commission concerning the abandonment of the public sector heavy vehicle project. Secretary, Planning Commission, wrote back on January 16, 1978 to say: "On perusal of our papers it is seen that the discussion on the heavy vehicle project was limited to the question of the provision to be made in the Five Year Plan and the Annual Plans. . . . We have no papers concerning the abandonment of the scheme by the administrative Ministry". Thereafter, this Commission again wrote to the Planning Commission for clarification after reproducing an extract from the Department of Heavy Industry's note prepared in May 1977 saying "subsequently the Planning Commission indicated that budgetary constraints precluded inclusion of this project in the Vth plan. On their advice, further processing of this proposed (sic.) was abandoned". To this Secretary, Planning Commission, replied on February 4, 1978 as follows:

> "I have got the records checked up again, and as stated in my earlier letter, Planning Commission has no papers concerning the abandonment of the scheme by the administrative Ministry. Based on the discussions held in May 1976 with the Ministry for the finalisation of the Fifth Plan, a provision of Rs. 10 crores was made for this project in the final Fifth Plan document for the two year period 1977–79 against Rs. 25 crores sought by the administrative Ministry.
>
> The Ministry did not, however, seek any provision for this project during the Annual Plans 1977-78 and 1978-79. Implicitly it could be inferred that the Ministry had, by then, decided not to proceed with the project.
>
> The Planning Commission had not attached high priority to this scheme. It was only at the instance of the Ministry that the provision of Rs. 10 crores was included in the Fifth Plan."

From this letter it would appear that the Department of Heavy Industry themselves did not seek any provision for the project during the Annual Plan for 1977-78 and had also made no provision for it in the revised estimates for 1976-77 even though a provision of Rs. 10

lacs had already been made for it in the budget for 1976-77 and Fifth Plan funds of Rs. 10 crores were available for 1977–79. A perusal of the Department of Heavy Industry File relating to the Plan provision for the year 1977-78 [File II-(3)(1)/76-TSW] supports what the Planning Commission's letter said. From the file it appears that the Department of Heavy Industry (Integrated Finance Wing) Office Memorandum No. G. 20012 (4)/B&A/HI/76 dated September 18, 1976 called upon all administrative sections to submit the revised estimates for 1976-77 and budget estimates for 1977-78 along with reasons for variations between the budget and the revised estimates for the current year and the budget estimates of the next financial year. The concerned section [AEI(1) Section] does not appear to have put up any note or proposal in respect of the public sector vehicle project. In continuation of the letter dated September 18, 1976 of the Integrated Finance Wing, all public sector units were written to on September 30, 1976 for data to be furnished to the Planning Commission for finalising the revised estimates for 1976-77 and the budget estimates for 1977-78. Shri S.M. Ghosh, Additional Secretary called a meeting in his room on November 9, 1976 to discuss the budget proposals of the public sector units. On November 15, 1976 Shri Mantosh Sondhi, Secretary, Heavy Industry, forwarded the detailed proposals of the 1977-78 Annual Plan Outlay and the revised estimate for 1976-77 to Secretary, Planning Commission. A statement annexed to this letter shows the plan outlay and the budgetary support in the case of commercial vehicle project in the public sector. While the budgetary support for 1976-77 was shown as Rs. 10 lacs, the revised estimate in the same year was shown as 1977-78 were also shown as nil, the total outlay for 1977–79 indicated was Rs. 10 crores. No reason was stated either for the variation of the revised estimate from the budget estimate or for not providing funds in the budget of the following year. On November 16 the Department of Heavy Industry forwarded to the Ministry of Finance, Department of Expenditure, copies of these proposals. Comments of the Industry and Minerals Division of the Planning Commission on the proposals of the Department of Heavy Industry, circulated in connection with the meeting to be held in Planning Commission on November 17, 1976 about the Annual Plan of the Department of Heavy Industry, did not include any comments on the commercial vehicle project presumably because the Department of Heavy Industry had made no budgetary proposals. In the statistical portion of the note, however, the fact that a provision of Rs. 10.10 crores had been assigned to the commercial vehicle project in the Fifth Plan balance for this project during 1978-79 was Rs. 10.10 crores was specified.

From the facts stated above one is left with the impression that all possible competition was removed in a planned way from the path of Maruti's venture in the field of Heavy Duty Vehicles.

After Shrimati Indira Gandhi's defeat in the General Elections held in March 1977, a letter was issued from the Department of Heavy Industry to Maruti Limited on May 10, 1977 on the subject of foreign collaboration agreement with MAN of West Germany. The letter said: ". . . import of capital goods was required for operating the collaboration agreement and implementation of the diversification scheme in respect of manufacture of heavy duty trucks. It has been reported that workers have been retrenched and civil suits have been filed by the dealers against you for refund of money deposited by them. Therefore, it appears that it will not be possible for you to apply for import of capital goods". It was therefore proposed to withdraw the approval accorded for foreign collaboration and cancel the approval given to the diversification scheme. It was added that "if no satisfactory reply in respect of the above proposals" was received by May 24, 1977, Government would be "proceeding further" in the matter. No reply was received to this letter and on June 4, 1977, the Department of Heavy Industry withdrew the approval given for foreign collaboration and cancelled the approval to the diversification scheme.

Maruti Technical Services Private Limited

In the beginning of this chapter it was mentioned that Maruti Technical Services Private Limited obtained import licences for importing some scientific instruments. The company made two applications on December 19, 1974 and June 3, 1975 for the purpose. Though there is no evidence that the company entered into an agreement with any foreign party to import these instruments, some facts concerning the grant of licence may be briefly stated. The first application made by Maruti Technical Services Private Limited was for a licence to import two machines, Spectro Photometer and Metallurgical Microscope. DGTD cleared the application from indigenous angle, that is, certified that these instruments were not manufactured in this country. This case was then placed before the Capital Goods *Ad hoc* Committee which decided to allow the import of Spectrophotometer with accessories and spares worth Rs. 2,05,354 from German Democratic Republic against Rupees payment sources subject to essentiality being certified by the Ministry of Industry and Civil Supplies and the matter was referred to them for this purpose. The object of essentiality certificate was to ensure that the item was needed for the purpose mentioned. The Ministry of Industry and Civil Supplies stated that the company was not enlisted with them. A unit which was not a production unit had to be registered with the Department of Science and Technology as a research unit or, if it was a consultancy organisation with the Ministry of Industry and Civil Supplies as a consultancy unit. The matter was again placed before the Capital Goods *Ad hoc* Committee on July 3, 1975 when the Committee endorsed its earlier decision and further stated that the applicant should be registered as a technical consultancy organisation with the Department of Industrial Development. The object of registration was to make certain that the organisation was carrying on bonafide activities. Shri B.D. Kumar who was Chief Controller of Imports and Exports from May 1974 till November 1975 has said that "normally where a unit is not registered its application is liable to be rejected", but "in this case the Committee did not take this firm stand" because this was "likely to be misconstrued" by Shri Sanjay Gandhi. The case came up again for consideration at a meeting of the Capital Goods *Ad hoc* Committee on February 6, 1976. At this meeting, presided over by Shri P.K. Kaul who took over charge as Chief Controller of Imports and Exports from January 31, 1976, the import of the aforesaid instruments was allowed without any reference to the conditions insisted upon by the Committee in the earlier meetings, Kaul's explanation is that that aspect of the matter was not brought to his notice, the only issue considered was a request for change in the source of import, from GDR to West Germany. The file came to Shri M.I. Singh who was controller of Imports and Exports, New Delhi. Mr Singh says, "I was fully conscious that this matter related to M/s Maruti Technical Services (P) Ltd. which was owned by Shri Sanjay Gandhi. If any letter had to be sent from the CCI&E office (Office of the Chief Controller of Imports and Exports) it would have gone under my signature only as Controller. I had that fear that any further processing by way of insisting or seeking further clarification on registration from the party as a consultancy organisation. . .as also insistence on the obtaining of essentiality certificate would have recoiled on me and landed me in great trouble. The emergency was in full swing then and the fate of Shri P.S. Bhatnagar of PEC (Project Equipments Corporation) and others for having tried to probe into Maruti affairs was quite fresh in my mind". Shri M.I. Singh adds that "under the prevailing atmosphere I was only eager to get rid of the case with the issue of import licence to the firm as quickly as possible". The import licence for (i) Spectrophotometer and (ii) Metallurgical Microscope with accessories and spares was issued on March 4, 1976.

In the meantime Maruti Technical Services Private Limited had made another application for the licence on June 3, 1975 in respect of three instruments including Gear Rolling Tester No. 895, which, it was said, were required for their laboratory for technical development and research purposes DGTD gave indigenous clearance only for the Gear Rolling Tester. It may be mentioned that prior to the application made by Maruti Technical Services, Maruti Limited had applied for import of Gear Rolling Tester but that application was rejected on the ground that import of capital goods was barred under the conditions of the licence issued to that company. This is another instance of how easily Maruti Limited could get round the prohibition by getting things done through Maruti Technical Services. Shri Nand Kumar who was then working in the officer of the Chief Controller of Imports and Exports as Joint Chief Controller noted on the file that the "applicant had not furnished any evidence that they have registered themselves with the Department of Science and Technology as per the procedure". In his statement to the Commission Shri Nand Kumar says, "the application being that of Maruti Technical Services (P) Ltd., connected with Shri Sanjay Gandhi and since it was being talked about that some action had been taken against certain officials of DGTD etc., including Shri A.S. Rajan, Development Officer of DGTD, and Shri Krishnaswamy of Heavy Industry for collecting details for answering Parliament Questions against Maruti Ltd., no officer was inclined to individually take the responsibility of deciding to insist on the requisite condition of registration and certification of essentiality as a pre-condition to the issue of import licence. That is why it was thought fit that the matter could be left to the Capital Goods *Ad hoc* Committee to take a decision. In the meeting of the Capital Goods *Ad hoc* Committee held on August 21, 1975 it was decided to refer the case to the Department of Science and Technology. The Department of Science and Technology replied that Maruti Technical Services Private Limited were not registered with them as a research and development unit. In the next meeting held on August 28, 1975 the Capital Goods *Ad hoc* Committee presided over by Shri B.D. Kumar, Chief Controller of Imports and Exports, decided to permit import of one Gear Rolling Tester from West Germany against West German Credit. Shri B.D. Kumar also speaks of prevailing atmosphere at that time and says that the conditions as to registration and essentiality were not insisted on in this atmosphere. Shri B.D. Kumar says further: "all the officers were aware of the treatment meted to those of the Department of Heavy Industry and DGTD when they were trying to collect information for answering questions in Parliament relating Maruti Ltd." Shri B.D. Kumar names one officer, Shri Krishnaswamy, in the Department of Heavy Industry, two in the Project Equipment Corporation, Mr. Kolay and Mr. Bhatnagar, and another officer in DGTD, Mr. Rajan.

Maruti Technical Services Private Limited got the import licences without complying with the rules. The officers were too terrified to insist on the rules, they know what happened to those who proved difficult to Shri Sanjay Gandhi.

CHAPTER X

Conclusion

There is hardly anything that remains to be said except to emphasise a point or two.

The affairs of the Maruti concerns described in the previous chapters appear to have brought about a decline in the integrity of public life and sullied the purity of administration. Legal and other requirements were brushed aside and accepted norms of behaviour were forgotten on many occasions when the interest of a Maruti company was involved. This was due to, as witness after witness repeated, an atmosphere of fear then prevailing; anything connected with the Maruti concerns was looked upon as a "sensitive matter". And the fear was real. Threat of detention under the Maintenance of Internal Security Act or a CBI inquiry or other forms of harassment made it hazardous for the officers to insist on the rules or the dealers and depositors to insist on the rules or the dealers and depositors to insist on their rights. Persons in public life were in danger of having their political careers ruined. That it was not an idle threat is proved by instances of persons in whose case the threat was carried out. Some of the officers who went out of their way to be helpful to Maruti have denied that they were under any fear or pressure. What then made them act in the way they did? No evidence has been found that any other kind of inducement was held out to them, and it is difficult to get direct evidence in such matters. In their case it may have been only a hope that in future, if an occasion arose, the services rendered by them would be remembered. It may have been power-worship which blurs judgement and makes one believe that the present trends will continue and whoever is in power at the moment is invincible. They could not enforce the laws against those who appeared to be the laws' masters.

Quite a few of the applications that Shri Sanjay Gandhi made and the letters he wrote to the authorities asking for something for his business concerns were undated or did not contain a proper signature; in some of them a scratch of the pen or a tick mark has to be taken as his signature. It seems Shri Sanjay Gandhi was convinced that making these applications or writing these letters were a mere formality, it was a predetermined that all he wanted would be granted to him — and in most cases they were. From the interest taken in Maruti's progress by men from the Prime Minister's Secretariat and the way even matters connected with the country's defence were subordinated to the interest of Maruti Limited, and the prevailing sense of fear that prompted implicit obedience, one is left in no doubt as to the origin of the power that made such a state of affairs possible. Shri Sanjay Gandhi exercised only a derivative power, its source was the authority of the Prime Minister.

A number of irregularities in the working of the Maruti companies have been noticed in the foregoing pages. The minutes books do not appear to have been kept in the prescribed manner, at least two resolutions stated to have been passed by the Board of Directors of Maruti Limited have not been recorded. Evidence has been adduced showing that shares of Maruti Limited were allotted to persons who know nothing about the transactions also that in February 1977 large sums of money were paid out of fictitious persons as refund of their dealership reservation money or deposits made by them along with their alleged applications for Maruti shares. All these indicate the presence of unaccounted money. It has not been possible for the Commission to examine all the vouchers, books of original entries and other records and documents. What is revealed in such examination as the Commission has been able to do suggests that if a joint and co-ordinated examination of the records of the Maruti companies is done by the Departments of Revenue and Company Affairs and their books of account are audited by a special team, many more irregularities are likely to come to light.

